World Historical Fiction Guide for Young Adults

World Historical Fiction Guide for Young Adults

By Lee Gordon and Cheryl Tanaka

Fort Atkinson, Wisconsin

Published by Highsmith Press LLC
W5527 Highway 106
P.O. Box 800
Fort Atkinson, Wisconsin 53538-0800
1-800-558-2110

© Lee Gordon, 1995

Cover Design: Frank Neu
All rights reserved. Printed in the United States of America.
Except as permitted under the United States Copyright Act of 1976, no part of this publication may be reproduced or distributed in any form or by any means, or stored in a database or retrieval system, without the prior written permission of the publisher.

The paper used in this publication meets the minimum requirements of American National Standard for Information Science —
Permanence of Paper for Printed Library Material.
ANSI/NISO Z39.48-1992.

Library of Congress Cataloging in Publication
Gordon, Lee
    World historical fiction guide for young adults / by Lee Gordon and Cheryl Tanaka.
    p.   cm.
    Includes bibliographical references and index.
    Summary: An annotated bibliography with review citations for over 800 of the best in recent and classic historical fiction from all over the world, excluding the United States.
    ISBN 0-917846-41-9
    1. Historical fiction--Bibliography. 2. Young adult fiction--Bibliography. [1. Historical fiction--Bibliography.]
I. Tanaka, Cheryl. II. Title.
Z5917.H6G67 1995
[PN3441]
016.80883 ' 81--dc20   95-9689
                                                    CIP

ISBN 0-917846-41-9

Contents

Introduction	ix
How to Use This Guide	xii

Index to World Historical Fiction

—Africa

Prehistoric Africa (Prior to 6500 B.C.)	1
—North of the Sahara	1
Egypt	1
Ethiopia	5
North Africa	6
—South of the Sahara	7
Burundi	7
Cameroun	7
East Africa	8
Liberia	8
Namibia	8
Nigeria	9
Sierra Leone	11
South Africa	11

—Asia

—Prehistoric Asia (Prior to 6500 B.C.)	16
—Southeast Asia	17
Cambodia	17
Singapore	18
Thailand	18
Tibet	19
Vietnam	19

World Historical Fiction Guide

Middle East	**20**
Ancient Civilization	20
Biblical	21
Byzantium (to A.D. 1100)	23
Iran/Iraq	25
Israel	25
Palestine	27
Syria	28
Turkey	28
Far East	**29**
China	29
China–Nineteenth Century	30
China–Twentieth Century	32
India	35
Nepal	37
Pakistan	37
Japan–Feudal	37
Japan–Twentieth Century	41
Korea	44

Australia/New Zealand/Oceania

Australia	45
New Zealand	47
Oceania	47

Europe (General by era)

Prehistoric Europe (Prior to 6500 B.C.)	**49**
Early European Civilizations (6500 B.C.–1000 B.C.)	**52**
Ancient Greece (500 B.C.–A.D. 476)	**54**
Ancient Rome	**59**
Early European Civilizations	**67**
Dark Ages (6th–11th Centuries)	**69**
Medieval Europe (11th–13th Centuries)	**83**
The Renaissance (14th–15th Centuries)	**99**
Age of Discovery and Reformation (15th–18th Centuries)	**113**
Enlightenment and Liberty (1714–1815)	**139**

Nineteenth Century	**156**
Twentieth Century (by nation)	**173**
England	**173**
Ireland	**177**
Scotland	**179**
Austria	**180**
Germany	**180**
Greece	**183**
Poland and Eastern Europe	**184**
Soviet Union	**185**
Spain	**190**
World War I	**191**
World War II	**193**
Holocaust	**210**

The Americas
The Caribbean	**223**
Central America	**225**
Mexico	**227**
Canada	**230**
South America	**233**

Bibliography and Suggested Reading — 237

Title Index — 239

Author Index — 249

Subject Index — 255

Chronological Index — 291

Introduction

Adolescents live in the present. They are oriented to their own immediate world and have little interest in people and places outside of their circle of interaction They have no connection with the past, but this is precisely the time in their development when they need to connect with the past on a personal and emotional level. Through literature, adolescents are able to experience history as a reality, know different cultures, and understand the universality of emotions and values, precisely what historical fiction enables readers to do.

As most teachers and school library media specialists know, historical fiction novels are not usually high on popularity lists with students. Students believe the books to be boring, very much on par with their history textbooks. Students and some teachers assume that the subjects of the books must be a major historical figure or event, one about which they are tired of hearing. Teachers and school library media specialists often have trouble locating historical fiction that will fit the needs of the curriculum. The three roadblocks combined result in less than interested readers and a less than exciting collection.

Finding a comprehensive list of world historical fiction for junior and senior high school students was difficult, which lead to this book. With the widening use of whole language or resource based instruction, the need for a source listing world historical fiction novels that could be found in school libraries or purchased today became more critical. Finding "good" historical fiction was also a challenge.

First was the need to find out what criteria identified historical fiction of quality. Christopher Collier, co-author of several award-winning historical fiction novels for young adults, admits that he is highly critical of much of the historical fiction available for it does not meet all four of his criteria. "The book must:
- focus on an important historical theme an understanding of which helps us to deal with the present
- center on an episode in which the theme inheres in fact
- attend to the historiographic elements
- present accurate detail." ("Criteria for Historical Fiction," *School Library Journal*, Aug. 1982, 33)

World Historical Fiction Guide

Most of the other authorities also echoed these four criteria in their own words, but Donelson and Nilson changed a list of criteria into a chart which delineates the qualities of good and bad historical fiction. For the classroom teacher or the school library media specialist, this is more useful than a list and more detailed. Every teacher who plans to use a novel in a classroom setting must carefully read and evaluate that novel before assigning it, even before purchasing it in class sets. These suggestions provide the framework for careful evaluation.

Suggestions for Evaluating Historical Fiction

A good historical novel usually has:	A poor historical novel may have:
A setting that is integral to the story.	A story that could have happened any time or any place. The historical setting is for visual appeal and to compensate for a weak story.
An authentic rendition of the time, place, and people being featured.	
An author who is so thoroughly steeped in the history of the period that he or she can be comfortably creative without making mistakes.	Anachronisms in which the author illogically mixes up people, events, speaking styles, social values, or technological developments from different time periods.
Believable characters with whom young readers can identify.	Awkward narration and exposition as the author tries to teach history through the characters' conversations.
Evidence that even across great time spans people share similar emotions.	
References to well-known events or people, or other clues through which the reader can place the happenings in their correct historical framework.	Oversimplification of the historical issues and a stereotyping of the "bad" and the "good" guys.
Readers who come away with the feeling that they know a time or place better. It is as if they have lived in it for at least a few hours.	Characters who fail to come alive as individuals who have something in common with the reader. They are just stereotyped representatives of a particular period.

Table 1: Suggestions for Evaluation Historical Fiction from Literature for Today's Young Adults, 4th ed. by Alleen Pace Nilsen and Kenneth L. Donelson. Copyright © 1993 by HarperCollins College Publishers. Reprinted by permission.

In addition to being able to evaluate the quality of the historical fiction, it is also necessary to evaluate the students who will be reading it. Choosing the wrong novel might cause students to turn away from historical fiction totally. Adults who guide students in their choice of novels must have read a wide variety of historical fiction in order to help students find the "right" book.

Introduction

The use of historical fiction in the classroom as an assigned text or as supplementary reading can be enriching, interesting, and exciting. The goals in such uses are varied. All teachers would agree that two primary goals are: to have students read good literature "which vividly and realistically portrays other times, place and people;" and to put "students in touch with these other times and cultures to help them overcome parochialism of time and place." (R. E. Heinly and K. Hilton, "Using Historical Fiction to Enrich Social Studies Courses," *The Social Studies*, (Jan./Feb 1982):21.

Historical fiction has been used as enrichment material for individual students, small groups, and entire classes. It has been used as primary source material in lieu of textbooks. It has also been used successfully in whole school districts such as the Rose Tree-Media District, Pennsylvania, in an enrichment reading program based in social studies classes in both junior and senior high schools. Teachers in this district reported eight major benefits from this program. Among them are: 1) "development of a sense of identity with the past;" 2) "humanizing experience;" 3) better understanding of "societal cause-effect relationships;" 4) strengthened "chronology and time sense;" 5) "tolerance, values clarification, moral development, and improved self-esteem;" 6) improvement of "higher thinking and reasoning abilities;" 7) "flexible teaching tool;" and 8) facilitation of "horizontal articulation of secondary curricula." (Heinly; 21-22) In a well-planned program like that of Rose Tree-Media District, these eight benefits to both students and teachers should be sufficient to justify the inclusion of historical fiction in the social studies curriculum or developmental reading program.

Works Cited

Collier, Christopher. "Criteria for Historical Fiction." *School Library Journal*, (Aug. 1982): 32-33.

Donelson, Kenneth L. and Allen Pace Nilsen. *Literature for Today's Young Adults*. 4th ed. Glenview, Ill: HarperCollins College Publishers, 1993.

Heinly, R. E. and Kenneth Hilton. "Using Historical Fiction to Enrich Social Studies Courses." *The Social Studies*, (Jan./Feb. 1982): 21-24.

How to Use This Guide

Selection Criteria

Historical Content

Though most books included are historical in content, there are books on the list that will not be considered as true historical fiction, especially those with a location in Third World countries. Purists may disagree with this, but until they have tried to find books for several classes of young adults who are single-minded in their interests, they need to understand the lack of choices. There are some areas of the world that are the subject of few historical fiction novels. Until such time that new books are written, it is better to provide period pieces and cultural works than nothing at all.

Location

All selected novels had to take place outside of the United States. A few exceptions were made for novels where a small portion of the plot occurred in the United States. Location took precedence over the nationality of the main characters.

Characters

The main characters could not be American. A few exceptions were made when only one of two or more main characters were American. Students need to see the world through different view points to try to counteract their ethnocentricity.

Time Periods

All time periods from prehistory to the present were considered. This also includes time travel novels that were historical in content.

Introduction

Publication Dates

Books that are still available for purchase or are likely to be found in school or public libraries were sought. The publication dates selected were 1970 to the present. "Classic" novels originally published before 1970 were included if more recent editions had been published.

Reviews

Simply providing a list of every world historical fiction novel written for young adults would not give teachers and librarians enough information about suitability. They need to know if reviews were favorable, what journals and publications reviewed the novels, and what grade levels were recommended. To be included, a novel must have been reviewed in two or more sources that would be readily available in school and public libraries. An exception was made for novels included in the *Wilson Senior High Catalog* and the *Wilson Junior High Catalog*. Books included in these sources have multiple reviews. Books which received more than one unfavorable review were not included. Therefore, this is not a complete bibliography, but one which provides a selective list, especially useful in school settings.

Reading an Entry

Each entry provides the basic imprint information of a book (author, title, publisher, copyright date, pagination, and ISBN and LC numbers). A short summary of the book is provided, followed occasionally by excerpts from reviews. A list of book review citations is provided for those who need to locate a more complete review. The sources of the reviews are abbreviated, and the list of abbreviations follows. Grade levels are provided for junior and high school readers. Books are indexed by author, title, geographical places/subjects. There is a separate chronological index.

Review Sources

BBSH: *Best Books for Senior High Readers.* ed by John T. Gillespie. New Providence, New Jersey: R. R. Bowker, 1991.
BBYA: Best Books for Young Adults, selected yearly by the American Library Association.
BCCB: *Bulletin of the Center for Children's Books* (periodical)
BFY: *Books for You: A Booklist for Senior High Students*, 10th and 11th ed. by Richard F. Abrahmson and Betty Carter. Illinois: National Council of Teachers of English, 1988 and 1993.
BL: *Booklist* (periodical)
BR: *The Book Report* (periodical)
CED: Children's Editor's Choice, selected yearly by *Booklist*

CRD: Children's Reviewer's Choice, selected yearly by *Booklist*
FFY: *Fiction for Youth: A Guide to Recommended Books*, 2nd ed. edited by Lillian L. Shapiro. New York: Neal Schuman Publishers, 1986.
HB: *Horn Book* (periodical)
LJ: *Library Journal* (periodical)
NCB: Notable Children's Book, selected yearly by the American Library Association.
PW: Publishers Weekly (periodical)
SLJ: *School Library Journal* (periodical)
TLS: *Times Literary Supplement* (periodical)
VOYA: *Voices of Youth Advocate* (periodical)
WJ: *Wilson's Junior High School Catalog* (serial), 4th, 5th, and 6th eds. New York: H. W. Wilson Co.
WS: *Wilson's Senior High School Catalog* (serial), 11th, 12th, 13th and 14th eds. New York: H. W. Wilson Co.
YAEC: Young Adult Editors' Choice, selected yearly by *Booklist*
YARC: Young Adult Reviewers' Choice, selected yearly by *Booklist* Classroom Activities

The most obvious, time-tested use of historical fiction novels is the historical fiction book report. Long used by English and language arts teachers, this can be a written summary which students often find dry. There are a multitude of ways to have students report on historical fiction that are much more interesting for both the students and the teacher.

An outstanding example of this appears in "Book Strategies: *The Second Mrs. Giaconda* by E. L. Konigsburg," by Pat Scales (*Book Links*. Nov. 15, 1990, 616-620). The author shows in great detail how a historical novel is used as a class reading assignment which would be appropriate for a world history class. The main objective is to introduce students to life during the Renaissance. Included in the article are suggestions for "setting classroom atmosphere," "initiating activities," "discussion points," and "creating and researching." A bibliography of coordinating non-fiction books is also included to aid students in research. The article ends with information about the author and short bibliography of sources.

This unit, or any similarly planned, needs the collaboration of both the classroom teacher and the school library media specialist. Students benefit when two knowledgeable teachers and the full resources of the school are offered to them.

Another successful unit begins as a book report, but branches out into research. Students begin by selecting a historical novel, perhaps suggested during book talks by the school library media specialist. After reading the book, a well-structured "book report" is written. As the teacher reads and evaluates the reports, he/she highlights three or four subjects that may be the basis of a research paper. People, places, events, objects, or time periods may be chosen. When the book reports are returned to the students, they choose one of the highlighted subjects to

Introduction

do a short research paper. The research paper serves to fill in the factual gaps left by the historical fiction, while the historical fiction provides the human and personal aspects omitted from factual works.

Following are other classroom activities and assignment which can be centered around historical fiction novels:

1. Create diary entries for the main character. Extend the entries to time before the story begins and after it ends.
2. Tell the story in four pictures with a 25 word description of each picture.
3. Stage a debate between the protagonist and the antagonist.
4. Make a scrapbook for the characters to show events and things that they would like (theater ticket stubs, post cards, party invitations, etc.)
5. Retell the climax of the story from the antagonist's or minor character's point of view.
6. If the novel does not explain political problems in the country, research the events and explain in more detail.
7. Write a series of letters from one character to another one.
8. Make Ven diagrams of values. What are the characters' values? What are yours? How are they the same or different? This could compare individual characters or two cultural groups.
9. Make a newspaper showing the main event of the story as the headline story.
10. Chart the differences in fashion, clothing, personal decoration, dance, household decoration, etc. between two groups in the book.
11. Research the characters in the book. Which were real and why are they remembered today?
12. Divide class into four groups. Each group researches one of four topics about the time period being studied: science and technology, arts, medicine, and literature. Each researches and presents information orally. Encourage use of visuals.
13. Construct a time line of the events of the book. If several students are reading novels that take place during the same time period, they may work together.

Discussion topics

When the entire class or smaller groups read the same novel, consider the following areas to use as discussion topics:
- Values/value conflicts

World Historical Fiction Guide

- Character's success or failure in meeting goals
- Decision makers, settling disputes, government, law
- Marriage, family, children, becoming an adult
- Status, social class, mobility
- Food, shelter, clothing
- Religions, beliefs, superstitions
- Art, architecture, music, dance, fashion, decoration
- Economics, money, property, jobs, natural resources, trade, advertising, capitalism or communism.
- Cause and effect

Other suggested resources and subject bibliographies

"The Blitz to the Bomb: WWII Fiction." *Booklist* (1 April 1977): 1174-1178.

Bruner, Katherine Everett. "Stereotypes in Juvenile Historical Fiction." *School Library Journal* (Sept. 1988): 124-125.

Caywood, Carolyn. "Roman through Historical Fiction." *School Library Journal* 40 (Sept. 1994): 152.

"Children's Books on Jewish Themes." *Booklist* (1 April 1977): 1174-1178.

Covey, Donita. *Novel Strategies for Young Adults*. Englewood, Colorado: Teacher Ideas Press, 1992.

Feicht, Sylvia. "Historical Fiction with a Twist in Time." *The Book Report* (Jan./Feb. 1990): 32-35.

Hathaway, Milton G. "The Second World War." *School Library Journal* (Feb. 1984): 36-37.

"The Holocaust: a Tragedy in Fact and Fiction." *Booklist* (1 Oct. 1984): 213-214.

Hotchkiss, Jeannette. *European Historical Fiction and Biography for Children and Young People*. 2nd ed. New Jersey: Scarecrow, 1972.

MacRae, Cathi. "The Young Adult Perplex." *Wilson Library Bulletin* (Sept. 1991): 102-103.

Muallem, Miriam and Frances A. Dowd. "Model Criteria for and Content Analysis of Historical Fiction about the Holocaust for Grades Four through Twelve." *Multicultural Review* 1 (April 1992): 43-55.

"Popular Reading--Historical Fiction." *Booklist* (1 Mar. 1988): 1189-1191.

"Popular Reading--Picture Books with Historical Settings." *Booklist* (1 Mar. 1987): 1058-1059.

Posner, Marcia W. "Echoes of the Shoah: Holocaust Literature--Part I." *School Library Journal* (Jan. 1988): 36-37.

Posner, Marcia W. "Echoes of the Shoah: Holocaust Literature--Part II." *School Library Journal* (Feb. 1988): 30-31.

Scales, Pat. "Book Strategies: *The Second Mrs. Giaconda* by E. L. Konigsburg." *Book Links* (15 Nov. 1990): 616-620 [This premiere issue of *Book Links* was located as a pull-out section of *Booklist* (15 Nov. 1990)].

Seybolt, Cynthia. "Looking to the East: Books on China" *School Library Journal* (Jan. 1976): 24-25.

Welton, Ann. "Historical Hooks: Leading Children Into the Past." *School Library Journal* (May 1990): 46-47.

Index to World Historical Fiction

Africa

Prehistoric Africa

Christopher, John. *Dom and Va*. New York: Macmillan, 1973. 154pp. ISBN 0-02-718320-1. LC 72-92434.
Prehistoric Africa. Dom, a boy from a fierce hunting tribe and Va, a girl from an agrarian society, have their friendship threatened by a clash of cultures. When Dom carries Va off as a captive after a tribal conflict, they learn to resolve their cultural differences. The conflict and resolution between the two cultures is convincing in this action-filled, suspenseful story.
Reviews: *WJ* 4; *BL* 9/15/73
Reading Level: Middle & Junior High School
Subject Areas: prehistoric man; Africa
Time Period: Neolithic Age; Stone Age ❑ Library owns

North of the Sahara

Egypt

Baumann, Hans; Richard and Clara Winston, trans. *The World of the Pharoahs*. New York: Pantheon Books, 1960. 255pp. ISBN 0-394-91840-1. LC 60-11491.
Ancient/Modern Egypt. Megdi, the son of a contemporary Egyptian archaeologist, and a learned old man who says he lived thousands of years ago visit all of the famous archeological sites where the old man explains what the artifacts show about ancient Egyptian life. This unusual novel contains vivid descriptions and much historical detail.

Africa—North of the Sahara

Reviews: *WJ*4
Reading Level: Middle–High School
Subject Areas: archeology; Egypt
Time Period: 3000 B.C. ❏ Library owns

Bell, Clare. *Tomorrow's Sphinx.* **New York: Macmillan/Margaret K. McElderry Books, 1986. 292pp. ISBN 0-689-50402-0. LC 86-8479.**
Ancient Egypt/Future. Two cheetahs, one who lived with the young pharaoh Tutankhamen and one struggling to survive in an ecologically ravaged futuristic world, communicate through mental links, each telling of its life. Exciting action scenes and many details of Egyptian life, such as training cheetahs, complement this story which is both historical and fantastic.
Reviews: *BBYA*; *BCCB* 11/86; *BL* 10/15/86; *WS*13; *SLJ* 11/86; *YAEC*
Reading Level: High School
Subject Areas: Egypt; Tutankhamen, King of Egypt; cheetahs; fantastic fiction
Time Period: 1350 B.C. ❏ Library owns

Bradshaw, Gillian. *The Beacon at Alexandria.* **Boston: Houghton Mifflin, 1986. 376pp. ISBN 0-395-41159-9. LC 86-3017.**
Alexandria, Egypt, fourth century. Fleeing an unacceptable arranged marriage to a brutish man, Charis, a young Roman noblewoman, flees to Alexandria, Egypt. There, disguised as a eunuch, she studies Hippocratic medicine and becomes a physician.
"In spellbinding fashion, Bradshaw uses Charis' studies and her subsequent career as a physician to reveal the extraordinary powers and riches, as well as the approaching downfall, of the empire." *Booklist*
Reviews: *BBSH*; *BFY*; *BL* 9/1/86
Reading Level: High School
Subject Areas: Egypt; physicians; Rome
Time Period: 300 ❏ Library owns

Carter, Dorothy Sharp. *His Majesty, Queen Hatshepsut.* **New York: Lippincott, 1987. 248pp. ISBN 0-397-32178-3; PLB 0-397-32179-1. LC 85-45855.**
Ancient Egypt. This fictionalized story of Queen Hatshepsut's life augments the known historical facts about the only woman who became pharaoh when her husband and half-brother lacked the ability to rule. The historical background provides an excellent history lesson that is also entertaining.
Reviews: *BCCB* 11/87; *BFY*; *BR* 3-4/88; *SLJ* 10/87★; *VOYA* 12/87
Reading Level: Middle–High School
Subject Areas: Egypt; Hatshepsut; pharaohs
Time Period: 1470 B.C. ❏ Library owns

Africa—North of the Sahara

Drury, Allen. *A God Against the Gods.* **New York: Doubleday, 1976. 310pp. ISBN 0-385-00199-1.** LC **75-41673.**
Ancient Egypt. Commentary on the "pomp and circumstance of the House of Thebes" under Queen Nefertiti and Pharaoh Akhenaten is given from the viewpoint of several characters. Akhenaten's displacement of the old gods in favor of one god brings him into disfavor.
Reviews: *BL* 6/15/76; *LJ* 7/76
Reading Level: High School
Subject Areas: Egypt; Amenhetep IV, King of Egypt; Nefertiti, Queen of Egypt; pharaohs
Time Period: 1300 B.C. ❑ Library owns

Drury, Allen. *Return to Thebes.* **New York: Doubleday, 1977. 272pp. ISBN 0-385-04199-3.** LC **76-23757.**
Ancient Egypt. Drury dramatizes the power struggle that marked the end of Pharaoh Akhenaten's reign with Nefertiti and paved the way for the succession of Tutankhamen. Though very historical in nature, the author creates realistic characters and situations. Sequel to *A God Against the Gods.*
Reviews: *BL* 2/1/77; *WS* 11
Reading Level: High School
Subject Areas: Egypt; Amenhetep IV, King of Egypt; Nefertiti, Queen of Egypt; Tutenkhamen, King of Egypt; pharaohs
Time Period: 1300 B.C. ❑ Library owns

Gedge, Pauline. *Child of the Morning.* **Cutchogue, NY: Buccaneer, 1986, c1977. 403pp. ISBN 0-89966-567-5.** LC **77-4385.**
Ancient Egypt. The life of Hatshepsut, Egypt's only woman pharaoh, is drawn with rich historical detail, showing her great power as well as her human needs and faults.
Reviews: *BBSH*; *BL* 9/1/77; *LJ* 6/15/77; *WS*11
Reading Level: High School
Subject Areas: Egypt; Hatshepsut, Queen of Egypt; pharaohs
Time Period: 1470 B.C. ❑ Library owns

Harris, Rosemary. *The Bright and Morning Star.* **New York: Macmillan, 1972. 254pp.** LC **73-171566.**
Ancient Egypt. In this third book of Harris's trilogy, the royal house of Kemi is endangered by a plot put in motion by the prince's priest/tutor, Hotep. Reuben arrives in Kemi to meet his wife Thamar, who is looking for a cure for their afflicted son. There he works with his friend Tahlevi to rescue the royal family. With moments of wit and satire, the plot moves along at a swift pace and is filled with assassinations, betrayal, and intrigue.
Reviews: *BL* 6/15/72; *HB* 4/72; *LB* 6/15/72

Africa—North of the Sahara

Reading Level: Middle–High School
Subject Areas: Egypt
Time Period: 2500 B.C. ❏ Library owns

Harris, Rosemary. *The Moon in the Cloud.* **Magnolia, MA: Peter Smith, 1969. 182pp. ISBN 0-8446-6429-4. LC 71-99121.**
Ancient Egypt. In this Carnegie medal-winning first book of Harris's trilogy, Reuben ventures into Egypt to find a royal cat and a brace of lions for Noah's Ark. Though dangerous, the success of the mission is of vital importance to Reuben, as he has been promised a place on the Ark and salvation from the flood for himself and his beloved wife Thamar. With a cast both human and animal, this is a witty, well-narrated story containing elements of villainy, virtue, sorrow and happiness.
Reviews: *BL* 4/15/70; *HB* 4/70; *LJ* 5/15/70
Reading Level: Middle–High School
Subject Areas: Egypt; Noah's Ark; adventure and adventurers; Bible stories
Time Period: 2500 B.C. ❏ Library owns

Harris, Rosemary. *The Shadow on the Sun.* **New York: Macmillan, 1970. 189pp. ISBN 0-571-09326-4. LC 78-543688.**
Ancient Egypt. Reuben and Thamar return in Harris's sequel, as do Noah and Mrs. Noah, all having been "delivered from the flood." This time, Reuben must help the Pharaoh of Kemi rescue and win his lady love, Meri-Mekhmet. Humor is found throughout the book, even in more serious moments that border on horror.
Reviews: *BL*12/1/70; *HB* 10/70; *LJ* 11/15/70; *TLS* 7/2/70
Reading Level: Middle & Junior High School
Subject Areas: Egypt
Time Period: 2500 B.C. ❏ Library owns

Leighton, Margaret (Carver). *Cleopatra; Sister of the Moon.* **New York: Farrar, 1969. 215pp. LC 75-85368.**
Ancient Egypt. Leighton's well-told story brings Cleopatra, Egypt's most famous queen, to life showing her to be an intelligent young woman proud of her divine lineage and prepared to meet her royal destiny.
Reviews: *BL* 11/15/69; *BCCB* 2/70; *LJ* 11/15/66
Reading Level: Middle–High School
Subject Areas: Egypt; Cleopatra, Queen of Egypt
Time Period: 50 B.C. ❏ Library owns

Rofheart, Martha. *The Alexandrian.* **New York: T.Y.Crowell, 1976. 320pp. ISBN 0-690-01148-2. LC 76-3659.**
Ancient Egypt. In first person narrative, the life of Cleopatra from young girl in a decaying court to queen seeking the best for her subjects is detailed. Using myth,

fantasy, and fact, the author re-creates the personalities of Cleopatra, Caesar, Pompey, and Marcus Antonius.
Reviews: *BL* 12/15/76; *LJ* 10/15/76
Reading Level: High School [Mature Reader]
Subject Areas: Egypt; Cleopatra, Queen of Egypt
Time Period: 50 B.C. ❑ Library owns

Waltari, Mika; Naomi Walford, trans. *The Egyptian.* **New York: Putnam, 1949. 503pp. OP.**
Ancient Egypt. Through the adventures of Sinuhe, a physician to the Pharaoh, Egyptian life more than 1000 years before Christ is described in rich detail.
Reviews: *WS*10
Reading Level: High School
Subject Areas: Egypt; physicians
Time Period: 1100 B.C. ❑ Library owns

Ethiopia

Levitin, Sonia. *The Return.* **New York: Atheneum, 1987. 213pp. ISBN 0-689-31309-8.** LC 86-25891.
Ethiopia, 1984-1985. Like many other Ethiopian Jews, feeling hated by the people of their remote mountain village as well as by the Communist government, Desta, her older brother and younger sister decide to make the arduous journey to Sudan with the hope of eventually emigrating to Israel. This sensitively written novel includes the use of many Ethiopian terms used in the text so that their meaning is clear to readers.
Reviews: *BBYA*, *BCCB* 3/87, *BL* 4/15/87★, *SLJ* 5/87, *VOYA* 6/87
Reading Level: Middle–High School
Subject Areas: Ethiopia; Jews--Ethiopia; antisemitism; Falashas; refugees
Time Period: 1984-1985 ❑ Library owns

Schlee, Ann. *The Guns of Darkness.* **New York: Atheneum, 1974. 238pp. ISBN 0-689-30145-6.** LC 73-84834.
Ethiopia, 1860s. Emperor Tewodros' reign in Ethiopia is seen through the eyes of 14-year-old Louisa Bell, daughter of an Ethiopian mother and an English father who is an advisor to the Emperor. Louisa witnesses the civil war and ensuing widespread starvation brought on by Tewodros' investment in military strength in pursuit of his dream of capturing Jerusalem. Due to the complexity of this novel, it may be more suitable for advanced readers.
Reviews: *BCCB* 10/74; *BL* 5/1/74★; *LJ* 5/15/74; *SLJ* 5/74
Reading Level: High School

Africa—North of the Sahara

Subject Areas: Ethiopia; Tewodros, Emperor of Ethiopia
Time Period: 1860 ❏ Library owns

North Africa

Myers, Walter Dean. *The Legend of Tarik.* New York: Viking, 1981. 185pp. ISBN 0-670-42312-2. LC 80-27655.
Medieval Northwest Africa. In this mythic tale, the black hero Tarik avenges his family against the white villain on his journey to self-discovery. In keeping with mythic form, the story contains monsters, journeys, and a final duel between good and evil.
"There are Islamic, Classical, Christian and traditional African elements." *School Library Journal*
Reviews: *BBYA*; *BL* 7/15/81; *HB* 8/81; *SLJ* 5/81; *VOYA* 10/81
Reading Level: Middle–High School
Subject Areas: fantastic fiction; Africa; adventure and adventurers
Time Period: Middle Ages ❏ Library owns

Ray, Mary. *The Windows of Elissa.* Winchester, MA: Faber & Faber, 1982. 183pp. ISBN 0-571-11831-3. LC 82-670147.
Carthage, North Africa, third century, B.C. Motherless Elissa and her family struggle to survive through the three-year siege of Carthage. Elissa fights to keep her younger sister from her religiously fanatic aunt and struggles to understand the Nomadic hostage living with them.
Reviews: *BCCB* 7-8/82; *BL* 5/15/82; *SLJ* 10/82
Reading Level: Middle & Junior High School
Subject Areas: Carthage; Africa
Time Period: 200 B.C. ❏ Library owns

Schlee, Ann. *The Consul's Daughter.* New York: Atheneum, 1972. 176pp. LC 72-175562.
Algiers, 1816. Based on an 1816 conflict between Britain and the Dey of Algeria over people captured by Algerian pirates and sold into slavery. This is the story of 14-year-old Ann McDonnel, the daughter of the British Consul to Algeria, who lives through this turbulent time, escaping from Algeria aboard a British sloop with her new stepmother and stepbrother. British Colonial attitudes and the social conditions in early nineteenth-century Algeria are described well.
Reviews: *BL* 9/1/72; *HB* 12/72; *LJ* 10/15/72; *TLS* 4/28/72
Reading Level: Middle–High School
Subject Areas: Algeria; pirates
Time Period: 1816 ❏ Library owns

South of the Sahara

Dickinson, Peter. *AK.* **New York: Delacorte, 1992. 192pp. ISBN 0-385-30608-3. LC 91-25628.**

A fictional former British colony, now independent. A 12-year-old orphan, Paul, caught up in a long civil war, is adopted by the leader of a guerilla band and trained to use his prized AK-47. When the war ends, Paul buries his AK, but a coup results in renewed fighting and Paul is called upon to fight. Though the country is fictional, it could be any war-torn African nation. This work poses thought provoking questions about the issues facing many Third World nations.

Reviews: *BL* 4/15/92; *CBBC* 5/92; *HB* 9/92; *KR* 6/5/94; *SLJ* 7/92; *VOYA* 6/92; *WS* 14

Reading Level: Middle–High School

Subject Areas: Africa; war

Time Period: 1980

❏ **Library owns**

Burundi

Clifford, Mary Louise; illustrated by Trevor Stubley. *Bisha of Burundi.* **New York: T. Y. Crowell, 1973. 140 pp. ISBN 0-690-14569-9. LC 72-83780.**

Contemporary Burundi. The nuns at the mission school encourage Bisha to go for teacher training, something no village girl has ever done. However, this is not "in line" with the traditional tribal values embraced by her father, who feels that "ambition is misplaced in a woman," or by her mother, who wants Bisha to marry to help her family advance politically.

Reviews: *BCCB* 10/73; *BL* 10/1/73; *HB* 8/73; *SLJ* 9/73

Reading Level: Middle & Junior High School

Subject Areas: Burundi; women

Time Period: 1970

❏ **Library owns**

Cameroun

Weaver-Gelzer, Charlotte. *In the Time of Trouble.* **New York: Dutton, 1993. 228 pp. ISBN 0-525-44973-6. LC 92-11146.**

Cameroun. The struggle for independence in Cameroun in 1958 is shown through the eyes of Jessie, daughter of missionaries who are abducted by political activists. Jessie must also deal with conflicts with her twin brother, her sisters, and her faith in God. Jesse's friendship with a local girl adds some cultural details, but also points out some of the hidden racism of the missionaries. There is a glossary of Basa and Bulu terms.

Reviews: *BL* 2/1/93; *BR* 9-10/93; *BCCB* 3/93; *SLJ* 7/93; *VOYA* 4/93

Reading Level: Middle–High School

Africa—South of the Sahara

Subject Areas: Cameroun; missionaries; twins; brothers and sisters
Time Period: 1955-1960   ❏ Library owns

East Africa

Scholefield, Alan. *Lion in the Evening.* **New York: William Morrow, 1974. 175pp. ISBN 0-688-00242-0.**
East Africa, 1916. Two man-eating lions become obstacles to the completion of a vital railroad being built by an American for the British, but desired by the Germans. The lions must be captured or destroyed by a crippled hunter. Though there are few characters, there is plenty of action, and the adventure is enjoyable.
Reviews: *WS*11
Reading Level: High School
Subject Areas: Africa, East; railroads; lions
Time Period: World War, 1914-1918   ❏ Library owns

Liberia

Bess, Clayton. *Story for a Black Night.* **Boston: Houghton/Parnassus Press, 1982. 84pp. ISBN 0-395-31857-2. LC 81-13396.**
Contemporary Liberia. Momo recalls a black night in his childhood when the arrival of a woman and her small-pox-infected baby set into motion events that tested the convictions of his grandmother, mother and their community. A strong image of village and family life is drawn. This is a good book for reading aloud and discussing.
Reviews: *BCCB* 6/82; *BL* 6/1/82; *HB* 8/92; *SLJ* 3/82
Reading Level: Middle & Junior High School
Subject Areas: Liberia; smallpox; villages
Time Period: Twentieth Century   ❏ Library owns

Namibia

Beake, Lesley. *Song of Be.* **New York: Holt, 1993. 95pp. ISBN 0-8050-2905-2. LC 93-11440.**
Namibia. Be, a member of the San or Bushman tribe in the Kalahari Desert region, receives word that her grandfather is in danger of losing his job on a farm unless she and her mother can help him. The actions of the Afrikaans farm owner and his wife ultimately lead to turmoil and tragedy, forcing Be to see the painful truth of her situation and that of her people. The author makes the current events of Namibia more important than its history, showing the personal side of change, and dealing with such complex issues as racial stereotypes.
Reviews: *BL* 12/1/93★; *BR* 5-6/94; *BCCB* 3/94; *SLJ* 3/94★; *NCB*
Reading Level: Middle–High School

Subject Areas: Africa; Namibia; San (African People); Bushmen; race relations
Time Period: 1990s ❏ Library owns

Linfield, Esther; Sam B. Hopson and George Carey Hobson, trans. *The Lion of the Kalahari.* **New York: Greenwillow Books/Morrow, 1976. 118pp. ISBN 0-688-80049-1; PLB 0-688-84049-3.** LC 76-3432.
The Kalahari Desert. Skankwan, grandson of the "Old Leopard," once headman of the Bushmen's Leopard band, grows into a master huntsman who avenges the wrong done to his family by Murák, the outsider who cheated Skankwan's family of their rightful place as headmen of the Leopard band.
Reviews: *BCCB* 2/77; *BL* 3/15/77; *SLJ* 3/77
Reading Level: Middle & Junior High School
Subject Areas: Africa; Kalahari Desert; Bushmen
Time Period: Nineteenth Century ❏ Library owns

Nigeria

Achebe, Chinua. *Arrow of God.* **New York: Anchor Literary Library, 1989, c1964. 287pp. ISBN 0-385-01480-5.** LC 75-79409.
Nigeria, 1960s. A story of the conflict between tribal customs and Westernization unfolds in a Nigerian village when Ezeulu, Chief Priest of Ulu, sends his son to missionary school. His son's absolute conversion to Christianity brings a final tragic clash between Ezeulu and the influences of the West, embodied in the English Administrator, Captain Winterbottom.
Reviews: *WS* 10
Reading Level: High School
Subject Areas: Africa; Nigeria; Ibo Tribe; British in Nigeria
Time Period: 1960s ❏ Library owns

Achebe, Chinua. *Things Fall Apart.* **New York: Crest/Fawcett, 1985, c1959. 215pp. ISBN 0-449-20810-9.** LC 59-7114.
Nigeria, late nineteenth century. A glimpse of bygone tribal days is seen in this story of Okonkwo, his three wives and their children. The advent of Christianity, through his favorite son's conversion, spells the end for Okonkwo and his tribal world.
Reviews: *WS* 10, 11, 12, 14
Reading Level: High School
Subject Areas: Africa; Nigeria; Ibo Tribe
Time Period: Nineteenth Century ❏ Library owns

Burchard, Peter. *Chinwe.* **New York: Putnam, 1979. 127pp. ISBN 0-399-20667-1.** LC 78-24401.
Ibo Nigeria, 1800s. Aboard a ship bound for Cuba, where she and many of her tribespeople will be sold as slaves, Chinwe proudly recalls her life in the Ibo

Africa—South of the Sahara

village where chiefs listened to her wise father, and whose wisdom sustains her and her brother as they become slaves, and keeps their hopes alive of one regaining their freedom. The descriptions of conditions aboard the slave vessel and of the collaboration of blacks in the capture of other blacks is notable.
Reviews: *BCCB* 10/79; *BL* 7/1/79; *HB* 8/79; *SLJ* 5/79
Reading Level: Middle–High School
Subject Areas: Africa; Ibo Tribe; slave trade
Time Period: Nineteenth Century ❏ Library owns

Emecheta, Buchi. *The Bride Price*. New York: Braziller, 1976. 168pp. ISBN 0-807609818-1. LC 75-46608.
Contemporary Nigeria. After her father's death, urban-bred and educated Aku-nna moves to Ibuza Village to live with her uncle. There she is bound by unfamiliar tribal customs such as the bride price her uncle expects to receive upon her marriage. She struggles with the choice between accepting the man her uncle has chosen or eloping with the village schoolmaster, an inferior match.
Reviews: *BL* 3/15/76; *SLJ* 9/76
Reading Level: High School [Mature Reader]
Subject Areas: Africa; Nigeria; marriage; Blacks--Nigeria
Time Period: Twentieth Century ❏ Library owns

Emecheta, Buchi. *The Slave Girl*. New York: Braziller, 1977. 179pp. ISBN 0-8076-0872-6. LC 77-77559.
Nigeria. An orphaned Nigerian girl's courage and dignity help her out of a "web of circumstances" and earn her passage into womanhood in Emecheta's third novel.
Reviews: *BL* 12/15/77; *SLJ* 2/78
Reading Level: High School [Mature Reader]
Subject Areas: Africa; Nigeria; orphans; Blacks--Nigeria
Time Period: Twentieth Century ❏ Library owns

Rupert, Janet E. *The African Mask*. New York: Clarion, 1994. 125pp. ISBN 0-395-67295-3. LC 93-7726.
Nigeria, 1100. In the city-state of Ifo, 12-year-old Layo finds that her elders have chosen a young man to be her husband. This poses a problem, as Layo has become a talented potter in her family's tradition. But if married, she will be expected to practice the trade of their husband's clans, and in this case, it means she would be working with bronze. She attempts to find a way to show that she should not be married. This book provides a look at family structure, the treatment of women and the importance of crafts in African society.
Reviews: *BL* 7/94; *SLJ* 9/94
Reading Level: Middle–High School

Subject Areas: Africa; Nigeria; Yoruba (Tribe)
Time Period: Twelfth Century   ❏ Library owns

Sierra Leone

Clifford, Mary Louise; illustrated by Elzia Moon. *Salah of Sierra Leona.* **New York: T. Y. Crowell, 1975. 184pp. ISBN 0-690-00908-9.** LC **75-9665.**
Sierra Leone, 1967. In the politically tense climate surrounding the 1967 elections in Sierra Leone, Salah is falsely accused of involvement in an attempted military takeover of the government because of his father's participation. He must decide whether to face a tribal jury or to escape to a modern life in Freetown.
Reviews: *BCCB* 2/76; *BL* 1/15/76; *HB* 2/76; *SLJ* 1/76
Reading Level: Middle & Junior High School
Subject Areas: Africa; Sierra Leone; Blacks--Sierra Leone
Time Period: 1967   ❏ Library owns

South Africa

Gordon, Sheila. *Waiting for the Rain: A Novel of South Africa.* **New York: Watts/Orchard/Richard Jackson Books, 1987. 224pp. ISBN 0-531-05726-7; PLB 0-531-08326-8.** LC **87-7638.**
Contemporary South Africa. Tengo, a black foreman's son, and Frikkie, nephew to the white farm owner, grow up as friends, but when the quest for education and entrance into the army bring them respectively to the city, they become embroiled in a political battle that changes the childhood friends into enemies. In this exciting docu-novel emphasis is on political and social conditions in South Africa.
Reviews: *BBYA*; *BCCB* 7-8/87; *BL* 8/87★; *HB* 9-10/87; *SLJ* 8/87; *VOYA* 12/87; *WJ* 6; *WS* 14
Reading Level: Middle–High School
Subject Areas: Africa; South Africa; apartheid; Blacks--South Africa; race relations
Time Period: Twentieth Century   ❏ Library owns

Duggan, William. *The Great Thirst.* **New York: Delacorte, 1985. 328pp. ISBN 0-385-29387-9.** LC **84-26863.**
South Africa. Mojomaje, a fictional BaNare tribesman, survives the hardships of nature, the Zulus, the Boers, diamond mines, and the English in a tale that mirrors the history of South Africa. Told in a manner meant to resemble the African oral tradition, this story clearly shows the ancient BaNare culture as it collides with modern ways.
Reviews: *BBSH*; *BL* 9/15/85; *BR* 5-6/86
Reading Level: High School
Subject Areas: Africa; South Africa
Time Period: Twentieth Century   ❏ Library owns

Africa—South of the Sahara

Jones, Toeckey. *Skindeep.* **New York: Charlotte Zolotow Books/Harper, 1986. 250pp. ISBN 0-06-023051-7; PLB 0-06-023052-5. LC 85-45843.**
Contemporary South Africa. This is initially the love story between students, Rhonda and Dave. However, all is not that simple for the South African teens as they face Dave's secret that he has been "passing for white." The teens' emotional and sexual relationship is set against racial prejudice and intolerance, against which they must act.
Reviews: *BCCB* 11/86; *HB* 3-4/87; *SLJ* 11/86★
Reading Level: High School [Mature Reader]
Subject Areas: Africa; South Africa; apartheid; race relations; love
Time Period: Twentieth Century ❑ Library owns

Linfield, Esther. *The Secret of the Mountain.* **New York: Greenwillow Books/ Morrow, 1986. 132pp. ISBN 0-688-05992-9. LC 85-9912.**
Pre-colonial Southeastern Africa. Anta, the son of the Xhosa chief, is destined to become chief, leaving his older half-brother very jealous. When the loss of cattle under Anta's care results in a battle with a neighboring tribe, Anta is too young to fight, but his half-brother does, planning to undermine Anta's claim to leadership. The people's interdependence and reverence for their cattle are vividly described.
Reviews: *BCCB* 4/86; *SLJ* 4/86
Reading Level: Middle–High School
Subject Areas: Africa; South Africa; Xhosa Tribe; brothers
Time Period: Eighteenth Century ❑ Library owns

Maartens, Maretha; Madeleine van Biljon, trans. *Paper Bird: A Novel of South Africa.* **Boston: Clarion Books, 1991. 148pp. ISBN 0-395-56490-5. LC 90-39675.**
Contemporary South Africa. Ten-year-old Adam supports his entire family, living in a black township in abject poverty, by selling newspapers in a nearby town. When political activists stage a "stay-at-home," Adam risks his wages and possible punishment to go to his job.
Reviews: *BL* 9/15/91★; *SLJ* 10/91
Reading Level: Middle & Junior High School
Subject Areas: Africa; South Africa; race relations; Blacks--South Africa; poverty
Time Period: 1986 ❑ Library owns

Michener, James. *The Covenant.* **New York: Random House, 1980. 877pp. ISBN 0-394-50505-0. LC 80-5315.**
South Africa. Michener employs fictional characters in an historical context to tell us the story of South Africa, from the time of the Bushmen to the present, through the generations of three families: Black, English and Dutch.
Reviews: *BBSH*; *BL* 91/80; *HB* 6/81; *WS* 11, 12, 13

Reading Level: High School [Mature Reader]
Subject Areas: Africa; South Africa
Time Period: Eighteenth–Twentieth Century ❏ Library owns

Naidoo, Beverley; illustrated by Eric Velasquez. *Chain of Fire.* **Philadelphia: Lippincott, 1990. 245pp. ISBN 0-397-32427-8. LC 89-27551.**
Contemporary South Africa. Sequel to *Journey to Jo'burg*. Naledi's village is faced with a forced removal to a "homeland," and Naledi and the other young people of the village become involved in a political confrontation which threatens her village's very existence and places people in jeopardy.
Reviews: *BBYA*; *BCCB* 5/90; *BL* 3/15/90★; *HB* 9/90; *SLJ* 5/90★; *VOYA* 6/90
Reading Level: Middle–High School
Subject Areas: Africa; South Africa; apartheid; race relations; revolutions
Time Period: Twentieth Century ❏ Library owns

Naidoo, Beverly; illustrated by Eric Velasquez. *Journey to Jo'burg: A South African Story.* **Philadelphia: Lippincott, 1990. 80pp. ISBN 0-397-32169-4. LC 85-45508.**
Contemporary South Africa. Naledi and Tiro, two South African youngsters must journey to Johannesburg, Jo'burg, to bring their mother home when their baby sister becomes gravely ill and must be hospitalized. Their journey takes them and the reader through the history and present of apartheid.
Reviews: *BCCB* 5/86; *BL* 3/15/86; *SLJ* 8/86★; *VOYA* 8/86
Reading Level: Middle & Junior High School
Subject Areas: Africa; South Africa; apartheid; race relations; Blacks--South Africa
Time Period: Twentieth Century ❏ Library owns

Paton, Alan. *Ah, But Your Land Is Beautiful.* **New York: Scribners, 1982. 271pp. ISBN 0-684-107830-3. LC 81-13547.**
South Africa 1952-58. Paton's novel chronicles South Africa's racial unrest, incorporating such events as the Suppression of Communism Act and the destruction of Sophiatown. Historic figures such as Trevor Huddleston, Patrick Duncan, Geoffrey Clayton, and Helen Joseph interact with fictional characters representing members from each segment of South Africa, allowing all voices to be heard.
Reviews: *WS* 13
Reading Level: High School
Subject Areas: Africa; South Africa; apartheid; race relations
Time Period: 1952-1958 ❏ Library owns

Africa—South of the Sahara

Paton, Alan. *Cry, The Beloved Country.* **New York: Collier/Macmillan, 1948, 1987. 304pp. ISBN 0-02-053210-5. LC 86-9674**
South Africa. A tragic novel about South Africa revolving around the sons and worlds of a Zulu parson and a white industrialist who become entangled by murder.
Reviews: *FFY*; *WS* 10, 11, 12, 14
Reading Level: High School
Subject Areas: Africa; South Africa; race relations
Time Period: Twentieth Century ❑ Library owns

Rochman, Hazel, ed. *Somehow Tenderness Survives: Stories of Southern Africa.* **New York: Harper, 1988. 118pp. ISBN 0-06-025023-2. LC 88-916.**
South Africa. In this collection of ten stories, South African writers, such as Peter Abrahams, Doris Lessing, Nadine Gordimer and Mark Mathabane, tell stories, sometimes autobiographical, of growing up under apartheid.
Reviews: *BBYA*; *BL* 8/88; *HB* 3-4/88; *SLJ* 12/88; *WS* 14
Reading Level: High School
Subject Areas: Africa; South Africa; apartheid; race relations; short stories
Time Period: Twentieth Century ❑ Library owns

Sacks, Margaret. *Beyond Safe Boundaries.* **New York: Dutton/Lodestar, 1989. 155pp. ISBN 0-525-67281-8. LC 88-27311.**
South Africa, early 1960s. Teenaged Elizabeth, growing up in an affluent Jewish family, knows little of apartheid and feels it has nothing to do with her. This changes when her older sister Evie has a romance with Willem, a multiracial student leader whose underground activity soon imperils both him and Evie.
Reviews: *BCCB* 7-8/89; *BL* 3/15/89★; *HB* 7-8/89; *SLJ* 7/89
Reading Level: Middle–High School
Subject Areas: Africa; South Africa; race relations; apartheid; sisters
Time Period: 1960 ❑ Library owns

Seed, Jenny. *The Great Thirst.* **New York: Dutton, 1974. 188pp. ISBN 0-87888-058-5. LC 73-80198.**
Southwest Africa, 1830s. This story of Garib and his quest for "the glory road" is set against the historical war between the westernized Hottentots, lead by Jonker Afrikaner, and the Herores, the Cattle People. After following Jonker Afrikaner in many successful raids on the Herores, Garib decides there must be another way to prove himself.
Reviews: *BCCB* 5/75; *BL* 2/15/75; *HB* 4/75; *SLJ* 2/75
Reading Level: Middle–High School
Subject Areas: Africa; Hottentots
Time Period: 1830 ❑ Library owns

Africa—South of the Sahara

Silver, Norman. *An Eye for Color.* **New York: Dutton, 1993. 192pp. ISBN 0-525-44859-4. LC 92-41525.**

Contemporary South Africa. In a set of interconnected stories, Basil is confronted by the inhumanity of apartheid, even in the peaceful white suburbs. In the final story, Basil pretends to be insane rather than join the military and be forced to brutalize blacks.

Reviews: *BCCB* 3/93; *BL* 1/15/93; *BR* 5/93; *SLJ* 7/93; *VOYA* 4/93
Reading Level: High School
Subject Areas: Africa; South Africa; apartheid; race relations
Time Period: Twentieth Century ❏ Library owns

Silver, Norman. *No Tigers in Africa.* **New York: Dutton, 1992. 100pp. ISBN 0-525-44733-4. LC 91-29121.**

Contemporary South Africa. Selwyn, a white South African teenager who has moved to England with his family, tries to repress memories of a black man whose death he caused. Filled with guilt, rejected by classmates, and watching his parents' lives fall apart, he attempts suicide, and then confronts the realities of his life.

Reviews: *BCCB* 9/92; *BL* 6/1/92; *BR* 1/93; *SLJ* 11/92; *VOYA* 10/92; *WS* 14
Reading Level: Middle–High School
Subject Areas: Africa; South Africa; apartheid; Great Britain; family problems; moving, household
Time Period: Twentieth Century ❏ Library owns

Van der Post, Laurens. *A Story Like the Wind.* **San Diego: Harcourt Brace Jovanovich, 1978. 370pp. ISBN 0-05-685261-6. LC 78-5688.**

South Africa. On a cooperative farm, 13-year-old Francois Joubert gains respect for Africa's ancient ways from his father, a teacher. His tutelage continues as he learns how to survive in the bush from a Matabele herdsman and a legendary game warden, Mopani Theron.

Reviews: *BL* 12/15/72; *WS* 10
Reading Level: High School
Subject Areas: Africa; South Africa; Bushmen
Time Period: Twentieth Century ❏ Library owns

Watson, James. *No Surrender.* **Pomfret, VT: Victor Gollancz/Trafalgar Square, 1993. 160pp. ISBN 0-575-04893-X.**

Contemporary South Africa. Malenga Nakale, daughter of an African resistance leader, is kidnapped in Angola by a South African army unit and taken to South Africa. She falls in love with a white fellow-prisoner and together they attempt to escape. The author shows a relationship between the rebels and the CIA in this sometimes brutal book.

Reviews: *BL* 7/93; *LJ* 7/93; *SLJ* 11/93

Asia—Prehistoric Asia

Reading Level: High School
Subject Areas: Africa; South Africa; Angola; prisoners
Time Period: Twentieth Century ❏ Library owns

Williams, Michael. *Crocodile Burning.* **New York: Lodestar, 1992. 192pp. ISBN 0-525-67401-2. LC 91-46197.**
Contemporary South Africa. Sowetan Seraki's role in a local musical allows him to escape the reality of his life in a black township. First simply through the act of performing and later through travel, when the musical is booked in New York. Seraki learns not only the unpleasant side of a theatrical life, but learns what is right for him.
Reviews: *BL* 8/92; *BR* 11/92; *HB* 9/92; *SLJ* 11/92; *VOYA* 10/92
Reading Level: Middle–High School
Subject Areas: Africa; South Africa; Blacks--South Africa; theater
Time Period: 1990 ❏ Library owns

Williams, Michael. *Into the Valley.* **New York: Philomel, 1993. 194pp. ISBN 0-399-22516-1. LC 92-25116.**
Contemporary South Africa. Walter, weighed down with his brother's death and his own draft into the South African Defense Force, leaves home to join a band defending Illongweni in Zululand from the ANC. He finds no clear cut lines between good and bad, and must make decisions about his actions.
Reviews: *BCCB* 9/93; *BL* 8/93; *SLJ* 10/93
Reading Level: Middle–High School
Subject Areas: Africa; South Africa; Zulu; war
Time Period: Twentieth Century ❏ Library owns

Asia

Prehistoric Asia

Linevski, A.; Maria Polushkin, trans. *An Old Tale Carved Out of Stone.* **New York: Crown, 1973. 230pp. ISBN 0-517-50263-1. LC 72-92386.**
Neolithic (Stone Age) Siberia. Liok, a neolithic Siberian, becomes his tribe's shaman, but goes against tradition and must flee the tribe with his brother. The two are adopted by a more advanced tribe whose knowledge could aid their former tribe.
Reviews: *BCCB* 3/74; *BL* 11/1/73; *HB* 12/73; *NCB*; *SLJ*★
Reading Level: Middle–High School
Subject Areas: prehistoric man; Siberia
Time Period: Stone Age ❏ Library owns

Osborne, Chester G. *The Memory String.* **New York: Atheneum, 1984. 154pp. ISBN 0-689-31020-X. LC 83-15633.**

Prehistoric Siberia. The story of Darath's tribe's journey in search of food to a legendary land of plenty, supports the theory of migration from Siberia to North America 30,000 years ago.

Reviews: *BCCB* 7/84; *BL* 4/1/84; *SLJ* 4/84; *VOYA* 6/84; *WJ* 5

Reading Level: Middle & Junior High School

Subject Areas: prehistoric man; Siberia

Time Period: Stone Age ❑ Library owns

Thomas, Elizabeth Marshall. *Reindeer Moon.* **Boston: Houghton Mifflin, 1987. 338pp. ISBN 0-395-42112-8. LC 86-18530.**

Prehistoric Siberia. Yanan becomes a spirit who must help the people of her lodge find food. As she guards her people, she reminisces about her youth.

Reviews: *BL* 11/15/86; *LJ* 1/87; *WS*

Reading Level: High School

Subject Areas: prehistoric man; Siberia

Time Period: Stone Age ❑ Library owns

Southeast Asia

Cambodia

Baillie, Allan. *Little Brother.* **New York: Viking, 1992. 144pp. ISBN 0-670-84381-4. LC 91-28797.**

Cambodia, 1970s. While fleeing the Cambodian Khmer Rouge in an effort to escape to Thailand, two brothers become separated. Vithy, fearing his brother's death, continues on, helped along the way by others. He makes his way to a refugee camp and to resettlement in Australia with a doctor he meets in the camp.

"This excellent tale of courage and survival lends real life flesh to textbook facts and will be welcomed in most collections. It should be mandatory reading for anyone working with Southeast Asian youth." *School Library Journal*

Reviews: *BCCB* 3/92; *BL* 1/15/92; *HB* 3/92 & 7/91; *SLJ* 3/92; *VOYA* 8/92

Reading Level: Middle & Junior High School

Subject Areas: Cambodia; refugees; orphans

Time Period: 1970s ❑ Library owns

Ho, Minfong. *The Clay Marble.* **New York: Farrar, 1991. 160pp. ISBN 0-374-31340-7. LC 91-14093.**

Cambodia, 1980s. Dara yearns to have life as it was before her family had to flee to a refugee camp in Thailand. When the camp is shelled, Dara is separated from her family and her best friend is mortally wounded. After the turmoil, Dara convinces her family to return home.

Asia—Southeast Asia

Reviews: *BCCB* 12/91; *BL* 11/15/91; *HB* 1/92; *SLJ* 10/01
Reading Level: Middle & Junior High School
Subject Areas: Cambodia; refugees
Time Period: 1980s ❏ Library owns

Singapore

Cheong, Fiona. *The Scent of the Gods.* New York: Norton, 1991. 224 pp. ISBN 0-393-03024-5. LC 91-22594.
Singapore, 1960s. Eleven-year-old orphan Su Yen lives with her extended family, headed by her grandmother. She relates her observations as Singapore and her family change around her.
Reviews: *BL* 9/15/91★; *LJ* 9/15/91; *SLJ* 3/92
Reading Level: High School
Subject Areas: Singapore; family life; orphans
Time Period: 1960s ❏ Library owns

Thailand

Boulle, Pierre; Xan Fielding, trans. *The Bridge Over the River Kwai.* New York: Bantam, 1990, c1952. 224pp. ISBN 0-553-24850-2.
World War II Thailand, 1939-1945. Boulle's satirical novel follows a British colonel who, even as a Japanese prisoner of war, is able to carry on with British discipline. He supervises the building of a bridge, even safeguarding his project from Allies sent to sabotage the Japanese.
Reviews: *BBSH*; *FFY*; *WS* 10, 12, 13, 14
Reading Level: High School
Subject Areas: Thailand; Great Britain. Army; prisoners of war
Time Period: World War, 1939-1945 ❏ Library owns

Ho, Minfong. *Rice Without Rain.* New York: Lothrop, 1990. 208pp. ISBN 0-688-06355-1. LC 86-33745.
Thailand, 1970s. Seventeen-year-old Jinda works with her family in an agricultural valley where a two-year drought has caused much hardship. She meets Ned, one of a group of radical students sent to work in the fields and falls in love with him. Jinda follows him to Bangkok, but finds her only interest in politics is in using it to help her imprisoned father. Jinda returns to her village without Ned.
Reviews: *BBYA*; *BL* 7/90★; *BR* 11/90; *HB* 11/90; *SLJ* 9/90★; *YAEC*
Reading Level: Middle–High School
Subject Areas: Thailand; revolutions
Time Period: 1970s ❏ Library owns

Asia—Southeast Asia

Tibet

Dickinson, Peter. *Tulku.* **New York: Dutton, 1979. 288pp. ISBN 0-525-41571-8. LC 78-11461.**

Tibet, 1900s. Theo, the son of an American missionary and a Chinese woman, is rescued after the Boxer Rebellion by a free-spirited English woman, Mrs. Jones, who is traveling to Tibet with a young Chinese lover. After much adventure on the road, they are taken in by Tibetan monks who believe Mrs. Jones is pregnant with their "tulku," or reincarnated spiritual leader.

Reviews: *BBYA*; *BCCB* 10/79; *BL* 1/15/79; *HB* 8/79; *SLJ* 5/79★

Reading Level: High School

Subject Areas: China; Tibet; orphans

Time Period: 1900-1910 ❏ Library owns

Vietnam

Bennett, Jack. *The Voyage of the Lucky Dragon.* **New York: Prentice Hall, 1982. 149pp. ISBN 0-13-944165-4. LC 81-19267.**

Saigon, Southeast Asia, Australia, late 1970s. Phan Thi Chi and his family, in Saigon at the end of the Vietnam War, are desperate to escape. The son, Quan, steals the family's confiscated boat back from the government, and they begin an arduous and dangerous journey in search of asylum in other Southeast Asian countries, Australia and America.

Reviews: *BL* 6/1/82; *SLJ* 5/82; *VOYA* 12/82; *WJ* 5

Reading Level: Middle–High School

Subject Areas: Vietnam; refugees; Australia; Vietnam War, 1961-1975

Time Period: 1970s ❏ Library owns

Garland, Sherry. *Song of the Buffalo Boy.* **San Diego: Harcourt, Brace, Jovanovich, 1992. 264pp. ISBN 0-15-277107-7. LC 91-31872.**

Vietnam, 1980s. Loi, an Amerasian teen growing up in a small village, has born insults and been rejected by her village because of her absent American father. Her family arranges Loi's marriage to a lecherous officer, but Loi, who loves Khai the buffalo herder, runs away to the city where she waits for him to join her. When he doesn't come, Loi lives on the street until she meets an American who is looking for his daughter and offers to take her instead.

Reviews: *BCCB* 7/92; *BL* 4/1/92; *BR* 9/92; *HB* 7/92; *SLJ* 6/92

Reading Level: Middle–High School

Subject Areas: Vietnam; Amerasians; prejudices

Time Period: 1980s ❏ Library owns

Asia—Middle East

Huong, Duong Thu; Phan Huy Duong and Nina McPherson, trans. *Paradise of the Blind.* **New York: Morrow, 1993. 270pp. ISBN 0-688-11445-8.** LC 92-18599.

Vietnam, 1970s. Growing up under repressive Communist rule, Hang and her family suffer in many ways. Hang's father disappeared years ago; her mother works hard to support Hang and her uncle, who denigrates the woman who supports him. when her mother is injured, Hang must quit school and ends up being sent to Russia as an "exported worker." This book was banned in Vietnam.

Reviews: *BR* 9/93; *LJ* 1/94; *SLJ* 7/93
Reading Level: High School
Subject Areas: Vietnam
Time Period: 1970s ❑ Library owns

Whelan, Gloria. *Goodbye, Vietnam.* **New York: Knopf/Borzoi, 1992. 136pp. ISBN 0-679-92263-6.** LC 91-3660.

Vietnam, 1970s. With the arrest of her grandmother and father imminent, Mai's family makes a run for freedom, slogging through swamps to the ocean where they gain passage on a small boat heading for Hong Kong. The trip is hard, but they do reach a refugee camp where they fear they will be sent back to Vietnam before relatives in America can be found.

Reviews: *BCCB* 10/92; *BL* 1/1/93; *BR* 1/93; *HB* 1/93; *SLJ* 9/92
Reading Level: Middle & Junior High School
Subject Areas: Vietnam; refugees; sea stories
Time Period: 1970s ❑ Library owns

Middle East

Ancient Civilization

Silverberg, Robert. *Gilgamesh the King.* **New York: Arbor House, 1984. 290pp. ISBN 0-87795-599-9.** LC 84-12434.

Sumer, 2700-538 B.C. In a retelling of the world's oldest tragedy, Gilgamesh, part god and part mortal, fulfills a prophecy which detailed his life. Unfortunately, he cannot avoid the tragic end that is also prophesied.

"Maintaining the integrity of the 5,000-year-old tale, Silverberg delivers this most human of stories in a wholly new form, while, it is hoped, inspiring readers to return to the original translations on which it is based." *Booklist*

Reviews: *BL* 9/1/84; *LJ* 10/15/84
Reading Level: High School
Subject Areas: Sumer; Gilgamesh
Time Period: 3000 B.C. ❑ Library owns

Biblical

Caldwell, Taylor. *Dear and Glorious Physician.* **New York: Bantam, 1984. 608pp. ISBN 0-553-25997-0 (paper).**

Biblical times, first century A.D. Caldwell presents the story of Saint Luke, or Lucanus, physician and author of one of the Gospels, whose wanderlust takes him from his boyhood home in Antioch to Judea where he embraces Christianity.

Reviews: *WS* 10

Reading Level: High School

Subject Areas: Judea; Saints; Christian Saints; Luke, Saint; Physicians; Bible stories

Time Period: First Century A.D. ❏ Library owns

Caldwell, Taylor. *Great Lion of God.* **Guilford, CT: Ulverscroft, 1976. 629pp. ISBN 0-85456-553-1.**

Biblical times. This novel is based on the life of St. Paul from his birth to his conversion to Christianity and his decision to go to Rome.

Reviews: *WS* 10

Reading Level: High School

Subject Areas: saints; Christian saints; Paul, Saint; Jesus Christ; Palestine; Bible stories

Time Period: First Century A.D. ❏ Library owns

Douglas, Lloyd C. *The Big Fisherman.* **Boston: Houghton, 1948. 581pp. ISBN 0-395-07630-7. LC 48-10352.**

Biblical times, first century A.D. The story follows Simon Peter (Saint Peter), the fisherman chosen by Christ to lead his disciples, and Fara, Arabian princess and Herod's daughter who learns love and forgiveness from Christ. The author makes references to many persons actual and fictitious who appeared in *The Robe*.

Reviews: *WS* 10

Reading Level: High School

Subject Areas: Peter, Saint; Jesus Christ; saints; Christian saints; Bible stories

Time Period: First Century A.D. ❏ Library owns

Holmes, Marjorie. *Three from Galilee: The Young Man from Nazareth.* **New York: Harper, 1985. 230pp. ISBN 0-06-015100-5. LC 82-48145.**

Biblical times, 1 A.D. In this sequel to *Two from Galilee*, Holmes portrays the young Jesus as the oldest and best loved of many siblings, who realizes and accepts his destiny when his mother begins to speak of his marriage.

Reviews: *BBSH*; *BL* 8/85; *LJ* 9/15/85

Reading Level: High School

Asia—Middle East

Subject Areas: Jesus Christ; Palestine; Bible stories
Time Period: First Century A.D. ❏ **Library owns**

Levitin, Sonia. *Escape from Egypt.* **Boston: Little, Brown, 1994. 267pp. ISBN 0-316-52273-2. LC 93-29376.**
Egypt and Israel, before 1200 B.C. Jesse, an Israelite teen, his family, and Jennat, a half-Egyptian, half-Syrian slave, undertake the exodus from Egypt, following Moses across the Red Sea and into the desert. There they face hardships and tests to their faith.
Reviews: *BL* 5/1/94★; *SLJ* 4/94; *BR* 11-12/94; *VOYA* 4/94
Reading Level: Middle–High School
Subject Areas: Egypt; Israel; Moses; Exodus, The; Jews; Bible stories
Time Period: 1200 B.C. ❏ **Library owns**

Lofts, Norah. *How Far to Bethlehem? A Novel.* **New York: Doubleday, 1965. 353pp. LC 65-15092.**
Bethlehem, Judea, Biblical times, 1 A.D. Lofts presents the Nativity from Mary's vision of the angel to Jesus' birth and homage by the three wise men.
Reviews: *WS* 10
Reading Level: High School
Subject Areas: Jesus Christ; Judea; Bible stories
Time Period: 1 A.D. ❏ **Library owns**

Mann, Thomas; H.T. Lowe-Porter, trans. *Joseph and His Brothers.* **New York: Knopf, 1948. 1207pp. ISBN 0-394-43132-4. LC 48-7040.**
Biblical times, before 1200 B.C. This anthology contains four titles now out of print in separate editions: *The Tales of Jacob* (1934); *Young Joseph* (1935); *Joseph in Egypt* (1938); *Joseph the Provider* (1944).
Reviews: *WS* 10, 11
Reading Level: High School
Subject Areas: Joseph the Patriarch; Bible stories
Time Period: 1200 B.C. ❏ **Library owns**

Morgan, Alison. *The Eyes of the Blind.* **New York: Oxford Univ. Press, 1987. 207pp. ISBN 0-19-271542-9.**
Judea and Jerusalem, 800-700 B.C. Benjamin, grandson of Isaiah, is caught up in an invasion by Assyrians. He aids the wounded son of the Assyrian commander who was left to die, and the two begin an odyssey seeking first safety, and then their destinies.
Reviews: *SLJ* 2/88; *School Librarian* 12/86
Reading Level: Middle–High School

Subject Areas: Jews; Assyrians; blind

Time Period: 800-700 B.C. ❏ Library owns

Murphy, Walter F. *Upon This Rock: The Life of St. Peter.* **New York: Macmillan, 1987. 538pp.** ISBN **0-02-588270-8.** LC **87-15896.**

Biblical times, first century A.D. The events of St. Peter's life are seen through the eyes of Quintus, a Greco-Roman follower, from the founding of Christianity to Peter's return to Rome to die in Nero's circus.

Reviews: *SLJ* 3/88; *LJ* 11/15/87

Reading Level: High School

Subject Areas: Peter, Saint; Rome; saints; Christian saints; Bible stories

Time Period: First Century A.D. ❏ Library owns

Speare, Elizabeth George. *The Bronze Bow.* **New York: Houghton, 1961. 255pp.** ISBN **0-395-07113-5; 0-395-13719-5 (paper).** LC **61-10640.**

Palestine, first century A.D. Young Daniel, whose parents are killed by the Romans, swears vengeance and joins a band of outlaws who find dangerous and violent ways to thwart the Romans. Returning to his village to care for his sister, Daniel is drawn to Rabbi Jesus and eventually becomes a convert to Jesus' teachings of peace and forgiveness.

Reviews: *WJ* 4; Newbery Medal 1962

Reading Level: Middle & Junior High School

Subject Areas: Jesus Christ; Palestine

Time Period: First Century A.D. ❏ Library owns

Walsh, John Evangelist. *The Man Who Buried Jesus.* **New York: Macmillan/ Collier, 1989. 160pp.** ISBN **0-02-045731-6.** LC **88-31166.**

Jerusalem; Biblical times; first century A.D. Nicodemus, an elder, visits the tomb of Jesus to gather evidence to verify reports he has heard of the Resurrection. He interviews a wide variety of people, including disciples and Roman guards, and comes to a spiritual conclusion.

Reviews: *BL* 4/15/89

Reading Level: High School

Subject Areas: Jesus Christ; Bible stories; Jerusalem

Time Period: First Century A.D. ❏ Library owns

Byzantium

Bradshaw, Gillian. *The Bearkeeper's Daughter.* **Boston: Houghton, 1987. 310pp.** ISBN **0-395-43620-6.** LC **87-2924.**

Sixth century A.D. Reign of Justinian I and Empress Theodora, Constantinople (Istanbul, Turkey). Bradshaw tells the tale of John, who learn's from his father's

Asia—Middle East

deathbed revelation that his mother is the Empress Theodora. The knowledge leads him to the glorious palace in Constantinople where he is acknowledged and rises in rank while refusing his mother's wish that he become emperor.

Reviews: *BL* 12/1/87; *LJ* 11/15/87

Reading Level: High School

Subject Areas: Constantinople; Byzantine Empire; Theodora, Empress of Byzantium

Time Period: Sixth Century ❏ Library owns

Bradshaw, Gillian. *Imperial Purple*. Boston: Houghton, 1988. 324pp. ISBN 0-395-43635-4. LC 88-11923.

Fifth century A.D., Constantinople/Tyre, Phoenicia (Lebanon). When state slave Demetrias is told to weave a large cloak of the imperial purple, worn only by emperors, she and her fisherman husband become involved in a dangerous political plot.

Reviews: *BBSH*; *BL* 11/1/88; *SLJ* 2/89

Reading Level: High School

Subject Areas: Constantinople; Byzantine Empire; slaves; kidnapping

Time Period: Fifth Century ❏ Library owns

Dickinson, Peter; illustrated by David Smee. *The Dancing Bear*. Boston: Atlantic/Little, 1973. 244pp. ISBN 0-316-184268. LC 72-11530.

Byzantium, sixth century A.D. When a Hun raid kills most of the household of the Byzantine Count of the Outfields and abducts his 14-year-old daughter, the survivors—Silvester, the household's Greek slave bearkeeper, his charge, Bubba, and a holy man—pursue the raiding party to free Ariadne.

Reviews: *BL* 7/1/73; *HB* 10/73; *NCB*

Reading Level: Middle–High School

Subject Areas: Byzantine Empire; Huns; kidnapping; humorous stories

Time Period: Sixth Century ❏ Library owns

Holland, Cecelia. *The Belt of Gold*. New York: Knopf, 1984. 301pp. ISBN 0-394-52791-7. LC 83-48854.

Constantinople, ninth century A.D. Returning from a pilgrimage to the Holy Land, Hagen, "a Frank of noble blood," becomes involved with a maid in service to the Empress Irene and gets drawn into the conflict between the factions for and against her.

Reviews: *BL* 2/1/84; *LJ* 2/15/84

Reading Level: High School

Subject Areas: Byzantine Empire; Irene, Empress of Byzantium

Time Period: Ninth Century ❏ Library owns

Asia—Middle East

Iran/Iraq

Laird, Elizabeth. *Kiss the Dust.* **New York: Dutton, 1992. 281pp. ISBN 0-525-44893-4.** LC **91-43517.**
Iraq, Iran, 1984. Tara and her family must flee Iraq during the Iran-Iraq War and ending up in an Iranian refugee camp where the living conditions are harsh. Her family later finds refuge in Britain.
Reviews: *BCCB* 6/92; *BL* 6/15/92; *BR* 9/92; *SLJ* 7/92
Reading Level: Middle–High School
Subject Areas: Iran; Iraq; refugees; Kurds
Time Period: 1984 ❏ Library owns

Barkhordar-Nahai, Gina. *Cry of the Peacock.* **New York: Crown, 1991. 341pp.** ISBN **0-517-57479-9.** LC **90-20311.**
Iran, 1800-1982. Peacock, a 116-year-old Jewish woman, awaits her fate after being arrested by the Islamic Revolutionary Guard. As she waits, the stories of earlier generations of her family and the events of the past two hundred years are revealed.
Reviews: *BL* 6/1/91; *SLJ* 11/91
Reading Level: High School [Mature Reader]
Subject Areas: Iran; Jews
Time Period: 1800-1982 ❏ Library owns

Israel

Forman, James D. *My Enemy, My Brother.* **New York: Scholastic, 1970, c1969. 304pp.** ISBN **0-590-04477-X.** LC **75-80282.**
Arab-Israeli War, 1948. After being released from a German concentration camp, Daniel Baratz emigrates to Israel and a kibbutz called "Promise of the Future," which for Daniel means peace. As a shepherd, he befriends an Arab youth and they pledge never to fight in the wars of their peoples, however both are eventually drawn in on opposite sides.
Reviews: *BCCB* 7/69; *BL* 9/1/69; *HB* 6/69; *WJ* 4, 5
Reading Level: Middle–High School
Subject Areas: Israel; Jews; Jewish-Arab relations; Israel-Arab War, 1948-49
Time Period: 1945-1948 ❏ Library owns

Hellman, Aviva. *To Touch a Dream.* **New York: Donald I. Fine, 1989. 544pp. ISBN 1-55611-055-3.** LC **87-81423.**
1912-1970s. Through Deborah Danziger's life, six generations of living and strife in Israel are explored.
Reviews: *BL* 10/15/89; *LJ* 5/15/89
Reading Level: High School [Mature Reader]

Subject Areas: Israel; Jews; Jewish–Arab relations
Time Period: 1912–1975 ❏ Library owns

Michener, James. *The Source.* **New York: Random House, 1965. 909pp. ISBN 0-394-44630-5.** LC **65-11255.**
Western Galilee (Israel/Palestine). Twentieth century/past. The objects found on an archaeological expedition in Western Galilee provide the link to stories from many different eras spanning the history of Israel.
Reviews: *BBSH*; *WS* 10, 11, 12, 13, 14
Reading Level: High School
Subject Areas: Israel; Palestine; Archeology; Jews; Arabs
Time Period: 2000 B.C.-1960 ❏ Library owns

Nurenberg, Thelma. *The Time of Anger.* **England: Abelard-Schuman, 1975. 207pp. ISBN 0-200-00153-1.** LC **75-2396.**
Eve of Arab-Israeli War of 1967. Two young girls, Jewish Aviva and Arabic Laila, become friends when Laila is admitted to Aviva's kibbutz as an experiment in intercultural relations. They find that they must face the hostility and prejudices of their friends, family and boyfriends.
Reviews: *BL* 1/15/76; *SLJ* 11/75
Reading Level: Middle–High School
Subject Areas: Israel; Jewish-Arab relations; Israel-Arab War, 1967; friendship; prejudice
Time Period: 1967 ❏ Library owns

Semel, Nava; Seymour Simckes, trans. *Becoming Gershona.* **New York: Viking, 1990. 128pp. ISBN 0-670-83105-0.** LC **89-24845.**
1958. In Tel Aviv, two years after the Sinai War, twelve-year-old Gershona is coping with becoming an adolescent. She is bothered by Holocaust and war memories, but when her grandfather comes to Israel she struggles with new emotions.
Reviews: *BCCB* 6/90; *BL* 9/1/90; *SLJ* 7/90
Reading Level: Middle & Junior High School
Subject Areas: Israel; Jews; adolescence; grandparent and child
Time Period: 1958 ❏ Library owns

Uris, Leon. *Exodus.* **New York: Doubleday, 1958. 626pp. ISBN 0-385-05082-8.** LC **62-16691.**
Nineteenth century—1940s. The story of a Christian nurse smuggling a group of Jewish children to Palestine in the 1940s, gives Uris the thread to weave a tale that covers the whole history of Zionism, from the nineteenth century including all the events that resulted in the formation of the modern state of Israel.
Reviews: *FFY*; *WS* 10, 11, 12, 13

Reading Level: High School
Subject Areas: Israel; Palestine; Zionism; Jewish-Arab relations
Time Period: 1850-1940 ❑ Library owns

Palestine

Jabbour, Hala Deeb. *A Woman of Nazareth.* **New York: Interlink/Olive Branch Press, 1990. 272pp. ISBN 0-940793-07-5. LC 88-2785.**
Palestine, Lebanon, 1948-1982. Amal, a Palestinian woman living in a Lebanese refugee camp, finds her society too restrictive for women and leaves the camp to search for freedom.
Reviews: *BL* 1/1/90; *PW* 1/12/90
Reading Level: High School [Mature Reader]
Subject Areas: Israel; Lebanon; Palestine; refugees; women
Time Period: 1948-1982 ❑ Library owns

Scott, Sir Walter. *The Talisman.* **Lanham, MD: Evman/Biblio Dist, 1980, (orig. pub. 1829). ISBN 0-0460-01144-8 (paper).**
The Third Crusade, 1189-1192. Sir Kenneth, Prince Royal of Scotland, disguises himself as a knight and joins the Crusade in the Holy Land under Richard Coeur de Lion, the Lionheart. There Richard's "noble enemy Saladin," disguises himself as a physician when he hears Richard is ill, then offers the ailing Richard a drink of spring water into which he has dipped his "talisman" to aid in Richard's healing.
Reviews: *WS* 10, 11
Reading Level: High School
Subject Areas: Israel; crusades; Richard I, King of England; Saladin
Time Period: 1189-1192 ❑ Library owns

Wiesel, Elie; Frances Frenaye, trans. *Dawn.* **New York: Hill & Wang, 1961. 89pp. ISBN 0-553-22536-7.**
Palestine; 1940s. In the night before he is to execute a British officer, 18-year-old Elisha is haunted by memories of the concentration camps, and then before dawn gets to know the man he is to kill. He realizes to his horror that he could become a friend, not an enemy.
Reviews: *BBSH*; *FFY*; *WS* 10
Reading Level: High School
Subject Areas: Palestine; concentration camps
Time Period: 1940s ❑ Library owns

Asia—Middle East

Syria

Schami, Rafik; Rika Lesser, trans. *A Handful of Stars.* **New York: Dutton, 1990. 224pp. ISBN 0-525-44535-8. LC 89-25991.**
Contemporary Damascus, Syria, twentieth century. Through journal entries, the narrator tells of his 14th through 18th during which he is forced to leave school to work and becomes involved in a very dangerous underground resistance movement, all at a time when the government is becoming more repressive.
"...there's a rich, vital, multicultural community. The narrator's family is Catholic, his best friend is Muslim, the barber is Armenian, the assistant comes from Persia, and the boy's beloved elderly mentor tells him stories from everywhere-- history, legend, and fable." *School Library Journal*
Reviews: *BBYA*; *BL* 2/15/90; *SLJ* 3/90
Reading Level: Middle–High School
Subject Areas: Syria; censorship; diaries; government, resistance to
Time Period: 1980s ❏ Library owns

Turkey

Hiçyilmaz, Gaye. *Against the Storm.* **Boston: Little, Brown/Joy Street Books, 1992. 200pp. ISBN 0-316-36078-3. LC 91-41155.**
Contemporary Turkey. Mehmet and his family leave their small village for Ankara, with hopes for the better life that has been promised by a rich uncle, but instead find squalid, dehumanizing conditions. Mehmet defies his uncle and prepares to leave his family to return to his village.
Reviews: *BBYA*: *BCCB* 4/92; *BL* 4/15/92; *HB* 5/92; *SLJ* 5/92; *VOYA* 6/92
Reading Level: Middle–High School
Subject Areas: Turkey; poverty
Time Period: 1980s ❏ Library owns

Mourad, Kenize; Sabine Destrée and Anna Williams, trans. *Regards from the Dead Princess: Novel of a Life.* **Boston: Arcade/Little, Brown, 1989. 560pp. ISBN 1-55970-019-X. LC 89-15096.**
Turkey, Lebanon, 1918-1938. When the Ottoman Empire falls, Selma, granddaughter of the Sultan, who has been living in royal splendor, suddenly tastes poverty. An arranged marriage leaves her feeling trapped by the restrictions on women in her society, and she escapes to Paris and personal freedom.
"Perhaps the most intriguing aspect of the novel is the fact that it is based on the life of the author's mother, whom she never knew... A sweeping, atmospheric tale..." *Booklist*
Reviews: *BL* 10/15/89; *LJ* 11/1/89
Reading Level: High School

Subject Areas: Turkey; Lebanon; women
Time Period: 1918-1938 ❏ Library owns

Far East

China

Carlson, Dale Bick; illustrated by John Gretzer. *The Beggar King of China.* **New York: Atheneum, 1971. 185pp.** LC **70-154750.**
Ming Dynasty, 1368-1644. Chu Yuan-chang, born the son of a poor farmer, rises to hero by leading the forces that drive the Mongols out of China. He becomes T'ai-tsu Ming, emperor of all China and founder of the Ming Dynasty.
Reviews: *BL* 4/1/72; *LJ* 12/15/71
Reading Level: Middle–High School
Subject Areas: China; Ming, T'ai-tsu, Emperor of China
Time Period: 1350-1400 ❏ Library owns

David, Kurt; Anthea Bell, trans.; illustrated by Hans Baltzer. *Black Wolf of the Steppes.* **Boston: Houghton, 1972. 251pp. ISBN 0-395-14329-2.** LC **72-2756.**
Mongolia, China, 1167-1227. Through the eyes of his boyhood friend Kara-Chono, we see Temujin's rise to power as the cruel, ruthless, and power-hungry Genghis Khan, leader of the Mongol tribes. Nomadic life on the steppes is described without being glamorized.
Reviews: *BL* 5/1/73; *HB* 5/1/73; *SLJ* 9/73
Reading Level: Middle–High School
Subject Areas: China; Genghis Khan
Time Period: 1167-1227 ❏ Library owns

Buck, Pearl. *Imperial Woman.* **New York: John Day, 1956. 376pp.**
End of the Manchu Dynasty, China. The life of Tzu-hsi, the last Empress of China, is related from the time she was first ordered to appear before the Emperor until her death in 1908. Historical details about the political workings of life within the Forbidden City and the fall of the Manchu Dynasty contribute greatly to this novel.
Reviews: *WS* 10
Reading Level: High School
Subject Areas: China; Tz'u-hsi, Empress Dowager of China
Time Period: 1840-1908 ❏ Library owns

Asia—Far East

China–Nineteenth Century

Buck, Pearl. *The Good Earth.* **Oxford: Oxford University Press, 1931, 1982. ISBN 0-19-581035-X.**
Late nineteenth century, China. An epic novel about a Chinese peasant's belief in owning land. This a story of poverty, struggle, and revolution won the 1932 Pulitzer Prize.
Reviews: *WS* 10, 12, 13, 14; *FFY; BBSH*
Reading Level: High School
Subject Areas: China
Time Period: 1880-1911   ❏ Library owns

Eden, Dorothy. *The Time of the Dragon.* **New York: Crest/Fawcett, 1975, 1981. 284pp. ISBN 0-449-23059-7. LC 75-22243.**
Peking, Britain, 1899. Peking and London are the alternating settings for this novel of the Carrington family whose fortune was made from treasures stolen during China's Boxer Rebellion.
Reviews: *BL* 12/15/75; *LJ* 12/15/75
Reading Level: High School [Mature Reader]
Subject Areas: China; Peking, siege of, 1900; London, England
Time Period: 1899   ❏ Library owns

Lee, C. Y. *The Second Son of Heaven.* **New York: Morrow, 1990. 384pp. ISBN 0-688-05140-5. LC 89-48315.**
China, mid-nineteenth century. This is a tale loosely based on the lives of two men on opposite sides of the Taiping Rebellion, which was an attempt to fight the corruption of Manchu rule and Western imperialism. The first is Hung Shiu-chu'an, leader of the Chinese Christian God-worshippers, who leads the rebellion and the other, British adventurer Charles George ("China") Gordon who commands the forces against them.
Reviews: *BL* 5/15/90; *LJ* 5/1/90
Reading Level: High School [Mature Reader]
Subject Areas: China; Taiping Rebellion, 1850-1864; Gordon, Charles George; Hung Shiu-chu'an; revolutions
Time Period: 1850-1864   ❏ Library owns

Monjo, F. N. *The Porcelain Pagoda.* **New York: Viking, 1976. 257pp. ISBN 0-670-56565-2. LC 75-38574.**
China, 1822. Kitty and her family travel to China with a ship full of trade goods. In a fog off Macao, their ships collides with another. In the ensuing chaos, Kitty meets and falls in love with the captain of the other ship, an opium smuggler. To

keep her away from him, her parents take her inland in China—where foreign women are forbidden by law—and the trouble begins.

Reviews: *BCCB* 10/86; *BL* 5/1/76; *HB* 8/76; *SLJ* 4/76★

Reading Level: Middle–High School

Subject Areas: China; sea stories

Time Period: 1822 ❏ Library owns

Paterson, Katherine. *Rebels of the Heavenly Kingdom.* **New York: Lodestar, 1983. 229pp. ISBN 0-525-66911-6. LC 83-1529.**

Taiping Rebellion, mid-nineteenth century. Farm boy Wang Lee is kidnapped by bandits, and then rescued by Mei Lin, a follower of the Taiping or Heavenly Kingdom cult. The cult is waging a "holy crusade" against the Manchu Dynasty in order to build a "Kingdom on Earth." Although at first drawn to the cult and its promises of education and equality, Wang Lee later begins to question its indiscriminately violent means toward a better life for China.

Reviews: *BL* 6/15/83; *SLJ* 9/83

Reading Level: Middle–High School

Subject Areas: China; Taiping Rebellion, 1850-1864; cults; revolutions

Time Period: 1850-1864 ❏ Library owns

Yep, Laurence. *Mountain Light.* **New York: Harper, 1985. 282pp. ISBN 0-06-026758-5; 0-06-026759-3. LC 85-42643.**

Red Turban Revolt, 1855. In this companion book to *The Serpent's Children*, Cassia and Tiny continue their battle to free the Middle Kingdom (China) from the "darkness" of the Manchu Dynasty. This novel introduces Squeaky Lau, a revolutionary comrade, who eventually travels to San Francisco, the land of "Mountain Light" to complete his journey into manhood.

Reviews: *BCCB* 11/85; *BL* 9/15/85; *SLJ* 1/86; *VOYA* 12/85

Reading Level: Middle–High School

Subject Areas: China: Taiping Rebellion, 1850-1864; emigration and immigration; revolutions

Time Period: 1855 ❏ Library owns

Yep, Laurence. *The Serpent's Children.* **New York: Harper, 1984. 277pp. ISBN 0-06-026809-3; PLB 0-06-026812-3. LC 82-48855.**

Kwangtung province, mid-nineteenth century. The spirited Cassia and her brother, whom villagers chide for having "serpent's blood," feel the effects of revolutionary actions against the Manchu Dynasty, such as the Taiping Rebellion, the hardships of life in a small village, and the promise of travel to "Gold Mountain" where fortunes can be made.

Reviews: *BCCB* 3/84; *BL* 5/1/84; *BR* 9/84; *HB* 8/84; *SLJ* 8/84; *VOYA* 8/84; *WJ* 5

Reading Level: Middle–High School

Subject Areas: China; Taiping Rebellion, 1850-1864; revolutions; family life
Time Period: 1850-1864 ❏ Library owns

China–Twentieth Century

Ballard, J. G. *Empire of the Sun; A Novel.* **New York: Simon & Schuster, 1984. 279pp. ISBN 0-671-53051-8; 0-671-503053-4.** LC 84-10630.
Shanghai, World War II, 1939-1945. Eleven-year-old Jim is separated from his parents when Shanghai is captured by the Japanese the day after Pearl Harbor. He then spends the better part of the war in a Japanese prison camp, where he faces the difficult task of surviving in grim circumstances.
Reviews: *BBSH*; *WS* 13, 14
Reading Level: High School
Subject Areas: prisoners of war; Shanghai (China); Sino-Japanese Conflict, 1937-1945; concentration camps
Time Period: 1941-1945 ❏ Library owns

Bell, William. *Forbidden City.* **New York: Bantam, 1990. 208pp. ISBN 0-553-07131-9.** LC 90-080951.
Tiananmen Square, Beijing, 1989. In the Spring of 1989, Canadian teenager Alex Jackson, a Chinese history and military strategy buff, accompanies his cameraman father on a trip to Beijing to cover Gorbachev's visit. There Alex learns about life in the People's Republic of China and develops a sympathetic understanding for its students that pulls him into the tragic events at Tiananmen Square that June.
"This is a blood-and-thunder story, and Bell tells it with gusto. Incidents are piled on one another, background descriptions are very convincing, and at times the readers will almost feel they are there. All this amounts to an incredibly compelling novel...this is an excellent tale, well-told, and a historical novel of note."
School Library Journal
Reviews: *BCCB* F 91; *BL* 1/15/91★; *SLJ* 3/91
Reading Level: Middle–High School
Subject Areas: China; Tiananmen Square Incident, 1989
Time Period: 1989 ❏ Library owns

Buck, Pearl S. *Dragon Seed.* **New York: John Day Co., 1942. 378pp.**
Nanking, China, 1930s. Ms. Buck's 1938 Nobel Prize winner is the story of farmer Ling Tan and his family in Nanking as the Japanese take over the city. Though propagandistic, it is an indictment of dictatorships and inhumanity in the widest sense.
Reviews: *WS* 10, 11
Reading Level: High School

Subject Areas: China; Sino-Japanese relations
Time Period: 1930s ❏ Library owns

Chen, Yuan-Tsung. *The Dragon Village.* **New York: Pantheon, 1980. 285pp. ISBN 0-394-50791-6. LC 79-3315.**
Shanghai, 1949. During the tumultuous founding of the People's Republic of China, 17-year-old Ling-ling decides to remain in the PRC instead of fleeing to Hong Kong with her wealthy family. She joins a theater group that goes to the remote Dragon Village of the title where she and her idealistic colleagues hope to effect land reforms.
Reviews: *BL* 7/1/80; *SLJ* 9/80; *YARC*; *VOYA* 12/80
Reading Level: High School
Subject Areas: China; revolutions; actors
Time Period: 1949 ❏ Library owns

Cordell, Alexander; illustrated by Victor Ambrus. *The Traitor Within.* **Nashville: Nelson, 1973. 126pp. ISBN 0-8407-6294-1. LC 72-13250.**
People's Republic of China. Ling, a 14-year-old Red Guard, wages battles to defend his father from suspicion and the villagers from attack by Taiwanese paratroopers. The Red communal life is seen in a sympathetic light.
Reviews: *BL* 9/15/73; *SLJ* 10/73
Reading Level: Middle & Junior High School
Subject Areas: China
Time Period: 1945-1950 ❏ Library owns

Cronin, A.J. *The Keys of the Kingdom.* **Boston: Little, Brown, 1941, 1984. 344pp. ISBN 0-316-16184-5.**
China, 1900-1930. Father Francis Chisholm, a Scottish Catholic priest, dedicates 30 years of his life to a mission in China where he cares for the physical and spiritual well-being of his converts. He and his colleagues experience the horrors of the famine and civil war that spread through China during these years.
Reviews: *WS* 10
Reading Level: High School
Subject Areas: China; missionaries
Time Period: 1900-1930 ❏ Library owns

Gaan, Margaret. *Little Sister.* **New York: Dodd, 1983. 208pp. ISBN 0-396-08096-0. LC 82-9576.**
Shanghai, May Thirtieth Movement of 1925. Alternately told by three young members of a unique family—their Chinese grandmother with traditionally bound feet is married to an American. This is a story about a family, and how its

members are affected by the revolutionary activity that preceded the Nationalist-Communist struggle for power in China.
Reviews: *BL* 6/15/83; *SLJ* 3/83; *YARC*
Reading Level: High School
Subject Areas: China; May Thirtieth Movement, 1925; revolutions; family life
Time Period: 1925 ❏ Library owns

Li, Leslie. *Bittersweet.* **Rutland, VT: Charles E. Tuttle, 1992. 388pp. ISBN 0-8048-1777-4. LC 92-15385.**
China, 1900-1980. From a woman's perspective, Bittersweet sums up Chinese society and history by relating her experiences from the time of the Boxer Rebellion to the 1970s.
Reviews: *LJ* 8/92; *SLJ* 4/93
Reading Level: High School
Subject Areas: China; women
Time Period: 1900-1980 ❏ Library owns

Lord, Bette Bao. *Spring Moon; A Novel of China.* **New York: Harper & Row, 1981. 464pp. ISBN 0-380-59923-6. LC 78-20210.**
Soochow, China, 1890-present. Lord tells the story of China's recent history from tradition to revolution and change, through the generations of an aristocratic Chinese family, focusing most of his story on Spring Moon who is taught to read and write, but must follow the traditional roles for women including bound feet and an arranged marriage.
Reviews: *BBSH*; *LJ* 10/15/81; *SLJ* 4/82; *WS* 13, 14
Reading Level: High School
Subject Areas: China; family life
Time Period: 1890-1970 ❏ Library owns

Malraux, André; Haakon M. Chevalier, trans. *Man's Fate.* **New York: Vintage/Random, 1990, c1934. 283pp. ISBN 0-679-72574-1.**
Shanghai, 1927 Insurrection. A small yet diverse group of revolutionaries (French, Russian, Japanese and Chinese) fight to better the fate of Chinese workers. What they find to be worse than their violent and bloody struggle is the problem of placing a value on human life.
Reviews: *BBSH*; *WS* 11
Reading Level: High School [Mature Reader]
Subject Areas: China; revolutions; Shanghai Insurrection, 1927
Time Period: 1927 ❏ Library owns

Tsukiyama, Gail. *Women of the Silk.* **New York: St. Martin's, 1991. 288pp. ISBN 0-312-06465-9.** LC **91-21006.**

China, 1919-1938. When Pei is eight years old, she is sent to work in a silk factory where she spends the next 20 years of her life. She gets support from her coworkers and forms a great friendship with Lin, who was also sent to the factory. The workers weather the Japanese threat and the communists and begin to demand better working conditions and more independence.

Reviews: *BBYA*; *BL* 9/15/91; *LJ* 5/1/92; *SLJ* 3/92

Reading Level: High School

Subject Areas: China; women; silk industry

Time Period: 1919-1938 ❏ Library owns

Vander Els, Betty. *The Bomber's Moon.* **New York: Farrar, 1985. 167pp. ISBN 0-374-30864-0.** LC **85-47591.**

China, India, World War II. From 1942 to 1946, Ruth and her brother Simeon, the children of missionaries, are separated from their parents. They are led on a four-year "odyssey" by their boarding school masters in an effort to flee the invading Japanese forces. Their travels take them from China to the Himalayan foothills of India.

Reviews: *SLJ* 8/85; *VOYA* 4/86

Reading Level: Middle & Junior High School

Subject Areas: China; India; missionaries; escapes; World War 1939-1945

Time Period: 1942-1946 ❏ Library owns

India

Courter, Gay. *Flowers in the Blood.* **New York: Dutton, 1990. 613pp. ISBN 0-525-24897-8.** LC **90-44085.**

Nineteenth century, India. Dinah Sassoon, part of a wealthy Jewish family, lives a life that is anything but dull. Over 50 years, Dinah experiences the murder of her mother, two unhappy marriages, exotic settings, and business dealings in the opium trade.

Reviews: *BL* 8/90; *LJ* 9/1/90; *SLJ* 2/91

Reading Level: High School [Mature Reader]

Subject Areas: India; Jews

Time Period: Nineteenth Century ❏ Library owns

Kipling, Rudyard. *Kim.* **New York: Penguin, 1987. First published 1901. ISBN 0-14-043281-7.**

Lahore, India. Kim, an Irish orphan, is brought up in the native quarter of Lahore, educated first by a Tibetan lama searching for the River of Immortality and then at a Catholic college in England. He is carefully groomed and well-prepared for his career with the British Secret Service, where he quickly proves himself on his first assignment in the Himalayas.

Reviews: *WJ* 4, 5

Reading Level: Middle–High School

Subject Areas: India; orphans; secret service; adventure and adventurers; spies

Time Period: Nineteenth Century ❏ Library owns

Rana, Indi. *The Roller Birds of Rampur.* **New York: Holt, 1993. 298pp. ISBN 0-8050-2670-3.** LC **92-33471.**

Modern India. Seventeen-year-old Sheila Mehta, who has been living in England for ten years, returns to India when a romance ends. She finds some comfort in her grandfather and attempts to balance her two cultures, each with contradictions and injustices.

Reviews: *BCCB* 5/92; *BL* 7/93; *SLJ* 5/93; *VOYA* 2/94

Reading Level: Middle–High School

Subject Areas: India; individuality

Time Period: 1980s ❏ Library owns

Smith, Rita Pratt. *In the Forest at Midnight.* **New York: Donald I. Fine, New York: 1989. 293pp. ISBN 1-55611-131-2.** LC **88-45859.**

India just after independence. Megan, a British colonial, falls in love with a young Indian revolutionary, despite experiencing the difficulties of her aunt's mixed marriage. When she becomes pregnant, she finds a new destiny awaits.

Reviews: *BL* 5/15/89; *LJ* 4/1/89

Reading Level: High School [Mature Reader]

Subject Areas: India; love; British in India

Time Period: 1948-50 ❏ Library owns

Yolen, Jane. *Children of the Wolf.* **New York: Viking, 1984. 136pp. ISBN 0-670-21763-8.** LC **83-16979.**

India, 1920s. Based a true story, Yolen recounts the story of two feral girls in India, found by a Christian missionary and brought to an orphanage to be civilized. Mohandas, the 14-year-old orphan who becomes the girls' protector and guide, soon sees that civilization can be as savage as the jungle they left.

Reviews: *BCCB* 6/84; *BL* 8/84★; *HB* 4/84; *SLJ* 3/84

Reading Level: Middle & Junior High School

Subject Areas: India; feral children; orphans

Time Period: 1920s ❏ Library owns

Nepal

Marks, James M.; illustrated by Goray Douglas. *Ayo Gurkha!* **Nashville, TN: Nelson, 1973. 253pp. ISBN 8407-6310-7. LC 73-7827.**

Nepal, Malaysia, World War II. To buy the land he dreams of owning, Aitahang, a hill country shepherd, enlists in the army. The story follows him from his hill country home to his army training and his experiences in tracking Chinese terrorists in Malaysia during World War II.

Reviews: *BL* 1/1/74; *LJ* 11/15/73
Reading Level: Middle–High School
Subject Areas: Nepal; Malaysia; family life; soldiers
Time Period: World War, 1939-1945 ❏ Library owns

Pakistan

Staples, Suzanne Fisher. *Shabanu: Daughter of the Wind.* **New York: Knopf, 1989. 256pp. ISBN 0-394-84815-2; PLB 0-394-94815-7. LC 89-2714.**

Cholistan Desert, Pakistan. In her nomadic family, Shabanu, at 12, is only one year away from an arranged marriage which she has been brought up to accept. But fate intervenes, plans change, and Shabanu must decide whether to follow her family's dictates or her own wishes.

Reviews: *BBYA*; *BCCB* 10/89; *BL* 10/1/89★; *HB* 1/90; *SLJ* 11/89; *VOYA* 4/90
Reading Level: Middle–High School
Subject Areas: Pakistan; family life; women; marriage
Time Period: Twentieth Century ❏ Library owns

Staples, Suzanne Fisher. *Haveli.* **New York: Knopf, 1993. 259pp. ISBN 0-0679-84157-1. LC 92-29054.**

Pakistan, present day. Sequel to *Shabanu: Daughter of the Wind*. Now married to an aging clan leader, and with a young daughter, Shabanu is allowed to visit her husband's family home. There she meets and falls in love with her husband's nephew. But when her husband is killed by his brother, who then wishes to take Shabanu as his wife, she fakes her death and goes into hiding.

Reviews: *BBYA*; *BL* 6/1/93; *BR* 2/94; *CED*; *SLJ* 8/93
Reading Level: Middle–High School
Subject Areas: Pakistan; women
Time Period: Twentieth Century ❏ Library owns

Japan–Feudal

Carlson, Dale Bick; illustrated by John Gretzer. *Warlord of the Genji.* **New York: Atheneum, 1970. 171pp. LC 73-115079.**

Twelfth century. Yoshitsune Minamoto, son of a defeated Genji chief, and his brother join forces to defeat a rival clan. After the victory, Yoshitshune's brother turns on him in an attempt to become the warlord.

Asia—Far East

Reviews: *BL* 1/1/71; *LJ* 10/15/70
Reading Level: Middle–High School
Subject Areas: Japan; brothers; Minamoto, Yoshitsune
Time Period: Twelfth Century   ❏ Library owns

Clavell, James. *Shogun; A Novel of Japan.* **New York: Delacorte, 1983, c1975. 802pp. ISBN 0-385-29224-4.** LC 74-77840.
Seventeenth century. John Blackthorne's adventures in feudal Japan are chronicled from the time of his shipwreck to his achievement of samurai status as he adapts to living in a world very different from his own.
Reviews: *BBSH*; *WS* 10, 11, 13, 14
Reading Level: High School [Mature Reader]
Subject Areas: Japan; Samurai
Time Period: Seventeenth Century   ❏ Library owns

Haugaard, Erik Christian. *The Samurai's Tale.* **Boston: Houghton-Mifflin, 1984. 234pp. ISBN 0-395-34559-6.** LC 83-22746.
Sixteenth century. The son of a lord, the sole survivor of a battle in which his entire family is killed, is taken in by the invading lord, stripped of his noble samurai rank, and given the name Taro. In this tale of Japanese military and court life, in the time of civil wars, Taro regains his status and adheres to the rigorous samurai code.
Reviews: *BL* 4/1/84; *BR* 11/84; *NCB*; *SLJ* 5/84
Reading Level: Middle–High School
Subject Areas: Japan; Samurai
Time Period: Sixteenth Century   ❏ Library owns

Haugaard, Erik Christian. *The Boy and the Samurai.* **Boston: Houghton Mifflin, 1991. 256pp. ISBN 0-395-56398-4.** LC 90-47535.
Sixteenth century. In this sequel to *The Samurai's Tale*, orphaned Saru lives on the streets by cunning. He meets an old samurai who is trying to save his wife by outsmarting a rival, and the two work together.
Reviews: *BCCB* 4/91; *BL* 5/1/91★; *BR* 9/91; *HB* 5/91; *SLJ* 4/91; *VOYA* 6/91
Reading Level: Middle–High School
Subject Areas: Japan; Samurai; orphans
Time Period: Sixteenth Century   ❏ Library owns

Namioka, Lensey. *The Coming of the Bear.* **New York: HarperCollins, 1992. 240pp. ISBN 0-06-020289-0.** LC 91-17331.
Sixteenth century. Zenta and Matsuzo, two samurai, are captured by the Ainu when their boat lands on the island of Hokkaido. They become embroiled in a

Asia—Far East

mystery concerning a marauding bear that should be hibernating, and in a conflict caused by Japanese trying to colonize the island.

Reviews: *BCCB* 3/92★; *BL* 3/1/92★; *SLJ* 3/92
Reading Level: Middle–High School
Subject Areas: Japan; Samurai; Ainu; mystery and detective stories
Time Period: Sixteenth Century ❏ Library owns

Namioka, Lensey. *Island of Ogres.* **New York: Harper & Row, 1989. 197pp. ISBN 0-06-024372-4; 0-06-024373-2. LC 88-22058.**

Sixteenth century. Kaijiro, an unemployed samurai, shows up at a castle claiming to be Zenta (who is being hidden by the commander's wife). The plot thickens to include murder, espionage, and rebellion, which Kaijiro, Zenta, and Matsuzo help along.

"Appearance versus reality permeates the plot; no one is exactly who he says he is at the beginning, except for the Samurai heroes." *School Library Journal*

Reviews: *BCCB* 2/89; *BL* 5/15/89; *SLJ* 3/89; *WS* 13
Reading Level: Middle–High School
Subject Areas: Japan; Samurai; mystery and detective stories
Time Period: Sixteenth Century ❏ Library owns

Namioka, Lensey. *The Samurai and the Long-nosed Devils.* **New York: McKay, 1976. 153pp. ISBN 0-679-20361-3. LC 76-12744.**

Sixteenth century. Zenta and Matsuzo find employment as the bodyguards of Portuguese missionaries. When the missionaries are suspected of killing a nobleman, the duo works to clear the missionaries while keeping themselves safe from the real killer.

Reviews: *BCCB* 1/77; *BL* 12/1/76
Reading Level: Middle–High School
Subject Areas: Japan; Samurai; missionaries; mystery and detective stories
Time Period: Sixteenth Century ❏ Library owns

Namioka, Lensey. *Valley of the Broken Cherry Trees.* **New York: Delacorte, 1980. 218pp. ISBN 0-440-09325-2. LC 79-53605.**

Sixteenth century. Once again Ronin Zenta and his companion Matsuzo find adventure and intrigue in their travels. This time there is the mysterious mutilation of sacred cherry trees and a power struggle between two warlords.

Reviews: *BBSH*; *BCCB* 6/80; *BL* 4/15/80; *HB* 6/80; *SLJ* 8/80; *VOYA* 8/80
Reading Level: Middle–High School
Subject Areas: Japan; Samurai; mystery and detective stories
Time Period: Sixteenth Century ❏ Library owns

Asia—Far East

Namioka, Lensey. *Village of the Vampire Cat.* **New York: Delacorte, 1981. 200pp. ISBN 0-440-09377-5. LC 80-68737.**
Sixteenth century. Ronin Zenta and Matsuzo travel to the snow country (northern Japan) where Zenta's tea master, Ikken, lives. Here they come to the aid of the villagers threatened by a vampire cat that kills women and bandits selling "protection" from it.
Reviews: *BCCB* 6/81; *BBYA*; *BL* 5/1/81; *HB* 8/81; *SLJ* 5/81; *VOYA* 10/81
Reading Level: Middle–High School
Subject Areas: Japan; Samurai; mystery and detective stories
Time Period: Sixteenth Century ❏ Library owns

Namioka, Lensey. *White Serpent Castle.* **New York: McKay, 1976. 154pp. ISBN 0-679-20362-1. LC 76-12743.**
Sixteenth century. Zenta and Matsuzo's travels take them to a warlord's castle where they aid the nine-year-old heir who is threatened by power-hungry rivals and solve the mystery of the White Serpent Ghost, which has made its appearance.
Reviews: *BL* 1/1/77; *SLJ* 1/77
Reading Level: Middle–High School
Subject Areas: Japan; Samurai; mystery and detective stories
Time Period: Sixteenth Century ❏ Library owns

Paterson, Katherine; illustrated by Haru Wells. *Of Nightingales That Weep.* **New York: T.Y. Crowell, 1974. 170pp. ISBN 0-690-00485-0. LC 74-8294.**
1180-1185. When Takiko's father, a famous samurai, is killed, she is taken into the court of the boy emperor to be a musician and personal servant. While there Takiko must resolve her conflicts about loyalty toward the court, a handsome samurai, and her peasant stepfather.
Reviews: *BCCB* 4/75; *BL* 12/1/74; *HB* 2/75; *NCB*; *SLJ* 1/75
Reading Level: Middle–High School
Subject Areas: Japan; Samurai
Time Period: Twelfth Century ❏ Library owns

Paterson, Katherine; illustrated by Haru Wells. *The Master Puppeteer.* **New York: Crowell, 1976. 179pp. ISBN 0-069-00913-5; PB 0-06-440281-9. LC 75-8614.**
Eighteenth century, Osaka. When Jiro runs away from his impoverished puppet-maker father and apprentices with the Hanaza puppet theater, he finds a mysterious link between the Robin Hood-like Saboro and the theater.
"The make-believe world of the Japanese puppet theatre merges excitedly with the hungry, desperate realities of eighteenth century Osaka in this better-than-average junior novel." *Bulletin of the Center for Children's Books*

Reviews: *BBYA*; *BCCB*; *BL* 3/1/76; *HB* 4/76; *NCB*; *SLJ* 3/76★; *WJ* 5
Reading Level: Middle & Junior High School
Subject Areas: Japan; puppets and puppet plays
Time Period: Eighteenth Century ❏ Library owns

Robson, Lucia St. Clair. *The Tokaido Road; A Novel of Feudal Japan.* **New York: Ballantine, 1991. 576pp. ISBN 0-345-37026-0. LC 90-93213.**
Feudal Japan. Lady Kinume ("Golden Plum"), tracked by her enemy's chief henchman, yet bent on avenging her father's death, assumes various disguises to travel the perilous Tokaido Road in search of Oishi, the samurai she is sure can help her cause.
Reviews: *BL* 4/1/91★; *LJ* 2/15/91
Reading Level: High School [Mature Reader]
Subject Areas: Japan
Time Period: Sixteenth Century ❏ Library owns

Japan–Twentieth Century

Maruki, Toshi. *Hiroshima No Pika.* **New York: Lothrop, 1982. unpag. ISBN 0-688-01297-3. LC 82-15365.**
Hiroshima, August 1945. Artist Toshi Maruki graphically depicts one family's experience of the atomic bomb blast that devastated Hiroshima toward the end of World War II, often using nude and definitely somber figures and shades. Although produced as children's picture book, caution and guidance are advised to help students understand the background, circumstances and complex issues, surrounding the bombings.
Reviews: *BCCB* 10/82; *HB* 10/82; *SLJ* 8/82★
Reading Level: Middle–High School
Subject Areas: Japan; Hiroshima; atomic bomb
Time Period: World War, 1939-1945 ❏ Library owns

Matsubara, Hisako; Ruth Hein, trans. *Samurai.* **New York: Times Books, 1980. 218pp. ISBN 0-8129-0852-X. LC 79-51443.**
1900-1960. The wealthy father of the Hayato family, who is descended from the samurai ruling class, sends his son, whom he adopted to marry his daughter and carry on the family name, Nagayuki to America to make a financial success. The task takes 60 years and separates Nagayuki from his wife, Tomiko.
Reviews: *BL* 1/15/80★; *LJ* 1/1/80; *WS* 11, 12
Reading Level: High School [Mature Reader]
Subject Areas: Japan; family life; Japanese in the United States
Time Period: Twentieth Century ❏ Library owns

Asia—Far East

Matsubara, Hisako; Leila Vennewitz, trans. *Cranes at Dusk.* **New York: Dial Press, 1984. 253pp. ISBN 0-385-27858-6. LC 84-7031.**
Kyoto, Post World War II. Ten-year-old Saya, the daughter of a Shinto priest, wakes up one morning to find the war over. This marks the beginning of a new way of life. There are the physical hardships as well as the opposing views held by her parents, her mother clinging to the traditions that her father now finds empty.
Reviews: *BBYA*; *BCCB* 5/85; *BL* 3/15/85; *SLJ* 5/85; *WS* 13
Reading Level: High School
Subject Areas: Japan; family life
Time Period: 1945   ❏ Library owns

Mattingley, Christobel; illustrated by Marianne Yamaguchi. *The Miracle Tree.* **San Diego: Gulliver/Harcourt Brace Javonovich, 1986. unpag. ISBN 0-15-20005-30-7. LC 86-4541.**
Post World War II. Taro, his wife Hanako, and her mother are separated by the war and the atomic bomb explosion that shatters Hanako physically and mentally. They rebuild their lives separately in post-war Japan, and are miraculously reunited years later by the pine tree Taro plants as a "plea for peace."
"The author...has once again caught the sufferings of families victimized by war, but the tone here is more tragic in keeping with the ultimate threat of nuclear holocaust. In spite of its picture-book format, this is a story for older readers."
Bulletin of the Center for Children's Books
Reviews: *BCCB* 12/86; *HB* 3/87; *SLJ* 12/86
Reading Level: Middle–High School
Subject Areas: Japan; Christmas stories; peace; atomic bomb
Time Period: 1945-1965   ❏ Library owns

Morris, Edita. *The Flowers of Hiroshima.* **New York: Viking, 1959. 187pp. LC 59-13712.**
1950s. Yuka Nakamura's family takes an American businessman in as a boarder to supplement their income. Through his friendship with Yuka and her family, the American learns about the continuing effects of radiation on Japanese families 14 years after the atomic bombs were dropped on Hiroshima and Nagasaki.
Reviews: *WS* 10
Reading Level: High School
Subject Areas: Japan; atomic bomb; Hiroshima; Americans in Japan
Time Period: 1959   ❏ Library owns

Morris, Edita. *The Seeds of Hiroshima.* **New York: Braziller, 1966. 118pp. LC 66-015753.**
1960s. In this sequel to *The Flowers of Hiroshima,* the story of Yuka and her sister Ohatsu, who represent survivors of the Hiroshima/Nagasaki atomic bomb-

ings, continues. Ohatsu marries and gives birth to a baby deformed by her exposure to atomic radiation.

Reviews: *WS* 10

Reading Level: High School

Subject Areas: Japan; atomic bomb; Hiroshima

Time Period: 1960 ❏ Library owns

Say, Allen. *The Ink-keeper's Apprentice.* **New York: Harper, 1979. 185pp. ISBN 0-06-025209-X. LC 78-20264.**

Post-World War II. Thirteen-year-old Kiyoi, like many post-war children, lives on his own even while going to school. He takes his fate in hand and asks a master cartoonist for an apprenticeship. As he begins to learn his chosen craft, he forms relationships with those around him.

Reviews: *BBYA*; *BCCB* 7/79; *BL* 5/15/79★; *CRC*; *HB* 6/79; *SLJ* 3/79

Reading Level: High School

Subject Areas: Japan; cartoonists; artists; orphans

Time Period: 1945-50 ❏ Library owns

Stroup, Dorothy. *In the Autumn Wind.* **New York: Scribners, 1987. 520pp. ISBN 0-684-18642-X. LC 86-10075.**

August, 1945-1954. While her husband is away at war, Chiyo Hara does what she can to provide for herself and her three children. When the bomb is dropped on Hiroshima, Chiyo must cope amidst the chaos and torment that follows with the loss of one child and the injuries to the two survivors.

Reviews: *BL* 2/15/87; *LJ* 2/15/87, *BBSH*

Reading Level: High School [Mature Reader]

Subject Areas: Japan; Hiroshima; atomic bomb; family life

Time Period: 1945-1954 ❏ Library owns

Sumii, Sué; Susan Wilkinson, trans. *The River With No Bridge.* **Rutland, VT: Charles E. Tuttle, 1990. 359pp. ISBN 0-8048-1590-9. LC 89-51715.**

Early 1900s. The rigidity of Japanese class structure is viewed through the eyes of Koji Hatanaka, whose family is among the three million "burakumin," who, because of the type of manual work they do, are social outcasts. Koji questions this system, but is too young and too powerless to change it.

Reviews: *LJ* 6/15/90; *SLJ* 11/90

Reading Level: High School

Subject Areas: Japan; social classes; prejudices

Time Period: 1900-1910 ❏ Library owns

Asia—Far East

Watkins, Yoko Kawashima. *So Far from the Bamboo Grove.* **New York: Lothrop, 1986. 183pp. ISBN 0-688-06110-9. LC 85-15939.**
North Korea/Japan 1945. Eleven-year-old Yoko and her family abruptly leave North Korea where her father has been a Japanese government official, and flee. During their escape, Yoko and her mother are separated from her father and brother, and Yoko is wounded. Eventually they arrive in Japan to find a war-torn country where conditions lead to further tragedy\.
Reviews: *BBSH*; *BCCB* 6/86; *BL* 8/86; *HB* 7/86; *NCB*; *SLJ* 8/86★; *VOYA* 8/86; *WJ* 6
Reading Level: Middle–High School
Subject Areas: Japan; Korea; refugees; Watkins, Yoko Kawashima; sisters
Time Period: World War, 1939-1945 ❏ Library owns

Korea

Brown, Diana. *The Blue Dragon.* **New York: St. Martin's Press, 1988. 473pp. ISBN 0-312-01393-0. LC 87-27473.**
Late nineteenth century Korea. Brown weaves the tale of Marigold Wilder, the daughter of a Victorian vicar who joins an Anglican mission in Korea. Through Marigold's view of Korea, the reader learns about the people as well as the internal political conflict fueled by ineffective leadership, and the encroachment of Japan, China and Russia.
Reviews: *BL* 3/15/88; *LJ* 3/15/88
Reading Level: High School
Subject Areas: Korea; missionaries
Time Period: Nineteenth Century ❏ Library owns

Choi, Sook Nyul. *Year of Impossible Goodbyes.* **Boston: Houghton Mifflin, 1991. 176pp. ISBN 0-395-57419-6. LC 91-10512.**
Korea, Post WWII. This autobiographical novel tells of Sookan's and her family's hardships, first at the hands of the occupying Japanese Army, then under the Russians. Her family decides to escape to South Korea and begins a long and terrifying journey where that includes betrayal and her mother's capture. The children continue on, hoping to find their father and older brothers in the south.
Reviews: *BCCB* 10/91★; *BBYA*; *BL* 9/15/91; *BR* 3/92; *HB* 1/92; *NCB*; *SLJ* 10/91★; *VOYA* 12/91
Reading Level: Middle–High School
Subject Areas: Korea; refugees
Time Period: 1945-1948 ❏ Library owns

Choi, Sook Nyul. *Echoes of the White Giraffe.* **Boston: Houghton Mifflin, 1993. 137pp. ISBN 0-395-64721-5. LC 92-17476.**

Korea, Korean War, 1950-1953. Sequel to *Year of Impossible Goodbyes.* Sookan, her brother, and mother live in a refugee camp in Pusan. Sookan and her brother keep busy with school and church activities, waiting for the end of the war. When the war finally ends, they return to their home in Seoul where they learn of her father's death. Sookan decides to carry on with her studies in hopes of getting into a university.

Reviews: *BCCB* 6/93; *BL* 4/1/93; *BR* 9/93; *SLJ* 5/93; *VOYA* 8/93

Reading Level: Middle–High School

Subject Areas: Korean War, 1950-1953; refugees

Time Period: 1950-1953 ❏ Library owns

Australia/New Zealand/Oceania

Australia

Cato, Nancy. *The Heart of the Continent.* **New York: St. Martin's, 1989. 604pp. ISBN 0-312-02927-6. LC 89-30124.**

Queensland, 1910-1950. A portrait of Aboriginal life between 1910 and 1950 emerges in this story of two courageous women, Alix and her daughter Caro, and their efforts to bring medical care to these isolated areas.

Reviews: *BL* 9/15/89; *Publishers' Weekly* 8/4/89

Reading Level: High School

Subject Areas: Australia; Australian Aborigines; medical care

Time Period: 1910-1950 ❏ Library owns

Collins, Alan. *Jacob's Ladder.* **New York: Lodestar, 1989. 149pp. ISBN 0-525-67272-9. LC 89-7647.**

Sydney, 1930s, Depression Era. Jacob is orphaned at 12 and taken, along with his younger sister Solly, to a Jewish orphan's home which also houses European children who are refugees from the Nazis. As he grows up, he experiences the usual adolescent interest in the opposite sex, begins to learn a trade, and confronts bigotry.

Reviews: *BBSH*; *BCCB* 5/89; *BL* 6/1/89; *HB* 9/89; *SLJ* 10/89; *VOYA* 8/89

Reading Level: Middle–High School

Subject Areas: Australia; Jews; orphans; adolescence; antisemitism; Jews and gentiles

Time Period: 1930-1945 ❏ Library owns

Australia/New Zealand/Oceania—Australia

Cotich, Felicia. *Valda.* **New York: Coward-McCann, 1983. 126pp. ISBN 0-698-20574-X. LC 82-12586.**
1930s Depression Era Australia. Hard hit by the Depression, Valda and her family wait for the return of her irresponsible father, whose actions have left the family in "dire straits." When he does return, Valda is sent to live with an aunt, but haunted by homesickness Valda returns to her family just in time to see the family disintegrate. Valda returns to live with her aunt where she will have an opportunity for an education.
Reviews: *BCCB* 4/83; *BL* 5/1/83; *SLJ* 8/83
Reading Level: Middle & Junior High School
Subject Areas: Australia; depressions, economic; poverty
Time Period: 1930s ❏ Library owns

Noonan, Michael. *Mckenzie's Boots.* **New York: Watts/Orchard Books, 1988. 240pp. ISBN 0-531-08348-9. LC 87-25031.**
Australia, World War II. Passing for an 18-year-old because of his size, 15-year-old Rod McKenzie is sent to fight in New Guinea. There Rod continues to grow both physically, especially his feet, and philosophically. He is influenced by the people he meets, especially a Japanese prisoner.
Reviews: BBSH; *BBYA*; *BL* 4/1/88; *BR* 11/88; *SLJ* 4/88
Reading Level: Middle–High School
Subject Areas: Australia; New Guinea; soldiers; friendship
Time Period: World War, 1939-1945 ❏ Library owns

Oodgeroo; illustrated by Bronwyn Bancroft. *Dreamtime: Aboriginal Stories.* **New York: Lothrop, 1994. 96pp. ISBN 0-688-13296-0. LC 93-79375.**
Australia. This selection of short stories, coming mostly from the Queensland area, shows how Aboriginal life has changed as white civilization has spread across Australia. The book includes some traditional Aboriginal stories.
Reviews: *BL* 10/1/94; *HB* 3/94; *PW* 7/4/94
Reading Level: Middle–High School
Subject Areas: Australia; Australian Aborigines; Aborigines; short stories; folklore
Time Period: World War, 1939-1945

Park, Ruth. *Playing Beatie Bow.* **New York: Atheneum, 1982. 196pp. ISBN 0-689-30889-2. LC 81-8097.**
Sydney, 1870s/Present. Fourteen-year-old Abigail Kirk must decide whether to let herself love and trust her father who has returned after having abandoned Abigail and her mother. One day, as she watches children play the game, Beatie Bow, she meets the original Beatie Bow and is swept back in time to the Bows' Victorian home where she meets Beatie's family, experiences Victorian working-

class life, and influences the Bows' destiny. She returns to her own time with a greater understanding of her own situation. An Australian prize winner.
Reviews: *BBYA*; *BCCB* 4/82; *BL* 6/1/82★; *HB* 8/82; *SLJ* 5/82★; *VOYA* 8/82
Reading Level: Middle–High School
Subject Areas: Australia; space and time; family life
Time Period: 1870s ❑ Library owns

Pople, Maureen. *A Nugget of Gold.* **New York: Holt, 1989. 183pp. ISBN 0-8050-0984-1. LC 88-13918.**
1870s Gold Rush/Present. Sally, a contemporary teen, finds a gold nugget with a mysterious inscription in an abandoned gold mine. In alternating chapters Ann, a teen living in the 1870s, tells about her life and the circumstances that led to the inscription on the gold nugget. Sally tells about her life and problems while trying to solve the mystery of the nugget.
Reviews: *BCCB* 4/89; *BL* 4/1/89; *SLJ* 4/89
Reading Level: Middle–High School
Subject Areas: Australia
Time Period: 1870s; 1970s ❑ Library owns

New Zealand

Anderson, Margaret J. *Light in the Mountain.* **New York: Knopf/distributed by Random, 1982. 151pp. ISBN 0-394-94791-6. LC 81-14266.**
Prehistoric New Zealand. The rhythm of Maori tribal life is captured in this fictionalized version of the Maori settlement of New Zealand. The story centers around two priestesses, one who leads the people to "the Land of Long White Clouds" and the one who follows her, both make personal sacrifices to become good leaders for their people.
Reviews: *BCCB* 4/82; *BL* 4/15/82; *HB* 6/82; *SLJ* 5/82
Reading Level: Middle–High School
Subject Areas: New Zealand; Maoris; islands
Time Period: Ninth Century ❑ Library owns

Oceania

Bosse, Malcolm. *Deep Dream of the Rain Forest.* **New York: Farrar, 1993. 179pp. ISBN 0-374-31757-7. LC 92-55095.**
Borneo, 1920s. Harry, an orphan, is visiting his uncle in Borneo when he is kidnapped by three members of the Iban tribe and forced to accompany them on a long and dangerous trek. Harry, who had thought of the natives as "simple," comes to know and respect the Iban.

Australia/New Zealand/Oceania—Oceania

Reviews: *BCCB* 10/93; *SLJ* 10/93★
Reading Level: Middle–High School
Subject Areas: Borneo; Iban; orphans; Great Britain--Colonies; British in Borneo
Time Period: 1920s   ❑ Library owns

Innes, Hammond. *The Last Voyage; Captain Cook's Lost Diary.* **New York: Knopf, 1979. 253pp. ISBN 0-394-50579-4. LC 78-20443.**
Oceania, eighteenth century. Through the device of a journal that Captain James Cook might have kept on his voyage to find a sea passage between the Atlantic and Pacific Oceans, Innes gives us a glimpse of the private person who history has recorded as a great sailor and explorer, while relating the adventures of Cook's voyage.
Reviews: *BL* 2/15/79; *WS* 11
Reading Level: High School
Subject Areas: Cook, James; Islands of the Pacific; voyages and travels; sea stories; explorers
Time Period: 1750-1779   ❑ Library owns

Myers, Christopher A. and Lynne Born. *Forest of the Clouded Leopard.* **Boston: Houghton, 1994. 112pp. ISBN 0-395-67408-5. LC 93-350.**
Borneo. While attending a government boarding school, 15-year-old Kenchendai is embarrassed when his grandfather appears in traditional Iban dress, expecting Kenchendai to accompany the male family members on a boar hunt. Kenchendai reluctantly goes, only to have his grandfather die and his father become ill. Kenchendai learns much about the rainforest and his people's traditions, choosing to remain in the jungle rather than return to the school.
Reviews: *BR* 9-10; *PW* 4/25/94; *SLJ* 5/94
Reading Level: Middle & Junior High School
Subject Areas: Borneo; Iban Tribe; rainforest
Time Period: Twentieth Century   ❑ Library owns

Nordhoff, Charles and Hall, James Norman; illustrated by N. C. Wyeth. *The Bounty Trilogy.* **Boston: Little, 1982, c1946. 691pp. ISBN 0-316-61161-1.**
Oceania, eighteenth century. This trilogy based on an actual mutiny on a British warship in 1787 begins with the famous *Mutiny on the Bounty* against the infamous Captain Bligh; continues with *Men Against the Sea* in which Bligh and his supporters are set adrift; and ends with *Pitcairn's Island* which follows the mutineers to the sanctuary of a Pacific island.
Reviews: *BFY*; *WS* 12, 13
Reading Level: High School
Subject Areas: Islands of the Pacific; Bounty (ship); Bligh, William; sea stories
Time Period: 1787   ❑ Library owns

Europe

Prehistoric Europe

Auel, Jean. *The Clan of the Cave Bear.* **New York: Crown, 1980. 468pp. ISBN 0-517-54202-1. LC 80-14581.**
Cro-Magnon Europe. Ayla, a Cro-Magnon child, is separated from her family, found and raised by a clan of Neanderthals, where she is nurtured by the clan medicine woman. However, as she matures she becomes a threat to the dominant males of the clan. The author's depiction of life in a cave-dwelling society is well-based in research, showing rituals, medicines, and hunting techniques, which adds to the realism.
Reviews: *BBYA*; *BL* 7/15/80; *LJ* 9/1/80; *SLJ* 11/80; *VOYA* 12/80; *WS* 11, 12, 13, 14; *YARC*
Reading Level: High School
Subject Areas: Neanderthals; Cro-Magnons; prehistoric man; anthropology
Time Period: Stone Age ❏ Library owns

Brennan, J. H. *Shiva: An Adventure of the Ice Age.* **New York: HarperCollins/Lippincott, 1990. 192pp. ISBN 0-397-32454-5. LC 89-77654.**
Ice Age Europe. Finding Doban, a Neanderthal boy, in the forest, Shiva, a Cro-Magnon girl, brings him back to her tribe where he is imprisoned. This is an exciting mixture of adventure, history, and myth with an important message about similarities and differences.
Reviews: *BL* 12/15/90; *SLJ* 12/90
Reading Level: Middle & Junior High School
Subject Areas: Cro-Magnons; Neanderthals; orphans; prehistoric man; prejudices
Time Period: Ice Age ❏ Library owns

Brennan, J. H. *Shiva's Challenge.* **New York: HarperCollins, 1992. 209pp. ISBN 0-06-020826-0. LC 91-40676.**
Ice Age Europe. In the third book of the series, Shiva's mystic powers are tested by the Ordeal by Poison. She wakes hours later lost in a deep cave and must find her way back. At the same time, Hiram, a hunter searches for her, and Thag, the overthrown ruler faces death. The three come together and help each other.
Reviews: *BL* 12/15/92; *BR* 5/93; *SLJ* 12/92; *VOYA* 4/93
Reading Level: Middle–High School
Subject Areas: Cro-Magnons; prehistoric man
Time Period: Ice Age ❏ Library owns

Europe—Prehistoric Europe

Brennan, J. H. *Shiva Accused: An Adventure of the Ice Age.* New York: HarperCollins, 1991. 288pp. ISBN 0-06-020742-6. LC 90-25888.

Ice Age Europe. In the second of a trilogy, Shiva is caught up in inter-tribal politics and prejudices when she discovers the body of the chief wise woman and is accused of murder by a rival tribe. Shiva's tribe and her friends, the Neanderthals, help to free her and place the blame where it belongs.

Reviews: *BL* 8/91; *BR* 3/92; *SLJ* 11/91
Reading Level: Middle–High School
Subject Areas: Cro-Magnons; Neanderthals; prehistoric man; prejudices
Time Period: Ice Age ❏ Library owns

Denzel, Justin. *Boy of the Painted Cave.* New York: Philomel, 1988. 158pp. ISBN 0-399-21599-X. LC 87-36609.

Stone Age Europe. Tao, a teenager with a crippled foot, longs to be a cave painter, but he is considered an outcast. When his tribe discovers that he has befriended a wolf and has been receiving painting lessons from the shaman, he is tested.

Reviews: *BL* 11/1/88; *SLJ* 11/88
Reading Level: Middle & Junior High School
Subject Areas: prehistoric man; physically handicapped; cave dwellers; cave drawings
Time Period: Stone Age ❏ Library owns

García, Ann O'Neal. *Spirit on the Wall.* New York: Holiday, 1982. 181pp. ISBN 0-8234-0447-1. LC 81-85094.

Cro-Magnon Europe, Upper Paleolithic period. When Em is born with a crooked leg, her mother wants to destroy her as is customary with deformed infants. Her grandmother, Mat-Maw, will not allow it and sets out on a journey with Em and her brother Tuk to find a place where they can live alone, against all clan customs.

Reviews: *BL* 6/1/82; *SLJ* 3/82; *VOYA* 10/82
Reading Level: Middle–High School
Subject Areas: cave dwellers; Cro-Magnons; physically handicapped; grandmothers; cave drawings
Time Period: Stone Age ❏ Library owns

Holland, Cecelia. *Pillar of the Sky.* New York: Knopf, 1985. 529pp. ISBN 0-394-53538-3. LC 84-48659.

Prehistoric England. Ladon, current chief, wants to insure that his son, not Moloquin, the son of his sister, will be the next chief. Moloquin, tradition, and tribal politics win, allowing him to build his dream, of a circular arrangement of stones that would be a portal between earth and heaven—Stonehenge.

Reviews: *BL* 4/1/85; *LJ* 6/1/85

Europe—Prehistoric Europe

Reading Level: High School
Subject Areas: prehistoric man; Stonehenge
Time Period: Stone Age ☐ Library owns

Kurtén, Björn. *Singletusk: A Novel of the Ice Age.* **New York: Pantheon, 1986. 195pp. ISBN 0-394-55352-7. LC 85-43460.**

Stone Age Europe. A sequel to *Dance of the Tiger*, the author gives an account of Neanderthal life, telling stories of family conflicts, belief in spirits, trade, language, and developing human feelings and responses.

Reviews: *BL* 8/86; *LJ* 7/86
Reading Level: High School [Mature Reader]
Subject Areas: Neanderthals; prehistoric man
Time Period: Stone Age ☐ Library owns

McGowen, Tom. *The Time of the Forest.* **Boston: Houghton, 1988. 110pp. ISBN 0-395-44471-3. LC 87-26191.**

Stone Age Europe. Wolf, from a hunter-gather tribe, and Bright Dawn, from a farming tribe, meet and fall in love. When war breaks out between the two groups, Wolf saves Bright Dawn, and a wiseman prophesies that they will together "make a new thing." They go against tribal wishes and pledge themselves to each other, knowing they will start a new tribe.

Reviews: *BCCB* 5/88; *BL* 4/1/88; *SLJ* 4/88
Reading Level: Middle & Junior High School
Subject Areas: prehistoric man; Denmark; war; prejudices
Time Period: Stone Age ☐ Library owns

Pryor, Bonnie. *Seth of the Lion People.* **New York: Morrow, 1988. 128pp. ISBN 0-688-07327-1. LC 88-18747.**

Prehistoric Europe. Crippled from early childhood, Seth knows he will not be able to follow his father as leader of the hunting Lion People, even though he has his father's gift of storytelling. Threatened by a member of his tribe, Seth journeys to find an agrarian tribe with different values, and develops the skills and courage that enable him to return and lead his tribe.

Reviews: *BL* 11/15/88; *BR* 3/89; *SLJ* 12/88
Reading Level: Middle & Junior High School
Subject Areas: prehistoric man; physically handicapped; storytelling; cave dwellers
Time Period: Stone Age ☐ Library owns

Wolf, Joan. *Daughter of the Red Deer.* New York: Dutton, 1991. 432pp. ISBN 0-525-93379-4. LC 91-12843.

Ice Age Europe. When the women of the patriarchal Tribe of the Horse die from poisoned water, the men steal women from the matriarchal Tribe of the Red Deer. Both the men and their captives have much to learn from each other, as they come from vastly different cultures. These differences cause much dissension, especially when the men of the Red Deer come to take back their women.

Reviews: *BL* 10/15/91; *SLJ* 6/92; *PW* 9/21/92

Reading Level: High School

Subject Areas: Cro-Magnons; prehistoric man; Ice Age

Time Period: Ice Age ❏ Library owns

Early European Civilizations

Anderson, Margaret J. *The Druid's Gift.* New York: Knopf, 1989. 176pp. ISBN 0-394-81936-5. LC 88-22028.

Scotland, 500 B.C. Orphaned Caitlan rebels against womanly duties and asks the Druids to teach her their skills. With her power she moves forward in time in a thousand-year leap and experiences the changes that will occur with the Viking invasion, in the eighteenth century, and in the nineteenth century. Returning to her time, she uses this knowledge to unify her people.

Reviews: *BCCB* 4/89; *BL* 8/89; *HB* 7/89; *SLJ* 3/89

Reading Level: Middle–High School

Subject Areas: Scotland; Kilda, Saint; Druids; space and time; islands; orphans

Time Period: 500 B.C. ❏ Library owns

Andrews, J. S. *The Man from the Sea.* New York: Dutton, 1971. 154pp. LC 70-157948.

Bronze Age, Ireland. After the men in Euan's fishing village are lost in a gale, and the village is starving, Euan discovers a shipwrecked stranger who helps feed the village by trading some of his bronze tools. Euan, the stranger, and five others leave to search for the lost men.

Reviews: *BL* 2/15/72; *HB* 12/71; *LJ* 1/15/72

Reading Level: Middle–High School

Subject Areas: Ireland

Time Period: Bronze Age ❏ Library owns

Caldecott, Moyra. *The Tall Stones.* New York: Farrar, Straus & Giroux, 1977. 234pp. ISBN 0-8090-9120-8. LC 77-23896.

Bronze Age, Britain. In a time when each village is led by a priest, three teenagers attempt to thwart the evil Wardyke who has taken control from Maal, the priest in their village.

Reviews: *LJ* 2/1/78; *SLJ* 5/78
Reading Level: High School
Subject Areas: Britain; extrasensory perception
Time Period: Bronze Age ❏ Library owns

Gardner, John; illustrated by Emil Antonucci. *Grendel*. New York: Knopf, 1971. 174pp. ISBN 0-394-47143-1.
Britain. This is a prose retelling of the epic poem *Beowulf*, from the monster Grendel's point of view.
Reviews: *WS* 10, 11, 12
Reading Level: High School
Subject Areas: Britain; Beowulf; monsters
Time Period: Sixth Century ❏ Library owns

Llywelyn, Morgan. *Bard: The Odyssey of the Irish*. Boston: Houghton, 1984. 463pp. ISBN 0-395-35352-1. LC 84-6645.
Ireland, fourth century B.C. A retelling of *Laebar Gabula*. Amergin, a bard and Druid who lived during the fourth century, acts as a visionary for his people as the Gaels attempt to invade Ireland. Amergin's brothers are warriors, his father is the clan chief, and his love is a Danann woman, one of the mythical little people.
Reviews: *BL* 9/1/84; *SLJ* 9/85
Reading Level: High School [Mature Reader]
Subject Areas: Ireland; Celts; Druids; Amergin
Time Period: Fourth Century B.C. ❏ Library owns

Llywelyn, Morgan. *The Horse Goddess*. Boston: Houghton, 1982. 417pp. ISBN 0-395-32514-5. LC 82-6234.
Austria, eighth century B.C. Epona, a woman with mystic powers who is destined to be a priestess in her Celtic tribe, runs away with Kazhak, a Scythian trader from the steppes. Due to the enormous differences in their cultures, their relationship is stormy. Epona's own tribe's priest tracks her and intends to kill her, but Epona's powers are greater, and she returns to fulfill her destiny.
Reviews: *BBYA*; *BL* 8/82★; *SLJ* 12/82; *YARC*
Reading Level: High School
Subject Areas: Austria; Celts; Scythians; extrasensory perception
Time Period: Iron Age; Eighth Century B.C. ❏ Library owns

Melling, Orla. *The Druid's Tune*. Chester Spring, PA: O'Brien Press; distributed by Dufour Editions, 1993. 196pp. ISBN 0-86278-285-6.
Ireland, Iron Age, contemporary. Two Canadian teens, sent to Ireland for the summer, discover a Druid lost in time and go back in time with him where they

Europe—Ancient Greece

are captured by warriors of Maeve, a warrior queen, as she is getting ready to attack Ulster. The attack is known today as Tain Bo Cuailnge or the Cattle Raid of Cooley.
Reviews: *BL* 2/15/93; *BL* 3/1/93
Reading Level: Middle–High School
Subject Areas: Ireland; Druids; space and time; fantastic fiction
Time Period: Iron Age ❏ Library owns

Ancient Greece

Bradley, Marion Zimmer. *The Firebrand.* **New York: Simon & Schuster, 1987. 590pp. ISBN 0-671-64177-8. LC 87-17283.**
Troy. Beginning with the birth of twins Paris and Kassandra, this is a retelling of the Trojan War from Kassandra's viewpoint. Kassandra must choose whether to devote her life to Apollo or the Earth Mother, but finds a third choice.
Reviews: *BL* 9/15/87; *LJ* 10/15/87
Reading Level: High School
Subject Areas: Greece; Troy; mythology, Greek; Cassandra (Greek mythology)
Time Period: 1200 B.C ❏ Library owns

Bradshaw, Gillian. *Horses of Heaven.* **Garden City, NY: Doubleday, 1991. 464pp. ISBN 0-385-41466-8. LC 90-43095.**
A Greek outpost in Asia. In the Ferghana Valley, a ruler wishing to strengthen his borders arranges a marriage to a young princess, sister of the neighboring Greek ruler. Her arrival signals the beginning of a love triangle between the old ruler, the young princess, and the ruler's son.
Reviews: *BL* 5/1/91; *LJ* 3/1/91; *SLJ* 9/91
Reading Level: High School
Subject Areas: Greece; love
Time Period: 100 B.C. ❏ Library owns

Caldecott, Moyra. *The Lily and the Bull.* **New York: Hill and Wang, 1979. 177pp. ISBN 0-8090-6572-X. LC 79-10805.**
Crete, Minoan Era, 2800-1200 B.C. An evil queen has plans for a teenage girl and a young acrobat, who become embroiled in conflicts between two religious cults.
"This novel's dramatic suspense and supernatural events should enthrall Caldecott fans." *Booklist*
Reviews: *BL* 7/1/79; *WS* 11
Reading Level: High School
Subject Areas: Crete
Time Period: 2000 B.C. ❏ Library owns

Europe—Ancient Greece

Davis, William Stearns. *A Victor of Salamis: A Tale of the Days of Xerxes, Leonidas, and Themistocles.* **New York: Macmillan, 1969, c1935. (orig. pub. 1907). 450pp. LC 70-15591.**
Greece, 481-479 B.C. The Isthmian games, Pan-Athenaic festival, and the battles of Thermopylaie, Salamis, and Plataea are recounted.
Reviews: *WS* 10
Reading Level: High School
Subject Areas: Greece; athletics; war; Themistokles; Xerxes; Leonidas
Time Period: 481-479 B.C. ❏ Library owns

Hoover, H. M. *The Dawn Palace: The Story of Medea.* **New York: Dutton, 1988. 244pp. ISBN 0-525-44388-6. LC 87-30602.**
Ancient/Mythical times. In this retelling of the Medea/Jason and the Argonauts myth, Medea is not portrayed as an evil matricidal woman. The clash between the old feminist culture and new masculine culture creates tension as a young Medea falls instantly in love with an opportunistic Jason who will use her powers and will try to leave her an outcast and pariah in his male-dominated world.
Reviews: *BBSH*; *BBYA*; *BL* 6/1/88; *BR* 3/89; *SLJ* 9/88
Reading Level: High School [Mature Reader]
Subject Areas: Greece; mythology, Greek; Jason (Greek mythology); Medea (Greek mythology)
Time Period: 1600–1200 B.C. ❏ Library owns

Johnston, Norma. *The Days of the Dragon's Seed.* **New York: Atheneum, 1982. 194pp. ISBN 0-689-30882-5. LC 81-10786.**
Ancient/Mythical times. Johnston retells the tragedy of the royal house of Thebes. Once again Oedipus tries to escape his destiny, but murders his father and marries his mother in the end, causing exile and suffering for both himself and his daughter Antigone.
Reviews: *BL* 4/15/82; *VOYA* 12/82
Reading Level: High School
Subject Areas: Greece; mythology, Greek; Oedipus (Greek mythology); Antigone (Greek mythology)
Time Period: 1600–1200 B.C. ❏ Library owns

Keaney, Brian. *No Need for Heroes.* **New York: Oxford University Press, 1989. 114pp. ISBN 0-19-271610-7. LC 88-38938.**
Minoan Era, 2800-1200 B.C. Keaney gives a contemporary retelling of the Theseus and the Minotaur myth. Here Minos' daughter Ariadne reacts to events as the feminist civilization begins to turn away from worship of the Magna Mater (Great Mother) in favor of the "new male cult of the Bull."

Europe—Ancient Greece

Reviews: *BCCB* 6/89; *SLJ* 7/89; *VOYA* 8/89
Reading Level: Middle & Junior High School
Subject Areas: Crete; mythology, Greek; Theseus (Greek mythology); Ariadne (Greek mythology); Minotaur (Greek mythology)
Time Period: 1600-1200 B.C. ❑ Library owns

Paton Walsh, Jill. *Children of the Fox.* **New York: Farrar, 1978. 115pp. ISBN 0-374-31242-7. LC 78-8138.**
Greece, 480-470 B.C. Athenian general, Themistokles, an actual historic figure in the Greek wars against Persia, is the unifying character in three tales of young people who have contact with him during that time of war.
Reviews: *BCCB* 1/79; *BL* 9/1/78; *HB* 10/78; *SLJ* 9/78
Reading Level: Middle & Junior High School
Subject Areas: Greece; Themistokles; short stories
Time Period: 500-449 B.C. ❑ Library owns

Polland, Madeleine A. *Daughter of the Sea.* **New York: Doubleday, 1973. 176pp. ISBN 0-385-07046-2. LC 72-90367.**
Ancient times/present. The modern-day romance between Sarah and Miklos is paralleled by that of Saran, a woman shipwrecked on her way to Crete and Mikolai, the nobleman's son who rescues her. Saran is taken to Crete where the people believe she is Poseidon's daughter, and expect her to keep the Greek invaders away.
Reviews: *BCCB* 10/73; *BL* 6/1/73; *LJ* 4/15/73; *SLJ* 4/73
Reading Level: Middle–High School
Subject Areas: Crete; love
Time Period: 1300 B.C. ❑ Library owns

Ray, Mary. *The Golden Bees.* **New York: Faber, dist. by Harper, 1984. 152pp. ISBN 0-571-13201-4. LC 83-25340.**
Greece, 1500 B.C. Kenofer, the blind bard to the royal court introduced in *Song of Thunder*, returns to tell his tale of adventure when he, as a youth, retrieved Princess Leda's lost golden bee earrings. His quest takes him throughout the Greek isles, where he encounters bandits, tyrants, and shipwrecks.
Reviews: *BCCB* 7/84; *HB* 8/84; *SLJ* 8/84
Reading Level: Middle & Junior High School
Subject Areas: Greece; adventure and adventurers
Time Period: 1500 B.C. ❑ Library owns

Renault, Mary. *The Bull from the Sea.* **New York: Vintage/Random, 1975. ISBN 0-394-71504-7.**
Greece, 1600-1200 B.C. In this sequel to *The King Must Die*, the tale of Theseus continues as he becomes the king of Athens, the lover of Amazon warrior Hippolyta, and husband of Cretan princess Phaedra.
Reviews: *FFY*; *WS* 10, 11
Reading Level: High School
Subject Areas: Greece; mythology, Greek; Theseus (Greek mythology)
Time Period: 1600-1200 B.C. ❏ Library owns

Renault, Mary. *Fire from Heaven.* **New York: Pantheon, 1969. 375pp. ISBN 0-394-42492-1. LC 72-98035.**
Greece, 356-336 B.C. Alexander the Great's life is traced from childhood to his succession of his murdered father, King Philip of Macedon, at the age of 20. Alexander's accomplishments are played against the politics, court and peasant life, and mores of the times. The impact of his tutor Aristotle is shown, and his homosexual relationship with Hephaistion is suggested.
Reviews: *BBSH; BL* 1/1/70; *HB* 4/70; *LJ* 12/15/69; *WS* 10
Reading Level: High School [Mature Reader]
Subject Areas: Greece; Alexander the Great
Time Period: 356-336 B.C. ❏ Library owns

Renault, Mary. *The King Must Die.* **New York: Pantheon, 1958. 338pp. ISBN 0-394-43195-2. LC 58-7202.**
Crete, Minoan Era, 2800-1200 B.C. In this version of the Theseus and the Minotaur myth, Theseus is sent to end the matriarchy of Eleusis and Crete. He joins a group of bull dancers and later takes advantage of the confusion caused by an earthquake to topple the Cretan civilization.
Reviews: *BBSH*; *FFY*; *WS* 10, 12, 13, 14
Reading Level: High School
Subject Areas: Crete; mythology, Greek; Theseus (Greek mythology)
Time Period: 1600-1200 B.C. ❏ Library owns

Renault, Mary. *The Last of the Wine.* **New York: Random, 1975, c1969. 389pp. ISBN 0-394-71653-1.**
Peloponnesian War, 431-404 B.C. During the last years of the Peloponnesian War, Alexias and Lysis, both students of Socrates, develop a friendship that mirrors the ethics of the time.
Reviews: *BBSH*; *FFY*; *WS* 10
Reading Level: High School [Mature Reader]

Europe—Ancient Greece

Subject Areas: Greece; Socrates
Time Period: 431-404 B.C.   ❏ Library owns

Renault, Mary. *The Mask of Apollo.* **New York: Vintage/Random, 1988. 384pp. ISBN 0-394-75105-1. LC 86-46177.**
Fourth century B.C. Actor Nikeratos travels between Syracuse and Athens to be in Greek plays, always carrying his antique mask of Apollo, which becomes his "artistic conscience." Through Niko the reader sees the power struggle between the philosopher and soldier Dion (who is a friend of Plato's) and the tyrannical Dionysios the Younger.
Reviews: *WS* 10
Reading Level: High School [Mature Reader]
Subject Areas: Greece; actors
Time Period: Fourth Century B.C.   ❏ Library owns

Renault, Mary. *The Praise Singer.* **New York: Random House, 1988, c1978. 290pp. ISBN 0-394-75102-7. LC.**
Greece, Sixth century B.C. The life and time of Simonides, a prolific poet, is told. This was a time of war with the Persians, of tyrants, and of great artistic achievement.
Reviews: *BBSH*; *BL* 11/1/78; *LJ* 10/1/78
Reading Level: High School
Subject Areas: Greece; Simonides, 556-667 B.C.; poets
Time Period: 556-667 B.C.   ❏ Library owns

Sutcliff, Rosemary. *The Flowers of Adonis.* **New York: Coward-McCann, 1970. 383pp. LC 76-96780.**
Peloponnesian Wars, 431-404 B.C. Alkibiades, seen by some as a Peloponnesian War hero and by other as a traitor, is recalled by a wide variety of people who had contact with him. These people, from all walks of life and both sides of the conflict, each tell their tale in first-person.
Reviews: *BL* 3/15/70; *HB* 4/70; *LJ* 1/1/70; *WS* 10
Reading Level: High School
Subject Areas: Greece; Peloponnesian Wars; Alcibiades
Time Period: 431-404 B.C.   ❏ Library owns

Wolfe, Gene. *Soldier of Arete.* **New York: Tor, distributed by St. Martin's, 1989. 320pp. ISBN 0-312-93185-9. LC 89-11784.**
Classical Greece. Persian prisoner-of-war Latro, still without the memory he gave up in return for a look at the gods, is involved in high-level intrigues and adventures in the rivalry between Athens and Sparta. Sequel to *Soldier of the Mist*.

Reviews: *BL* 8/89; *LJ* 10/15/89
Reading Level: High School [Mature Reader]
Subject Areas: Greece
Time Period: 500 B.C.

❏ Library owns

Ancient Rome

Anderson, Paul L. *With the Eagles.* Cheschire, CT: Biblio & Tannen, 1965, c1929. 279pp. ISBN 0-8196-0100-4. LC 57-9447.
Gaul. In this installment in the "Roman Life and Times series," a "Gallic boy joins Caesar's army..., eventually winning a place in Caesar's famous Tenth Legion." *Wilson's Senior High School Catalog*
Reviews: *WS* 10
Reading Level: High School
Subject Areas: Gaul; soldiers; Roman Legion
Time Period: 56-49 B.C.

❏ Library owns

Breem, Wallace. *Eagle in the Snow: A Novel.* New York: Putnam, 1970. 320pp. LC 76-124275.
Germanic territory. Told with great, graphic detail, this is the story of Rome's last stand against the Teutonic tribes.
Reviews: *BL* 1/15/71; *LJ* 11/15/70
Reading Level: High School [Mature Reader]
Subject Areas: Germany; Rome; Roman Legion
Time Period: Second Century

❏ Library owns

Bulwer-Lytton, Sir Edward. *The Last Days of Pompeii.* Cutchogue, NY: Buccaneer Bks., 1983 repr. (orig. pub. 1834). 308pp. ISBN 0-89966-309-5.
Pompeii. Glaucus and Ione, both of Greek descent and both of pure and noble character, are attracted to each other, but Ione's guardian, Arbaces, of low character works to keep Ione for himself.
Reviews: *WS* 10
Reading Level: High School
Subject Areas: Rome; Pompeii; love
Time Period: 79 A.D.

❏ Library owns

Costain, Thomas B. *The Darkness and the Dawn: A Novel.* New York: Doubleday, 1959. 478pp. LC 59-11583.
Fifth Century A.D. Attila the Hun's campaign to capture Rome lends the historical backdrop to this story of Nicolan. Aetius, dictator of Rome appears in the story.
Reviews: *WS* 10

Europe—Ancient Rome

Reading Level: High School
Subject Areas: Rome; Attila; Huns
Time Period: 470 ❏ Library owns

Costain, Thomas B.; illustrated by Burt Silverman. *The Silver Chalice.* **New York: Doubleday, 1964. 533pp. LC 52-8754.**
Rome, Antioch, Jerusalem. This is the story of Basil of Antioch, a young slave artisan who creates a decorative case for the silver chalice used by Christ at his Last Supper, and experiences the persecution of Christians by the Romans.
Reading Level: High School
Subject Areas: Rome; Jerusalem; Antioch; church history; Grail; Bible stories
Time Period: 40 A.D. ❏ Library owns

Davis, Lindsey. *The Iron Hand of Mars.* **New York: Crown, 1993. 320pp. ISBN 0-517-59240-1. LC 93-19265**
Rome, Germanic territory, 71 A.D. In the fourth of a series, private investigator Marcus Didius Falco is sent on a mission into barbarian territory while there to deliver a tribute to the 14th Legion, he is to investigate its leadership. Falco is more interested in locating his missing lover who was last seen in the same area.
Reviews: *BL* 9/15/93; *LJ* 8/93; *SLJ* 3/94
Reading Level: High School
Subject Areas: Rome; Germany; mystery and detective stories
Time Period: 71 A.D. ❏ Library owns

Davis, Lindsey. *Shadows in Bronze.* **New York: Crown, 1991. 343pp. ISBN 0-517-57612-0. LC 90-25078.**
Rome, 70 A.D. In the second in a series, Marcus Didius Falco, private eye to Emperor Vespasian, uncovers a plot to depose Vespasian and must keep one step ahead of those trying to kill him. Falco is also in love with a noblewoman well above his station in life and won't take no for an answer.
"Roman life comes alive in Falco's descriptions of clothes, meals, inns, mansions...This is adult historical fiction that good high school readers will enjoy. Latin classes should make it required reading--no dead language here!" *The Book Report*
Reviews: *BL* 3/1/91; *BR* 11/91; *LJ* 2/15/92; *SLJ* 7/91; *VOYA* 10/91
Reading Level: High School
Subject Areas: Rome; mystery and detective stories
Time Period: 70 A.D. ❏ Library owns

Davis, Lindsey. *Silver Pigs.* **New York: Crown, 1989. 288pp. ISBN 0-517-57363-6. LC 89-1139.**

Rome 70 A.D. Private informer, Marcus Didius Falco rescues a beautiful girl from kidnappers, then must solve the mystery of her death that is somehow intertwined with silver smuggling in Roman Britain and a plot to undermine the empire.

Reviews: *BBSH*; *BL* 8/89; *LJ* 9/1/89

Reading Level: High School

Subject Areas: Rome; mystery and detective stories

Time Period: 70 A.D. ❑ Library owns

Davis, Lindsey. *Venus in Copper.* **New York: Crown, 1992. 288pp. ISBN 0-517-58477-8. LC 91-37297.**

Rome, 70 A.D. Marcus Didius Falco, in his third adventure, investigates a possible gold-digging widow who has three dead husbands. Marcus is too late to save the fourth and finds a cast of possible suspects, not all of whom live to tell their tales.

Reviews: *BL* 3/15/92; *LJ* 3/1/92; *SLJ* 2/93

Reading Level: High School

Subject Areas: Rome; mystery and detective stories

Time Period: 70 A.D. ❑ Library owns

Dillon, Eilís. *The Shadow of Vesuvius.* **New York: Elsevier/Nelson, 1977. 159pp. ISBN 0-525-66569-2. LC 77-21941.**

Pompeii. Accompanying his itinerant artist master to Pompeii to paint frescoes for wealthy patrons, young Timon assists a merchant's niece who wishes to avoid an arranged marriage.

Reviews: *HB* 2/78; *SLJ* 11/77; *WJ* 4

Reading Level: Middle–High School

Subject Areas: Rome; Pompeii; slaves

Time Period: Fourth Century ❑ Library owns

Douglas, Lloyd C. *The Robe.* **Boston: Houghton, 1942. 472pp. ISBN 0-395-07635-8.**

Rome, 30-40 A.D. A parable for our times, follows the story of a Roman senator whose son, in charge of the Crucifixion, keeps the robe of Jesus, and whose belief in Christianity sends him to his death.

Reviews: *BBSH*; *WS* 10, 11, 12, 13

Reading Level: High School

Subject Areas: Rome; Jesus Christ; Caligula; Tiberius; church history; persecution

Time Period: 30-40 A.D. ❑ Library owns

Europe—Ancient Rome

Graves, Robert. *I, Claudius: from the Autobiography of Tiberius Claudius, Born B.C. 10, Murdered and Diefied A.D. 54.* **New York: Modern Library, 1983, c1934. 432p.p. ISBN 0-394-60811-9. LC 34-27150, 89-40099.**
Rome, 10 B.C.-54 A.D. Written as an autobiography, Graves shows Claudius, a stutterer and a cripple, to be a great observer of the political intrigues of the Roman nobility, particularly his grandmother Livia who arranges the murders of those who stand in the way of her son. Claudius outwits and outlives them all and becomes emperor. It is followed by *Claudius, The God and His Wife Messalina*.
Reviews: *BBSH*; *FFY*; *WS* 13, 14
Reading Level: High School [Mature Reader]
Subject Areas: Rome; Augustus, 63 B.C.-14 A.D., Emperor of Rome; Claudius, 10 B.C.-54 A.D., Emperor of Rome
Time Period: 10 B.C.-30 A.D. ❏ Library owns

Hersey, John. *The Conspiracy; A Novel.* **New York: Knopf, 1972. 274pp. ISBN 0-394-47929-7. LC 75-173775.**
64 A.D. Through a series of supposedly intercepted letters and other documents, Hersey constructs the plot of a conspiracy which resulted in the death of the poet Lucan and several prominent citizens of Seneca and Rome.
Reviews: *WS* 10
Reading Level: High School [Mature Reader]
Subject Areas: Rome; Nero, Emperor of Rome; Lucan
Time Period: A.D. 64 ❏ Library owns

Jaro, Benita Kane. *The Door in the Wall.* **Sag Harbor, NY: Permanent Press, 1994. 220pp. ISBN 1-877946-38-9. LC 93-36292.**
Rome, 100 B.C.-44 B.C. Through the journal of Marcus Caelius Rufus, a military commander, Julius Caesar's life is narrated, touching on his youth and concentrating on his rise to power. Other historical figures who enter this story are Cicero and Pompey the Great.
Reviews: *LJ* 12/93; *SLJ* 9/94
Reading Level: High School [Mature Reader]
Subject Areas: Rome; Julius Caesar
Time Period: 100 B.C.-44 B.C. ❏ Library owns

Nichols, Ruth. *The Left-Handed Spirit.* **New York: Margaret K. McElderry Bks./Atheneum, 1978. 220pp. ISBN 0-689-50120-X. LC 78-5573.**
Roman Empire/China, second century A.D. Teenaged Marianna who believes she derives her healing and psychic powers from the god Apollo, is kidnapped by Paulus, the ambassador from China. She makes the arduous journey along the

Europe—Ancient Rome

Silk Road arriving in China where she comes to terms with her gifts, finds love, and eventually returns to her family in Rome.
Reviews: *BCCB* 1/79; *BL* 11/1/78; *SLJ* 10/78; *WJ* 4
Reading Level: Middle–High School
Subject Areas: Rome; Asia; China; kidnapping; parapsychology; love
Time Period: Second Century ❏ **Library owns**

Ray, Mary. *The Ides of April.* **New York: Farrar, 1975. 177pp. LC 75-1322.**
Rome, 54-68 A.D. In this mystery, Roman slave Hylas escapes arrest after his master is murdered. With the help of a young military tribune and a porter, Hylas seeks the truth to save not only himself, but all of the household slaves who will be executed as suspects in the murder.
Reviews: *BL* 9/1/75; *HB* 6/75; *SLJ* 5/75
Reading Level: Middle–High School
Subject Areas: Rome; slaves; mystery and detective stories
Time Period: 60 A.D. ❏ **Library owns**

Ray, Mary. *Rain from the West.* **Faber & Faber, 1980. 175pp. ISBN 0-571-11532-2.**
Roman Britain, 71 A.D. Continues the story of Hylas and Camillus, the tribune who freed him. Hylas and Camillus meet two newcomers to Britain during an uprising of the Celts. The Romans easily defeat the Celts, but the experience changes the lives of each of these four Romans.
Reviews: *SLJ* 9/80; *Growing Point* 7/80
Reading Level: Middle–High School
Subject Areas: Rome; Great Britain--Roman period
Time Period: 71 A.D. ❏ **Library owns**

Robinson, Kathleen. *Heaven's Only Daughter.* **New York: St. Martin's, 1993. 336pp. ISBN 0-312-09304-7. LC 94-2966.**
Rome, 410 A.D. When the Goths invade Rome, Princess Placidia is taken hostage by Bold Wolf, brother of Alaric, and is forced to march with the Goths through Italy as they forage for food. Placidia at first loathes Bold Wolf, but soon an attraction develops, prompting her to help Bold Wolf. Here true love is born.
Reviews: *BL* 8/93; *LJ* 7/93
Reading Level: High School
Subject Areas: Rome; Goths; love
Time Period: 410 ❏ **Library owns**

Europe—Ancient Rome

Sienkiewicz, Henryk. *Quo Vadis.* **Cutchogue, NY: Buccaneer, 1990 (first pub. 1896). ISBN 0-89966-694-9.**

Rome, 50-60 A.D. The Nobel Prize-winning author paints a picture of Rome in the days of Nero and at the beginnings of Christianity. The characters are a mix of pagans, both noble and evil, and Christians struggling for survival.

Reviews: *BBSH*; *WS* 10, 11
Reading Level: High School
Subject Areas: Rome; church history
Time Period: 50-60 A.D. ❏ Library owns

Sutcliff, Rosemary. *The Eagle of the Ninth.* **New York: Oxford Univ. Press, 1986, c1954. 225pp. ISBN 0-19271037-0.**

Britain, first century A.D. Marcus Flavius and his freed slave journey to Britain to find the lost Ninth Legion, which disappeared under Marcus' father's command years ago. It is the first of a trilogy of novels about Roman legions in Britain.

"During the first century, a Roman legion marched off to battle and disappeared. Nearly 1,800 years later, the legion's standard was found in an excavation. The combination of these two mysteries is the basis of this novel." *The Book Report*

Reviews: *BFY*; *BR* 1-2/87
Reading Level: High School
Subject Areas: Rome; Great Britain--Roman period; mystery and detective stories
Time Period: First Century ❏ Library owns

Sutcliff, Rosemary. *Frontier Wolf.* **New York: Dutton, 1981. 196pp. ISBN 0-525-30260-3. LC 80-39849.**

Britain, fourth century A.D. As a punishment, Centurion Alexios is sent to command the Frontier Wolves, a band of fierce British soldiers in a wild corner of Britain. He and his men come to respect each other, and are tested in a bloody battle where Alexios proves his worth as a leader.

Reviews: *BCCB* 7-8/81; *BL* 7/1/81; *HB* 8/81; *SLJ* 9/81; *VOYA* 10/81
Reading Level: Middle–High School
Subject Areas: Rome; Great Britain--Roman period; soldiers; war
Time Period: Fourth Century ❏ Library owns

Sutcliff, Rosemary; illustrated by Richard Cuffari. *The Capricorn Bracelet.* **New York: Walck, 1973. 149pp. ISBN 0-8098-3113-9. LC 72-1065.**

Roman Britain, 61-383 A.D. A bracelet awarded for bravery to a Roman centurion is traced through six generations of Roman soldiers serving near Hadrian's Wall, covering the departure of the Romans from Britain and the cultural changes to the soldiers that stayed.

Reviews: *BL* 6/15/73; *WJ* 4
Reading Level: Middle–High School
Subject Areas: Great Britain--Roman period; soldiers; Rome
Time Period: 61-383 A.D.   ❏ Library owns

Tarr, Judith. *Throne of Isis.* **New York: Tor/Forge; distributed by St. Martin's, 1994. 384pp. ISBN 0-312-85363-7.**
Rome, Egypt, 30 B.C. A retelling of the story of Cleopatra and Marc Antony, where Cleopatra is regal but homely and Marc Antony is all too power hungry. A large cast of Romans and Egyptians are involved in Cleopatra's political intrigues as she tries to save her lover and her country.
Reviews: *BL* 4/15/94
Reading Level: High School
Subject Areas: Rome; Egypt; Cleopatra; Marc Antony
Time Period: 30 B.C.   ❏ Library owns

Wallace, Lew. *Ben Hur.* **Cutchogue, NY: Buccaneer Bks., 1981 repr. (orig. pub. 1880). 450pp. ISBN 0-89966-289-7.**
Rome, 35-30 B.C. The Roman Empire at the time of Christ provides the milieu for this story of Jewish Judah Ben-Hur whose family and fortune are ruined when he is falsely accused of attempting to assassinate the new governor of Jerusalem. After avenging himself in a chariot race, Ben-Hur approaches Christ to help his mother and sister who have contracted leprosy while imprisoned, and witnesses the Crucifixion at Calvary as one of Christ's converts.
Reviews: *BBSH*; *WJ* 4; *WS* 10, 12, 13
Reading Level: Middle–High School
Subject Areas: Rome; church history; Jews
Time Period: 35-30 B.C.   ❏ Library owns

Waltari, Mika; Joan Tate, trans. *The Roman.* **New York: Putnam, 1966. 637pp. LC 66-15593.**
Rome, 30-64 A.D. In this second entry in the trilogy begun with *The Egyptian* and ending with *The Etruscan*, the adventures of Minutus Lausus Manilianus, a Roman consul, offers a panorama of the Roman Empire under Claudius and Nero, revealing social customs and Christian persecution.
Reviews: *WS* 10
Reading Level: High School
Subject Areas: Rome; church history
Time Period: 30-64 A.D.   ❏ Library owns

Europe—Ancient Rome

White, Edward Lucas. *The Unwilling Vestal; A Tale of Rome Under the Caesars.* **New York: Dutton, 1918. 317pp.**
Rome, 161-191 A.D. "A story dealing with the time of Marcus Aurelius and his son, Commodus: both figures appear prominently. Illustrates especially the status of the Vestals." *Wilson's Senior High School Catalog*
Reviews: *WS* 10
Reading Level: High School
Subject Areas: Rome; Aurelius Antonius Marus, Emperor of Rome; vestal virgins
Time Period: 161-191 A.D. ❑ Library owns

Wilder, Thornton. *The Ides of March.* **New York: Harper, 1987, c1948. 256pp. ISBN 0-06-0914303-3. LC 86-46110.**
Rome, 62-30 B.C. Through letters, interviews, journals, and other imaginary documents, the life of Julius Caesar just prior to his assassination is related.
Reviews: *WS* 10
Reading Level: High School
Subject Areas: Rome; Caesar, Julius
Time Period: 62-30 B.C. ❑ Library owns

Yarbro, Chelsea Quinn. *Four Horses for Tishtry.* **New York: Harper, 1985. 218pp. ISBN 0-06-026638-4. LC 84-48341.**
First century A.D. Tishtry, a Roman slave, works as a trick horse rider, and hopes that by becoming better, she will be able to share in enough winnings to buy her and her family's freedom. As Tishtry grows older and increases in her abilities, she must take risks, not only with the horses, but with her life.
Reviews: *BCCB* 6/85; *BL* 6/15/85; *SLJ* 5/85; *VOYA* 8/85
Reading Level: Middle–High School
Subject Areas: Rome; slaves; horses; trick riding
Time Period: First Century ❑ Library owns

Yarbro, Chelsea Quinn. *Locadio's Apprentice.* **New York: Harper, 1984. 219pp. ISBN 0-06-026637-6. LC 84-47632.**
Pompeii, 79 A.D. Enecus Cano is Dr. Locadio Priscus' apprentice in this account of the last days of Pompeii. The eruption of Vesuvius puts Enecus' novice medical skills to a difficult test.
Reviews: *BR* 3-4/85; *SLJ* 10/84
Reading Level: Middle–High School
Subject Areas: Rome; Pompeii; Vesuvius, Mt.; physicians
Time Period: 79 A.D. ❑ Library owns

Early European Civilizations

Bradley, Marion Zimmer. *Forest House.* New York: Viking, 1994. 476pp. ISBN 0-670-84454-3. LC 93-33686.

Roman Briton. A clash between two cultures is brought about when Eilan, a Druid girl raised by priestesses, falls in love with Gaius, a half-Briton whose father is an officer in the Roman Legions.

Reviews: *BL* 1/15/94; *LJ* 3/15/94; *PW* 2/28/94; *SLJ* 10/94
Reading Level: High School
Subject Areas: Great Britain--Roman Period; Celts; Druids; love
Time Period: 100 A.D. ❏ Library owns

Gard, Joyce. *The Mermaid's Daughter.* New York: Holt, 1969. 319pp. LC 77-80316.

Scilly Islands, Britain. Astria, the mortal daughter of a sea-goddess, rescues an Iberian man from drowning, falls in love, and marries him. He leaves her to help repel invaders from his homeland and is reported killed two years later. Astria marries again, goes to Britain, and foils a Roman plot to destroy her sea-goddess cult.

Reviews: *BCCB* 7/70; *BL* 1/1/70; *HB* 4/70; *NCB*
Reading Level: Middle–High School
Subject Areas: Great Britain--Roman period; cults; Scilly Islands
Time Period: First–Fourth Century ❏ Library owns

Gárdonyi, Géza; Andrew Feldmar, trans.; illustrated by Victor C. Ambrus. *Slave of the Huns.* New York: Bobbs-Merrill, 1970. 357pp. ISBN 0-672-50500-2. LC 70-84166.

Europe, 450 A.D. Zeta, captured and made a slave in his youth but now freed, accompanies a delegation from Rome to Attila the Hun. Zeta, wishing to rejoin the Huns, forges a letter giving himself to the household of a young woman with whom he has fallen in love. He works first as a slave, then as a warrior, and finally becomes Attila's scribe.

Reviews: *BL* 7/1/70; *WS* 10
Reading Level: Middle–High School
Subject Areas: Europe; Huns; Attila
Time Period: 450 ❏ Library owns

Hunter, Mollie. *The Stronghold.* New York: Harper, 1975. 259pp. ISBN 06-022653-6. LC 73-14340.

Scotland. Brochs are mysterious Bronze Age forts found only in Scotland. This is the story of Coll, who was crippled in a Roman attack, and the brochs he designs in order to protect his people from further raids.

Europe—Early European Civilizations

Reviews: *WJ* 4
Reading Level: Middle & Junior High School
Subject Areas: Scotland; Celts; Druids; physically handicapped
Time Period: Bronze Age ❏ Library owns

Llywelyn, Morgan. *Druids.* **New York: Morrow, 1991. 448pp. ISBN 0-688-08819-8. LC 90-44292.**
Gaul, 58-51 B.C. Fifteen-year-old Ainvar, from one of the many Celtic tribes of Europe, becomes the hope of his people against the armies of Caesar. He also becomes the heir of the chief Druid, learning much of lore of his people and the mystical arts.
Reviews: *BBSH*; *BL* 12/1/90★; *LJ* 1/91; *SLJ* 7/91
Reading Level: High School [Mature Reader]
Subject Areas: Gaul; Europe; Celts; Druids
Time Period: 58-51 B.C. ❏ Library owns

Rayson, Steven. *The Crows of War.* **New York: Atheneum, 1975. 269pp. ISBN 0-689-30455-2. LC 74-19355.**
Britain, 43 A.D. Despite her mystic powers, Airmid, daughter of a Celtic chieftain, is unable to stop the Romans from defeating her people at Mai-Dun, losing her sight in the attack.
Reviews: *BL* 3/15/75★; *HB* 6/75; *SLJ* 4/75
Reading Level: Middle–High School
Subject Areas: Great Britain--Roman Period; Celts
Time Period: 43 A.D. ❏ Library owns

Sutcliff, Rosemary; illustrated by Charles Keeping. *The Lantern Bearers.* **New York: Oxford, 1979. 248pp. ISBN 0-19-27082-9.**
Britain, fifth century A.D. Aquila, whose father was killed by a band of Saxons, must accept that his sister has married one of those Saxons and chooses to protect her son with his life.
Reviews: *WJ* 4; *WS* 12
Reading Level: Middle–High School
Subject Areas: Great Britain--to 1066; Anglo-Saxons
Time Period: Fifth Century ❏ Library owns

Sutcliff, Rosemary. *Song for a Dark Queen.* **New York: Crowell, 1979, c1978. 181pp. ISBN 0-690-03911-5. LC 78-19514.**
Britain, 61 A.D. Boudicca, queen of the Iceni tribe, is treated with great cruelty by the Romans. Avenging the barbaric treatment of her and her family, Boudicca organizes her tribes and leads a revolt that destroys three cities they are stopped.

Reviews: *BCCB* 7/79; *BL* 4/1/79★; *HB* 6/79; *SLJ* 4/79; *WJ* 4, 5; *WS* 11, 12
Reading Level: Middle–High School
Subject Areas: Great Britain--Roman period; Boudicca, Queen; Celts
Time Period: 61 A.D. ❏ Library owns

Sutcliff, Rosemary. *Sun Horse, Moon Horse.* **New York: Dutton, 1978, c1977. 111pp. ISBN 0-525-40495-3. LC 77-25440.**
Britain, Iron Age. Lubrin's father and the other members of his tribe are killed by a tribe fleeing from the Roman invaders. Lubrin, to express his sorrow, draws a huge white horse on the side of a cliff to set his tribe's spirits free, knowing that only with his death will this happen. (There is a white horse on a cliff at Uffington today.)
Reviews: *BL* 5/15/78★; *HB* 6/78; *SLJ* 5/78; *WJ* 4
Reading Level: Middle & Junior High School
Subject Areas: Great Britain--Roman Period; Celts
Time Period: Iron Age ❏ Library owns

Dark Ages

Benchley, Nathaniel. *Beyond the Mists.* **New York: Harper, 1975. 160pp. ISBN 0-06-020460-5. LC 75-9389.**
Scandinavia, eleventh century. Old Gunnar Egilsen retells stories from his Viking life which includes expeditions with Leif Erikson to North America, and life as a sea-going merchant.
Reviews: *BL* 10/15/75; *HB* 10/75; *SLJ* 11/75; *WJ* 4
Reading Level: Middle–High School
Subject Areas: Vikings; Scandinavia; Erikson, Leif; adventure and adventurers; sea stories; explorers
Time Period: Middle Ages; Eleventh Century ❏ Library owns

Bloch, Marie Halun; illustrated by Edward Kozak. *Bern, Son of Mikula.* **New York: Atheneum, 1972. 177pp. LC 73-175549.**
Russia, tenth century. Based on an actual event, this is the story of Bern, who has spent several years as a captive of the Pechenihs, a nomadic people. He is recaptured by his own people, the Kiyans, and brought to Kiev. Despite being with his own people, he is unhappy and plans to betray the city when the Pechenihs attack.
Reviews: *BCCB* 7/72; *BL* 5/15/72; *LJ* 6/15/72
Reading Level: Middle & Junior High School
Subject Areas: Russia; Kiev
Time Period: Middle Ages; Tenth Century ❏ Library owns

Europe—Dark Ages

Bond, Nancy. *A String in the Harp.* **New York: Atheneum, 1976. 370pp. ISBN 0-689-50036-X. LC 75-28181.**

Wales, sixth century and contemporary. Contemporary teen Peter, who has recently moved to Wales, finds a sixth century artifact—a tuning key for a harp—which draws him into the past. He witnesses episodes in the life of Taliesin, a bard. Unable to resist the power of the key, he begins to see a purpose in what he witnesses.

Reviews: *BCCB* 7/76; *BL* 4/1/76★; *HB* 6/76; *SLJ* 4/76
Reading Level: Middle & Junior High School
Subject Areas: Wales; fantastic fiction; Taliesin; space and time
Time Period: Sixth Century ❏ Library owns

Burford, Lolah. *The Vision of Stephen.* **New York: Macmillan, 1972.**

England, Anglo-Saxon days and nineteenth century. Stephen, son of an Anglo-Saxon is able to travel through time to visit a nineteenth century household where he becomes friends with the children.

Reviews: *BL* 11/15/72; *BL* 9/1/72; *LJ* 8/72
Reading Level: Middle–High School
Subject Areas: Great Britain; Anglo-Saxons; fantastic fiction; space and time
Time Period: Sixth Century; Nineteenth Century ❏ Library owns

Castle, Frances. *The Sisters' Tale.* **Boston: Little, Brown, 1969. 249pp. LC 73-81877**

Ireland, sixth century. A story in two parts: the first tells of Yseult who, after the death of her mother, acquires a beautiful stepmother who is possibly a witch. It also tells of Yseult's marriage to a dashing outlaw. The second part is about Yseult's sister Blaina, who undertakes a dangerous journey to locate her lover who was kidnapped by Vikings.

Reviews: *BL* 3/15/70; *LJ* 2/15/70
Reading Level: Middle–High School
Subject Areas: Ireland; love
Time Period: Middle Ages; Sixth Century ❏ Library owns

Clements, Bruce. *Prison Window, Jerusalem Blue.* **New York: Farrar, 1977. ISBN 0-374-36121-6 LC 77-10081.**

Scandinavia, 831 A.D. Brother and sister, Jules and Sydne, who were kidnapped in England by Vikings and enslaved, scheme to gain their freedom from the Viking lord by revealing a plot to overthrow him.

Reviews: *BL* 10/15/77; *HB* 4/78; *SLJ* 11/77
Reading Level: Middle & Junior High School

Subject Areas: Scandinavia; Vikings; slaves
Time Period: 831; Middle Ages ❏ Library owns

Eberhart, Dikkon. *Paradise.* **Owens Mills, MD: Stemmer House, 1983. 295pp. ISBN 0-916144-52-6. LC 83-4392.**
Ireland, North America, sixth century. A well-traveled, pagan black man, Finbar, who has been shipwrecked on a small Irish island, is discovered by a small religious group and taken with them where, after a stormy ride, they arrive in North America.
Reviews: *LJ* 6/15/83; *SLJ* 1/84
Reading Level: High School [Mature Reader]
Subject Areas: Ireland; North America; adventure and adventurers; sea stories; explorers
Time Period: Sixth Century ❏ Library owns

Furlong, Monica. *Wise Child.* **New York: Knopf, 1987. 228pp. ISBN 0-394-99105-2. LC 87-3063.**
Scotland, sixth century. Set in the time when the old religion was giving way to Christianity, this is the story of an abandoned child, Wise Child, who is taken in by Juniper, a practitioner of the old religion, but considered a witch by the villagers. Wise Child is educated by the gentle Juniper, but when her rich mother returns, Wise Child goes with her, only to make a shocking discovery.
Reviews: *BCCB* 2/88; *BL* 12/1/87; *HB* 3-4/88; *SLJ* 9/87
Reading Level: Middle & Junior High School
Subject Areas: Scotland; witchcraft
Time Period: Sixth Century ❏ Library owns

Haugaard, Erik C.; illustrated by Leo and Diane Dillon. *Hakon of Rogen's Saga.* **Boston: Houghton, 1963. 132pp. ISBN 0-395-16037-5. LC 63-10901.**
Scandinavia, eleventh century. When his father dies, young Hakon, the rightful heir to Rogen island, must keep his treacherous uncle from taking the island.
Reviews: *WJ* 4
Reading Level: Middle & Junior High School
Subject Areas: Scandinavia; Vikings
Time Period: Middle Ages; Eleventh Century ❏ Library owns

Haugaard, Erik C. *A Slave's Tale.* **Boston: Houghton, 1965. 217pp. ISBN 0-395-06804-5. LC 65-12171.**
Scandinavia, eleventh century. Sequel to *Hakon of Rogen's Saga*. Helga, a stowaway slave girl, tells the tale of a Viking raid on Brittany.
Reviews: *WJ* 4

Europe—Dark Ages

Reading Level: Middle & Junior High School
Subject Areas: Scandinavia; Vikings; slaves
Time Period: Middle Ages; Eleventh Century ❏ Library owns

Kingman, Lee; illustrated by Richard Cuffari. *Escape from the Evil Prophecy.* **Boston: Houghton, 1973. 188pp. ISBN 0-395-17515-1 LC 73-7902.**
Iceland, eleventh century. As the people of Iceland begin to embrace Christianity, Thordis and her younger brother become embroiled in their foster-mother's attempts to fulfill a prophecy of their traditional beliefs. Thordis and Ketil defy the ancient ways, demand changes, and save themselves from death.
Reviews: *BL* 12/1/73; *HB* 10/73; *LJ* 10/15/73
Reading Level: Middle–High School
Subject Areas: Iceland; Christianity; brothers and sisters
Time Period: Middle Ages; Eleventh Century ❏ Library owns

Lewis, Hilda. *Harold Was My King.* **New York: McKay, 1970. 246pp. LC 71-20209.**
England, 1066. Edmund Edmundson, devoted squire to King Harold of England, refuses to swear allegiance to William the Conqueror, and joins a band of rebels. When their revolt fails, Edmund must concede that William has brought peace to England, finally swears allegiance to him, and is rewarded.
Reviews: *BL* 3/15/71; *WS* 10
Reading Level: High School
Subject Areas: Great Britain--Norman Period; Harold, II, King of England; William I, the Conqueror, King of England
Time Period: 1066 A.D.; Middle Ages ❏ Library owns

Llywelyn, Morgan. *Lion of Ireland: The Legend of Brian Boru.* **Boston: Houghton, 1980. 522pp. ISBN 0-395-28588-7. LC 79-21768.**
Ireland, tenth century. Brian Boru, legendary Irish hero, rises from a lowly position helping his older brother to fight Vikings to become the king that unites Ireland and finally defeats the invaders.
Reviews: *BBSH*; *BL* 2/1/80; *LJ* 1/15/80
Reading Level: High School [Mature Reader]
Subject Areas: Ireland; Brian Boru
Time Period: Middle Ages; Tenth Century ❏ Library owns

Maiden, Cecil; illustrated by Cary. *A Song for Young King Wenceslaus.* **Reading, Mass.: Addison-Wesley, 1969. 173pp. LC 70-88689.**
Bohemia, tenth century. The story of King Wenceslaus, who, though young, must defend his country and his faith.

Europe—Dark Ages

Reviews: *BL* 5/1/70; *LJ* 4/15/70
Reading Level: Middle & Junior High School
Subject Areas: Bohemia; Wenceslaus, Saint, Duke of Bohemia
Time Period: Middle Ages; Tenth Century ❏ Library owns

McGraw, Eloise. *The Striped Ships.* **New York: Macmillan/Margaret K. McElderry, 1991. 240pp. ISBN 0-689-50532-9. LC 91-7729.**
Great Britain, 1066. When her world is destroyed by Norman invaders, Juliana, daughter of a Saxon thane (a freeman who has been granted land by the king as a reward for his military service), finds a new life, becoming an embroiderer of the Bayeaux Tapestry in Canterbury.
Reviews: *BCCB* 10/91; *BL* 11/15/91; *BR* 5-6/92; *HB* 1/92; *SLJ* 9/91; *VOYA* 12/91
Reading Level: Middle–High School
Subject Areas: Great Britain--Norman Period; Anglo-Saxons; Bayeaux Tapestry
Time Period: 1066; Middle Ages ❏ Library owns

Muntz, Hope. *The Golden Warrior; The Story of Harold and William.* **New York: Scribner, 1970, c1949. 354pp. LC 76-107243.**
Great Britain, 1022-1066. A recreation of the life of King Harold of England, with particular emphasis on the Norman Invasion and the Battle of Hastings, where Harold lost his life.
Reviews: *WS* 10
Reading Level: High School
Subject Areas: Great Britain--Norman Period; Harold II, King of England; William I, the Conqueror, King of England; Hastings, The Battle of
Time Period: 1022-1066; Middle Ages ❏ Library owns

Seton, Anya. *Avalon.* **Boston: Houghton, 1965. 440pp.**
Great Britain, eleventh century. French, English and Viking characters come together in this story of a poetic French prince, a peasant girl with Viking blood, and her Viking relatives who kidnap her from Cornwall.
Reviews: *WS* 10
Reading Level: High School
Subject Areas: Great Britain--to 1066; Vikings
Time Period: Middle Ages; Eleventh Century ❏ Library owns

Stiles, Martha Bennett. *The Star in the Forest: A Mystery of the Dark Ages.* **New York: Scholastic, 1979. 256pp. ISBN 0-590-07537-3. LC 78-22284.**
France, sixth century. Valrada, daughter of a lord, falls in love with a poor man, but fears her father will arrange her marriage to a treacherous cousin. Valrada witnesses her brother's murder and must take steps to thwart the killer.

Europe—Dark Ages

Reviews: *BL* 10/1/79; *SLJ* 3/79★
Reading Level: Middle–High School
Subject Areas: Gaul; France--to 987; mystery and detective stories
Time Period: Sixth Century ❏ **Library owns**

Stolz, Mary. *Pangur Ban.* **New York: Harper, 1988. 182pp. ISBN 0-06-025862-4. LC 87-35049.**
Ireland, ninth century. When it becomes evident that Cormac's obsession with drawing will make him useless on the farm, his father sends him to the monastery. There, his talent develops and he becomes an illustrator of manuscripts. When a Viking invasion is imminent, Cormac hides his prized manuscript so carefully that it isn't discovered until twelfth century by another monk.
Reviews: *BL* 11/1/88; *BR* 5-6/89; *SLJ* 11/88
Reading Level: Middle–High School
Subject Areas: Ireland; religious life; artists; monks
Time Period: Middle Ages; Ninth Century ❏ **Library owns**

Sutcliff, Rosemary. *Blood Feud.* **New York: Dutton, 1977. 144pp. ISBN 0-525-26730-1. LC 76-58502.**
Russia, Istanbul, tenth century. When he comes to his master's aid, Jestyn, a 17-year-old slave, is freed by his Viking master, Thormod. Together they begin a journey that takes them to Juteland, Russia, and Istanbul, following the men who murdered Thormod's father. Thormod is killed and Jestyn is crippled by the last of the men they have sworn to kill. Jestyn must choose between final revenge or life and love in Istanbul, studying to be a healer.
Reviews: *BBSH*; *BL* 7/15/77; *HB* 10/77; *SLJ* 9/77; *WJ* 4, 5
Reading Level: Middle–High School
Subject Areas: Vikings; Istanbul (Turkey); Byzantium; adventure and adventurers
Time Period: 900; Middle Ages ❏ **Library owns**

Sutcliff, Rosemary. *The Shining Company.* **New York: Farrar, 1990. 296pp. ISBN 0-374-36807-4. LC 89-46142.**
Great Britain, 600 A.D. This retelling of "The Gododdin" centers around Prosper, shieldbearer for one of the 300 younger sons who make up the Company of the Three Hundred, an army whose purpose is to destroy the Saxons. Prosper witnesses the final bloody battle of the Company, where only two survive. Prosper makes it back to his people and there immortalizes the lost warriors in song.
Reviews: *BBYA*; *BL* 6/15/90★; *BR* 1-2/91; *CNB*; *SLJ* 7/90★; *WS* 14; *YAEC*
Reading Level: Middle–High School

Subject Areas: Great Britain--to 1066; Anglo-Saxons; war
Time Period: 600 ❏ Library owns

Sutcliff, Rosemary. *Tristan and Iseult.* **New York: Dutton, 1971. 150pp.**
Ireland, sixth century. A retelling of the story of Tristan and Iseult. Iseult was an Irish princess who married the king of Cornwall and then had a hopeless love affair with Tristan, one of the king's knights, resulting in their deaths.
Reviews: *BCCB* 4/72; *BL* 1/15/72; *HB* 12/71
Reading Level: Middle–High School
Subject Areas: Ireland; love
Time Period: Sixth Century ❏ Library owns

Tarr, Judith. *His Majesty's Elephant.* **San Diego: Harcourt, 1993. 224pp. ISBN 0-15-200737-7. LC 93-12878.**
Holy Roman Empire, 780. Rowan, one of Charlemagne's daughters overhears a sorcerer's plot to put her father under a spell, allowing the sorcerer to take a talisman containing a piece of the cross of the crucifixion. With the help of a stable boy and an elephant, Rowan discovers powers within herself and is able to help her father.
Reviews: *BL* 1/1/94; *BR* 5-6/94; *HB* 1/94; *VOYA* 2/94
Reading Level: Middle–High School
Subject Areas: Charlemagne, Emperor; magic; fantastic fiction
Time Period: 780 ❏ Library owns

Todd, Catherine. *Bond of Honour.* **New York: St. Martin's, 1982. 224pp. ISBN 0-312-08763-2. LC 81-51638.**
Great Britain, 1050-1066. This is an accessible and sympathetic treatment of William the Conqueror's life beginning with his defense of Normandy against the French, his marriage to Mathilda of Flanders despite his bastard status, the battle for England between the Normans and Saxons, the eventual Norman victory and finally, his coronation in Westminster Abbey.
Reviews: *BL* 3/1/82; *LJ* 2/15/82; *SLJ* 2/82
Reading Level: High School [Mature Reader]
Subject Areas: Great Britain--Norman period; William I, the Conqueror, King of England
Time Period: 1050-1066; Middle Ages ❏ Library owns

Wolf, Joan. *Born of the Sun.* **New York: NAL/Dutton, 1989. 416pp. ISBN 0-453-00666-3. LC 88-39422.**
England, sixth century. Niniane, a British princess, and Ceawlin, the illegitimate son of a Saxon king, marry and try to bring their two tribes together. When

Ceawlin accidentally kills his brother, he and Niniane are forced to flee. Upon their return, their hopes for peace between the tribes is realized.
Reviews: *BL* 8/89; *LJ* 7/89
Reading Level: High School [Mature Reader]
Subject Areas: Great Britain--to 1066; Anglo-Saxons
Time Period: Sixth Century ❏ Library owns

Wolf, Joan. *The Edge of Light*. New York: NAL/Dutton, 1990. 384pp. ISBN 0-453-00738-4. LC 89-77094.
England, ninth century. Alfred the Great attempts to hold the competing Saxon kingdoms together to fight a common foe, the invading Danes.
Reviews: *BL* 7/90; *LJ* 6/15/90
Reading Level: High School [Mature Reader]
Subject Areas: Great Britain--to 1066; Alfred the Great, King of England; Anglo-Saxons
Time Period: Middle Ages; Ninth Century ❏ Library owns

Wright, Patricia. *I Am England*. New York: St. Martin's, 1987. 397pp. ISBN 0-312-01045-1. LC 87-16665.
England, 70 A.D, 891, 1068, 1450, 1550. Five stories are joined by their location, a ridge in Sussex and its surrounding area. The stories follow the history of England, telling of a hunting-gathering tribe, Saxons, Normans, three men of the fifteenth century, and a man in the sixteenth century.
Reviews: *BL* 11/15/87; *LJ* 11/15/87
Reading Level: High School [Mature Reader]
Subject Areas: Great Britain--Norman Period
Time Period: 70 A.D.; 891; 1068; 1450; 1550; Middle Ages ❏ Library owns

Arthurian Tales

Bradley, Marion Zimmer. *The Mists of Avalon*. New York: Knopf, 1983. 858pp. ISBN 0-394-52406-3. LC 82-47810.
England. Through the eyes of three women, Morgaine, Arthur's sister; Viviane, Arthur's aunt; and Guinevere, we hear the story of King Arthur.
"Bradley evokes with compelling precision the time and ideals of feudal aristocracy and the clash of Christianity with paganism that led ultimately to the demise of Camelot." *Booklist*
Reviews: *BL* 11/15/82★; *LJ* 12/15/82; *WS* 14
Reading Level: High School [Mature Reader]

Subject Areas: Great Britain--to 1066; Arthur, King; Guinevere; Druids; knights and knighthood

Time Period: Sixth Century ❏ Library owns

Bradshaw, Gillian. *Hawk of May*. New York: Simon & Schuster, 1980. 313pp. ISBN 0-671-25093-0. LC 79-27135.

England. The first volume of a trilogy. Recognizing the dark forces that rule his mother, Morgawse, Gwalchmai flees to Arthur, where he becomes a powerful warrior with a magic sword.

Reviews: *BL* 7/15/80; *SLJ* 8/80

Reading Level: High School

Subject Areas: Great Britain--to 1066; Arthur, King; knights and knighthood; fantastic fiction

Time Period: Sixth Century ❏ Library owns

Bradshaw, Gillian. *In Winter's Shadow*. New York: Simon & Schuster, 1982. 320pp. ISBN 0-671-43512-4. LC 82-3267.

England. The third volume of a trilogy. Queen Gwynhwyfar chronicles the end of Arthur's empire, caused partly by the treachery of Medraut, illegitimate son of Arthur and his half-sister Morgawse, and partly by Gwynhwyfar's affair with Bedwyr.

Reviews: *BL* 7/82; *SLJ* 11/82

Reading Level: High School

Subject Areas: Great Britain--to 1066; Arthur, King; Guinevere; knights and knighthood

Time Period: Sixth Century ❏ Library owns

Bradshaw, Gillian. *Kingdom of Summer*. New York: Simon & Schuster, 1981. 288pp. ISBN 0-671-25472-3. LC 81-274.

England. The second of a trilogy. Rhys ap Sion, servant to Gwalchmai, finds himself caught in a struggle between the evil Morgawse and Gwalchmai who possesses the power of Light.

Reviews: *BL* 4/1/81; *SLJ* 9/81

Reading Level: High School

Subject Areas: Great Britain--to 1066; Arthur, King; knights and knighthood; fantastic fiction

Time Period: Sixth Century ❏ Library owns

Europe—Dark Ages

Newman, Robert; illustrated by Richard Cuffari. *The Testing of Tertius.* **New York: Atheneum, 1973. 186pp. LC 72-86944.**
England. Sequel to *Merlin's Mistake*. Three friends, with the help of Arthur, journey to France to break the spell that holds Merlin in a near-death state, a spell placed by Urlik the Black in his quest to conquer Britain.
Reviews: *BL* 9/15/72; *HB* 8/73; *SLJ* 9/73
Reading Level: Middle–High School
Subject Areas: Great Britain--to 1066; France--to 986; Arthur, King; Merlin; Arthurian romances
Time Period: Sixth Century ❏ Library owns

Newman, Sharan. *Guinevere.* **New York: St. Martin's, 1981. 257pp. ISBN 0-312-35318-9. LC 80-21753.**
England. The tale of Guinevere, Concentrating on her early life, including her protected childhood, and her romance with the bumbling Arthur.
Reviews: *BL* 2/15/81; *LJ* 4/1/81; *SLJ* 4/81
Reading Level: High School
Subject Areas: Great Britain--to 1066; Guinevere; Arthur, King; chivalry
Time Period: Sixth Century ❏ Library owns

Pyle, Howard. *The Story of the Grail and the Passing of Arthur.* **New York: Scribner, 1985. 258pp. ISBN 0-684-18483-4. LC 85-40302.**
England. Originally published in 1910. The final chapter to the story of Arthur—the search for the Holy Grail, after which the Round Table dissolves and Arthur's reign ends.
Reviews: *BFY*; *BL* 12/15/85
Reading Level: Middle–High School
Subject Areas: Great Britain--to 1066; Arthur, King; Lancelot; knights and knighthood; Holy Grail
Time Period: Sixth Century ❏ Library owns

Rice, Robert. *Last Pendragon.* **New York: Walker, 1992. 209pp. ISBN 0-8027-1180-4. LC 91-22428.**
England. Eleven years after Arthur's death, Bedwyr travels back to Britain to complete his final task—casting Arthur's sword Caliburn into the lake. As he travels through a ravaged Britain, he helps the remaining tribes repel the Saxons.
Reviews: *PW* 1/1/92; *SLJ* 5/92
Reading Level: High School
Subject Areas: Great Britain--to 1066; Arthurian romances; knights and knighthood
Time Period: Sixth Century ❏ Library owns

Stewart, Mary. *Mary Stewart's Merlin Trilogy.* **New York: Morrow, 1980. 919pp. ISBN 0-688-00347-8. LC 80-210019.**
England. An omnibus edition of *The Crystal Cave, The Hollow Hills* and *The Last Enchantment*, each entered separately below.
Reviews: *WJ* 5; *WS* 13, 14
Reading Level: Middle–High School
Subject Areas: Great Britain--to 1066; Arthur, King; Merlin
Time Period: Sixth Century ❏ Library owns

Stewart, Mary. *The Crystal Cave.* **New York: Morrow, 1970. 521pp. ISBN 0-449-20644-0.**
England. The Arthur legend begins in this volume with Merlin's youth, as he masters the magical arts and awaits the birth of Arthur.
"[Stewart] creates a dramatic and colorful picture of fifth-century England, Wales, and Brittany, showing Welsh, Saxons, and Britons in a bitter power struggle while Christians sought to destroy the old druidic and Roman religions." *Wilson's Senior High School Catalog* (from *Booklist*)
Reviews: *WS* 10, 12
Reading Level: High School
Subject Areas: Great Britain--to 1066; Merlin; Arthurian romances
Time Period: Sixth Century ❏ Library owns

Stewart, Mary. *The Hollow Hills.* **New York: Morrow, 1973. 499pp. ISBN 0-688-00179-3.**
England. The second volume of the trilogy begins with Arthur's birth and follows as, he is raised secretly under Merlin's guardianship and away from his father's court. In his 15th year, Arthur and Merlin reunite as Arthur pulls his sword from the stone.
Reviews: *BBYA*; *BL* 1/15/74★; *WS* 10, 11
Reading Level: High School
Subject Areas: Great Britain--to 1066; Merlin; Arthur, King
Time Period: Sixth Century ❏ Library owns

Stewart, Mary. *The Last Enchantment.* **New York: Morrow, 179. 538pp. ISBN 0-688-03481-0. LC 79-12937.**
England. The third of the trilogy. Arthur's early adult life is chronicled, including battles with the Saxon, his marriages to two Guineveres, and birth of Mordred. Merlin's story includes his love for Nimuë in his final years, who uses it to entrap him.
Reviews: *BL* 9/1/79★; *WS* 11
Reading Level: High School

Europe—Dark Ages

Subject Areas: Great Britain--to 1066; Arthur, King; Merlin; knights and knighthood
Time Period: Sixth Century ❏ Library owns

Stewart, Mary. *The Wicked Day.* **New York: Morrow, 1983. 452pp. ISBN 0-688-02507-2. LC 83-12091.**
England. In this fourth volume, Mordred's life is retold. He is raised by stepparents who are unaware of his heritage, and later is introduced to Arthur's court and the evil Queen Morgause.
Reviews: *BL* 9/1/83; *FFY; YARC*
Reading Level: High School
Subject Areas: Great Britain--to 1066; Arthur, King; Mordred (legendary character)
Time Period: Sixth Century ❏ Library owns

Sutcliff, Rosemary. *The Road to Camlann: The Death of King Arthur.* **New York: Dutton, 1982. 143pp. ISBN 0-525-44018-6. LC 82-9481.**
England. In this final volume of a trilogy which begins with *The Light Beyond the Forest* and *The Sword and the Circle,* we see the arrival of Mordred, the death of Lancelot and the end of Arthur and Camelot.
Reviews: *BBYA*; *BL* 2/1/83; *BR* 5-6/83; *SLJ* 1/83★
Reading Level: Middle–High School
Subject Areas: Great Britain--to 1066; Arthur, King; knights and knighthood
Time Period: Sixth Century ❏ Library owns

Twain, Mark. *A Connecticut Yankee in King Arthur's Court.* **New York: Morrow, 1988. 374pp. ISBN 0-688-06346-2. LC 87-62879.**
England. First published in 1889. A Yankee is transported through time to the court of King Arthur where he has many adventures and tries to right some injustices.
Reviews: *BL* 2/15/89; *WJ* 4, 5; *WS* 10, 11, 12, 13, 14
Reading Level: Middle–High School
Subject Areas: Great Britain--to 1066; Arthur, King; chivalry; space and time
Time Period: Sixth Century ❏ Library owns

Wein, Elizabeth. *The Winter Prince.* **New York: Atheneum, 1993. 224pp. ISBN 0-689-31747-6. LC 91-39129.**
England. This novel concentrates on Medraut (Mordred) and his relationship with his half-brother Lleu, the legitimate heir to Camlan. Medraut's love-envy feelings for his brother are exploited by Morgause, his mother, who wishes to control Lleu.
Reviews: *BL* 11/15/93; *BR* 1/94; *HB* 3/94; *SLJ* 10/93; *VOYA* 12/93
Reading Level: Middle–High School

Subject Areas: Great Britain--to 1066; Arthur, King; Arthurian romances; Brothers; Mordred (legendary character)
Time Period: Sixth Century ❏ Library owns

White, T. H. *The Book of Merlyn; The Unpublished Conclusion to the Once and Future King.* **University of Texas Press, 1977. 137pp. ISBN 0-292-70769-X. LC 77-3454.**

England. Sequel to *The Once and Future King.* Arthur, now old, defeated, and despondent, is led by Merlyn to overhear what the animals are saying about humans.

"Writing during World War II, White vented his feelings about the futility of war with a fierceness that sometimes overwhelms the intriguing mixture of fantasy, humor, and rationality which pervaded the tetralogy." *Wilson's Senior High School Catalog* 14 (from *Booklist*)

Reviews: *WJ* 5; *WS* 11, 12, 13, 14
Reading Level: Middle–High School
Subject Areas: Great Britain--to 1066; Arthur, King; Merlin; war
Time Period: Sixth Century ❏ Library owns

White, T. H. *The Once and Future King.* **New York: Putnam, 1958. 677pp. ISBN 0-425-09116-3 (Berkeley Paper). LC 58-10760.**

England. An omnibus volume of the author's complete story of the Arthurian legend, includes: *The Sword in the Stone, The Witch in the Wood* which is now called *The Queen of Air and Darkness, The Ill-Made Knight,* and *The Candle in the Wind.*

Reviews: *FFY*; *WJ* 5; *WS* 10, 11, 12, 13, 14
Reading Level: Middle–High School
Subject Areas: Great Britain--to 1066; Arthur, King
Time Period: Sixth Century ❏ Library owns

White, T. H. *The Sword in the Stone.* **New York: Putnam, 1939. 311pp. ISBN 0-399-10783-5. LC 39-27014.**

England. The beginning volume of *The Once and Future King.* This is an account of Wart's (Arthur's) youth as he plays and works at a manor house, and how Merlin makes him aware of what is to be.

Reviews: *WJ* 4, 5
Reading Level: Middle–High School
Subject Areas: Great Britain--to 1066; Arthur, King; Merlin
Time Period: Sixth Century ❏ Library owns

Europe—Dark Ages

Wooley, Persia. *Child of the Northern Spring.* **New York: Poseidon, 1987. 418pp. ISBN 0-671-62200-5. LC 87-2294.**
England. First volume of a trilogy. Guinevere tells her own story as well as that of Arthur. Guinevere reveals her childhood, her meeting with Arthur, their wedding, the founding of the Round Table and war.
Reviews: *BBYA*; *BL* 5/15/87; *LJ* 6/1/87
Reading Level: High School
Subject Areas: Great Britain--to 1066; Arthur, King; Guinevere
Time Period: Sixth Century ❏ Library owns

Wooley, Persia. *Guinevere: The Legend in Autumn.* **New York: Poseidon, 1991. 432pp. ISBN 0-671-70831-7.**
England. The third volume of a trilogy. Guinevere recalls the wonders of Camelot as she awaits her final dawn, when she will be burned at the stake.
"Wooley grounds the Arthurian legends firmly in the Dark Ages, surrounding them with enough facts to make the book more historical fiction than fantasy..." *Booklist*
Reviews: *BL* 10/1/91; *PW* 10/11/91
Reading Level:
Subject Areas: Great Britain--to 1066; Guinevere; Arthur, King
Time Period: Sixth Century ❏ Library owns

Woolley, Persia. *Queen of the Summer Stars.* **New York: Simon & Schuster/Poseidon, 1990. 415pp. ISBN 0-671-62201-3. LC 90-33441.**
England. The second of a trilogy. Guinevere, now married to Arthur, is sent to Lancelot's home for protection. While there she is raped by a cousin, rescued and nursed back to health by Lancelot. Lancelot, fearing his feelings for Gwen, leaves Camelot. Gwen returns to Arthur and learns the truth about Mordred and Morgause. Lancelot comes back to Camelot and pledges his loyalty to both Arthur and Gwen.
Reviews: *BBSH*; *BBYA*; *BL* 5/1/90; *BR* 1-2/91; *SLJ* 9/90
Reading Level: High School
Subject Areas: Great Britain--to 1066; Arthur, King; Guinevere; chivalry
Time Period: Sixth Century ❏ Library owns

Medieval Europe

Amoss, Berthe. *Lost Magic.* **Westport, CT: Hyperion; distributed by Little, Brown, 1993. 192pp. ISBN 1-56282-573-9. LC 93-10082.**
Great Britain. Ceridwen, an abandoned child, is found by an old wise woman and trained in the healing arts and magic. Ceridwen is called upon to cure the lord of the castle, which she does, and is rewarded with an offer to live there. The lord's wife is grateful to her, but she must also deal with the governess, who wishes to eliminate her.
Reviews: *BL* 11/1/93; *SLJ* 9/93
Reading Level: Middle & Junior High School
Subject Areas: Great Britain--1154-1399; healers; witchcraft; orphans
Time Period: Middle Ages ❑ Library owns

Andrews, J. S. *Cargo for a King.* **New York: Dutton, 1973. 173pp. ISBN 0-525-27460-X. LC 72-89834.**
Isle of Man, thirteenth century. High adventure marks this story of teenager Ragnor MacHelli, an inhabitant of the Isle of Man, who sets out to help King John take Ulster back from the treacherous Hugh de Lacy. Ragnor uses his family's trading ship to help capture pirates working for de Lacy.
Reviews: *BL* 5/15/73; *HB* 6/73; *SLJ* 9/73
Reading Level: Middle–High School
Subject Areas: Great Britain--1154-1399; pirates; sea stories
Time Period: Middle Ages; Thirteenth Century ❑ Library owns

Attanasio, A. A. *Kingdom of the Grail.* **New York: HarperCollins, 1992. 500pp. ISBN 0-06-017965-1. LC 91-50467.**
Wales, twelfth century. An aging, abused baroness is sent to the Holy Land during the Crusades by her son, who has taken her castle. While in the Holy Land, the Baroness Ailena finds a young, orphaned Jewish girl who looks exactly as the Baroness did in her youth. She spends ten years training Rachel to take her place back in Wales—claiming a miracle of rejuvenation—and help her gain revenge. Rachel complies, but not without inner conflicts.
Reviews: *BL* 2/15/92; *BR* 11-12/92
Reading Level: High School
Subject Areas: Wales; Crusades; Jews
Time Period: Middle Ages; Twelfth Century ❑ Library owns

Beckman, Thea. *Crusade in Jeans.* **New York: Scribners, 1976. 275pp. ISBN 0-684-14399-2. LC 75-13415.**
Germany, 1212. Dolf Hefting is transported by a time machine from contemporary Amsterdam to the middle of the Children's Crusade. He finds the children

threatened by hunger, disease, suspicious villagers, and wild animals. With his twentieth century knowledge, he tries to bring order to the crusade, but ends up on trial as a heretic. Dolf exposes the monks' true motive for sending the children on the Crusade, and returns home.
Reviews: *BL* 4/15/76; *SLJ* 4/76
Reading Level: Middle–High School
Subject Areas: Europe--476-1492; Germany; Children's Crusade, 1212; Crusades; space and time
Time Period: 1212 ❏ **Library owns**

Bosse, Malcolm. *Captives of Time.* **New York: Delacorte, 1987. 267pp. ISBN 0-385-29583-9. LC 86-32943.**
Europe. After witnessing the brutal murder of their parents, Anne and her mute younger brother undertake an arduous journey to their Uncle Albrecht's. Anne is fascinated by Albrecht's plans to build a giant clock. Albrecht is caught up in a power struggle with the church, a duke, and the local merchants who all want control of the clock. Anne survives the hardships of the time, including the Black Plague and rape, living to begin designing a town clock.
Reviews: *BBSH; BBYA; BFY; BL* 1/1/88; *BR* 11-12/87; *SLJ* 10/87★; *VOYA* 12/87
Reading Level: High School
Subject Areas: Europe--476-1492; clocks and watches; survival
Time Period: Middle Ages ❏ **Library owns**

Cervantes, Miguel de; translated by Magda Bogin. *Don Quixote de La Mancha.* **Stewart, Tabori & Chang; distributed by Workman, 1991. 144pp. ISBN 1-55670-201-9.**
Spain. The gentleman knight-errant and his squire Sancho Panza travel the countryside and wage battles with windmills that appear to be giants and become involved in many other fantastic adventures. First published in Spain in two parts, 1605 and 1615. This new edition is illustrated by the Spanish artist Manuel Boix.
Reviews: *BL* 12/15/91; *SLJ* 1/92; *WJ* 5, 6; *WS* 11, 12, 13, 14
Reading Level: Middle–High School
Subject Areas: Spain; knights and knighthood; adventures and adventurers
Time Period: Middle Ages ❏ **Library owns**

Chadwick, Elizabeth. *The Running Vixen.* **New York: St. Martin's, 1992. 336pp. ISBN 0-312-07793-9. LC 92-1098.**
Wales, twelfth century. This swash-buckling adventure is centered around Adam de Lacey, land owner and errand boy for King Henry I. Adam is sent to the continent to escort Henry's sharp-tongued daughter and heir home. Then he is sent on

a mission to secure a husband for her. If these disagreeable duties aren't enough, he is caught up in a feud with a traitorous former lover of his wife.
Reviews: *BL* 4/15/92; *LJ* 4/1/92
Reading Level: High School
Subject Areas: Wales; Henry I, King of England; adventures and adventurers
Time Period: Middle Ages; Twelfth Century ❏ Library owns

Chadwick, Elizabeth. *The Wild Hunt.* **New York: St. Martin's, 1991. 370pp. ISBN 0-312-06491-8. LC 91-4337.**
Wales, twelfth century. By order of King William Rufus, 28-year-old Guyon marries 16-year-old Judith in order to gain lands from her uncle. The marriage begins with Guyon angry at having to marry a little girl, and with Judith terrified, expecting to be abused as her mother was by her father. Each begins to appreciate the other. The political situation and medieval setting create an atmosphere that support this believable romance.
Reviews: *LJ* 9/1/91; *SLJ* 3/92
Reading Level: High School
Subject Areas: Wales; marriage; love
Time Period: Middle Ages; Twelfth Century ❏ Library owns

Chester, Deborah. *The Sign of the Owl.* **New York: Scholastic/Four Winds, 1981. 219pp. ISBN 0-590-07729-5. LC 80-69998.**
France. Fifteen-year-old Wint is on his own after his ruthless uncle kills his father and takes over the family land. Wint has a quest—he must find the family sword which will make him the true ruler. During his journey, he befriends an English girl who is fleeing from an arranged marriage. Together, they both achieve their goals.
Reviews: *BBYA*; *BCCB* 12/81; *BL* 7/15/81; *HB* 8/81; *SLJ* 9/81
Reading Level: Middle–High School
Subject Areas: France
Time Period: Middle Ages ❏ Library owns

Coolidge, Olivia. *Tales of the Crusades.* **Boston: Houghton, 1970. 225pp. ISBN 0-395-06720-0.**
Europe, Middle East, 1094-1464. Recreating the flavor of the times, these twelve stories about priests, knights, peasants, and children explore the hopes, motivations and the tragic realities of a pilgrimage to the Holy Land.
Reviews: *BL* 7/15/70; *WJ* 4
Reading Level: Middle–High School

Europe—Medieval Europe

Subject Areas: Europe--476-1492; Middle East; Crusades; knights and knighthood; short stories
Time Period: 1094-1464; Middle Ages ❏ Library owns

Collins, Meghan. *Maiden Crown.* **Boston: Houghton, 1979. 192pp. ISBN 0-395-28639-5. LC 79-16201.**
Denmark, twelfth century. Sophie, a Russian princess, marries King Valdemar of Denmark to seal a political alliance. She is surprised to find that they get along quite well—until she discovers that Valdemar has a mistress. Tove, the mistress, spreads rumors about Sophie which cause Sophie and Valdemar to argue violently with tragic results. This story is based on a Danish ballad.
Reviews: *BCCB* 3/80; *BL* 12/1/79; *HB* 4/80; *SLJ* 2/78; *VOYA* 2/80
Reading Level: Middle–High School
Subject Areas: Denmark; Valdemar I, King of Denmark
Time Period: Middle Ages; Twelfth Century ❏ Library owns

Costain, Thomas B. *The Black Rose.* **New York: Doubleday, 1945. 403pp. LC 45-7847.**
England, Asia, thirteenth century. A young English nobleman journeys to Asia and the Mongol Empire. When, after many battles, he arrives, he falls in love with an Asian girl. After he returns home, he finds he must choose between an English heiress and the girl he met in Asia.
Reviews: *WS* 10, 11
Reading Level: High School
Subject Areas: Great Britain--1154-1399; Asia; adventure and adventurers
Time Period: Middle Ages; Thirteenth Century ❏ Library owns

Cushman, Karen. *Catherine, Called Birdy.* **New York: Clarion, 1994. 174pp. ISBN 0-395-68186-3. LC 93-23333.**
England, 1290. In her diary, 14-year-old Birdy tells all of the intimate details of her life as the daughter of a minor lord. This includes not only how many fleas she has killed in a day, and of the tedium of a woman's life, but the numerous suitors that her father has proposed, and she has rejected. Her diary reveals the routine of medieval life with wit and insight.
Reviews: *BL* 4/15/94; *SLJ* 6/94★; *BBYA*; *BR* 1-2/95
Reading Level: Middle–High School
Subject Areas: Great Britain--1154-1399; diaries; women
Time Period: 1290; Middle Ages ❏ Library owns

Europe—Medieval Europe

Doherty, P.C. *Murder Wears a Cowl.* **New York: St. Martin's, 1994. 249pp. ISBN 1-312-10506-1. LC 93-35844.**
England, ca. 1300. When a serial murderer, who had been killing prostitutes, kills the pious widow of a friend of Edward I, Hugh Corbett, a spy for Edward, and his bawdy servant track down the killer. During his investigation, Hugh uncovers bizarre behavior at a half-built cathedral and the arrival of a rival spy. Based on actual events, this provides a colorful look at medieval life.
Reviews: *PW* 2/14/94; *SLJ* 9/94
Reading Level: High School [Mature Reader]
Subject Areas: Great Britain; mystery and detective stories
Time Period: 1300; Middle Ages ❑ Library owns

Doherty, P. C. *The Whyte Hart.* **New York: St. Martin's, 1988. 256pp. ISBN 0-312-02318-9. LC 88-17670.**
England, fourteenth century. After King Richard II is deposed from the throne, Matthew Jankyn reluctantly joins the Whyte Harte. He uncovers a conspiracy that involves members of the royal class and the church and must ensure his own survival through deceit and double-cross.
Reviews: *BBSH*; *BL* 12/1/88
Reading Level: High School
Subject Areas: Great Britain--1154-1399; Richard II, King of England; mystery and detective stories
Time Period: Middle Ages; Fourteenth Century ❑ Library owns

Follett, Ken. *The Pillars of the Earth.* **New York: Morrow, 1989. 975pp. ISBN 0-688-04659-2. LC 89-9405.**
England, twelfth century. An epic concerning the partnership between two men, one a devout monk and the other an ambitious stonemason, who join forces to build a magnificent cathedral. But many obstacles, including political maneuvering, warfare, and natural disasters delay the completion. Death necessitates that the stonemason's stepson help complete his dream. Throughout are the minute details of medieval life.
Reviews: *BBSH*; *BL* 6/15/89★; *LJ* 7/89
Reading Level: High School [Mature Reader]
Subject Areas: Great Britain--Norman Period; cathedrals
Time Period: Middle Ages; Twelfth Century ❑ Library owns

Garwood, Julie. *Saving Grace.* **New York: Simon & Schuster, 1993. 372pp. ISBN 0-6771-74422-4. LC 93-7531.**
England, Scotland, thirteenth century. Sixteen-year-old widow, Lady Johanna, is relieved when her brother arranges a marriage to a Scottish laird, instead of waiting

87

for King John to marry her off. She has much to learn about life and customs in Scotland, and must decide how to make her husband fall in love with her. Despite some errors in the historical details, the characters bring the period to life.

Reviews: *BL* 5/15/93; *LJ* 6/15/93; *SLJ* 1/94

Reading Level: High School [Mature Reader]

Subject Areas: Scotland; love; marriage

Time Period: 1206; Middle Ages ❏ Library owns

Godwin, Parke. ***Robin and the King.*** **New York: Morrow, 1993. 324pp. ISBN 0-688-05274-6. LC 92-42216.**

England, eleventh century. Sequel to *Sherwood*. After eight years of quiet family life, Robin finds he must once again fight injustice when Ranulf of Bayeux tries to illegally seize property. Together with his old friends and allied with his old enemy, the sheriff of Nottingham, Robin must choose between his principles and his loyalty to the crown.

Reviews: *BL* 6/1/93; *BL* 6/15/93; *LJ* 5/15/93

Reading Level: High School

Subject Areas: Great Britain--Norman Period; Robin Hood

Time Period: Middle Ages; Eleventh Century ❏ Library owns

Godwin, Parke. ***Sherwood.*** **New York: Morrow, 1991. 384pp. ISBN 0-688-05264-9. LC 90-28565.**

England, eleventh century. Going against tradition, the author places Robin Hood in the eleventh century and makes him a leader in the Anglo-Saxon resistance against the Normans. The sheriff of Nottingham is a young Norman knight, who does not understand the Anglo-Saxon ways. A great deal of history is skillfully integrated into this imaginative work.

Reviews: *BL* 6/1/91; *LJ* 7/91

Reading Level: High School

Subject Areas: Great Britain--Norman Period; Robin Hood; Anglo-Saxons

Time Period: Middle Ages; Eleventh Century ❏ Library owns

Goldman, James. ***Myself As Witness.*** **New York: Random, 1979. 340pp.**

England, 1167-1216. This is the fictionalized story of John Plantagenet, sometimes known as John Lackland because he inherited so small a portion of his family's wealth. John was the last child of Henry II and Eleanor of Aquitaine. His stormy relations with the nobility precipitated the Magna Carta and the first Baron's War.

Reviews: *BL* 2/1/80; *FFY*; *LJ* 12/15/79

Reading Level: High School

Subject Areas: Great Britain--1154-1399; John, King of England
Time Period: 1167-1216; Middle Ages ❏ Library owns

Gray, Elizabeth Janet; illustrated by Robert Lawson. *Adam of the Road.* **New York: Viking, 1942. 317pp. ISBN 0-670-10435-3. LC 42-10681.**
England, thirteenth century. Winner of the 1943 Newbery Medal. When Adam is separated from his minstrel father and his dog, he begins a search which takes him to London, Winchester, and Oxford, where they are reunited. Through his eyes life and history in medieval England are revealed.
Reviews: *Wilson Children's Catalog*
Reading Level: Middle & Junior High School
Subject Areas: Great Britain, 1154-1399; minstrels
Time Period: Middle Ages; Thirteenth Century ❏ Library owns

Hall, Lynn. *Dog of Bondi Castle.* **Chicago: Follett, 1979. 124pp. ISBN 0-695-41255-8. LC 78-21646.**
France. Isabelle gives her betrothed, Aubry. a staghound puppy which grows to a large and devoted dog. When Aubry is finally knighted and has wedding plans underway, his jealous squire kidnaps the dog. In a rage at being forced to return the dog, he murders Aubry. Isabelle has her revenge with the dog as a weapon. This is based on a French legend.
Reviews: *BL* 3/1/79; *SLJ* 5/79
Reading Level: Middle–High School
Subject Areas: France; dogs; love
Time Period: Middle Ages ❏ Library owns

Harding, Paul. *The Nightingale Gallery: Being the First of the Sorrowful Mysteries of Brother Athelstan.* **New York: Morrow, 1992. 256pp. ISBN 0-688-11225-0. LC 91-37351.**
England. When the king dies leaving noblemen and merchants to maneuver for political positions, a prominent merchant is murdered. Brother Athelstan, a Dominican friar, and the chief coroner, begin an investigation that leads to all social classes, and poses a threat to their safety.
Reviews: *BL* 4/15/92; *LJ* 4/1/92
Reading Level: High School
Subject Areas: Great Britain--1159-1399; mystery and detective stories
Time Period: Middle Ages ❏ Library owns

Europe—Medieval Europe

Harding, Paul. *Red Slayer: Being the Second of the Sorrowful Mysteries of Brother Athelstan.* **New York: Morrow, 1994. 283pp. ISBN 0-688-12569-7. LC 93-5348.**

England, fourteenth century. When the constable of the Tower of London is found murdered in his locked chamber, Sir John Cranston and his clerk Brother Athelstan are called in to solve the mystery. Their quest takes them into some unsavory corners of London.

Reviews: *BL* 3/15/94; *LJ* 2/1/94; *SLJ* 9/94.

Reading Level: High School

Subject Areas: Great Britain; mystery and detective stories

Time Period: Middle Ages; Fourteenth Century ❏ Library owns

Haycraft, Molly (Costain). *The King's Daughters.* **Philadelphia: Lippincott, 1971. 247pp. LC 76-154847.**

England, 1272-1307. The romantic lives of Edward I's five daughters are revealed through their sister Elizabeth, called Bette. Although marriages were arranged to promote profitable political alliances, Bette is able, after the death of her first husband, to marry the man she truly loves.

Reviews: *BL* 12/1/71; *LJ* 9/15/71; *SLJ* 4/72

Reading Level: Middle–High School

Subject Areas: Great Britain--1154-1399; Edward I, King of England; Elizabeth, Princess of England; marriage

Time Period: 1272-1307; Middle Ages ❏ Library owns

Hendrey, Frances Mary. *Quest for a Maid.* **New York: Farrar, 1990. 273pp. ISBN 0-374-36162-2. LC 89-46396.**

Scotland, thirteenth century. Meg overhears her older sister putting a death spell on King Alexander III. When the king dies, Meg is chosen to accompany an eight-year-old princess back to Scotland from Norway to marry Prince Edward. The journey is stormy, and, cursed by Meg's sister, the ship is wrecked. In legend, the Maid of Norway dies, but here she and Meg live.

Reviews: *BBYA*; *BL* 7/90; *BR* 5-6/91; *SLJ* 12/90

Reading Level: Middle–High School

Subject Areas: Scotland; witchcraft; adventure and adventurers

Time Period: Middle Ages; Thirteenth Century ❏ Library owns

Hill, Pamela. *The Woman in the Cloak.* **New York: St. Martin's, 1990. 160pp. ISBN 0-312-03956-5. LC 89-27128.**

Spain, thirteenth century. When Margaret is born a dwarf and blind, the shame of her wealthy parents, she is kept hidden from sight for years. At the age of 17, she is taken to a shrine to pray for a cure, and she is abandoned when the cure fails.

Despite her handicaps, Margaret of Metola becomes a person who brings joy and solace to others. This is based on historical fact.
Reviews: *BL* 1/1/90; *PW* 12/1/89
Reading Level: High School
Subject Areas: Spain; saints; Christian saints; Margaret of Metola, Saint; blind
Time Period: Middle Ages; Thirteenth Century ❏ Library owns

Holland, Cecelia; illustrated by Richard Cuffari. *The King's Road.* **New York: Atheneum, 1970. 151pp.**
Sicily, ca. 1210. Twelve-year-old Federigo, who is King of Sicily in name only, overhears a plot to kill him while playing with friends on the street. He and two friends flee from Palermo on a pirate ship and experience a series of adventures before he returns. Through his travels he becomes aware of his strengths, which serve him well when he becomes Frederick II, Holy Roman Emperor.
Reviews: *BL* 2/1/71; *HB* 12/70; *LJ* 10/15/70
Reading Level: Middle & Junior High School
Subject Areas: Italy; Sicily; Friedrich II, Emperor of Germany
Time Period: 1210; Middle Ages ❏ Library owns

Jones, Ellen. *The Fatal Crown.* **New York: Simon & Schuster, 1991. 435pp. ISBN 0-671-72464-9. LC 90-49918.**
England, 1130-1142. This is a romantic account of the struggle between Matilda, daughter of Henry I, and her cousin Stephen for the throne of England. Even though they were involved in a love affair, when Stephen becomes king, he forces Matilda to leave England.
Reviews: *BL* 1/15/91; *PW* 11/23/90
Reading Level: High School
Subject Areas: Great Britain--Norman Period; Matilda, Empress of Germany; Stephen, King of England; love
Time Period: 1130-1142; Middle Ages ❏ Library owns

Koenig, Alma Johanna; translated by Anthea Bell. *Gudrun.* **New York: Lothrop, 1979. 187pp. ISBN 0-688-51899-0. LC 79-917.**
Scandinavia, Normandy, thirteenth century. Gudrun is kidnapped from her home and taken to Normandy, where she is enslaved to the evil Lady Gerlind. After a very long year, Gudrun's betrothed rescues her. This is a retelling of an ancient Norse poem.
Reviews: *BL* 1/1/80; *SLJ* 10/79
Reading Level: High School
Subject Areas: Normandy; Gudrun; knights and knighthood
Time Period: Middle Ages; Thirteenth Century ❏ Library owns

Europe—Medieval Europe

Konigsburg, E. L. *A Proud Taste for Scarlet and Miniver.* **New York: Atheneum, 1973. 201pp. ISBN 0-689-30111-1. LC 73-76320.**
England, twelfth century. Eleanor of Aquitaine is in heaven waiting impatiently with her mother-in-law and several friends for Henry II to join her. Each member of the group gives a glimpse from a different part of Eleanor's earthly life.
Reviews: *BCCB* 7/79; *BL* 11/1/73; *HB* 6/79; *NCB*; *SLJ* 4/79; *WJ* 4, 5
Reading Level: Middle–High School
Subject Areas: Great Britain--1154-1399; Eleanor, Queen of England; Henry II, King of England
Time Period: 1180s; Middle Ages ❏ **Library owns**

Mackin, Jeanne. *The Queen's War.* **New York: St. Martin's, 1991. 452pp. ISBN 0-312-04960-9. LC 90-15542.**
England, twelfth century. Set in 1173, this is an account of Eleanor of Aquitaine's and her two sons' revolt against Henry II. Not only are the historical facts presented, but many interesting minor characters are included who bring interest to the story.
Reviews: *BL* 5/15/91; *LJ* 3/15/91
Reading Level: High School
Subject Areas: Great Britain--1154-1399; Eleanor, Queen of England; Henry II, King of England
Time Period: 1173; Middle Ages ❏ **Library owns**

Newman, Sharan. *Death Comes As Epiphany.* **New York: Tor, 1993. 318pp. ISBN 0-312-85419-6. LC 93-12761.**
France, twelfth century. Set after Abelard's and Heloise's tragic love affair when each has entered a religious community. Heloise sends a young scholar, Catherine, to help Abelard. Someone has been forging Abelard's works and Catherine must find out the identity of the forger. As she progresses Catherine is in danger of losing her life.
Reviews: *SLJ* 2/94; *PW* 6/7/93
Reading Level: High School
Subject Areas: France; Abelard, Peter; mystery and detective stories
Time Period: Middle Ages; Twelfth Century ❏ **Library owns**

O'Dell, Scott. *The Road to Damietta.* **Boston: Houghton, 1985. 230pp. ISBN 0-395-38923-2. LC 85-11720.**
Italy, thirteenth century. Francis Bernardone, later to be known as Francis of Assisi, was as a young man a wastrel and pleasure seeker. Ricca di Montanaro, a young noblewoman, was in love with him and pursued him. Through her eyes we see the change in Francis as he becomes devoted to God and peace. It is only after

Europe—Medieval Europe

banishment by her family, the Fifth Crusade, and a trip to Damietta, Egypt, with Francis that she realizes he will never love her.
Reviews: *BCCB* 12/85; *SLJ* 12/85; *VOYA* 2/86
Reading Level: Middle–High School
Subject Areas: Italy; Francis of Assisi, Saint; Christian saints; saints; crusades
Time Period: 1205-1220; Middle Ages ❑ Library owns

Oldenbourg, Zoé; translated by Anne Carter. *The Heirs of the Kingdom*. New York: Pantheon, 1971. 563pp. ISBN 0-394-46835-X.
France, Jerusalem, 1096-1099. Following Peter the Hermit, a group of weavers from Arras join the First Crusade. It takes them three years to reach Jerusalem where they storm the city with the help of knights.
Reviews: *WS* 10
Reading Level: High School
Subject Areas: France; Jerusalem; crusades
Time Period: 1096-1099; Middle Ages ❑ Library owns

Pargeter, Edith. *The Heaven Tree Trilogy*. New York: Warner, 1993. 912pp. ISBN 0-446-51708-9.
England, Wales, thirteenth century. In three novels, the history of a thirteenth century family of stonecarvers is traced. Harry Talvace begins it all when he is apprenticed to Lord Isambard who wants to build a cathedral. Harry designs and begins to build it, but power struggles interfere. When Harry is murdered, Harry's youngest son returns to Wales to avenge his father's death. Contains *The Heaven Tree* (1960), *The Green Branch* (1962), and *The Scarlet Seed* (1963).
Reviews: *BL* 10/1/93★; *LJ* 10/1/93
Reading Level: High School [Mature Reader]
Subject Areas: Great Britain--1154-1399; Wales; cathedrals
Time Period: Middle Ages; Thirteenth Century ❑ Library owns

Penman, Sharon Kay. *Falls the Shadow*. New York: Holt, 1988. 580pp. ISBN 0-8050-0300-2. LC 87-32255.
England, 1216-1272. This is the story of Henry III, an erratic leader forced to sign the Magna Carta, and Simon de Montfort, once a favorite of Henry's turned adversary. Along with the historical details of the Baron's War and the Magna Carta are romance, chivalry and the Crusades.
Reviews: *BBSH*; *BL* 3/15/88; *BR* 5-6/88; *SLJ* 9/88
Reading Level: High School
Subject Areas: Great Britain--1154-1399; Henry III, King of England; Magna Carta; Montfort, Simon de, Earl of Leicester
Time Period: 1216-1272; Middle Ages ❑ Library owns

Europe—Medieval Europe

Penman, Sharon Kay. *Here Be Dragons.* **New York: Holt, 1985. 704pp. ISBN 0-03-062773-7. LC 84-23480.**

England, Wales, thirteenth century. The arranged marriage of 14-year-old Joanna, illegitimate daughter of King John, to Llewelyn, Prince of Wales, 20 years her senior, is made to smooth relations between England and Wales. However, true love develops between these two very different people amidst political intrigues, battles, and less than perfect social conditions.

Reviews: *BBSH*; *SLJ* 9/85; *VOYA* 4/86

Reading Level: High School [Mature Reader]

Subject Areas: Great Britain--1154-1399; Wales; marriage; love

Time Period: Middle Ages; Thirteenth Century ❏ Library owns

Penman, Sharon Kay. *The Reckoning.* **New York: Holt, 1991. 593pp. ISBN 0-8050-1014-9. LC 90-27099.**

England, Wales, thirteenth century. Through the story of the romance of Llewelyn, Prince of Wales, and his bride Eleanor, daughter of Simon de Montfort, we see the takeover of Wales by Edward I. Due to internal fighting, the Welsh are weakened, allowing English forces to take over. Llewelyn is killed and all the members of Llewelyn's family are dispersed to prisons and convents.

Reviews: *BBYA*; *BL* 8/91; *LJ* 9/1/91; *SLJ* 7/92

Reading Level: High School

Subject Areas: England--1154-1399; Wales; Edward I, King of England

Time Period: 1283; Middle Ages ❏ Library owns

Peters, Ellis. *The Confession of Brother Haluin.* **New York: Mysterious Press; distributed by Ballantine, 1989. 176pp. ISBN 0-89296-349-2. LC 88-15141.**

England, twelfth century. Brother Cadfael, a Benedictine monk and herbalist, is accompanying Brother Haluin on a pilgrimage to the tomb of a former loved one. When they find the body of a murder victim, Cadfael finds a connection to Haluin's past. Medieval life is well-integrated into this novel. This is volume 13 of the Brother Cadfael series.

Reviews: *BL* 2/1/89; *PW* 1/6/89

Reading Level: High School

Subject Areas: Great Britain--Norman Period; monks; mystery and detective stories

Time Period: Middle Ages; Twelfth Century ❏ Library owns

Peters, Ellis. *A Rare Benedictine: The Advent of Brother Cadfael.* **New York: Mysterious Press; distributed by Ballantine, 1989. 118pp. ISBN 0-89296-397-2. LC 89-42603.**

England, twelfth century. This contains three stories which explain the origins of Brother Cadfael. The first story sees him returning from war in 1120, a soldier and a scribe. In his first mystery he saves the life of his master, but not his property, which prompts him to seek the stable life of the Benedictine monks.

Reviews: *BL* 1/1/90

Reading Level: High School

Subject Areas: Great Britain--Norman Period; monks; mystery and detective stories

Time Period: 1120; Middle Ages   ❏ Library owns

Peters, Ellis. *The Potter's Field.* **New York: Mysterious Press; distributed by Ballantine, 1990. 240pp. ISBN 0-89296-419-7. LC 90-6340.**

England, twelfth century. Brother Cadfael finds the buried body of a woman in a field that is being plowed. As his abbot, the sheriff and he search for her identity, Cadfael fears that the most likely suspects are fellow monks. This is the 17th novel in the series.

Reviews: *BL* 11/15/90; *PW* 10/12/90

Reading Level: High School

Subject Areas: Great Britain--Norman Period; monks; mystery and detective stories

Time Period: Middle Ages; Twelfth Century   ❏ Library owns

Peters, Ellis. *The Holy Thief.* **New York: Mysterious Press; distributed by Ballantine, 1993. 246pp. ISBN 0-89296-524-X. LC 92-50451.**

England, twelfth century. With the abbey hosting guests, the bones of their patron saint are stolen. A guest is murdered and young monk is accused. Brother Cadfael must not only solve the murder and free the innocent monk, he must find the stolen relic to save himself from embarrassment and accusations. He took the bones years ago and buried them according to the last wishes of the saint.

Reviews: *BL* 3/1/93; *SLJ* 7/93

Reading Level: High School

Subject Areas: Great Britain--Norman Period; monks; mystery and detective stories

Time Period: Middle Ages; Twelfth Century   ❏ Library owns

Polland, Madeleine A. *To Kill a King.* **New York: Holt, 1971. 187pp. ISBN 03-084264-6. LC 79-98917.**

England, eleventh century. Sequel to *The Queen's Blessing.* Merca and her brother Dag, who were orphaned in the Norman Conquest, are taken in by King

Malcolm and Queen Margaret of Scotland. Merca wishes to enter a convent to escape the miseries of life. She is forced to travel to London with King Malcolm where he is to pay homage to William I. There she meets Edward, who is intent on killing William, and Merca is tempted to join in his plan.
Reviews: *BL* 4/1/71; *HB* 6/71; *LJ* 4/15/71; *TLS* 10/30/70
Reading Level: Middle–High School
Subject Areas: Great Britain--Norman Period; Malcolm III, King of Scotland; Margaret, Saint, Queen of Scotland; orphans
Time Period: Middle Ages; Eleventh Century ❏ Library owns

Rosen, Sidney and Rosen, Dorothy. *The Magician's Apprentice.* **New York: Carolrhoda, 1994. 155pp. ISBN 0-87614-809-7. LC 93-10781.**
France, England, thirteenth century. Jean has been educated at an abbey in France. When he is accused of possessing a heretical document, 15-year-old Jean agrees to spy on Roger Bacon in England. Jean takes a job in Bacon's laboratory at Oxford and must decide what to tell the Grand Inquisitor in France.
Reviews: *BL* 5/1/94
Reading Level: Middle & Junior High School
Subject Areas: Great Britain--1154-1399; France; Bacon, Roger; Inquisition; scientists; orphans
Time Period: Middle Ages; Thirteenth Century ❏ Library owns

Rosefield, James. *The Lion and the Lily.* **New York: Dodd, 1972. 209pp.**
England, France, 1180-1189. Fifteen-year-old King Philip II of France, much to the consternation of his mother and uncles who each want to become regent, chooses to exercise his right to rule. Henry II in England gives each of his sons a dukedom in France, thinking that his sons will then challenge Philip. Instead, they join forces with Philip to fight against their father.
Reviews: *BL* 5/1/73; *LJ* 3/15/73
Reading Level: High School
Subject Areas: France; Great Britain--1154-1399; Henry II, King of England; Philip II, King of France
Time Period: 1180-1189; Middle Ages ❏ Library owns

Scott, Sir Walter. *Ivanhoe.* **New York: New American Library. 192pp. ISBN 0-451-51876-4.**
England, ca. 1190. In a sweeping, swashbuckling tale, Wilfred, knight of Ivanhoe, does not want to marry the woman his father has chosen for him. He is in love with the fair Rowena. Other characters that have large roles are Richard I and Robin Hood. This was first published in 1819.
Reviews: *WJ* 4, 5

Reading Level: Middle–High School
Subject Areas: Great Britain--1154-1399; Richard I, King of England; Robin Hood; knights and knighthood
Time Period: 1190; Middle Ages ❏ Library owns

Skurzynski, Gloria. *Manwolf.* **Boston: Clarion Books, 1981. 177pp. ISBN 0-395-30079-7. LC 80-22393.**
Poland, fourteenth century. Adam, illegitimate son of a mysterious knight, develops red teeth, skin that is disfigured, and hairiness, leading the villagers to believe that he is a werewolf. In hopes of a cure, he stops Queen Jadwiga's carriage one day, scaring her, and prompting the villagers to cage him. He is freed and taken in by the monks of a local monastery.
Reviews: *BBYA*; *CRC*; *HB* 8/81; *SLJ* 5/81; *VOYA* 8/81; *WJ* 5
Reading Level: Middle–High School
Subject Areas: Poland; superstition
Time Period: Middle Ages; Fourteenth Century ❏ Library owns

Skurzynski, Gloria. *What Happened in Hamelin.* **New York: Scholastic/Four Winds, 1979. 177pp. ISBN 0-590-07625-6. LC 79-12814.**
Germany, 1284. Gast, a flute-playing stranger, appears in Hamelin, and convinces the city elders that he can solve the problem they have with rats. Geist, a baker's apprentice, is fascinated by Gast and his apparent powers in swaying people. When the village elders choose not to honor their agreement with Gast, he gets his revenge by luring away the children. Geist observes, but is powerless to stop him. The author's research provides a credible explanation to the legendary events in Hamelin.
Reviews: *BL* 1/1/80★; *CRC*; *SLJ* 1/80
Reading Level: Middle–High School
Subject Areas: Germany; Pied Piper of Hamelin
Time Period: 1284; Middle Ages ❏ Library owns

Strauss, Victoria. *The Lady of Rhuddesmere.* **New York: Warne, 1982. 218pp. ISBN 0-7232-6210-1. LC 81-19706.**
England. Geraint, illegitimate son of the baron of Wallestoke, is sent to live at the estate at Rhuddesmere. He is pleased to go since he has been barely tolerated at Wallestoke, and at first is happy with new friends. He is naturally curious about the religion of those at Wallestoke. When he discovers that they are Manichaens (a non-Christian religion begun in Persia), he reveals this to the baron who takes steps to have Wallestoke and those who live there destroyed.
Reviews: *BL* 7/82; *SLJ* 5/82
Reading Level: Middle–High School

Subject Areas: Great Britain--1154-1399; Manichaeism; heresies and heretics
Time Period: Middle Ages ❏ **Library owns**

Sutcliff, Rosemary. *The Witch's Brat.* **New York: Walck, 1970. 143pp. ISBN 0-8098-3095-7. LC 73-119575.**
England, twelfth century. Hunchbacked Lovel is driven from his village after the death of his herbalist grandmother. He takes shelter with the monks at Minster, who discover his healing skills and knowledge of herbs. Rahere, jongleur to King Henry I, convinces Lovel to leave Minster and travel to London where he has a hand in founding Saint Bartholomew's Hospital.
Reviews: *BL* 2/1/71; *HB* 12/70; *LJ* 12/15/70; *NCB*
Reading Level: Middle & Junior High School
Subject Areas: Great Britain--Norman Period; physically handicapped; physicians
Time Period: Middle Ages, Twelfth Century ❏ **Library owns**

Temple, Frances. *The Ramsay Scallop.* **New York: Orchard, 1994. 310pp. ISBN 0-531-08686-0. LC 93-29697.**
England, Spain, 1300. When Thomas returns from the Crusades, he and Elenor are reluctant to get married. Their priest sends them on a pilgrimage to Spain. Their journey brings them new sights, new friends, adventures, and time to get to know one another. Information on everyday life and the arts is included in this story.
Reviews: *BL* 3/15/94; *SLJ* 5/94; *BCCB* 4/94; *BR* 9-10/94; *PW* 3/14/94; *VOYA* 4/94.
Reading Level: High School
Subject Areas: Great Britain--1154-1399; Spain; pilgrims and pilgrimages; marriage
Time Period: 1300; Middle Ages ❏ **Library owns**

Thorne, Victoria. *Longsword.* **New York: St. Martin's, 1982. 252pp. ISBN 0-312-49679-6. LC 81-23220.**
England. Escaping the clutches of a villainous uncle, Gervase Escot finds himself at the castle of a woman to whom he is engaged, though they have never met. He saves her from an attack, but does not reveal his identity, choosing to wait until his problems with his uncle are settled and he is able to resume his noble position.
Reviews: *BL* 7/82; *LJ* 7/82
Reading Level: High School
Subject Areas: Great Britain--1154-1399; chivalry
Time Period: Middle Ages ❏ **Library owns**

Trease, Geoffrey. *The Baron's Hostage.* Nashville, TN: Nelson, 1975. 160pp. ISBN 0-8407-6434-0. LC 75-11638.

England, 1200s. As Prince Edward is being held prisoner by Simon de Montfort, his page Michael becomes involved in an attempt to free the Prince. A courageous and adventurous lady in waiting aids his plan.

Reviews: *BL* 11/15/75; *HB* 12/75; *SLJ* 9/75

Reading Level: Middle & Junior High School

Subject Areas: Great Britain--1154-1399; Montfort, Simon de, Earl of Leicester; Baron's War, 1263-1267

Time Period: 1263-1267; Middle Ages ❑ Library owns

Undset, Sigrid; translated by Arthur G. Chater. *The Master of Hestviken.* New York: Knopf, 1978. 4v in 1p. ISBN 0-452-26034-5.

Norway. Through four novels, the story of two young lovers in medieval Norway are developed. This contains *The Axe* (1928), *The Snake Pit* (1929), *In the Wilderness* (1929); *The Son Avenger* (1930).

Reviews: *WS* 10

Reading Level: High School

Subject Areas: Norway

Time Period: Middle Ages ❑ Library owns

Undset, Sigrid. *Kristin Lavransdatter.* New York: Knopf, 3v in 1p. ISBN 0-394-43262-2.

Norway, thirteenth and fourteenth century. The life of a woman in medieval Scandinavia is described in three novels: *The Bridal Wreath* (1923), *The Mistress of Husaby* (1925), and *The Cross* (1927). Kristin convinces her father to let her marry Erlend, her lover. Erlend's farm is unsuccessful and he leaves her. When he does return, he is killed in a fight. Kristin's six sons all take different paths in life. Undset won the Nobel Prize in Literature in 1928.

Reviews: *BBSH*; *FFY*; *WS* 10, 11, 12, 13, 14

Reading Level: High School

Subject Areas: Norway; women

Time Period: Middle Ages; Thirteenth–Fourteenth Century ❑ Library owns

The Renaissance

Barnes, Margaret Campbell. *The Tudor Rose.* Philadelphia: Macrae Smith Co., 1953. 313pp.

England, 1455-1485. To create a political affiliation, Elizabeth, daughter of Edward IV, is married to Henry VII. This marriage ends the War of the Roses and

Europe—The Renaissance

begins the Tudor dynasty, but gives Elizabeth a marriage she does not want and a husband who refuses to give up his mistresses.

Reviews: *WS* 10, 11, 12
Reading Level: High School
Subject Areas: Great Britain--1399-1485; War of the Roses, 1455-1485; Elizabeth, consort of Henry VII; Henry VII, King of England; marriage
Time Period: 1455-1485 ❑ Library owns

Carr, Robyn. *The Everlasting Covenant.* **Boston: Little, Brown, 1987. 393pp. ISBN 0-316-12979-8. LC 86-33771.**
England, 1455-1485. This is the love story between Anne Gifford and Dylan DeFraynes. Born to already feuding families that also take opposing sides in the War of the Roses, their love endures though time, circumstances and marriages to other people intervene.
Reviews: *BL* 7/87; *LJ* 6/15/87
Reading Level: High School
Subject Areas: Great Britain--1399-1485; War of the Roses, 1455-1485; love
Time Period: 1444-1485 ❑ Library owns

Chute, Marchette. *The Innocent Wayfaring.* **New York: Dutton, 1955, c1943. 199pp. ISBN 0-525-32558-1.**
England, fourteenth century. Two runaways, Anne who is fleeing a convent and a young poet who is escaping parental demands, meet on the road and travel together for three days. During those three days, they fall in love and decide to return home to be married.
Reviews: *WJ* 4
Reading Level: Middle & Junior High School
Subject Areas: Great Britain--1154-1399; love; runaways
Time Period: Middle Ages; Fourteenth Century ❑ Library owns

Dana, Barbara. *Young Joan.* **New York: HarperCollins, 1991. 371pp. ISBN 0-06-021423-6. LC 90-39494.**
France, 1422-1461. This is an unusual treatment of the life of Joan of Arc, focusing on her childhood and the foundations of her religious fervor. The story ends as Joan leaves her family's farm. Rural fifteenth century life in France is described well.
Reviews: *BCCB* 4/91★; *BL* 5/15/91★; *SLJ* 5/91; *VOYA* 6/91
Reading Level: Middle–High School
Subject Areas: France; Joan of Arc, Saint; saints; Christian saints
Time Period: 1422-1461 ❑ Library owns

Darby, Catherine. *The Love Knot.* **New York: St. Martin's, 1991. 240pp. ISBN 0-312-04996-X. LC 90-15548.**

England, 1360-1400. Pregnant with the child of the master of the household where she is in service, Philippa accepts an arranged marriage to a poet named Chaucer. This is her story and the story of the times in which she lived, which included the Hundred Years War and the Black Death.

Reviews: *BL* 2/15/91; *LJ* 2/15/91
Reading Level: High School [Mature Reader]
Subject Areas: Great Britain--1154-1399; Chaucer, Geoffrey; marriage
Time Period: 1360-1400 ❏ Library owns

Doyle, Sir Arthur Conan. *The White Company.* **New York: Morrow, 1988 reissue. 366pp. ISBN 0-688-07817-6. LC 87-62625.**

Great Britain, France, 1340-1377. Alleyne joins the White Company, which serves Edward III, and travels throughout France experiencing many adventures, all the while hoping to impress a fair lady with his valiant deeds. Said to be Doyle's favorite book, it was first published in 1891.

Reviews: *BR* 9-10/88; *WS* 10, 11
Reading Level: High School
Subject Areas: Great Britain--1154-1399; France; Hundred Years' War, 1339-1453; adventure and adventurers; chivalry
Time Period: 1340-1377; Middle Ages ❏ Library owns

Goodwin, Marie D. *Where the Towers Pierce the Sky.* **New York: Four Winds, 1989. 192pp. ISBN 0-02-736871-8. LC 89-1055.**

France, 1429. In South Bend, Indiana, contemporary teen Lizzie is surprised when Jacques, an astrologer's assistant, appears in her bedroom, the result of a few time travel miscalculations. Jacques had planned to travel only a few years ahead in time to see what became of Jeanne d'Arc. Lizzie is pulled back in time with Jacques and becomes involved with Jeanne d'Arc's efforts as a nurse and healer, becoming a double agent in return for transport back to her own time. The descriptions of social conditions in war-torn France are vivid.

Reviews: *BCCB* 11/89; *BL* 12/1/89; *BR* 5/90; *SLJ* 11/89; *VOYA* 12/89
Reading Level: Middle–High School
Subject Areas: France; Joan of Arc, Saint; space and time
Time Period: 1429; Middle Ages ❏ Library owns

Grace, C. L. *Shrine of Murders: Being the First of the Canterbury Tales of Kathryn Swinbrooke, Leech and Physician.* **New York: St. Martin's, 1993. 208pp. ISBN 0-312-09388-8. LC 93-474.**

England, fifteenth century. Pilgrims visiting the shrine in Canterbury are being poisoned and Colum Murtagh, sent to restore order after the War of the Roses,

Europe—The Renaissance

consults with Kathryn Swinbrooke for information on poisons. Together they explore Canterbury to find the killer's identity.
Reviews: *BL* 4/15/93; *PW* 3/22/93
Reading Level: High School
Subject Areas: Great Britain--1485-1603; Canterbury (England); physicians; mystery and detective stories
Time Period: Fifteenth Century ❏ Library owns

Harnett, Cynthia. *The Cargo of the Madalena*. Minneapolis: Lerner, 1984 reissue. 235pp. ISBN 0-8225-0890-7. LC 83-24874.
England. When a shipment of paper is not delivered, Bendy solves the mystery for printer William Caxton just after the printing press was introduced to England.
Reviews: *BL* 9/15/84
Reading Level: Middle & Junior High School
Subject Areas: Great Britain--1399-1485; printing; Caxton, William; mystery and detective stories
Time Period: Fifteenth Century ❏ Library owns

Harnett, Cynthia. *The Merchant's Mark*. Minneapolis: Lerner, 1984. 181pp. ISBN 0-8225-1891-5. LC 83-24879.
England, 1439. In 1439, Nicholas, the son of a wealthy wool merchant uncovers a plot to ruin his father's business.
Reviews: *BL* 9/15/84
Reading Level: Middle & Junior High School
Subject Areas: Great Britain--1399-1485; mystery and detective stories
Time Period: 1439 ❏ Library owns

Harnett, Cynthia. *The Sign of the Green Falcon*. Minneapolis: Lerner, 1984. 217pp. ISBN 0-8225-0888-5. LC 83-24831.
England, France, 1415. The story unfolds as Henry V battles domestic unrest while also trying to secure the French throne.
Reviews: *BL* 9/15/84
Reading Level: Middle & Junior High School
Subject Areas: Great Britain--1399-1485; France; Henry V, King of England
Time Period: 1415 ❏ Library owns

Harnett, Cynthia; illustrated by Gareth Floyd. *The Writing on the Hearth*. Minneapolis: Lerner, 1984, c1971. 299pp. ISBN 0-8225-0889-3. LC 83-23904.
England, 1430-1455. The events leading to the War of the Roses provide the backdrop for the story of Stephen, whose father's heroic death at Agincourt has

bestowed Stephen with the opportunity to receive an education. Stephen is fascinated by a design left by an Oxford master on the hearth of a local witch, the significance of which becomes known to him years later.
Reviews: *BL* 6/15/73; *WJ* 4
Reading Level: Middle & Junior High School
Subject Areas: Great Britain--1399-1485
Time Period: 1430-1455 ❏ Library owns

Haugaard, Erik Christian. *Leif the Unlucky.* **Boston: Houghton, 1982. 206pp. ISBN 0-395-32156-5. LC 82-1053.**
Greenland, fifteenth century. Decimated by cold, hunger, and disease, the remaining members of an abandoned Norse colony wish to return to Norway, but have no way to get there. Two factions develop and vie for power among the younger members. One group is led by Leif, who wants to get everyone to cooperate; the other is led by Egil, who leads through violence.
Reviews: *BCCB* 7-8/82; *HB* 8/82; *SLJ* 3/82; *WJ* 5
Reading Level: Middle–High School
Subject Areas: Greenland; Vikings
Time Period: Fifteenth Century ❏ Library owns

Holland, Cecelia. *The Lords of Vaumartin.* **Boston: Houghton, 1988. 344pp. ISBN 0-395-48828-1. LC 88-12836.**
France, fourteenth century. Not expecting him to return, 14-year-old Everard de Vaumartin's guardians send him into battle against the English, hoping to keep his title and land for themselves. Everard lives, but pretends to be a commoner, knowing one day he will regain his rightful title.
Reviews: *BL* 10/15/88; *SLJ* 1/89; *BBSH*
Reading Level: High School
Subject Areas: France
Time Period: Fourteenth Century ❏ Library owns

Hugo, Victor. *The Hunchback of Notre Dame.* **Mattituck, NY: Amereon, 1976. ISBN 0-8488-0534-8.**
France, fourteenth century. With a vivid background draws from medieval life, we view the lives of three characters: Quasimodo, the hunchbacked, faithful servant who is ordered to kidnap the beautiful gypsy dancer, Esmeralda, for the Archdeacon Frolla, who desires her.
Reviews: *WS* 10, 11, 12, 13, 14
Reading Level: High School
Subject Areas: France; Notre Dame Cathedral; physically handicapped
Time Period: Middle Ages; Fourteenth Century ❏ Library owns

Europe—The Renaissance

Jarman, Rosemary Hawley. *The King's Grey Mare.* **Boston: Little, 1973. 448pp. ISBN 0-316-45781-7. LC 73-7766.**
England, 1470-1483. Having been previously married to John Grey, Elizabeth Woodville, Edward IV's queen, is known as his "Grey Mare." In this story about her life, amid the intrigue of Lancaster, York, and Tudor, she emerges as a victim of the political workings of the times. The author draws a new conclusion about the death of Elizabeth's two sons in the Tower of London.
Reviews: *BL* 9/15/73; *WS* 10
Reading Level: High School
Subject Areas: Great Britain--1399-1485; War of the Roses, 1455-1485; Elizabeth, consort of Edward IV; Edward IV, King of England
Time Period: 1470-1483 ❏ Library owns

Jarman, Rosemary Hawley. *We Speak No Treason.* **Boston: Little, 1971. 575pp. LC 77-152400.**
England, 1452-1485. The life of Richard III is detailed through the eyes of one of his men-at-arms, his lover, and the court jester. They show him to be a courageous, honorable man, instead of the demented despot he has been characterized as.
Reviews: *HB* 4/72; *LJ* 10/1/71; *WS* 10
Reading Level: High School
Subject Areas: Great Britain--1399-1485; Richard III, King of England
Time Period: 1452-1485 ❏ Library owns

Keneally, Thomas. *Blood Red, Sister Rose.* **New York: Viking, 1975. 384pp. ISBN 0-670-17433-5.**
France, 1420-1431. Showing her to have very human emotions and sometimes a not so saintly demeanor, the author tells of the life of Joan of Arc.
Reviews: *BL* 11/15/74; *LJ* 1/15/75; *WS* 10
Reading Level: High School
Subject Areas: France; Joan of Arc, Saint; saints; Christian saints
Time Period: 1420-1431 ❏ Library owns

Kelly, Eric P.; illustrated by Janina Domanska. *The Trumpeter of Krakow.* **New York: Macmillan, 1991, c1929. 224pp. ISBN 0-689-71571-4. LC 91-26879.**
Poland, fifteenth century. A story of intrigue and adventure, in which Andrew and his son, Joseph use legend and the power of music to alert the city to a Tartar attack.
Reviews: *WJ* 4, 5
Reading Level: Middle & Junior High School

Subject Areas: Poland
Time Period: Middle Ages; Fifteenth Century ❏ Library owns

Konigsburg, E. L. *The Second Mrs. Giaconda.* **New York: Atheneum, 1975. 153pp. ISBN 0-689-30480-3. LC 75-6946.**
Italy, 1480-1500. In the middle years of his life, Leonardo da Vinci was influenced by Salai, his street-wise servant, and Beatrice, the wife of Leonardo's patron. These two people bring some gaiety into his normally serious life. Why Leonardo chose to paint the portrait of a merchant's wife, now known as Mona Lisa, is imaginatively explained.
Reviews: *BL* 9/1/75; *HB* 10/75; *SLJ* 9/75★
Reading Level: Middle–High School
Subject Areas: Italy; Leonardo da Vinci; Salai, Andrea; Beatrice d'Este, consort of Lodovico Sforza, il Moro, Duke of Milan; Mona Lisa; Milan; painters; artists
Time Period: 1480-1500; Renaissance ❏ Library owns

La Mure, Pierre. *The Private Life of Mona Lisa.* **Boston: Little, 1976. 406pp. ISBN 0-316-51300-8. LC 76-16811.**
Italy, 1480-1510. The life of Lisa de' Gherardini del Giaconda is played against the social and economic history of the Renaissance in Florence, including invasions by foreign powers, the exile of the Medicis, the rise of the Borgias, and finally her encounter with Leonardo da Vinci.
Reviews: *BL* 10/1/76; *LJ* 8/76
Reading Level: High School [Mature Reader]
Subject Areas: Italy; Mona Lisa
Time Period: 1480-1510; Renaissance ❏ Library owns

Llorente, Pilar Molina; translated by Robin Longshaw; illustrated by Alonso, Juan Ramón. *The Apprentice.* **New York: Farrar, 1993. 101pp. ISBN 0-374-30389-4. LC 92-54648.**
Italy, fifteenth century. Thirteen-year-old Arduino has achieved his dream of being apprenticed to an artist, Cosimo de Forli. Not only is life hard, and de Forli ill-tempered, but Arduino discovers that de Forli has been taking credit for another artist's work, who he has chained in an attic room. Arduino frees the real artist, who works with him on a grand project.
Reviews: *BL* 8/93; *NCB*; *SLJ* 9/93; *PW* 8/9/93
Reading Level: Middle & Junior High School
Subject Areas: Italy; Florence (Italy); artists; apprentices
Time Period: Renaissance; Fifteenth Century ❏ Library owns

Europe—The Renaissance

Lofts, Norah. *Knight's Acre.* **New York: Doubleday, 1975. 253pp. ISBN 0-385-03551-9. LC 74-5918.**
England, 1451. Finally able to afford a house for his family, but still needing funds to furnish it properly, Sir Godfrey Tallboys accepts an invitation to a tournament in Spain where he is sure he can make his fortune. However, while there, Sir Godfrey is kidnapped and enslaved by the Moors, so his family must struggle to survive until he is able to escape and return to them.
Reviews: *BL* 5/75; *WS* 10
Reading Level: High School
Subject Areas: Great Britain--1399-1485; Spain; knights and knighthood; Moors
Time Period: 1451; Middle Ages ❏ Library owns

MacCoun, Catherine. *The Age of Miracles.* **Boston: Atlantic Monthly Press/ distributed by Little Brown, 1989. 318pp. ISBN 0-87113-312-1. LC 88-39299.**
England, fourteenth century. Eighteen-year-old Ingrid Fairfax, renowned for her healing skills, is cloistered in gloomy Grayleigh Convent where she was abandoned by her father twelve years earlier. Enter worldly troubadour Jack Rudd whose injury brings the two together, disturbing Ingrid's heretofore "saintly" existence.
Reviews: *BL* 7/89; *LJ* 6/15/89
Reading Level: High School [Mature Reader]
Subject Areas: Great Britain--1154-1399; love
Time Period: Middle Ages; Fourteenth Century ❏ Library owns

Mannix, Daniel Pratt; illustrated by Janny Wurts. *The Wolves of Paris: A Novel.* **New York: Dutton, 1978. 235pp. ISBN 0-525-23587-6. LC 77-18004.**
France, 1439-40. In the winter of 1439-40, a wolf pack, lead by Courtaud, half dog, half wolf, held Paris under siege. This details the social conditions of the times, bloody details of wolf attacks, and medieval warfare tactics by the humans.
Reviews: *BL* 10/1/78; *LJ* 7/78
Reading Level: High School [Mature Reader]
Subject Areas: France; Paris (France); wolves
Time Period: 1439; Middle Ages ❏ Library owns

Marcuse, Katherine; illustrated by Paul Zepelinsky. *The Devil's Workshop.* **Nashville, TN: Abingdon, 1979. 157pp. ISBN 0-687-10506-4. LC 78-24121.**
Germany, 1430. Twelve-year-old runaway Johann becomes an apprentice with Johann Gutenberg in Mainz. Colored with the events of everyday life, young Johann and Gutenberg each have dreams that Gutenberg's press makes possible.
Reviews: *BCCB* 7/79; *BL* 4/1/79; *SLJ* 4/79
Reading Level: Middle & Junior High School

Subject Areas: Germany; Gutenberg, Johann; printing; apprentices
Time Period: 1430 ❑ Library owns

McCaughrean, Geraldine. *A Little Lower Than the Angels.* **New York: Oxford, 1987. 133pp. ISBN 0-19-271561-5.**
England, 1347-1351. Gabriel escapes from his apprenticeship with a cruel stonemason to join a traveling group of actors who stage "miracle" cures for naive peasants. Gabriel at first believes that the cures are real, just like the peasants, but discovers the truth. Despite all of his troubles, Gabriel decides he has found his life's work.
Reviews: *BCCB* 4/88; *BL* 1/1/88; *SLJ* 4/88
Reading Level: Middle–High School
Subject Areas: Great Britain--1154-1399; theater; actors
Time Period: 1347-1351; Middle Ages ❑ Library owns

Pargeter, Edith. *The Bloody Field.* **New York: Viking, 1973. 313pp. ISBN 0-670-17435-1. LC 72-11061.**
England, 1403. The story begins in 1399 and culminates in July 1403 when three Henrys. Henry III of Lancaster; his son Henry IV (Hal), the young Prince of Wales; and Henry Percy, Hal's mentor, also known as "Hotspur," meet in a battle between Henry of Lancaster and Henry Percy, which tests Hal's loyalty to both.
Reviews: *BL* 9/15/73; *HB* 12/73; *LJ* 5/15/73; *WS* 10
Reading Level: High School
Subject Areas: Great Britain--1399-1485; Henry IV, King of England; Henry V, King of England; Percy, Sir Henry
Time Period: 1403 ❑ Library owns

Phillips, Ann. *The Peace Child.* **New York: Oxford University Press, 1988. 150pp. ISBN 0-19-271560-7.**
England, fourteenth century. In order to end a feud, two families each trade a child at birth. When at age ten, Alys discovers that she is a "peace child," she sets off on an adventure to find her real parents. Her journey takes her to London and back home again several times. Her travels expose her to many and varied rogues as well as dangers such as the Black Death.
Reviews: *BL* 12/1/88; *HB* 11/88; *SLJ* 11/88
Reading Level: Middle & Junior High School
Subject Areas: Great Britain--1154-1399; adventures and adventurers
Time Period: Middle Ages; Fourteenth Century ❑ Library owns

Europe—The Renaissance

Plaidy, Jean. *Madonna of the Seven Hills.* **New York: Putnam, 1974. 300pp. ISBN 0-399-11456-4.**
Italy, 1480-1519. This novel details the life of one of history's infamous women, Lucrezia Borgia, daughter of Pope Alexander VI. The author presents her as an innocent young woman, forced into a political marriage which was annulled by her father. She becomes aware of her role in the Borgia's rise to power.
Reviews: *WS* 10
Reading Level: High School
Subject Areas: Italy; Borgia, Lucrezia; Borgia family
Time Period: 1480-1519 ❏ Library owns

Plaidy, Jean. *Passage to Pontefract.* **New York: Putnam, 1982. 366pp. ISBN 0-399-12750-X. LC 82-7645.**
England, 1350-1400. In this tenth novel in the Plantagenet series, two brothers, Edward the Black Prince and John of Gaunt, vie for the throne of England. Their two sons, Richard II and Henry IV, also clash in their grasps for power. Henry IV is banished to France by Richard II, but Richard is unable to preserve his power. The previous volume in this series is *The Vow on the Heron.*
Reviews: *BBSH*; *BL* 9/1/82
Reading Level: High School
Subject Areas: Great Britain--1399-1484; Henry IV, King of England; Richard II, King of England
Time Period: 1370-1400 ❏ Library owns

Plaidy, Jean. *The Star of Lancaster.* **New York: Putnam, 1982. 320pp. ISBN 0-399-12758-5. LC 82-7705.**
England, 1380-1422. The story begins with the marriage of Henry IV to Mary of Bohun and relates the births of their children, and Henry's struggles to retain land and power. The story continues with his son Harry, the future Henry V, who joins with Sir John Falstaff for some merriment before assuming his kingly duties. As Henry V, he goes to battle at Agincourt, where his early death sets the stage for his son Henry VI.
Reviews: *BBSH*; *BL* 9/1/82
Reading Level: High School
Subject Areas: Great Britain--1399-1485; Henry IV, King of England; Henry V, King of England
Time Period: 1380-1422 ❏ Library owns

Pyle, Howard. *Men of Iron.* **New York: Airmont, 1891. 328pp. ISBN 0-8049-0093-0.**
England, 1380-1413. In this classic novel of knights and chivalry, a young nobleman is trained for knighthood in order to eliminate the enemies of family.

Reviews: *WJ* 4, 5
Reading Level: Middle–High School
Subject Areas: Great Britain--1399-1495; Henry IV, King of England; knights and knighthood
Time Period: 1380-1413   ❑ Library owns

Riley, Judith Merkle. ***In Pursuit of the Green Lion.*** **New York: Delacorte, 1990. 440pp. ISBN 0-385-30089-1. LC 90-32498.**
Europe, fourteenth century. Sequel to *A Vision of Light*. Margaret de Vilers and her daughters are kidnapped by the family of her scribe, and Margaret is then forced to marry him so that his family can obtain her estate. Her new husband, who isn't as bad as his family, is captured in France while recording the events of the Hundred Years War. Margaret and her friends, who include two ghosts and an alchemist, go off to find him, using alchemical trickery.
Reviews: *BBYA*; *BL* 10/15/90; *SLJ* 2/91; *WS* 14
Reading Level: High School
Subject Areas: Great Britain--1154-1399; France; marriage; adventure and adventurers
Time Period: Middle Ages; Fourteenth Century   ❑ Library owns

Riley, Judith Merkle. ***A Vision of Light.*** **New York: Delacorte, 1989. 442pp. ISBN 0-440-50109-1. LC 88-17514.**
England, fourteenth century. Because women were not educated in the Middle Ages, Margaret of Ashbury must hire a hungry monk in order to be able to record the story of her life. The monk considers this a waste of money, but is so in need, that he decides to oblige her. Margaret has led a life of real adventure while managing to survive poverty, the Black Death, and a trial for witchcraft. Margaret shines as an intelligent, witty, resourceful woman held down by the time in which she lived.
Reviews: *BL* 11/1/88; *LJ* 1/89; *SLJ* 12/89
Reading Level: High School
Subject Areas: Great Britain--1154-1399; women
Time Period: Middle Ages; Fourteenth Century   ❑ Library owns

Rofheart, Martha. ***Fortune Made His Sword.*** **New York: Putnam, 1972. 445pp. LC 78-175254.**
England, 1387-1422. The life of Henry V is told by five narrators; Henry himself as a boy and then as a man, his wife Katharine, his mistress Morgan, the court jester Hercules, and the knight John Page, each giving a different perspective on his true character.
Reviews: *BL* 4/15/72; *LJ* 2/1/72
Reading Level: High School

Europe—The Renaissance

Subject Areas: Great Britain--1399-1485; Henry V, King of England
Time Period: 1387-1422; Middle Ages ❏ Library owns

Russell, Jennifer. *The Threshing Floor.* **Mahwah, NJ: Paulist Press, 1987. 401pp. ISBN 0-8091-0394-X. LC 87-9203.**
England, fourteenth century. William, a scholar, his brother Nicholas, a knight, and Nicholas' wife Marion go on a pilgrimage to Canterbury. The story weaves in various people from all walks of medieval life that the trio encounters, shedding light on the Medieval workings of the class system.
Reviews: *BR* 5-6/88; *LJ* 8/87
Reading Level: High School
Subject Areas: Great Britain--1154-1399; pilgrims and pilgrimages; Canterbury (England)
Time Period: Middle Ages; Fourteenth Century ❏ Library owns

Seton, Anya. *Katherine.* **Boston: Houghton, 1954. 588pp.**
England, fourteenth century. This is the story of the romance between Katherine Swynford and John of Gaunt, and the time in which they lived.
Reviews: *WS* 10, 12, 13
Reading Level: High School
Subject Areas: Great Britain--1154-1399; Katherine, Duchess of Lancaster; John of Gaunt, Duke of Lancaster; love
Time Period: Middle Ages; Fourteenth Century ❏ Library owns

Scott, Sir Walter. *Quentin Durward.* **New York: Oxford, 1992. 616pp. ISBN 0-19-282658-1.**
France, 1461-1480. In this tale of life in the French nobility, a young member of the Scottish Guard, Quentin Durward, falls in love with Isabelle, Countess of Croye, who has another suitor, the Duke of Orleans. Quentin saves the life of Louis XI and is able to win the hand of Isabelle. Many of the historic figures that filled the royal court of France are found on these pages. First published in 1823.
Reviews: *WS* 10, 11
Reading Level: High School
Subject Areas: France; Louis XI, King of France
Time Period: 1461-1480; Middle Ages ❏ Library owns

Sedley, Kate. *The Plymouth Cloak: The Second Tale of Roger the Chapman.* **New York: St. Martin's, 1993. 192pp. ISBN 0-312-08875-2. LC 92-33372.**
England, 1470. Roger Chapman, a snoopy traveling peddler, is hired by Richard, Duke of Gloucester, to protect a royal messenger on a critical mission. When the messenger is murdered, Roger must find the murderer to complete his assignment.
Reviews: *BL* 2/1/93; *PW* 11/2/92

Reading Level: High School
Subject Areas: Great Britain--1399-1485; mystery and detective stories
Time Period: 1470; Middle Ages ❏ Library owns

Shellabarger, Samuel. *The King's Cavalier.* **Boston: Little, 1950. 377pp.**
France, 1520s. The events of the Bourbon conspiracy against Francis I provide the backdrop for a love story between a young Frenchman and a young English woman.
Reviews: *WS* 10
Reading Level: High School
Subject Areas: France; Francis, I, King of France
Time Period: 1520s; Renaissance ❏ Library owns

Shellabarger, Samuel. *Prince of Foxes.* **Boston: Little, 1947. 433pp.**
Italy, 1476-1507. Andrea Orsini, a mercenary soldier hired by Cesare Borgia, falls in love with one of Borgia's intended victims. Because of this, he decides to change sides and fights against Borgia, helping to defeat him.
Reviews: *WS* 10
Reading Level: High School
Subject Areas: Italy; Borgia, Cesare
Time Period: 1476-1507; Renaissance ❏ Library owns

Shulman, Sandra. *The Florentine.* **New York: Morrow, 1973. 314pp. LC 72-10201.**
Italy, fifteenth century. Francesca de' Narni escapes the destruction of her family in the Pazzi Conspiracy. Disguised as a boy, she becomes apprenticed to the painter Ghirlandaio. Her work comes to the attention of other painters such as Da Vinci and Botticelli, and the Medici become her patrons.
Reviews: *BL* 4/15/73; *SLJ* 5/73
Reading Level: High School
Subject Areas: Italy; painters; artists; Medici, Lorenzo de, il Magnifico
Time Period: Renaissance; Fifteenth Century ❏ Library owns

Stevenson, Robert Louis. *The Black Arrow.* **New York: Airmont, 1963. 253pp. ISBN 0-8049-0020-5.**
England, 1455-1485. Set during a minor battle of the War of the Roses, young Dick Shelton tries to outwit his guardian, Sir Daniel Brackley, who does not have Dick's best interests in mind.
Reviews: *BFY*; *WJ* 4, 5
Reading Level: Middle–High School

Subject Areas: Great Britain; 1399-1485; War of the Roses, 1455-1485; Richard III, King of England
Time Period: 1455-1485; Fifteenth Century   ❏ Library owns

Stone, Irving. *The Agony and the Ecstasy: A Novel of Michelangelo.* **New York: Doubleday, 1961. 664pp. ISBN 0-385-01092-3. LC 61-6520.**
Italy, 1475-1564. The entire life of Michelangelo Buonarotti is created with great splendor. Beginning at the age of 13 when he was apprenticed to Ghirlandaio, his life—with all its triumphs and difficulties—is created, as well as a vivid picture of Renaissance Italy.
Reviews: *WS* 10, 14
Reading Level: High School
Subject Areas: Italy; Michelangelo Buonarroti; artists
Time Period: 1475-1564; Renaissance   ❏ Library owns

Tey, Josephine. *The Daughter of Time.* **Cutchogue, NY: Buccaneer Bks., 1952. ISBN 0-89966-184-X. LC 52-7599.**
England, 1480-1485. Contemporary policeman Alan Grant, recovering from an injury and bored, becomes interested in Richard III and the assumption that he murdered the two princes in the Tower of London. Grant begins research to see whether he can solve the murders five centuries after they happened.
Reviews: *WS* 13, 14
Reading Level: High School
Subject Areas: Great Britain--1399-1485; Richard III, King of England; mystery and detective stories
Time Period: 1480-1485   ❏ Library owns

Turner, Ann. *The Way Home.* **New York: Crown, 1982. 116pp. ISBN 0-517-544261. LC 82-19880.**
England, 1349. Because of her harelip, Anne is considered cursed or a witch, and is beaten and turned out to fend for herself. While she is living in the forest, the Black Death strikes her village, killing almost everyone, including her family. After three months of surviving the hardships in the wild, she returns to the village where she finds sorrow, but also hope for the future.
Reviews: *BCCB* 2/83; *BL* 1/1/83; *HB* 4/83; *SLJ* 2/83; *VOYA* 6/83
Reading Level: Middle & Junior High School
Subject Areas: Great Britain--1154-1399; Black Death; survival
Time Period: 1349; Middle Ages   ❏ Library owns

Twain, Mark. *Personal Recollections of Joan of Arc, by the Sieur Louis De Conte (Her Page and Secretary)*. Hartford, CT: Stowe-Day, 1980. 596pp. ISBN 0-917482-16-6. LC 78-8051.

France, 1412-1431. Told by a man who began as her childhood playmate and followed her until the day of her death, the life of Joan of Arc is presented as a glowing picture of the goodness and greatness. De Conte details her life from childhood through the excitement of the campaigns with her army to her execution. First published in 1896.

Reviews: *WS* 10
Reading Level: High School
Subject Areas: France; Joan of Arc, Saint; saints; Christian saints
Time Period: 1412-1431; Middle Ages ❑ Library owns

Wheeler, Thomas Gerald. *All Men Tall*. Chatham, NY: S.G. Phillips, 1969. 256pp. ISBN 0-87599-157-2. LC 70-77313.

England, 1323. Betrayed by the queen, Thomeline of Tournai leaves in haste. He finds his way to Hugh the Armourer in the Wealdon Forrest and is taken in. Here Thomeline helps Hugh in the development of gun powder.

Reviews: *BL* 4/1/70; *LJ* 4/15/70
Reading Level: Middle–High School
Subject Areas: Great Britain--1154-1399; artillery; gun powder
Time Period: 1323; Middle Ages ❑ Library owns

Age of Discovery and Reformation

Anand, Valerie. *Women of Ashdon*. New York: St. Martin's, 1993. 373pp. ISBN 0-312-09417-5. LC 93-15062.

England, sixteenth century. Spanning two lifetimes, this is the story of Suzanna Whitmead and Christina, her granddaughter. Each leads a proper lady's life. However, Christina does not produce the heir necessary for her to keep her lands. The events and social conditions at the beginning of the Tudor reign are included. This is part of the "Bridges Over Time" Series.

Reviews: *SLJ* 11/93; *PW* 6/7/93
Reading Level: High School
Subject Areas: Great Britain--1485-1603; women
Time Period: Middle Ages; Sixteenth Century ❑ Library owns

Arthur, Ruth M.; illustrated by Margery Gill. *Requiem for Princess*. New York: Atheneum, 1967. 182pp. ISBN 0-689-70419-4. LC 67-2667.

England, sixteenth century. When taunted by classmates because she is an adoptee, contemporary Willow becomes ill with worry and is sent to recuperate at a private guest home. There she sees the portrait of a sixteenth century Spanish girl who was adopted by the owners of the house. Willow identifies with the girl in the portrait and has mystical dreams at night, reliving the life of the Spanish girl, Isabel.

Reviews: *WJ* 4
Reading Level: Middle & Junior High School
Subject Areas: Great Britain--1485-1603; adoption; dreams
Time Period: Middle Ages; Sixteenth Century ❏ Library owns

Bacon, Martha Sherman. *In the Company of Clown: A Commedia.* **Boston: Atlantic-Little, 1973. 153pp. ISBN 0-316-07510-8. LC 72-12893.**

Italy, sixteenth century. While trying to get back the donkey he was tricked out of by a commedia player, orphan Gian-Piero meets Harlequin who asks him to join his troupe of actors. He does, but finds he is unhappy and homesick. When Harlequin is falsely charged with murder by another player, Gian-Piero is able to save him.

Reviews: *BCCB* 12/73; *BL* 9/15/73; *HB* 8/73; *SLJ* 9/73
Reading Level: Middle & Junior High School
Subject Areas: Italy; Commedia dell' Arte; actors; theater; orphans
Time Period: Sixteenth Century ❏ Library owns

Beatty, John Louis and Patricia Beatty. *Holdfast.* **New York: Morrow, 1972. 222pp. LC 75-187902.**

England, 1558-1603. Twelve-year-old Irish orphan Catriona is taken to England to become a ward of Elizabeth I. She is placed with a titled English family and is separated from her only friend, her Irish wolfhound. The dog, Holdfast, becomes a bull and bear baiter. Catriona and her dog are reunited at a sports arena where Holdfast is to fight.

Reviews: *BL* 10/15/72; *HB* 12/72; *SLJ* 11/72
Reading Level: Middle & Junior High School
Subject Areas: Great Britain--1485-1603; orphans; dogs
Time Period: Middle Ages; Sixteenth Century ❏ Library owns

Beatty, John Louis and Patricia Beatty. *King's Knight's Pawn.* **New York: Morrow, 1971. 224pp. LC 78-155988**

England, 1649. Christopher Barlow runs away from home and goes to London where he witnesses the beheading of Charles I. He is befriended by Capt. Peter Dell, and together they go to Ireland to fight with Christopher's godfather, Sir Arthur Aston. In moves much like a chess game, events seem to move inevitably forward toward the bloody massacre of the Irish and Cavaliers by Cromwell's forces.

Reviews: *BCCB* 12/71; *BL* 11/1/71; *HB* 12/71
Reading Level: Middle–High School

Subject Areas: Great Britain--1642-1660; Ireland; runaways
Time Period: 1649 ❑ Library owns

Beatty, John Louis and Patricia Beatty. *Master Rosalind.* **New York: Morrow, 1974. 221pp. LC 74-5050.**
England, seventeenth century. Rosalind Broome, disguised as a boy for safety, is kidnapped and taken to London where she is to be trained as a pickpocket. Since she is not a good pickpocket, she joins a group of players and becomes involved in court intrigues, murder, and hidden identities.
Reviews: *BCCB* 2/75; *BL* 12/1/74; *HB* 2/75
Reading Level: Middle & Junior High School
Subject Areas: Great Britain--1485-1603; mystery and detective stories; theater
Time Period: Seventeenth Century ❑ Library owns

Belle, Pamela. *Alethea.* **New York: Berkley, 1985. 578pp. ISBN 0-425-08397-7.**
England, seventeenth century. Eleven-year-old Alethea Heron is sent to study painting in London, making her half-brother jealous. Her studies progress well, and Alethea decides to devote her life to art, but there are setbacks and difficulties which include a pregnancy, old jealousies, and family feuds, all set against a backdrop of Restoration England. This novel follows *The Moon in the Water* and *The Chains of Fate*.
Reviews: *BBSH*; *SLJ* 1/86
Reading Level: High School
Subject Areas: Great Britain--1603-1714; artists
Time Period: Seventeenth Century ❑ Library owns

Bibby, Violet. *Many Waters Cannot Quench Love.* **New York: Morrow, 1975. 160pp. ISBN 0-688-32042-2. LC 75-14446.**
England, seventeenth century. The marshland inhabitants, fenmen, resent the Dutch engineers who have been hired to drain the marsh, and so they plot to sabotage the engineers work. Constancy, daughter of a fenman who has been betrothed to Will, leader of the saboteurs, falls in love with Henrik, son of a Dutch engineer. She seeks the help of Goody Tomlin, a wise woman.
Reviews: *BL* 12/15/75; *SLJ* 11/75
Reading Level: Middle & Junior High School
Subject Areas: Great Britain--1603-1714; love
Time Period: 1603-1649 ❑ Library owns

Burton, Hester; illustrated by Victor G. Ambrus. *Beyond the Weir Bridge.* **New York: Crowell, 1970. 221pp. ISBN 0-690-14052-5.**
England, 1642-1660. Three friends overcome the political and religious divisions of their time. Richard is the son of a Roundhead, Richenda is becoming involved

with the Quakers, and Thomas' family is Royalist. This is the story of their commitment to each other and their beliefs.
Reviews: *BL* 11/15/70; *HB* 12/70; *LJ* 7/71; *NCB*
Reading Level: Middle–High School
Subject Areas: Great Britain--1642-1660; friendship
Time Period: 1642-1660 ❏ Library owns

Burton, Hester; illustrated by Victor G. Ambrus. *Kate Ryder.* **New York: Crowell, 1975. 177pp. ISBN 0-690-00978-X. LC 75-8576.**
England, 1642-1660. Twelve-year-old Kate Ryder is caught up in the English Civil War and must deal with the unwelcome changes in her life. Her father and brother Adam are fighting on opposite sides, another brother has gone to sea, and she must take care of her sister-in-law and niece in Colchester.
Reviews: *BL* 12/1/75★; *WJ* 4
Reading Level: Middle & Junior High School
Subject Areas: Great Britain--1642-1660
Time Period: 1642-1660 ❏ Library owns

Burton, Philip. *You, My Brother: A Novel Based on the Lives of Edmund and William Shakespeare.* **New York: Random House, 1973. 561pp. ISBN 0-394-48478-9. LC 73-5009.**
England, 1595-1616. Providing insight into the theatrical world in Elizabethan England, this is the story of Ned Shakespeare, younger brother of William, who follows William to London and becomes a promising actor.
Reviews: *WS* 10
Reading Level: High School
Subject Areas: Great Britain--1603-1714; theater; Shakespeare, William; Shakespeare, Edmund; actors
Time Period: Sixteenth – Seventeenth Century ❏ Library owns

Carter, Peter. *Children of the Book.* **New York: Oxford, 1984. 271pp. ISBN 0-19-271456-2.**
Austria, Poland, Istanbul, 1683. Using three sets of characters in three locations, the author details the invasion of Austria by the Turks including the siege on Vienna.
Reviews: *BCCB* 11/84; *BL* 12/1/84; *SLJ* 3/85
Reading Level: Middle–High School
Subject Areas: Austria; Poland; Istanbul; Vienna (Austria), Siege of, 1683
Time Period: 1683 ❏ Library owns

Europe—Age of Discovery and Reformation

Cheetham, Ann. *The Pit.* **New York: Holt, 1990. 154pp. ISBN 0-8050-1142-0. LC 89-26868.**

England, 1665. Modern day Oliver is intrigued by artifacts uncovered at a nearby construction site, and is drawn deeper into the past when excavators find a plague pit. He becomes a member of a family who are all dying of the plague, living in the same house that he occupies 400 years later.

Reviews: *BL* 6/1/90; *SLJ* 6/90
Reading Level: Middle & Junior High School
Subject Areas: Great Britain--1603-1714; London (England); plague; space and time
Time Period: 1665 ❑ Library owns

Clarke, Mary Stetson. *Piper to the Clan.* **New York: Viking, 1970. 239pp. LC 71-102925.**

Scotland, 1650. Companion volume to *The Iron Peacock*. Ross McRae, a young Scotsman, is among those captured by Cromwell's forces at Dunbar and forced to march from Dunbar to Durham Castle and imprisonment. Later, Ross is chosen to become an indentured servant in the New World.

Reviews: *BL* 7/15/70; *LJ* 5/15/70
Reading Level: Middle–High School
Subject Areas: Scotland; Great Britain--1642-1660; prisons and prisoners
Time Period: 1650 ❑ Library owns

Clynes, Michael. *White Rose Murders.* **New York: St. Martin's, 1993. 244pp. ISBN 0-312-08920-1. LC 92-43889.**

England, 1513. Roger Shallot, a rogue, saved from the gallows by Benjamin Daubney, is enlisted to help ensure the safety of Queen Margaret, widow of James IV of Scotland, who may be the target of Yorkists. The tangled web of intrigues lead him to Paris, described in all its raunchiness, and back again as he tries to protect not only the Queen and his master, but himself as well.

Reviews: *BL* 3/1/93; *LJ* 2/15/93; *SLJ* 8/93
Reading Level: High School [Mature Reader]
Subject Areas: Great Britain--1485-1603; mystery and detective stories; Paris (France)
Time Period: 1513; Middle Ages ❑ Library owns

Cowell, Stephanie. *Nicholas Cooke: Actor, Soldier, Physician, Priest.* **New York: Norton, 1993. 440pp. ISBN 0-393-03543-3. LC 92-42488.**

England, sixteenth century. Nick Cooke, on a search for self-knowledge, is at various times an actor, a soldier, a physician, and a priest. Each occupation gives a different perspective on Elizabethan life, as do his friends who include Christopher Marlowe and Shakespeare.

Reviews: *LJ* 8/93; *SLJ* 3/94
Reading Level: High School
Subject Areas: Great Britain--1485-1603
Time Period: Sixteenth Century ❑ Library owns

Defoe, Daniel. *A Journal of the Plague Year*. New York: AMS Press, 1974. ISBN 0-404-07919-9. LC 74-13469.
England, 1665. When this was first published in 1722, the journal was thought to be a true account of the plague epidemic of 1665. Defoe has written in such detail that it is easy to see why this work of fiction relating reactions to the coming of the plague was taken as fact.
Reviews: *WS* 10, 11
Reading Level: High School
Subject Areas: Great Britain--1603-1714; London (England); plague
Time Period: 1665 ❑ Library owns

Dumas, Alexandre. *The Black Tulip*. Cutchogue, NY: Buccaneer, 1990. 248pp. ISBN 0-89966-684-1.
Netherlands, 1672-5. Written in 1850. This love story set during the Haarlem tulip craze, when the Dutch began growing tulips, contains scenes from Dutch history specifically concerning William of Orange.
Reviews: *WS* 10, 11
Reading Level: High School
Subject Areas: Netherlands; William II, of Orange, King of the Netherlands
Time Period: 1672-1675 ❑ Library owns

Dumas, Alexandre. *The Man in the Iron Mask*. Philadelphia: Lippincottt, 1976. ISBN 0-89968-146-8.
France, 1630-50. With the identity of the man in the mask still a mystery, this novel follows the Three Musketeers and their captain, D'Artagnan, to the end of their adventures together.
Reviews: *WS* 10
Reading Level: High School
Subject Areas: France; adventure and adventurers
Time Period: 1630-50 ❑ Library owns

Dumas, Alexandre. *The Three Musketeers*. Cutchogue, NY: Buccaneer Books, 1984. ISBN 0-89966-486-5. LC 84-50433.
France, 1625. Originally published in 1844. With intrigues of the court of Louis XIII and Cardinal de Richelieu swirling in the background, the story is carried along by the swashbuckling adventures of three of the king's musketeers and

D'Artagnan, a naive country lad who they befriend. They become involved in intrigues of the court and of the heart.

Reviews: *WJ* 4, 5; *WS* 12, 13, 14

Reading Level: Middle–High School

Subject Areas: France; adventure and adventurers; friendship

Time Period: 1625   ❏ Library owns

Du Maurier, Daphne. *The King's General.* **New York: Avon, 1972, c1946. 731pp. ISBN 0-380-00210-8. LC 46-4572.**

England, 1642-1660. Filled with many details about life in seventeenth century Cornwall, this is the story of Honor Harris who is crippled just days before she is wed to Sir Richard Grenville. Honor recalls the story of Sir Richard and of the parliamentary wars as she remembers them many years later.

Reviews: *WS* 10

Reading Level: High School

Subject Areas: Great Britain--1642-1660; Grenville, Sir Richard; Cornwall; physically handicapped

Time Period: 1642-1660   ❏ Library owns

Dunlop, Eileen. *The Valley of Deer.* **New York: Holiday, 1989. 139pp. ISBN 0-8234-0766-7. LC 89-1931.**

Scotland, seventeenth century. In 1954 in Scotland, Anne is bored as she accompanies her archaeologist parents on a dig. Poking around, she finds a Bible from the late 1600s. After reading an inscription about Alice Jardyne with the words "Blot from the Book of Life" added to it, she decides to find out all she can about Alice, who was accused of witchcraft. A charm stone found by her parents sends her back in time to become Alice.

Reviews: *BCCB* 11/89; *BL* 10/15/89; *SLJ* 1/90

Reading Level: Middle & Junior High School

Subject Areas: Scotland; archeology; witchcraft; time and space

Time Period: Seventeenth Century   ❏ Library owns

Frohlich, Newton. *1492.* **New York: St. Martin's, 1990. 448pp. ISBN 0-312-05041-6. LC 90-36882.**

Spain, 1492. In 1492, Columbus, an unknown sea captain, embarks for the Spice Islands, and Spain becomes Christian again. The author tries to bring the time and people to life.

Reviews: *BL* 10/1/90; *LJ* 10/1/90

Reading Level: High School [Mature Reader]

Subject Areas: Spain; explorers; Columbus, Christopher

Time Period: 1492   ❏ Library owns

Europe—Age of Discovery and Reformation

Garner, Alan. *Red Shift.* **New York: Macmillan, 1973. 197pp. ISBN 0-02-735870-4. LC 73-584.**

England, Roman period, 1642-1660, modern. Linked only by the locale—a hill near Barthomley village—and a stone axe, these are three separate stories. The first is about the lost Roman Ninth Legion, the second about a massacre during the English Civil War, and the last about two lovers in 1973. The axe appears in each story, bringing each its discoverers some type of protection.

Reviews: *BL* 3/15/74; *FFY*; *HB* 10/73

Reading Level: High School

Subject Areas: Great Britain--Roman Period; Great Britain--1642-1660; space and time

Time Period: 200; 1642-1660 ❏ Library owns

Gidley, Charles. *Armada.* **New York: Viking, 1988. 437pp. ISBN 0-670-81807-0. LC 87-40296.**

Spain, Portugal, England, late 1500s. Set against the religious feuding between Protestant England and Catholic Spain and Portugal is the story of Tristam, son of a Cornish fisherman who uses the turbulence of the times for his own gain as a privateer. Tristam is tossed overboard at sea by his father, survives and is enslaved in Portugal, escapes back to England where he is trained to be a spy, and experiences political intrigues, family conflicts and romance.

Reviews: *BBSH*; *BL* 1/1/88; *LJ* 1/88

Reading Level: High School [Mature Reader]

Subject Areas: Spain; Portugal; Great Britain--1485-1603; spies; sea stories; Spanish Armada, 1588

Time Period: 1588 ❏ Library owns

Golstein, Lisa. *Strange Devices of the Sun and Moon.* **New York: Tor; distributed by St. Martin's, 1993. 304pp. ISBN 0-312-85460-9. LC 92-21572.**

England, 1590. Alice Wood, a widowed bookseller, is drawn into the intrigues of the fairy folk who have come back to London to claim Alice's missing son, Arthur, as their new king. As conspirators plot against Elizabeth I and plague travels through the city, everyone looks for Arthur including, an alchemist and Christopher Marlowe.

Reviews: *BL* 2/15/93; *LJ* 12/92; *VOYA* 8/93

Reading Level: High School

Subject Areas: Great Britain--1485-1603; fantastic fiction; fairies

Time Period: 1590; Middle Ages ❏ Library owns

Goudge, Elizabeth. *The Child from the Sea.* **New York: Coward-McCann, 1970. 736pp.**

England, 1650-70. Lucy Walter, a resourceful Welsh woman, meets Charles II before he takes the throne, falls in love and secretly marries him. Due to the political workings of the time, she and Charles never reveal their marriage, and Charles marries another after he becomes king.

Reviews: *WS* 10

Reading Level: High School

Subject Areas: Great Britain--1603-1714; Walter, Lucy; Charles II, King of Great Britain; love

Time Period: 1650-70 ❏ Library owns

Greene, Jacqueline Dembar. *One Foot Ashore.* **New York: Walker, 1994. 208pp. ISBN 0-8027-8281-7. LC 93-22961.**

Netherlands, 1654-6. Sequel to *Out of Many Waters*. Maria, one of two Jewish sisters who escape from virtual slavery in a Brazilian monastery, stows away on a ship headed for Amsterdam. Upon arriving she is taken in by the Rembrandt household, whose members try to help her find her family. Rembrandt is well characterized. Though totally fictional, the setting of the Netherlands during the time of the Spanish Inquisition provides a factual base.

Reviews: *BCCB* 6/94; *BL* 4/1/94; *SLJ* 6/94; *VOYA* 6/94

Reading Level: MIddle & Junior High School

Subject Areas: Netherlands; Jews in the Netherlands; Rembrandt, Harmenszoon van Rijn; artists

Time Period: 1654 ❏ Library owns

Hardwick, Mollie. *Blood Royal.* **St. Martin's, 1989. 320pp. ISBN 0-312-02548-3. LC 88-30604.**

England, 1490-1540. Instead of focusing on Henry VIII, this novel focuses on the ill-fated Boleyn family. Beginning with the marriage of Elizabeth Howard to Thomas Boleyn, the story follows their children, George, Mary, and Anne. The relationships that Mary, as mistress, and Anne, as wife, had with Henry VIII are detailed.

Reviews: *BL* 3/15/89; *PW* 1/27/89

Reading Level: High School [Mature Reader]

Subject Areas: Great Britain--1485-1603; Henry VIII, King of England; Boleyn, Anne; Boleyn family

Time Period: 1490-1540; Middle Ages ❏ Library owns

Europe—Age of Discovery and Reformation

Hardwick, Mollie. *I Remember Love.* **New York: St. Martin's, 1983. 335pp. ISBN 0-312-40265-1. LC 82-17069.**

England, 1455-1485, 1530s, 1865. This is the story of three couples, each living in a different time period. During the War of the Roses, Yolande is willing to accept her life as a squire's wife until she meets Sir Joscelyn Conyers. Then Clement and Margery inadvertently become involved in a plot involving the Canterbury Shrine and King Henry VIII. Finally, a couple meet by chance in 1865.

Reviews: *LJ* 2/15/83; *SLJ* 8/83

Reading Level: High School

Subject Areas: Great Britain--1399-1485; Great Britain--1485-1603; love

Time Period: 1455-1485; 1530s; 1865 ❏ Library owns

Hardwick, Mollie. *The Merrymaid.* **New York: St. Martin's, 1985. 187pp. ISBN 0-312-53019-6. LC 85-1715.**

England, 1553-1558. Orphaned, Jacquette Valency is rescued from a group of superstitious peasants by a lady who eventually plans her marriage to a dull merchant. Jacquette longs for the exciting life she knew with her performer father, and plans to elope with a traveling fortune teller. The lives of traveling minstrels and performers are described, including the everyday tragedies of the times, such as the plague and persecution.

Reviews: *BBSH*; *BL* 6/1/84; *SLJ* 11/85

Reading Level: High School

Subject Areas: Great Britain--1485-1603; orphans; actors; minstrels

Time Period: 1553-1558; Middle Ages ❏ Library owns

Harnett, Cynthia. *Stars of Fortune.* **Minneapolis: Lerner, 1984, 1956. 173pp. ISBN 0-8225-0892-3. LC 83-24826.**

England, sixteenth century. Young ancestors of George Washington help Queen Elizabeth flee England.

Reviews: *BL* 9/15/84

Reading Level: Middle–High School

Subject Areas: Great Britain--1485-1603; Elizabeth I, Queen of England; mystery and detective stories

Time Period: 1545-50; Middle Ages ❏ Library owns

Harnett, Cynthia. *The Great House.* **Minneapolis: Lerner, 1984, 1967. 173pp. ISBN 0-8225-0893-1. LC 83-24880.**

England, 1669. Set during the time of Christopher Wren, this story follows Barbara and Geoffrey as they travel with their architect father, who is to build a large, modern house on a country estate.

Reviews: *BL* 9/15/84

Reading Level: Middle–High School
Subject Areas: Great Britain--1603-1714; architects; country life
Time Period: 1669 ❏ Library owns

Haugaard, Erik Christian. *Cromwell's Boy.* **Boston: Houghton, 1978. 214pp. ISBN 0-395-27203-3. LC 78-14392.**
England, 1642-1660. Sequel to *A Messenger for Parliament*. Oliver dedicates himself to Cromwell. Beginning as a messenger, he soon finds himself spying behind enemy lines. After some close calls, he returns to report his findings to Cromwell.
Reviews: *BBYA*; *BL* 12/1/78; *HB* 12/78; *SLJ* 12/78★; *WJ* 4, 5
Reading Level: Middle–High School
Subject Areas: Great Britain--1642-1660; spies
Time Period: 1642-1660 ❏ Library owns

Haugaard, Erik Christian. *A Messenger for Parliament.* **Boston: Houghton, 1976. 218pp. ISBN 0-395-24392-0. LC 76-21737.**
England, 1642-1660. After his mother dies and he gets separated from his father, Oliver finds friendship among a band of boys who decide that war is not the fun they thought it would be. Jack and Oliver find shelter with a printer who sends them on a dangerous journey to Oxford with a secret message for Cromwell.
Reviews: *BBYA*; *BL* 10/15/76; *SLJ* 11/76★; *WJ* 4, 5
Reading Level: Middle–High School
Subject Areas: Great Britain--1642-1660
Time Period: 1642-1660 ❏ Library owns

Haugaard, Erik Christian; illustrated by Leo and Diane Dillon. *The Untold Tale.* **Boston: Houghton, 1971. 211pp.**
Denmark, seventeenth century. Seven-year-old Dag, an orphan, is caught up in the events leading to the Massacre of Christianopolos.
Reviews: *BL* 9/15/71; *HB* 6/71; *LJ* 9/15/71; *NCB*
Reading Level: Middle–High School
Subject Areas: Denmark; orphans; massacres
Time Period: Seventeenth Century ❏ Library owns

Heaven, Constance. *The Queen and the Gypsy.* **New York: Coward, McCann, 1977. 275pp. ISBN 0-698-10794-2. LC 76-44004.**
England, 1558-1603. The triangle between Robert Dudley, Earl of Leicester; Queen Elizabeth, his social and intellectual equal; and Robert's wife Amy, whom he loves yet outgrows, is explored with the social and political events of the times as backdrop.
Reviews: *BL* 7/15/77; *LJ* 2/15/77; *SLJ* 5/77

Europe—Age of Discovery and Reformation

Reading Level: High School [Mature Reader]
Subject Areas: Great Britain--1485-1603; Elizabeth I, Queen of England; Dudley, Amy Robsart, Lady; Leicester, Robert Dudley, Earl of; love
Time Period: 1558-1603 ❏ Library owns

Hersom, Kathleen. *The Half Child.* **New York: Simon & Schuster, 1991. 139pp. ISBN 0-671-74225-6. LC 90-24079.**
England, 1650. When Lucy's sister Sarah is born with a mental handicap, everyone except Lucy believes that she is a changeling who might be reclaimed by the fairies. When Sarah disappears, no one is upset except Lucy. Fifty-five years later Lucy explains what happened to her little sister in this tale that brings rural England in the seventeenth century to life.
Reviews: *BCCB* 9/91; *BL* 10/1/91; *SLJ* 11/91★; *VOYA* 12/91
Reading Level: Middle & Junior High School
Subject Areas: Great Britain--1603-1714; sisters; superstition; mentally handicapped
Time Period: 1650 ❏ Library owns

Hilgartner, Beth. *A Murder for Her Majesty.* **Boston: Houghton, 1986. 241pp. ISBN 0-395-41451-2. LC 86-10316.**
England, 1558-1603. Rich in suspense and filled with details of Elizabethan and choir life, the story of Alice Tuckfield begins as she witnesses her father's murder and flees to York in search of a family friend who will protect her. In York she disguises herself as a member of the York Cathedral Boy's Choir while she continues her search for Lady Jenny, who she knows will protect her.
Reviews: *BCCB* 9/86; *BL* 9/15/86; *BR* 3-4/87; *SLJ* 10/86; *VOYA* 12/86
Reading Level: Middle–High School
Subject Areas: Great Britain--1485-1603; mystery and detective stories; cathedrals; choirs
Time Period: 1558-1603 ❏ Library owns

Hodges, Cyril Walter. *Playhouse Tales.* **New York: Coward, 1974. 168pp. ISBN 0-598-20268-6. LC 72-94147.**
England, 1558-1603. Six short stories tell of the life and times of Elizabethan literary and theatrical figures such as Ben Jonson, poet and playwright George Peele, the Burbage family who built the Globe Theater, and the dancer-actor Will Kemp.
Reviews: *BCCB* 6/75; *BL* 3/1/75; *HB* 12/74; *SLJ* 3/75
Reading Level: Middle & Junior High School
Subject Areas: Great Britain--1485-1603; theaters; actors
Time Period: 1558-1603 ❏ Library owns

Europe—Age of Discovery and Reformation

Holland, Cecelia. *The Sea Beggars.* **New York: Knopf, 1982. 305pp. ISBN 0-394-50406-2. LC 81-48115.**

Netherlands, sixteenth century. When the Spanish Inquisition reaches the Netherlands, siblings Jan and Hanneke are separated after the execution of their father and suicide of their mother. Jan joins the Sea Beggars to help defeat the Spanish. Hanneke kills the Spaniard who rapes her and escapes to Germany and William of Orange. The two are reunited in a tragic ending at a battle at Brill.

Reviews: *BR* 1-2/83; *LJ* 5/1/82; *SLJ* 9/82; *VOYA* 10/82; *YARC*

Reading Level: High School

Subject Areas: Netherlands; Inquisition

Time Period: Sixteenth Century   ❏ Library owns

Holt, Victoria. *My Enemy the Queen.* **New York: Doubleday, 1978. 348pp. ISBN 0-385-14111-4. LC 77-11366.**

England, 1558-1603. Lettice Knollys, Queen Elizabeth's lady-in-waiting, attracts the notice of Robert Dudley, favorite of the queen, although she is married to the Earl of Essex. She becomes one of his mistresses, marries Robert when her husband dies, and then betrays him. Throughout, her relationship with Elizabeth is revealed.

Reviews: *BL* 9/15/78; *WS* 11

Reading Level: High School [Mature Reader]

Subject Areas: Great Britain--1485-1603; Elizabeth I, Queen of England; Knollys, Lettice

Time Period: 1558-1603   ❏ Library owns

Hunter, Mollie. *The 13th Member: A Story of Suspense.* **New York: Harper, 1971. 214pp. ISBN 0-06-022662-5.**

Scotland, 1567-1603. Gilly, a young kitchen maid, unwittingly becomes the 13th member of a witches' coven that is planning King James VI's death. Gilly's strange actions prompt Adam, a servant, to speak with the village alchemist. Together they save both Gilly and King James.

Reviews: *BL* 10/15/71; *HB* 10/71; *LJ* 12/15/71

Reading Level: Middle–High School

Subject Areas: Scotland; Great Britain--1485-1603; James VI, King of Scotland; witchcraft

Time Period: 1567-1603   ❏ Library owns

Hunter, Mollie. *You Never Knew Her As I Did.* **New York: Harper, 1981. 216pp. ISBN 0-06-022678-1. LC 81-47114.**

Scotland, 1567. Will Douglas, illegitimate son of the man charged with the supervision of the imprisoned Mary Queen of Scots, is infatuated with Mary and sympathetic to her plight. He and an uncle plot to hasten her escape so that she can regain the throne.

Reviews: *BL* 9/1/81; *WJ* 5

Reading Level: Middle–High School

Subject Areas: Scotland; Great Britain--1485-1603; Mary Stuart, Queen of Scots; escapes

Time Period: 1567 ❏ **Library owns**

Irwin, Margaret. *Elizabeth, Captive Princess.* **Guilford, CT: Ulverscroft, 1974. 246pp. ISBN 0-85456-640-6.**

England, 1553-1558. Sequel to *Young Bess*. Two years in the tempestuous life of Princess Elizabeth are drawn, beginning in 1553 with the death of Edward VI and culminating in Mary Tudor's marriage to Philip of Spain. Part of the "Shadows of the Crown" Series.

Reviews: *WS* 10

Reading Level: High School

Subject Areas: Great Britain--1485-1603; Elizabeth I, Queen of England

Time Period: 1553-1555 ❏ **Library owns**

Irwin, Margaret. *Young Bess.* **Guilford, CT: Ulverscroft, 1974. 274pp. ISBN 0-85456-638-4.**

England, 1533-1547. Providing many details about Court life, Irwin follows the early life of Elizabeth I from childhood through adolescence, including her father's tumultuous reign and the jockeying for power following his death. Part of the "Shadows of the Crown" Series.

Reviews: *WS* 10

Reading Level: High School

Subject Areas: Great Britain--1485-1603; Elizabeth I, Queen of England

Time Period: 1533-1547 ❏ **Library owns**

Kells, Susannah. *A Crowning Mercy.* **New York: Viking, 1983. 480pp. ISBN 0-670-20068-9. LC 83-47869.**

England, 1642-1660. Dorcas, daughter of a cruel Puritan man, falls in love with the dashing Toby, even though her father has arranged her marriage to another. When her father dies, she discovers a clue to a fortune that may be hers. Toby arrives and together they solve the mystery, experience the horrors of Civil War, and narrowly escape death.

Reviews: *LJ* 8/83; *SLJ* 1/84

Reading Level: High School

Subject Areas: Great Britain--1642-1660; mystery and detective stories; adventure and adventurers
Time Period: 1642-1660 ❏ **Library owns**

Kimmel, Eric A. *The Tartar's Sword.* **New York: Coward, McCann, 1974. ISBN 0-698-20243-0. LC 72-89758.**
Ukraine, seventeenth century. After killing his master, 15-year-old Hrisha, journeys far to find the Cossacks. Along the way he meets a misfit band of people who wish to kill both the Tartars and the gentry. When he does find the Cossacks, he is assimilated and proves to be a worthy addition to their ranks.
Reviews: *BL* 3/1/74; *HB* 8/74; *LJ* 9/15/74; *SLJ* 9/74
Reading Level: Middle–High School
Subject Areas: Russia; Ukraine; Cossacks; adventure and adventurers
Time Period: Seventeenth Century ❏ **Library owns**

Kingsley, Charles. *Westward Ho!* **, Cutchogue, NY: Buccaneer, 1982. ISBN 0-89966-399-0.**
England, 1558-1603. First published in 1855. Kingsley's tale focuses on the sea power held by both England and Spain during Elizabeth's reign and the sea battles that ensued between the Royal Navy and the Spanish Armada.
Reviews: *WS* 10
Reading Level: High School
Subject Areas: Great Britain--1485-1603; Armada, 1588; sea stories
Time Period: 1558-1603 ❏ **Library owns**

Laker, Rosalind. *Circle of Pearls.* **New York: Doubleday, 1990. 496pp. ISBN 0-385-26305-8. LC 89-29458.**
England, 1642-1660. Julia Pallister, a girl from a Royalist family, maturing amidst many social, religious, and political conflicts, manages to find romance and adventure during the time of the Civil War.
Reviews: *BBSH*; *BL* 6/15/90; *SLJ* 10/90
Reading Level: High School
Subject Areas: Great Britain--1642-1660
Time Period: 1642-1660 ❏ **Library owns**

Laker, Rosalind. *The Golden Tulip.* **New York: Doubleday, 1991. 585pp. ISBN 0-385-41560-5. LC 90-27591.**
Netherlands, seventeenth century. Just before Francesca Visser begins an apprenticeship with the painter Jan Vermeer, she discovers that her father has betrothed her to a wealthy, but loathsome man, in exchange for the payment of his debts. Help comes and Francesca goes to Delft to paint. She meets Pieter van Doorne, love blossoms with his tulips, and she achieves her goal with help from her sisters and Pieter.

Europe—Age of Discovery and Reformation

Reviews: *BL* 9/1/91; *SLJ* 4/92
Reading Level: High School
Subject Areas: Netherlands; artists; painters; love
Time Period: Seventeenth Century   ❑ Library owns

Lane, Jane. *Bridge of Sighs.* **New York: Day, 1975, c1973. 198pp. ISBN 0-381-98277-7.**
England, 1650-1701. Mary of Modena married James II of England when she was quite young. She shared both his crown and his exile and gave birth to a future king.
Reviews: *WS* 10
Reading Level: High School
Subject Areas: Great Britain--1603-1714; Mary, of Modena, consort of James II; James II, King of England
Time Period: 1650-1701   ❑ Library owns

Lane, Jane. *The Severed Crown.* **New York: Simon & Schuster, 1973. 210pp. ISBN 0-671-21567-1. LC 73-1127.**
England, 1646-1649. Built upon excerpts from fictional letters, diaries, and memoirs, this novel set during the English Civil War details the last days of Charles I before he was executed by Cromwell's forces.
Reviews: *BL* 11/1/73; *LJ* 8/73
Reading Level: High School [Mature Reader]
Subject Areas: Great Britain--1642-1660; Charles I, King of England
Time Period: 1642-1660   ❑ Library owns

Lewis, Hilda Winifred. *I Am Mary Tudor.* **New York: McKay, 1972. 422pp. LC 70-185132.**
England, 1516-1553. The reigns of Henry VIII and Edward VI are seen through the eyes of Mary Tudor, daughter of Henry VIII and Catherine of Aragon. Her view of the times is that of a staunch Catholic, and covers the years from her birth to her ascension to the throne.
Reviews: *BL* 6/15/72; *LJ* 6/15/72
Reading Level: High School
Subject Areas: Great Britain--1485-1603; Mary I, Queen of England; Henry VIII, King of England
Time Period: 1516-1553   ❑ Library owns

Litowinsky, Olga. *The High Voyage.* **New York: Viking, 1977. 147pp. ISBN 0-670-37155-6. LC 77-24893.**
Atlantic Ocean, 1502-04. Christopher Columbus's 13-year-old son, Fernando, accompanies him on his fourth and final voyage to the New World. Fernando, at

first excited with the coming adventure, soon learns of the hardships of sea travel as he and the crew deal with storms, shipwreck, and mutiny.
Reviews: *BL* 11/1/77; *HB* 4/78; *SLJ* 11/77
Reading Level: Middle & Junior High School
Subject Areas: Columbus, Christopher; Columbus, Ferdinand; sea stories; explorers; America; adventure and adventurers; voyages and travels
Time Period: 1502-04 ❏ Library owns

Llywelyn, Morgan. *Grania: She-King of the Irish Seas.* **New York: Crown, 1986. 437pp. ISBN 0-517-55951-X. LC 85-29975.**
Ireland, sixteenth century. Grace O'Malley spent 40 years on the high seas as trader, pirate, and sea captain, trying to keep Elizabeth I's forces from invading Ireland. Not a typical woman of her day, she went through two husbands, political intrigue, battles, lovers, and prison.
Reviews: *BL* 1/15/86; *LJ* 3/1/86; *WS* 13; *YAEC*
Reading Level: High School
Subject Areas: Ireland; sea stories; adventure and adventurers; women
Time Period: Sixteenth Century ❏ Library owns

Lofts, Norah (Robinson). *The King's Pleasure.* **New York: Doubleday, 1969. 372pp. LC 79-79966.**
England, 1485-1536. Lofts' story follows the life of Katharine of Aragon, Henry VIII's first wife, from her childhood in Spain to marriage to the Prince of Wales and finally to Henry VIII. Through her eyes we see Henry sympathetically, his good points balancing those that are overbearing.
Reviews: *BL* 12/15/69; *FFY*
Reading Level: High School
Subject Areas: Great Britain--1485-1603; Catherine of Aragon, consort of Henry VIII; Henry VIII, King of England
Time Period: 1485-1536 ❏ Library owns

Luke, Mary. *The Ivy Crown.* **New York: Doubleday, 1984. 456pp. ISBN 0-385-18823-4. LC 82-46014.**
England, 1509-1547. Katherine Parr, the sixth wife of King Henry VIII and the least known, was educated along side of Henry's daughter and was married several times before she married Henry. This is the colorful story of Katherine's life and of her times.
Reviews: *BL* 3/1/84; *LJ* 3/1/84
Reading Level: High School [Mature Reader]

Subject Areas: Great Britain--1485-1603; Henry VIII, King of England; Parr, Katherine, consort of Henry VIII
Time Period: 1509-1547 ❏ Library owns

Malvern, Gladys. *The Six Wives of Henry VIII*. New York: Vanguard, 1972. 200pp. ISBN 0-8149-0665-6. LC 71-134678.
England, 1491-1547. Here are the fictionalized biographies of Henry VIII's wives, all diverse in background and character, and their fates.
Reviews: *WS* 10
Reading Level: High School
Subject Areas: Great Britain--1485-1603; Henry VIII, King of England; queens
Time Period: 1491-1547 ❏ Library owns

Marshall, James Vance. *The Wind at Morning*. New York: Morrow, 1973. 208pp. ISBN 0-688-00188-2.
1519-1521. Young Juan Vizcaya signs on with Magellan's fleet, but is unaware of the hardships ahead. When he returns, he has seen more cruelty and misery than is imaginable for one person, but he also understands what drives Magellan on.
Reviews: *WS* 10
Reading Level: High School
Subject Areas: Magellan, Ferdinand; sea stories; explorers; voyages and travels
Time Period: 1519-1521 ❏ Library owns

Marston, Edward. *The Queen's Head*. New York: St. Martin's, 1989. 288pp. ISBN 0-312-02970-5. LC 89-30098.
England, 1588-1603. Marston sets his mystery against the Elizabethan era when the Royal Navy and Spanish Armada clashed. Hero Nicholas Bracewell, a theater troupe's stage manager and bookholder, searches for the person who has killed the troupe's major actor, causing the troupe to fall on hard times.
Reviews: *BL* 6/1/89; *LJ* 6/1/89
Reading Level: High School
Subject Areas: Great Britain--1485-1603; theater; actors; mystery and detective stories
Time Period: 1588-1603 ❏ Library owns

Martin, Susan; illustrated by Tom la Padula. *I Sailed With Columbus*. New York: Overlook, 1991. 128pp. ISBN 0-87951-431-1. LC 91-2820.
Spain, Atlantic Ocean, 1492. With a fleet partially manned by convicts who speaks of mutiny, Columbus makes his way to the New World. This story is told from the viewpoint of Diego de la Acevedo and his friend Luis, both ship's boys who see the harsh conditions and unpleasant realities not always included in accounts of Columbus' voyage.

Europe—Age of Discovery and Reformation

Reviews: *BCCB* 10/91; *BL* 9/1/91; *BR* 3/92; *SLJ* 9/91
Reading Level: Middle & Junior High School
Subject Areas: Spain; Columbus, Christopher; explorers; America; sea stories; voyages and travels
Time Period: 1492 ❏ Library owns

McLeod, Alison. *Prisoner of the Queen.* **Boston: Houghton, 1973. 191pp. LC 72-9077.**
England, 1567-1586. Undertaking a mission on behalf of his Catholic brethren in Protestant England, a young Jesuit priest becomes embroiled in religious politics and the attempts to bring Mary Queen of Scots to the throne.
Reviews: *BL* 6/15/73; *LJ* 7/73
Reading Level: High School [Mature Reader]
Subject Areas: Great Britain--1485-1603; Mary Queen of Scots; priests
Time Period: 1567-1586 ❏ Library owns

Miles, Rosalind. *I, Elizabeth.* **New York: Doubleday, 1994. 608pp. ISBN 0-385-47160-2.**
England. 1533-1603. In her later years, Elizabeth I writes her memoirs, vividly portraying life in Tudor England and the colorful people who greatly influenced her such as her father Henry VIII, sister Bloody Mary, and cousin Mary Queen of Scots. She also reveals how frightened she was when, as a young girl, she became queen, and how she matured to a shrewd and scholarly monarch.
Reviews: *BL* 7/94; *LJ* 5/15/94; *PW* 5/30/94
Reading Level: High School [Mature Reader]
Subject Areas: Great Britain; Elizabeth I, Queen of England
Time Period: 1533-1603 ❏ Library owns

Newth, Mette; translated by Tina Nunally and Steve Murray. *The Abduction.* **New York: Farrar, 1989. 247pp. ISBN 0-374-30008-9. LC 89-045615.**
Greenland, Norway, seventeenth century. Norwegian traders kidnap two Inuit teenagers and take them back to Norway to become slaves. The two, especially Osugo who is brutally raped, are treated cruelly. In Norway, Christine, a crippled servant girl whose father died on the expedition, is in charge of their care. The prejudices and cruelty of "civilized" people against other cultures are graphically conveyed. This book won the Norwegian State Prize.
Reviews: *BBSH*; *BBYA*; *BCCB* 11/89; *BL* 12/1/89; *HB* 1/90★; *SLJ* 12/89★; *VOYA* 2/90; *WS* 13
Reading Level: High School
Subject Areas: Norway; Greenland; Inuit; kidnapping; slaves
Time Period: Seventeenth Century ❏ Library owns

Europe—Age of Discovery and Reformation

O'Connor, Genevieve A.; illustrated by Rick Britton. *The Admiral and the Deck Boy: One Boy's Journey With Christopher Columbus.* **Crozet, VA: Shoe Tree Press; Betterway, 1991. 168pp. ISBN 1-55870-218-0. LC 91-17978.**

Spain, Atlantic Ocean, 1492. Told by Carlos, a 12-year-old deck boy, this is the story of Columbus' voyage. Carlos admires Columbus and does not let the crew's superstitions and mutterings deter him.

Reviews: *BR* 3/92; *SLJ* 1/92

Reading Level: Middle–High School

Subject Areas: Spain; Columbus, Christopher; explorers; America; sea stories; voyages and travels

Time Period: 1492 ❏ Library owns

O'Dell, Scott. *The Hawk That Dare Not Hunt by Day.* **Boston: Houghton, 1975. 222pp. ISBN 0-395-21892-6. LC 75-17029.**

England, 1524-1534. Based on William Tyndale's outlawed ambition to translate the Bible into English, this tale of smuggling and religious politics takes orphan Tom Barton from England to Germany and back again many times in his attempt to help the doomed Tyndale.

Reviews: *BCCB* 2/76; *BL* 10/15/75; *SLJ* 12/75

Reading Level: Middle–High School

Subject Areas: Great Britain--1485-1603; Tyndale, William; printing; smuggling; Reformation; Europe--1517-1648

Time Period: 1524-1534; Reformation ❏ Library owns

Paton Walsh, Jill. *A Parcel of Patterns.* **New York: Farrar, 1983. 136pp. ISBN 0-374-35750-1. LC 83-048143.**

England, 1665. Sixteen-year-old Mall Percival describes the course of the plague as it reaches her small town of Eyam. The village volunteers to cut itself off from the world to contain the plague, but Mall's suitor will not agree and comes to see her. The religious beliefs and daily life of the village all contribute to their fate.

Reviews: *BBYA*; *BL* 3/1/84; *HB* 4/84; *SLJ* 2/84; *VOYA* 4/84; *WJ* 5

Reading Level: Middle–High School

Subject Areas: Great Britain--1603-1714; plague; village life

Time Period: 1665 ❏ Library owns

Plaidy, Jean. *The Captive Queen of Scots.* **New York: Putnam, 1970, c1963. 410pp.**

England, 1571-1587. Sequel to *Royal Road to Fotheringay*. The last 18 years of Mary Queen of Scots' life are traced from imprisonment by Scottish enemies to a dramatic escape to England where a more royal imprisonment meets her.

Reviews: *BL* 5/15/70; *WS* 10

Reading Level: High School
Subject Areas: Great Britain--1485-1603; Mary Stuart, Queen of Scots
Time Period: 1571-1587 ❏ Library owns

Plaidy, Jean. *The Murder in the Tower.* **New York: Putnam, 1974, c1964. 286pp. ISBN 0-399-11396-7.**
England, 1603-1625. Twelve-year-old Frances Howard is married to the Earl of Essex who goes abroad to finish his education while Frances stays home. Two years later, Frances meets Robert Carr, a favorite of King James I, and becomes his mistress, vowing to marry him, regardless of the consequences. Her solution to her problem includes witchcraft and murder.
Reviews: *BL* 10/15/74; *WS* 10
Reading Level: High School [Mature Reader]
Subject Areas: Great Britain--1603-1714; Somerset, Robert Carr, Earl of; Somerset, Frances (Howard) Carr, Countess of
Time Period: 1603-1625 ❏ Library owns

Plaidy, Jean. *Queen of This Realm.* **New York: Putnam, 1985. ISBN 0-399-12985-5. LC 84-17895.**
England, 1533-1603. Follows *Myself My Enemy* in the "Queens of England" Series. For those who cannot get enough of Queen Elizabeth I, this novel covers her entire life, focusing on her relationships with the Earl of Leicester and the Earl of Essex and her role in the imprisonment and execution of Mary, Queen of Scots.
Reviews: *BL* 10/15/84; *LJ* 2/1/85
Reading Level: High School
Subject Areas: Great Britain--1485-1603; Elizabeth I, Queen of England
Time Period: 1533-1603 ❏ Library owns

Plaidy, Jean. *Myself My Enemy.* **New York: Putnam, 1984. 396pp. ISBN 0-399-12877-8. LC 83-9684.**
England, 1625-49. First of the "Queens of England" Series. Henriette Marie, wife of King Charles I of England, begins as a child bride, spoiled by her life as daughter of Henry IV of France. During 25 years of marriage, Henriette matures through all of the political and religious conflicts of the times and Charles' eventual beheading.
Reviews: *BBSH*; *BL* 10/15/83; *LJ* 12/1/83
Reading Level: High School
Subject Areas: Great Britain--1603-1714; Charles I, King of England; Henriette Marie, consort of Charles I
Time Period: 1625-1649 ❏ Library owns

Europe—Age of Discovery and Reformation

Plaidy, Jean. *The Three Crowns: The Stuart Saga.* **New York: Putnam, 1977, c1965. 363pp. ISBN 0-399-11892-6. LC 76-55937.**

England, 1662-94. Mary, daughter of James II, marries William of Orange of Holland, and must decide whether to follow her father into exile or to stay with her husband. Mary chooses William and the two of them rule England jointly after Mary declares him king instead of prince consort.

Reviews: *WS* 11
Reading Level: High School
Subject Areas: Great Britain--1603-1714; William III, King of Great Britain; Mary II, Queen of Great Britain
Time Period: 1662-1694; Seventeenth Century ❑ Library owns

Reade, Charles. *The Cloister and the Hearth.* **Heritage Press. 1932, 745pp.**

Europe, 1460-1500. This is the tragic love story of the parents of the philosopher Erasmus. Gerard, a writer, receives a forged letter telling him of the death of his wife Margaret. Heartbroken, he becomes a monk in the Dominican order. However, Margaret is not dead and has given birth to Erasmus. Years later, they meet again, but Gerard will not break his religious vows. Margaret dies of the plague, and Gerard dies of a broken heart. First published in 1861.

Reviews: *WS* 10
Reading Level: High School
Subject Areas: Reformation; love
Time Period: 1460-1500; Reformation ❑ Library owns

Schmitt, Gladys. *Rembrandt: A Novel.* **New York: Random House, 1961. 657pp.**

Netherlands, 1606-1669. The full span of the Dutch painter Rembrandt's life follows him from his humble beginnings, through his success and to his declining years. He is shown to be a man of brilliant talent with a very imperfect human side, including rudeness and an inability to handle money.

Reviews: *WS* 10
Reading Level: High School
Subject Areas: Netherlands; Rembrandt Hermanszoon van Rijn; Painters; artists
Time Period: 1606-1669 ❑ Library owns

Scott, Sir Walter. *Kenilworth.* **Ulverscroft, Guilford, CT, 1982. ISBN 0-7089-8028-7.**

England, 1558-1603. Originally published in 1821. Scott portrays the love triangle formed by Queen Elizabeth I, Robert, the Earl of Leicester, and Amy, Robert's unhappy neglected wife who meets a tragic end.

Reviews: *WS* 10, 11

Reading Level: High School
Subject Areas: Great Britain--1485-1603; Elizabeth I, Queen of England; Leicester, Robert Dudley, Earl of; Dudley, Amy Robsart, Lady
Time Period: 1558-1603   ❏ Library owns

Smith, A. C. H. *Lady Jane.* **New York: Holt, 1985. 186pp. ISBN 0-03-006168-7. LC 85-13181.**
England, 1537-1554. Based upon the screenplay of the same name, this is a fictionalized account of Lady Jane Grey's marriage to the Duke of Northumberland's wastrel son, her ascent to the throne and eventual beheading. Students unfamiliar with the period may have trouble understanding the plot.
Reviews: *BFY*; *BR* 3-4/86
Reading Level: High School
Subject Areas: Great Britain--1485-1603; Grey, Lady Jane
Time Period: 1537-1554   ❏ Library owns

Stolz, Mary. *Bartholomew Fair.* **New York: Morrow/Greenwillow, 1990. 152pp. ISBN 0-688-09522-4. LC 89-27230.**
England, 1597. Bartholomew Fair with its attractions entices Queen Elizabeth, two schoolboys, a wealthy cloth merchant, an overworked apprentice, and a scullery maid to attend. A mystery arises as the reader learns early in the story that one of these characters will not return. The characters experience the color and pageantry of a medieval fair.
Reviews: *BCCB* 10/90; *BR* 3/91; *BL*★; *HB* 7/90; *SLJ* 11/90; *VOYA* 4/91
Reading Level: Middle & Junior High School
Subject Areas: Great Britain--1485-1603; fairs; London (England)
Time Period: 1597   ❏ Library owns

Sutcliff, Rosemary. *Bonnie Dundee.* **New York: Dutton, 1984. 205pp. ISBN 0-525-44091-1. LC 84-8149.**
Scotland, seventeenth century. In the story centered around the religious and political conflicts of King James II and his foes, young Hugh Herriot leaves home to join the rebels led by John Graham of Claverhouse. Hugh serves Graham as a messenger, and when Graham is killed, follows King James into exile to France. Readers will find some knowledge of the times helpful.
Reviews: *BBSH*; *BCCB* 9/84; *BL* 8/84; *BR* 3-4/85; *HB* 9/84; *SLJ* 9/84
Reading Level: High School
Subject Areas: Scotland; Dundee, John Graham of Claverhouse, Viscount; Jacobites
Time Period: 1689-1714   ❏ Library owns

Treviño, Elizabeth Borton de. *I, Juan de Pareja.* New York: Farrar, 1965. 180pp. ISBN 0-374-33531-1. LC 65-19330.

Spain, Italy, 1620-1660. Juan de Pareja, a black slave, is owned by the Spanish painter Velázquez, helping him to prepare paints and canvases. Over the years, the two men grow to respect each other and become friends. Velázquez not only gives Juan his freedom, but teaches him to be a respected painter as well.

Reviews: Newbery Award, 1966.

Reading Level: Middle–High School

Subject Areas: Spain; Italy; Pareja, Juan de; Velázquez, Diego Rodriguez de Silva y; painters; artists; slaves

Time Period: 1620-1660 ❑ Library owns

Twain, Mark. *The Prince and the Pauper.* Berkeley, CA: Univ. of Calif. Press, 1983. 324pp. ISBN 0-520-05088-6.

England, 1537-1547. Revealing the English court life of Henry VIII's reign, the story revolves around a prince, Edward VI, who slips away to explore life outside the palace by changing places with a commoner who looks exactly like him. Originally published in 1881.

Reviews: *WJ* 4, 5; *WS* 13, 14

Reading Level: Middle–High School

Subject Areas: Great Britain--1485-1603; Edward VI, King of England; adventure and adventurers

Time Period: 1537-1547 ❑ Library owns

Vining, Elizabeth Gray. *Take Heed of Loving Me.* Philadelphia: Lippincott, 1964. 352pp. LC 63-20398.

England, 1573-1613. In this life of the poet and clergyman John Donne, set in Elizabethan and Jacobean England, Donne comes to life as a person whose character and talents lead him to success in his chosen fields and in his courtship and marriage to Anne More.

Reviews: *WS* 10

Reading Level: High School

Subject Areas: Great Britain--1603-1714; Donne, John; More, Anne; poets

Time Period: 1573-1613 ❑ Library owns

Von Canon, Claudia. *The Moonclock.* Boston: Houghton, 1979. 159pp. ISBN 0-395-27810-4. LC 79-1076.

Austria, 1683. In 1682, 20-year-old Barbara marries a much older man, Jacob. Here she chronicles her life with her unusually broad-minded husband, describing social conditions and superstitions, as well as the Siege of Austria by the Turks.

Reviews: *BL* 7/15/79; *HB* 6/79; *SLJ* 3/80★

Europe—Age of Discovery and Reformation

Reading Level: Middle–High School
Subject Areas: Austria; marriage; Vienna (Austria), Siege of, 1683
Time Period: 1683 ❏ Library owns

Von Canon, Claudia. *The Inheritance.* **Boston: Houghton, 1983. 212pp. ISBN 0-395-33891-3. LC 82-23418.**
Spain, Switzerland, 1580-1620. Miguel, studying medicine in Padua, is called home where he learns his father has become a victim of the Inquisition. He finds himself suspect and escapes to an old family friend in Switzerland, where he falls in love. Miguel seeks and has his final revenge on the man who betrayed his family.
Reviews: *BCCB* 9/83; *BL* 6/1/83; *BR* 9-10/83; *HB* 8/83; *SLJ* 9/83; *VOYA* 12/83
Reading Level: High School
Subject Areas: Spain; Switzerland; Inquisition; printing
Time Period: 1580-1620 ❏ Library owns

Watson, Sally. *Linnet.* **New York: Dutton, 1971. 224pp. LC 76-157952.**
England, 1558-1603. Fourteen-year-old runaway Linnet, who is befriended by Sir Colin Collyngewood, is fearful when she finds out that he runs a group of young pickpockets. Colin, however, has special plans for Linnet and wants her to help uncover a plot against Queen Elizabeth.
Reviews: *BCCB* 1/72; *BL* 4/1/72; *HB* 2/72; *LJ* 12/15/71
Reading Level: Middle–High School
Subject Areas: Great Britain--1485-1603; London (England); runaways; Elizabeth I, Queen of England
Time Period: 1558-1603 ❏ Library owns

Weir, Rosemary; illustrated by Richard Cuffari. *Blood Royal.* **New York: Farrar, 1973. 167pp. ISBN 0-374-30845-4. LC 73-75177.**
England, 1642-1660. During the English Civil War, Gil and his father are left in charge of the greyhounds when their master goes off to war. The years are hard and the estate suffers fire, looting, and threats to the dogs.
Reviews: *BCCB* 1/74; *BL* 9/15/73; *HB* 6/73; *SLJ* 5/73
Reading Level: Middle & Junior High School
Subject Areas: Great Britain--1642-1660; dogs
Time Period: 1642-1660 ❏ Library owns

Weir, Rosemary. *The Lion and the Rose.* **New York: Farrar, 1970. 167pp. LC 73-125152.**
England, 1670-1700. Jem runs away to London where he is hired by a stone mason, and eventually becomes his apprentice. The picture of London and stone-

masonry during an exciting time architecturally, as Christopher Wren was rebuilding St. Paul's Cathedral, is particularly interesting.
Reviews: *BL* 3/1/71; *LJ* 12/15/70
Reading Level: Middle & Junior High School
Subject Areas: Great Britain--1603-1714; London (England); architecture; stone; apprentices
Time Period: 1670-1700 ❏ Library owns

Welch, Ronald. *The Hawk.* **New York: Criterion Books, 1969. 224pp. LC 68-15243.**
England, 1558-1603. An action-packed sea adventure story set in the time of Elizabeth I concerns Harry Carey, son of the Earl of Aubigny and lieutenant on his father's galleon, the Hawk. Young Harry proves himself when he captures valuable cargo bound for Spain from Brazil and when he goes undercover to stop a plot against the queen.
Reviews: *BL* 5/1/70; *HB* 4/70; *LJ* 11/15/70
Reading Level: Middle–High School
Subject Areas: Great Britain--1485-1603; sea stories; adventure and adventurers; spies
Time Period: 1558-1603 ❏ Library owns

Willard, Barbara. *A Cold Wind Blowing.* **New York: Dutton, 1973. 175pp. ISBN 0-525-28125-8. LC 73-77453.**
England, 1509-1547. This story in Willard's Medley/Mallory family saga, shows the effects the Reformation has on ordinary lives. Piers Medley promises his dying clergyman uncle that he will protect a sick young woman, Isabella, who turns out to be a nun absolved of all her oaths, except that of chastity. Piers weds Isabella and when she becomes pregnant, they are forced to flee and tragedy follows. Sequel to *The Sprig of Broom.*
Reviews: *BL* 2/1/74; *HB* 12/73; *LJ* 1/15/74
Reading Level: Middle–High School
Subject Areas: Great Britain--1485-1603
Time Period: 1509-1547 ❏ Library owns

Willard, Barbara. *The Iron Lily.* **New York: Dutton, 1974. 175pp. ISBN 0-525-32592-1. LC 74-7195.**
England, 1509-1547. Sequel to *A Cold Wind Blowing.* Lilias, the illegitimate daughter of Piers Medley, suspects, but is not positive that Piers is her father. With her strong will and determination, she rises in status to become a prosperous ironmaster, but when her daughter Ursula falls in love with Piers's son, the two women come into conflict as Lilias tries to dissuade Ursula from her love, fearing that it may be incestuous.

Europe—Enlightenment and Liberty

Reviews: *BCCB* 2/75; *BL* 12/15/74; *HB* 2/75; *NCB*; *SLJ* 1/75
Reading Level: Middle–High School
Subject Areas: Great Britain--1485-1603; orphans
Time Period: 1509-1547   ❏ Library owns

Willard, Barbara. *The Sprig of Broom.* **New York: Dutton, 1972. 184pp. ISBN 0-525-39805-8. LC 72-78083.**
Great Britain, 1500-1509. Young Piers Medley is orphaned after his enigmatic father disappears and his mother is stoned to death on suspicion of witchcraft. He is taken in by an aristocratic family, the Mallorys. When Catherine Mallory says she loves him, Piers decides he must find out who his father was. This story explains the mysterious of the disappearance of Richard Plantagenet after the Battle of Bosworth. Sequel to *The Lark and Laurel.*
Reviews: *BL* 1/15/73; *HB* 2/73; *LJ* 1/15/73
Reading Level: Middle–High School
Subject Areas: Great Britain--1485-1603; orphans
Time Period: 1500-1509   ❏ Library owns

Enlightenment and Liberty

Aiken, Joan. *The Smile of the Stranger.* **New York: Doubleday, 1978. 280pp. ISBN 0-385-13634-X. LC 77-25573.**
England, eighteenth century. This gothic romance revolves around the life of Juliana Paget, whose father returns to England only to die and leave her an orphan in the hands of her Aunt Caroline, who wishes to marry her to an older man. Enter dashing Captain Davenport and adventurous Count van Welcker to bring romance, adventure and, danger into Juliana's life.
Reviews: *BL* 2/15/79; *LJ* 11/1/78; *SLJ* 3/79
Reading Level: High School
Subject Areas: Great Britain--1714-1837; orphans; adventure and adventurers
Time Period: Eighteenth Century   ❏ Library owns

Allen, Hervey. *Anthony Adverse.* **Rinehart, 1933. 1124pp.**
Italy, France, England, Spain, New World, 1775-1850. Orphaned and raised in a Catholic convent, Anthony Adverse is apprenticed to a merchant and becomes his heir. While checking on business interests, Anthony embarks on a series of adventures that bring him into contact with the slave trade, Napoleon, and finally exploration of the New World. He never gives up hope of finding his true identity.
Reviews: *WS* 10
Reading Level: High School [Mature Reader]

Europe—Enlightenment and Liberty

Subject Areas: Italy; France; Spain; America; orphans; adventure and adventurers
Time Period: 1775-1850 ❏ Library owns

Bourliaguet, Léonce; translated by John Buchanan-Brown. *The Guns of Valmy.* **London: Abelard-Schulman, 1969. 159pp. LC 69-10300.**
Germany, France, 1792. Thirty years after the event, Moses Koppman, Goethe's secretary, recounts the events of the Battle of Valmy when French forces fought German forces.
Reviews: *BL* 9/1/69; *LJ* 7/69
Reading Level: Middle–High School
Subject Areas: France; Germany; Valmy, Battle of, 1792
Time Period: 1792 ❏ Library owns

Burton, Hester; illustrated by Victor G. Ambrus. *The Rebel.* **New York: Crowell, 1972. 153pp. ISBN 0-690-69010-X. LC 71-181529.**
England, France, 1789. During his second trip to France during the French Revolution, Stephen, a student at Oxford, is arrested and imprisoned as an enemy of the Commune. He is freed, but the horror of the experience leaves him forever changed. Slowly he recovers and becomes a teacher to children living in poverty.
Reviews: *BCCB* 9/72; *BL* 9/15/72; *HB* 10/72; *SLJ* 10/72
Reading Level: Middle–High School
Subject Areas: Great Britain--1714-1837; France--1789; revolutions
Time Period: 1789 ❏ Library owns

Burton, Hester. *Riders of the Storm.* **New York: Crowell, 1973. 200pp. ISBN 0-690-70074-1. LC 73-4404.**
England, eighteenth century. Sequel to *The Rebel*. Stephen Parkin, teaching in a slum school in Manchester, becomes involved in a radical group of social reformers and is charged with treason.
Reviews: *BL* 11/1/73; *WJ* 4
Reading Level: Middle–High School
Subject Areas: Great Britain--1714-1837; teachers; reformers
Time Period: Eighteenth Century ❏ Library owns

Burton, Hester. *To Ravensrigg.* **New York: Crowell, 1977. 143pp. ISBN 0-690-01354-X. LC 76-54292.**
England, 1789. After a shipwreck kills the man she thought was her father and leaves her stranded, Emmie is taken in by a Quaker family. She discovers a clue to her true identity and travels to Ravensrigg where she learns the shocking truth.
Reviews: *BCCB* 9/77; *BL* 6/15/77; *HB* 10/77; *SLJ* 9/77★
Reading Level: Middle–High School

Subject Areas: Great Britain 1714-1837; slave trade; abolitionists; Society of Friends
Time Period: 1780 ❑ **Library owns**

Calvert, Patricia. *Hadder Maccoll.* **New York: Scribners, 1985. 134pp. ISBN 0-684-18447-8. LC 40292.**
Scotland, 1745. Hadder's family has been torn by their divided loyalties in the Jacobite Rebellion; Hadder and her father are true to Scotland, but her older brother is not. The Battle of Culloden brings tragedy and new hardships for Culloden.
Reviews: *BCCB* 11/85; *SLJ* 10/85
Reading Level: Middle–High School
Subject Areas: Scotland; Great Britain--1714-1837; Jacobite Rebellion
Time Period: 1745 ❑ **Library owns**

Cordell, Alexander. *The Healing Blade.* **New York: Viking, 1971. 156pp.**
Ireland, 1798. Sequel to *Witches' Sabbath*. John Regan is sent to France to protect Wolfe Tone, an Irish rebel leader who is helping to plan an invasion by French forces. Unfortunately, Tone is captured and sentenced to death. John smuggles a knife to him which Wolfe uses to thwart the British one last time.
Reviews: *BL* 6/1/71; *LJ* 6/15/71
Reading Level: Middle & Junior High School
Subject Areas: Ireland; France--1798; revolutions
Time Period: 1798 ❑ **Library owns**

Cordell, Alexander. *Witches' Sabbath.* **New York: Viking, 1970. 157pp. LC 75-123023.**
Ireland, 1798. Sequel to *The White Cockade*. Caught up in the Irish rebellion of 1798, John Regan, a messenger for the rebel forces, experiences the exciting, but bloody, events of the times and comes in contact with prominent historical figures.
Reviews: *BCCB* 7/71; *BL* 1/1/71
Reading Level: Middle & Junior High School
Subject Areas: Ireland; revolutions
Time Period: 1798 ❑ **Library owns**

Cornwell, Bernard. *Sharpe's Enemy: Richard Sharpe and the Defense of Portugal, Christmas, 1812.* **New York: Viking, 1984. 351pp. ISBN 0-670-63940-0. LC 83-47925.**
Spain, 1812. During the Napoleonic Wars, British Capt. Richard Sharpe must capture a Spanish village with only his small troop of men. First he must rout a group of army deserters who have captured the shrine. With that task accom-

Europe—Enlightenment and Liberty

plished, Sharpe finds he must plan the battle campaign by himself, a battle that proves to be gruesome and deadly.
Reviews: *BL* 1/1/84; *LJ* 4/1/84
Reading Level: High School
Subject Areas: Spain; Europe--1798-1900; soldiers
Time Period: 1812 ❑ Library owns

Cornwell, Bernard. *Sharpe's Regiment: Richard Sharpe and the Invasion of France, June to November, 1813.* **New York: Viking, 1986. 301pp. ISBN 0-670-81148-3. LC 85-29541.**
Spain, 1813. Sequel to *Sharpe's Honour*. Shocked that his second battalion is to be disbanded just before they enter France to fight Napoleon's army, Sharpe and his sergeant return to England to uncover treachery in the War Dept. and to try to prevent someone from killing them to assure their silence.
Reviews: *BBSH*; *BL* 7/86; *BFY*; *BR* 1-2/87
Reading Level: High School
Subject Areas: Great Britain--1714-1837; soldiers
Time Period: 1813 ❑ Library owns

Cornwell, Bernard. *Sharpe's Siege: Richard Sharpe and the Winter Campaign: 1814.* **New York: Viking, 1987. 316pp. ISBN 0-670-80866-0. LC 86-45850.**
France, 1814. Major Richard Sharpe, stranded behind enemy lines with 200 riflemen, must face a French force of 2,000 soldiers.
Reviews: *BBSH*; *BL* 4/1/87; *BFY*; *PW* 3/20/87
Reading Level: High School
Subject Areas: France; soldiers
Time Period: 1814 ❑ Library owns

Costain, Thomas B. *The Last Love.* **New York: Doubleday, 1963. 434pp.**
France, 1815-1821. A look at the last years of Napoleon's life on St. Helena where he is the guest of the Balcombes, whose 15-year-old Betsy is infatuated with him.
Reviews: *WS* 10
Reading Level: High School
Subject Areas: Napoléon I, Emperor of the French; Balcombe, Betsy
Time Period: 1815-1821 ❑ Library owns

Cross, Gilbert B. *A Hanging at Tyburn.* **New York: Atheneum, 1983. 233pp. ISBN 0-689-31007-2. LC 83-6331.**
England, mid-eighteenth century. Orphaned 14-year-old George Found is fortunate to be part of the Duke of Bridgewater's plan to construct a canal to Manchester. George is falsely accused of a crime by an enemy of the Duke and narrowly escapes the gallows.
Reviews: *BCCB* 11/83; *BL* 10/1/83; *HB* 4/84; *SLJ* 12/83
Reading Level: Middle–High School
Subject Areas: Great Britain--1714-1837; canals; orphans
Time Period: 1750s ❏ Library owns

Delderfield, Ronald Frederick. *Too Few for Drums.* **New York: Simon & Schuster, 1971. 253pp. ISBN 0-671-65195-1.**
Spain, 1800-1815. Confronted with getting his eight men back to the British forces on the other side of the Tagus River, Ensign Graham is aided by a camp follower who knows the terrain and gives him the confidence to become a competent leader.
Reviews: *BL* 1/1/72; *LJ* 2/15/72
Reading Level: High School
Subject Areas: Spain; soldiers
Time Period: Napoleonic Wars, 1800-1815 ❏ Library owns

Dickens, Charles. *Barnaby Rudge.* **Lanham, MD: Evman/Biblio Distribution Ctr., 1966. ISBN 0-460-00076-4.**
England, 1780. Dickens' story is based on the facts surrounding the events of lawlessness of the anti-Catholic Gordon Riots of 1780, in which Lord George Gordon, an actor and leader of the Protestant Association, played a pivotal role. First published in 1841.
Reviews: *WS* 10, 12, 12
Reading Level: High School
Subject Areas: Great Britain--1714-1837; Gordon Riots, 1780
Time Period: 1780 ❏ Library owns

Dickens, Charles. *A Tale of Two Cities.* **Cutchogue, NY: Buccanneer Books, 1982. ISBN 0-89966-371-0.**
England, France, 1789. Two men, Charles Darnay and Sydney Carlton, are both in love with Lucie Manette. When Darnay is arrested in Paris during the French Revolution, Carlton takes his place at the guillotine so that Lucie will have the man she loves. First published in 1859.
Reviews: *WJ* 4, 5; *WS* 10, 11, 12, 13, 14
Reading Level: Middle–High School

Subject Areas: France--1789; Revolutions; love
Time Period: French Revolution, 1789-1799 ❏ Library owns

Du Maurier, Daphne. *The Glass-Blowers.* **New York: Doubleday, 1963. 348pp.**
France, 1745-1845. The lives of the members of the Busson family, the father and five sons and daughters, are each changed in different ways by the events of the French Revolution and the ensuing civil war.
Reviews: WS 10
Reading Level: High School
Subject Areas: France--1789; revolutions; family life
Time Period: 1745-1845 ❏ Library owns

Forester, C. S.; illustrated by N. C. Wyeth. *Captain Horatio Hornblower.* **Boston: Little, Brown, 1939. 662pp. ISBN 0-316-28893-4.**
Pacific and Atlantic Oceans, 1800-1815. A trilogy consisting of *Beat to Quarters, Ship of the Line,* and *Flying Colours.* Hornblower, captain of the Lydia during the Napoleonic Wars, is involved in battles with the Spanish and French. Hornblower is the epitome of the British hero, brave, intelligent, and handsome.
Reviews: *WS* 10, 11, 12, 13
Reading Level: Middle–High School
Subject Areas: Great Britain--1714-1837; sea stories; adventure and adventurers; Great Britain. Navy
Time Period: Napoleonic Wars, 1800-1815 ❏ Library owns

Forester, C. S. *The Horation Hornblower Series.* **Boston: Little, Brown.**
The other titles in this series are: *Mr. Midshipman Hornblower* (ISBN 0-316-28909-4); *Lieutenant Hornblower* (ISBN 0-316-28907-8); *Hornblower and the Hotspur* (ISBN 0-316-28899-3); *Hornblower and the Atropos* (ISBN 0-316-28911-6); *Commodore Hornblower* (ISBN 0-316-28894-4); *Lord Hornblower* (ISBN 0-316-28908-6); *Admiral Hornblower in the West Indies* (ISBN 0-316-28901-9); *Hornblower During the Crisis* (ISBN 0-316-28915-9).
Reviews: *BBSH*; *WJ* 5
Reading Level: Middle–High School
Subject Areas: Great Britain--1714-1837; sea stories; adventure and adventurers; Great Britain. Navy.
Time Period: 1790-1830 ❏ Library owns

Forman, James D. *Prince Charlie's Year.* **New York: Scribners, 1991. 136pp. ISBN 0-684-19242-X. LC 90-26898.**
Scotland, 1745. In North Carolina in 1780, Scotsman Colin MacDonald recounts his experiences in the Jacobite Rebellion in 1745. He joined Bonnie Prince

Charlie's forces as a 14-year-old boy. When the rebellion fails, Colin is imprisoned and sent to the colonies as an indentured servant.
Reviews: *BCCB* 1/92; *BL* 12/1/91; *BR* 3/92; *SLJ* 2/92; *VOYA* 4/92
Reading Level: Middle–High School
Subject Areas: Scotland; Great Britain--1714-1837; Jacobite Rebellion, 1745
Time Period: 1745   ❑ Library owns

Garfield, Leon. *The Apprentices.* **New York: Viking, 1978. 315pp. ISBN 0-670-12978-X. LC 77-21770.**
England, eighteenth century. The lives of London apprentices in the eighteenth century are explored through twelve stories linked by recurring characters. Students may stumble over the strong British vernacular, but the different occupations of the time, midwives, apothecaries, and the like, as well as appealing characters, may help to carry them.
Reviews: *BL* 7/15/78; *WJ* 4
Reading Level: Middle–High School
Subject Areas: Great Britain 1714-1837; London (England); apprentices; short stories
Time Period: Eighteenth Century   ❑ Library owns

Garfield, Leon. *The Drummer Boy.* **New York: Pantheon, 1970. 185pp. LC 69-13455.**
France, England, eighteenth century. Charlie Samson, a drummer boy, is idealistic before his first battle in the wars with France. But after seeing senseless death, the cowardliness of survivors, and the ruthlessness of those in power, he is in deep despair until two people who truly love him help him recover.
Reviews: *BL* 7/15/70; *HB* 8/70; *LJ* 7/70
Reading Level: Middle–High School
Subject Areas: Great Britain--1714-1837
Time Period: Eighteenth Century   ❑ Library owns

Garfield, Leon. *The Empty Sleeve.* **New York: Delacorte, 1988. 205pp. ISBN 0-440-50049-4. LC 87-37580.**
England, eighteenth century. This suspenseful and action-packed story of ghosts and supernatural happenings revolves around Peter and Paul, twins born at the stroke of noon, which one man present prophesies will make one see ghosts. Sly Peter and saintly Paul grow up together until Peter is apprenticed to a locksmith. There he finds a way to steal enough money so he can go to sea, earning him that prophesied meeting with a ghost.
Reviews: *BCCB* 10/88; *BL* 9/15/88★; *BR* 11-12/88; *SLJ* 10/88
Reading Level: Middle–High School

Europe—Enlightenment and Liberty

Subject Areas: Great Britain--1714-1837; ghosts; twins; brothers; apprentices
Time Period: Eighteenth Century ❏ Library owns

Garfield, Leon; illustrated by Antony Maitland. *Smith.* **New York: Peter Smith, 1991, c1967. 218pp. ISBN 0-8446-6455-3. LC 67-20223.**
England, eighteenth century. Twelve-year-old Smith, a talented but illiterate pickpocket, steals a document just seconds before the owner is murdered by men looking for the paper. He hides it hoping it will bring him wealth, but it draws him into trouble and Newgate Prison.
Reviews: *BFY*; *HB* 12/67; *LJ* 11/15/67
Reading Level: Middle–High School
Subject Areas: Great Britain--1714-1837; London (England); pickpockets
Time Period: Eighteenth Century ❏ Library owns

Garfield, Leon; illustrated by John Lawrence. *The Sound of Coaches.* **New York: Viking, 1974. 256pp. ISBN 0-670-65834-0. LC 73-20931.**
England, eighteenth century. Sam Chichester has been raised by a coachman and his wife whose only connection to him is that they were driving the coach in which his mother traveled the night she died. He is tossed out after he carelessly wrecks that same coach. Sixteen-year-old Sam sets off for London where he joins a band of traveling players, one of whom turns out to be his biological father.
Reviews: *BL* 4/1/74★; *HB* 10/74; *LJ* 5/15/74
Reading Level: High School
Subject Areas: Great Britain--1714-1837; actors
Time Period: Eighteenth Century ❏ Library owns

Hall, Aylmer. *Beware of Moonlight.* **Nashville, TN: Nelson, 1970. 224pp. LC 70-119357.**
Ireland, 1765. Fifteen-year-old Larry has been raised by the housekeeper of his late uncle, a wealthy landlord, after his mother's death and his father's banishment. When his cousin, Lord Corcalee, arrives for a visit and cruelly evicts several of the poor tenants on his land, Larry's loyalties are torn between the family that has provided for him and the poor farmers with whom he identifies. He becomes involved with the "Whiteboys" and Captain Moonlight.
Reviews: *BL* 2/15/71; *HB* 2/71; *LJ* 1/15/71
Reading Level: Middle & Junior High School
Subject Areas: Ireland; Great Britain--1714-1837; poverty
Time Period: 1765 ❏ Library owns

Heaven, Constance. *The Wind from the Sea.* **New York: St. Martin's Press, 1993. 503pp. ISBN 0-312-08921-X. LC 92-37731.**

England, France, 1789. Isabelle and her brother seek refuge from the French Revolution at the home of their English uncle. Treated more like servants than family, Isabelle nonetheless manages to find romance and become involved in intrigue and a dangerous adventure.

Reviews: *LJ* 2/15/93; *SLJ* 6/93

Reading Level: High School

Subject Areas: Great Britain--1714-1837; France--1789-1799

Time Period: French Revolution, 1789-1799   ❏ Library owns

Holt, Victoria. *The Devil on Horseback.* **New York: Doubleday, 1977. 358pp. ISBN 0-385-13209-3. LC 77-72414.**

England, France, 1788-89. A young British schoolmistress is swept off her feet by a French count. She is caught up in the terrible events at the beginning of the French Revolution.

Reviews: *WS* 11

Reading Level: High School

Subject Areas: Great Britain--1714-1837; France--1789; teachers

Time Period: 1788-1789   ❏ Library owns

Holt, Victoria. *The Queen's Confession.* **New York: Doubleday, 1968. 430pp.**

France, 1755-1793. Written in the form of a memoir, this relates the life of Marie Antoinette. She is a spoiled Austrian Archduchess who becomes the misunderstood consort of Louis XVI.

Reviews: *WS* 10

Reading Level: High School

Subject Areas: France; Marie Antoinette, consort of Louis XVI

Time Period: 1755-1793   ❏ Library owns

Hunter, Mollie. *The Lothian Run.* **New York: Funk & Wagnalls, 1970. 212pp. LC 70-100653.**

Scotland, 1736. Welcoming the change, Sandy Maxwell, a bored lawyer's clerk, is asked to help the Customs Service track down a smuggler. Chosen because he knows the fishermen and the coastal area, Sandy not only finds the smugglers but uncovers a Jacobite plot to overthrow the government, both of which prove dangerous for Sandy.

Reviews: *BL* 5/15/70; *HB* 6/70; *LJ* 5/15/70

Reading Level: Middle–High School

Subject Areas: Scotland; Great Britain--1714-1837; smugglers; Jacobite Rebellion, 1745

Time Period: 1736 ❏ Library owns

Kent, Alexander. *Colors Aloft!* **New York: Putnam, 1986. 286pp. ISBN 0-399-12988-X. LC 86-3193.**

England, Mediterranean, 1800-1815. Promoted to admiral, Richard Bolitho takes a new squadron of ships to the Mediterranean to fight the French during the Napoleonic Wars. Not only is the French admiral a formidable enemy, Bolitho must also battle a jealous colleague.

Reviews: *BBSH*; *BL* 7/86

Reading Level: High School

Subject Areas: Great Britain--1714-1837; Great Britain. Navy; adventures and adventurers; sea stories

Time Period: Napoleonic War, 1800-1815 ❏ Library owns

Kent, Alexander. *Enemy in Sight!* **New York: Putnam, 1970. 350pp. LC 71-105584.**

England, Atlantic Ocean, 1794-1799. Captain Richard Bolitho, captain of the Hyperion, must engage the French off the coast of Spain. Not only does Bolitho have his own ship to worry about, he is forced to assume command of the English fleet when the squadron commander is unfit to continue his command. He must also deal with a difficult personal loss.

Reviews: *BBSH*; *BL* 7/15/70; *LJ* 10/15/70; *PW* 3/16/70

Reading Level: High School

Subject Areas: Great Britain--1714-1837; Great Britain. Navy; sea stories; adventures and adventurers

Time Period: 1794-1799 ❏ Library owns

Kent, Alexander. *Form Line of Battle!* **New York: Putnam, 1969. 320pp. LC 69-18182.**

England, 1793. Captain Bolitho, of the Royal Navy, sails from Gibraltar aboard the Hyperion, a 74-gun ship of the line, to join Lord Hood, who is leading British naval operations against the French revolutionary forces at Toulon. A victory over the French and his wedding to Cheney Seton, climax this adventure tale.

Reviews: *BL* 9/1/69; *LJ* 7/69

Reading Level: High School

Subject Areas: Great Britain--1714-1837; Great Britain. Navy; sea stories; adventure and adventurers

Time Period: 1793 ❏ Library owns

Kent, Alexander. *Stand Into Danger.* **New York: Putnam, 1981. 296pp. ISBN 0-399-12539-6. LC 80-23766.**
England, 1774. This entry into the Bolitho series, finds Richard Bolitho, newly promoted to third lieutenant aboard the frigate Destiny, involved in intrigue on a secret mission that takes him from Rio de Janeiro to the Spanish Main to the Indies in search of Spanish bullion.
Reviews: *BL* 3/15/81; *LJ* 2/1/81
Reading Level: High School
Subject Areas: Great Britain--1714-1837; Great Britain. Navy; sea stories; adventure and adventurers; voyages and travels
Time Period: 1774   ❏ **Library owns**

Kent, Alexander. *Success to the Brave.* **New York: Putnam, 1983. 284pp. ISBN 0-399-12878-6. LC 83-11238.**
Atlantic Ocean, 1802. Now a vice admiral and expecting his first child, Bolitho is ordered into American waters to give the island of San Felipe back to France as per the Peace Treaty of Amiens. He runs into hostility from the American government, his flagship is mysteriously fired upon, and he finds the San Felipe harbor blockaded, all events that challenge his ingenuity as a leader.
Reviews: *BL* 12/15/83; *SLJ* 3/84; *BBSH*
Reading Level: High School
Subject Areas: Great Britain--1714-1837; Great Britain. Navy; sea stories; adventure and adventurers
Time Period: 1802   ❏ **Library owns**

Laker, Rosalind. *The Silver Touch.* **New York: Doubleday, 1987. 356pp. ISBN 0-385-23745-6. LC 86-24199.**
England, eighteenth century. Hester Needham is seen from her orphaned childhood spent with her London tavern-keeper brother and his wife, to her meeting with the apprentice goldsmith she marries. Hester raises six children, all of whom become involved in the family business, and becomes one of the finest silversmiths in London.
Reviews: *BL* 8/87; *LJ* 7/87
Reading Level: High School
Subject Areas: Great Britain--1714-1837; silversmiths; family life; London (England)
Time Period: Eighteenth Century   ❏ **Library owns**

Lofts, Norah. *The Lost Queen.* **New York: Doubleday, 1969. 302pp.**
Denmark, 1762-1780. Married off to Christian, Crown Prince of Denmark, Caroline Matilda, sister of George III of England, finds that her sadistic, syphilitic husband is mentally ill. George III must send a warship to rescue her after she is

falsely imprisoned for adultery and her children are taken away from her. This book also examines many of the social injustices of the times at all social levels.
Reviews: *WS* 10
Reading Level: High School
Subject Areas: Denmark; Caroline Mathilde, consort of Christian VII; Christian VII, King of Denmark
Time Period: 1762-1780 ❏ Library owns

Lofts, Norah. *A Rose for Virtue: The Very Private Life of Hortense, Stepdaughter of Napoleon I, Mother of Napoleon* **III. New York: Doubleday, 1971. 348pp.**
France, 1783-1840. Beginning with her mother's marriage to Napoleon I, this is the story of Hortense who is devoted to her step-father and unhappily married to his brother. With Napoleon's defeat at Waterloo, Hortense's life changes as her son, Napoleon III, begins his rise to power.
Reviews: *WS* 10
Reading Level: High School
Subject Areas: France; Hortense, consort of Louis, King of Holland
Time Period: 1783-1840 ❏ Library owns

Monjo, F. N.; illustrated by Don Bolognese & Elaine Raphael. *Letters to Horseface, Being the Story of Wolfgang Amadeus Mozart's Journey to Italy, 1769-1770, When He Was a Boy of Fourteen.* **New York: Viking, 1975. 91pp. ISBN 0-670-42738-1. LC 74-23766.**
Italy, 1769-1770. In a series of letters to his sister, 14-year-old Mozart details his trip with his father to Italy. He describes not only his own concerts and accomplishments (including the first performance of his first opera) but also includes details about daily life in Italy.
Reviews: *BCCB* 4/76; *BL* 1/15/76★; *HB* 2/76; *NCB*; *SLJ* 12/75
Reading Level: Middle & Junior High School
Subject Areas: Italy; Mozart, Wolfgang Amadeus; music
Time Period: 1769-1770 ❏ Library owns

Orczy, Baroness. *The Scarlet Pimpernel.* **Cutchogue, NY: Buccaneer Books, 1983. 321pp. ISBN 0-8996-459-8.**
France, 1792. An Englishman, in disguise as the Scarlet Pimpernel, risks all to save aristocratic families during the French Revolution. Originally published in 1905.
Reviews: *BBSH*; *BFY*; *FFY*; *WS* 13, 14
Reading Level: High School

Subject Areas: France--1789-1799; adventure and adventurers
Time Period: 1792   ❏ **Library owns**

Parkinson, Cyril Northcote. *Devil to Pay.* **Boston: Houghton, 1973. 273pp. ISBN 0-395-15483-9. LC 72-6731.**
England, 1794. Richard Delancey wins his way back into the graces of the Royal Navy, fallen from favor after testifying against his commanding officer, by commanding a revenue cutter which leads to his captaincy of a British privateer. This gives him an opportunity to prove that Spain has agreed to help France in the war against England.
Reviews: *BL* 7/1/73; *LJ* 3/1/73
Reading Level: High School
Subject Areas: Great Britain--1714-1837; Great Britain. Navy; sea stories; adventure and adventurers
Time Period: 1794   ❏ **Library owns**

Parkinson, Cyril Northcote. *Touch and Go.* **Boston: Houghton, 1977. 230pp. ISBN 0-395-25592-9. LC 77-7665.**
England, 1794-1799. In this adventure, Delancey is in charge of a British sloop, assigned to the Mediterranean trade route, protecting merchant convoys from the French.
Reviews: *BL* 9/15/77; *LJ* 11/15/77
Reading Level: High School
Subject Areas: Great Britain--1714-1837; Great Britain. Navy; sea stories; adventure and adventurers
Time Period: 1794-1799   ❏ **Library owns**

Paul, Barbara. *The Frenchwoman.* **New York: St. Martin's, 1977. 278pp. ISBN 0-312-30537-0. LC 76-62787.**
England, France, 1799-1815. After the death of her French father, Juliette is sent to her mother's home in England, where she is to marry a stranger. There she discovers that someone is trying to kill her and that perhaps she is in love with the wrong man. Conspiracies and plots involving the French Revolution and her family's past all contribute to the intrigue.
Reviews: *BL* 4/1/84; *SLJ* 4/78
Reading Level: High School
Subject Areas: Great Britain--1714-1837; mystery and detective stories
Time Period: 1799-1815   ❏ **Library owns**

Europe—Enlightenment and Liberty

Peyton, K.M. *The Right-Hand Man.* **New York: Oxford, 1979, c1977. 217pp. ISBN 0-19-271391-4. LC 81-113589.**

England, eighteenth–nineteenth century. The adventure tale of coachman Ned Rowlands and Lord Ironminster, involves their passion for horses and racing, as the two join forces to thwart Lord Ironmaster's evil cousins. In this story that reveals the polar yet parallel worlds of the rich and poor, Ned becomes the means by which Lord Ironminster can still achieve his dreams.

Reviews: *BBYA*; *BL* 10/1/79; *SLJ* 1/80★; *WJ* 4; *WS* 11
Reading Level: Middle–High School
Subject Areas: Great Britain--1714-1837; horse racing
Time Period: 1714-1837 ❑ Library owns

Plaidy, Jean. *Queen in Waiting.* **New York: Putnam, 1985. 399pp. ISBN 0-399-13101-9.**

England, 1714-27. Set during the reign of George I, George's son and daughter-in-law plot to increase their power and access to the throne, most notably through court intrigues.

Reviews: *BBSH*; *BL* 10/1/85
Reading Level: High School
Subject Areas: Great Britain--1714-1837; George I, King of England
Time Period: 1714-1727 ❑ Library owns

Sabatini, Rafael. *Scaramouche, The King-Maker.* **New Orleans, LA: River City Press, reprint 1931. ISBN 0-89190-744-0.**

France, 1789. André-Louis Moreau, in order to avenge the death of his revolutionary friend uses his own natural eloquence to further the cause of the French Revolution.

Reviews: *WS* 10
Reading Level: High School
Subject Areas: France--1789-1799
Time Period: French Revolution, 1789-1799 ❑ Library owns

Selinko, Annemarie. *Désirée.* **New York: Morrow, 1953. 594pp. ISBN 0-688-01448-8. LC 52-9706.**

France, 1760s-1840s. With her life tied to Napoleon I in many ways, this is the story of Désirée who was once engaged to Napoleon, only to have that engagement broken to free Napoleon for Josephine. Désirée married French General Jean Baptiste Bernadotte, who was elected to the throne of Sweden in 1810, only to then defy Napoleon.

Reviews: *WS* 10
Reading Level: High School

Subject Areas: France--1799-1815; Sweden; Desideria, consort of Charles XIV John, King of Sweden and Norway; Charles XIV John, King of Sweden and Norway

Time Period: 1760-1840 ❏ Library owns

Seton, Anya. *Devil Water.* **Boston: Houghton, 1962. 526pp. LC 62-7256.**

England, eighteenth century. Set in Northumberland, London and Virginia, this tale follows Charles Radcliffe and his family, as they are torn apart by two Jacobite rebellions that heighten their differing beliefs and loyalties. Charles, a Newgate Prison escapee, also manages to maintain a strong relationship alive with Jenny, his daughter from a secret marriage. This contains many descriptions of daily life and customs.

Reviews: *WS* 10

Reading Level: High School

Subject Areas: Great Britain--1714-1837; Virginia; Radcliffe, Charles; Jacobite Rebellions

Time Period: 1714-1750 ❏ Library owns

Sherwood, Frances. *Vindication.* **New York: Farrar, 1993. 405pp. ISBN 0-374-28390-7. LC 92-41934.**

England, 1759-1797. This is a fictionalized biography of the fascinating and difficult life of the feminist, Mary Wollstonecraft. To escape an abusive home, she becomes a seamstress and a governess, at the same time developing as the intellectual equal of many of the philosophers of her day. Despite having written a major work on the equality of women, she seems less successful and often unhappy with the men she chooses to love. She finally marries William Godwin, but dies giving birth to Mary, who will one day marry Percy Shelley.

Reviews: *BL* 5/15/93; *LJ* 3/15/93; *PW* 3/1/93

Reading Level: High School [Mature Reader]

Subject Areas: Great Britain--1714-1837; Wollstonecraft, Mary; feminists; Godwin, William

Time Period: 1759-1797 ❏ Library owns

Stendhal; translated by C. K. Scott-Moncrieff. *The Charterhouse of Parma.* **New York: Liveright, 1953. 2v in 1p. ISBN 0-87140-835-X.**

Italy, 1789-1820. Set during and just after the Napoleonic era, Fabrizio del Dongo fights in the battle of Waterloo, gets entangled in court intrigues, pursues love, and experiences imprisonment, finally finding peace in the priesthood and a monastery. Originally published in 1839.

Reviews: *WS* 11

Reading Level: High School

Europe—Enlightenment and Liberty

Subject Areas: Italy
Time Period: 1789-1820 ❏ Library owns

Stendhal; translated by C. K. Scott-Moncrief. *The Red and the Black.* **Cutchogue, NY: Buccaneer Books, 1987. 532pp.ISBN 0-89966-619-1.**
France, 1799-1815. In this psychological novel, Julien Sorel, a handsome but ruthless man, uses his love affairs to further his station in life. He tries to murder his first mistress when she betrays him. The novel includes an historical examination of Napoleon's military class (the red) and the French clergy (the black). Originally published in 1830.
Reviews: *WS* 10, 11, 12, 13, 14
Reading Level: High School
Subject Areas: France--1799-1815
Time Period: 1799-1815 ❏ Library owns

Stevenson, Robert Louis. *The Master of Ballantrae.* **Mattituck, NY: Amereon, 1987. 273pp. ISBN 0-89190-738-6.**
Scotland, 1745. The Drurie family is divided as two brothers claim opposite loyalties in the Jacobite Rebellion and are consumed with hatred for each other. Originally published in 1888.
Reviews: *BFY*
Reading Level: High School
Subject Areas: Scotland; Great Britain--1714-1837; brothers; Jacobite Rebellion, 1745
Time Period: 1745 ❏ Library owns

Sutcliff, Rosemary. *Flame-Colored Taffeta.* **New York: Farrar, 1986. 130pp. ISBN 0-374-32344-5. LC 86-18351.**
England, mid-eighteenth century. Set in Sussex where smuggling is the norm during the waning days of the Jacobite rebellion, Damaris, a farmer's daughter, and her friend Peter rescue a young man they believe to be a smuggler, with the help of the village healing woman.
Reviews: *BCCB* 12/86; *BL* 11/15/86★; *CED*; *HB* 3-4/87; *SLJ* 2/87; *VOYA* 2/87; *WJ* 6
Reading Level: Middle–High School
Subject Areas: Great Britain--1714-1837; smuggling; adventure and adventurers; Jacobite Rebellion, 1745
Time Period: 1745 ❏ Library owns

Suyin, Han. *The Enchantress.* New York: Bantam, 1985. 352pp. ISBN 0-553-05071-0. LC 84-41585.

Switzerland, Orient, eighteenth century. Telepathic twins Colin and Bea each have a talent. Bea can predict the future, and Colin is gifted at clockmaking and creating androids. When Colin travels to China to make clocks for the emperor, Bea accompanies him, but events arise that require them flee to Thailand for safety. Colin has a tragic love affair and Bea's powers are unable to help her in a court intrigue.

Reviews: *BL* 11/1/84; *LJ* 3/15/85; *SLJ* 5/85
Reading Level: High School
Subject Areas: Switzerland; China; Thailand; twins; adventure and adventurers
Time Period: Eighteenth Century ❏ Library owns

Tolstoy, Leo. *War and Peace.* New York: Penguin, 1982. ISBN 0-14-044417-3.
Russia, 1799-1820. This epic novel with a multitude of characters from all walks of life, both French and Russian, gives a vast picture of the invasion of Russia by Napoleon's army.
"Interwoven with the story of the war are narrations of the lives of several main characters, especially those of Natasha Rostova, Prince Andrey Bolkonsky, and Pierre Bezukhov. These people are shown as they progress from youthful uncertainties and searchings toward a more mature understanding of life." *Wilson's Senior High School Catalog* 14

Reviews: *WS* 10, 11, 12, 13, 14
Reading Level: High School [Mature Reader]
Subject Areas: Russia--1799-1820; Napoleon I, Emperor of the French
Time Period: 1799-1820 ❏ Library owns

Wilson, Robert Anton. *The Earth Will Shake.* Boston: Houghton, 1982. 369pp. ISBN 0-87477-211-7. LC 82-10490.

Italy, eighteenth century. Fourteen-year-old Sigismundo Celine, confused by the violent events of his time, comes of age in Naples where the Inquisition is still strong and Freemasonry is widespread, at a time when revolutionary ideas are being discussed all over Europe. During the story, Sigismundo begins his passage into adulthood with both physical and philosophical awakenings.

Reviews: *LJ* 12/15/82; *SLJ* 5/83
Reading Level: High School [Mature Reader]
Subject Areas: Italy; Freemasonry; adolescence
Time Period: Eighteenth Century ❏ Library owns

Nineteenth Century

Aiken, Joan. *Bridle the Wind.* **New York: Delacorte, 1983. 242pp. ISBN 0-395-29301-1. LC 83-5355.**

Spain, France, 1820s. Sequel to *Go Saddle the Sea*. Shipwrecked on the French coast while traveling to Spain, 13-year-old Felix is rescued and taken to a monastery where he meets Juan (really Juana). Threatened by the abbot, who seems to be possessed, Felix and Juan escape and make their way back to Spain, having many adventures along the way, with the abbot in pursuit.

Reviews: *BCCB* 11/83; *BL* 11/1/83; *BR* 5-6/84; *HB* 12/83; *SLJ* 1/84; *VOYA* 12/83; *WJ* 5

Reading Level: Middle–High School

Subject Areas: France--1800-1899; Spain; friendship; adventure and adventurers

Time Period: 1820s ❑ **Library owns**

Aiken, Joan. *Go Saddle the Sea.* **New York: Doubleday, 1977. 312pp. ISBN 0-385-13225-5. LC 77-76958.**

Spain, England, 1821. Twelve-year-old Felix, orphaned and ill-treated in his Spanish grandfather's house, leaves home, determined to get to England and his father's family. After an arduous journey in which he finds a true friend, Sam, and spiced with adventures involving assassins and kidnappers, he reaches England. He finds the answers to his questions, and after a taste of English schooling, decides to return to Spain.

Reviews: *BL* 12/1/77; *HB* 4/78; *SLJ* 2/78

Reading Level: Middle & Junior High School

Subject Areas: Spain; Great Britain--1800-1899; friendship; adventure and adventurers

Time Period: 1821 ❑ **Library owns**

Aiken, Joan. *The Teeth of the Gale.* **New York: Harper, 1988. 307pp. ISBN 0-06-020045-6. LC 87-35050.**

Spain, 1827. Sequel to *Bridle the Wind*. Summoned home from the university by his grandfather, 18-year-old Felix is asked to help a woman whose children have been kidnapped by their escaped convict father. Felix agrees, unaware of the dangers and political intrigues, and travels with Juana, now a novice nun, and Doña Conchita, the children's petulant mother. After a series of escapes, the children are found and the villain unmasked.

Reviews: *BCCB* 11/88; *BL* 9/15/88; *BR* 5-6/89; *HB* 11-12/88; *SLJ* 11/88; *WJ* 6

Reading Level: Middle–High School

Subject Areas: Spain; kidnapping; adventure and adventurers
Time Period: 1827 ❏ Library owns

Banks, Lynne Reid. *Dark Quartet: The Story of the Brontës.* **New York: Delacorte Press, 1977. 432pp. ISBN 0-440-01657-6. LC 76-29727.**
England, 1821-1849. This very creative, but short-lived, period in the lives of Charlotte, Emily, Branwell and Anne Brontë, leads to novels, poems, and plays. "Banks' touching [fictionalized] biography reveals how a family pattern of failure and precarious physical and emotional health was converted into success." *Wilson's Senior High School Catalog* 11
Reviews: *FFY*; *SLJ* 9/77; *WS* 11, 12
Reading Level: High School
Subject Areas: Great Britain--1800-1899; Brontë family; authors; family life
Time Period: 1816-1850 ❏ Library owns

Black, Laura. *Albany.* **New York: St. Martin's, 1984. 244pp. ISBN 0-312-01708-1. LC 84-11729.**
Scotland, 1850s. At 17, Leonora Albany leaves the safety of her aunt's home to live at Glenalban Castle after she discovers that she is related to Prince Charles. As she waits for her inheritance, she also discovers that someone is trying to eliminate her to keep her from that inheritance.
Reviews: *BL* 11/15/84; *LJ* 11/15/84
Reading Level: High School
Subject Areas: Great Britain--1800-1899; mystery and detective stories
Time Period: 1850s ❏ Library owns

Branson, Karen; illustrated by Jane Sterrett. *The Potato Eaters.* **New York: Putnam, 1979. 160pp. ISBN 0-399-20678-7. LC 78-24330.**
Ireland, 1846. The O'Connor's, a typical Irish family, are hard hit by the potato famine. They barely manage to survive famine, disease, death, and injustice. Looking for a better life, Mr. O'Connor and his three remaining children go to America while Mrs. O'Connor stays with of consumption. The role of absentee English landlords is detailed.
Reviews: *BL* 9/1/79; *WJ* 4
Reading Level: Middle & Junior High School
Subject Areas: Ireland; Great Britain--1800-1899; famines; family life
Time Period: 1846 ❏ Library owns

Brindley, Louise. *In the Shadow of the Brontës.* **New York: St. Martin's, 1983. 272pp. ISBN 0-312-41167-7. LC 83-2928.**
England, 1830-40. Lizzie bears an amazing resemblance to Anne Brontë, so much so that she develops a psychic link to Anne and her sisters. Lizzie must also

deal with the death of someone she loves and battle against ruthlessness and destruction.
Reviews: *BL* 6/15/83; *LJ* 6/1/83
Reading Level: High School
Subject Areas: Great Britain--1800-1899; extrasensory perception; Brontë family
Time Period: 1830-1840 ❏ **Library owns**

Bunting, Eve. *The Haunting of Kildoran Abbey.* **New York: Warne, 1978. 159pp. ISBN 0-7232-6152-0. LC 77-84601.**
Ireland, 1847. Finn and Columb, homeless, orphaned twins, join up with a small group of youths who are stealing food from the English landlords to feed the starving Irish people during the potato famine. Their leader is Christopher, who is staying with the hated Lord Blunt. Most of the band is captured during a raid, except Columb, who manages to find help to save his brother and friends from deportation to Australia.
Reviews: *BCCB* 10/78; *BL* 7/1/78; *SLJ* 9/78; *WJ* 4
Reading Level: Middle & Junior High School
Subject Areas: Ireland; Great Britain--1800-1899; famines; orphans
Time Period: 1847 ❏ **Library owns**

Carter, Peter. *The Black Lamp.* **Nashville, TN: Nelson, 1975. 174pp. ISBN 0-8407-6468-5. LC 75-19100.**
England, nineteenth century. Set during the Industrial Revolution in the cloth mills, this is the melancholy tale of Daniel Cregg, a young mill engineer, and his father who attempts to organize the weavers in protest to the change to mechanization. Mr. Cregg is injured at a bloody protest, Daniel goes into hiding, and the mill owner presses Daniel's sister into child labor.
Reviews: *BL* 1/1/76; *SLJ* 10/75
Reading Level: High School
Subject Areas: Great Britain--1800-1899; Industrial Revolution
Time Period: Nineteenth Century ❏ **Library owns**

Chukovsky, Kornei; translated by Beatrice Stillman. *The Silver Crest: My Russian Boyhood.* **New York: Holt, 1976. 182pp. ISBN 0-03-014241-5. LC 75-32248.**
Russia, 1893. The author recalls his Russian childhood, telling of his expulsion from school and his unsuccessful efforts to get back in so that he wouldn't distress his mother. When he realizes that he won't be going back to school, he tries his hand at several jobs before returning to complete his education. His descriptions of Russian life and customs are realistic and memorable.
Reviews: *BL* 5/15/76; *HB* 8/76; *NCB*; *SLJ* 4/76★

Reading Level: Middle & Junior High School
Subject Areas: Russia
Time Period: 1893

❏ Library owns

Cookson, Catherine. *The Love Child.* **New York: Summit, 1991. 366pp. ISBN 0-67-72836-9. LC 91-20676.**
England, late nineteenth century. Anna, one of five children born out of wedlock, faces the cruelty of the villagers and their assumption that she, too, will act as her mother has. Anna defies them with courage.
Reviews: *BL* 9/1/91; *LJ* 9/1/91
Reading Level: High School
Subject Areas: Great Britain--1800-1899
Time Period: Nineteenth Century

❏ Library owns

Crichton, Michael. *The Great Train Robbery.* **New York: Knopf, 1975. 288pp. ISBN 0-394-49401-6. LC 74-25422.**
England, 1855. Based on an actual train robbery that took a year to plan, Crichton takes us along for this historic train ride with Edward Pierce, the mastermind behind a plan to steal £12,000 of gold bullion bound for British troops in the Crimea on the London-Paris train.
Reviews: *BBSH*; *BL* 7/15/75★; *FFY*; *SLJ* 9/75; *WS* 10, 11
Reading Level: High School
Subject Areas: Great Britain--1800-1899; London (England); crime and criminals; railroads
Time Period: 1855

❏ Library owns

Cross, Gillian. *The Iron Way.* **New York: Oxford University Press, 1979. 131pp. ISBN 0-19-271430-9. LC 78-40909.**
England, early nineteenth Century. Jem Penfold and his sisters, Kate and Martha, take in a "navvy" (a man working to build the new steam railway) border, even though there is resentment toward navvys and their rowdy antics. Oldest sister Kate makes this risky choice to keep them out of the workhouse, after their mother has died and their father is sent to prison for poaching.
Reviews: *BL* 1/80; *SLJ* 2/80
Reading Level: Middle–High School
Subject Areas: Great Britain--1800-1899; railroads; family life
Time Period: Nineteenth Century

❏ Library owns

Delderfield, R. F. *God Is an Englishman.* **New York: Simon & Schuster, 1970. 687pp. ISBN 0-671-20502-1.**

England, 1857-1866. Reflecting Victorian life, this is the story of Adam Swann, returning from military service in the Crimea and in India, who sets up a freight-hauling business and marries Henrietta Rawlinson, the local mill owner's daughter.

Reviews: *WS* 10

Reading Level: High School [Mature Reader]

Subject Areas: Great Britain--1800-1899

Time Period: 1857-1866   ❏ Library owns

Doherty, Berlie. *Street Child.* **New York: Orchard, 1994. 149pp. ISBN 0-531-08714-X. LC 93-5020.**

England, ca. 1860-1880. Jim finds himself on his own when his fatherless family is evicted from their home and his mother dies a few days later. He survives by stealth after escaping from a workhouse—until he is kidnapped and forced to work on a coal barge. Once again he escapes, only to find a friend dying of hunger. Desperate, Jim finds his way to Dr. Bernardo, who runs a home for destitute children. Dr. Bernardo is an historical figure who, inspired by a real-life Jim Jarvis, established homes for homeless children.

Reviews: *BL* 9/1/94; *SLJ* 10/94

Reading Level: Middle & Junior High School

Subject Areas: Great Britain; London (England); poverty; orphans; homeless persons

Time Period: 1860-1880   ❏ Library owns

Dumas, Alexandre; translated by A. Craig Bell. *Fernande.* **New York: St. Martin's Press, 1989. 114pp. ISBN 0-312-02575-0. LC 88-30624.**

France, 1835. Maurice is ill with heartbreak over the end of his relationship with the courtesan Fernand. In hopes of raising his spirits, his mother secretly arranges to transport her to Maurice at their country estate. Unfortunately, Fernande becomes embroiled in social intrigue in this old-fashioned, carefully plotted novel.

Reviews: *BL* 12/15/88; *SLJ* 8/89

Reading Level: High School

Subject Areas: France--1800-1899

Time Period: 1835   ❏ Library owns

Fisher, Leonard Everett. *Across the Sea from Galway.* **New York: Four Winds, 1975. 103pp. LC 75-9513.**

Ireland, 1847. Patrick, stunned survivor of a shipwreck which kills his siblings, tells the story of the Irish potato famine which sent him across the ocean without his parents. His descriptions of famine and hardship are heart-wrenching and haunting.

Reviews: *BL* 2/15/76; *SLJ* 1/76
Reading Level: Middle & Junior High School
Subject Areas: Ireland; famines; shipwrecks
Time Period: 1847   ❏ Library owns

Forster, Margaret. *Lady's Maid: A Novel of the Nineteenth Century.* **New York: Doubleday, 1991. 544pp. ISBN 0-385-41792-6. LC 90-45290.**
England, Italy, 1845-1861. This unusual look at Elizabeth Barrett and Robert Browning is a good example of social class and life in the Victorian era. Lily, Elizabeth's underpaid, undervalued, but loyal maid, relates life with her mistress of 20 years.
Reviews: *BL* 2/15/91; *LJ* 1/91
Reading Level: High School [Mature Reader]
Subject Areas: Great Britain--1800-1899; Italy; authors; poets; household employees; social classes
Time Period: 1845-1861   ❏ Library owns

Garfield, Leon. *Footsteps.* **New York: Delacorte, 1980. 196pp. ISBN 0-440-02634-2. LC 80-65834.**
England, nineteenth century. David Jones's father's pacing footsteps marked his guilty conscience over having cheated his business partner, and after his death, his guilty conscience is taken over by David who can still hear those pacing footsteps. Determined to right the wrong his father committed, David sets out for London, in search of his father's partner, where he encounters a Dickensien cast of characters and mystery.
Reviews: *BCCB* 9/80; *BL* 10/15/80★; *CRC*; *HB* 10/80; *SLJ* 10/80
Reading Level: Middle & Junior High School
Subject Areas: Great Britain--1800-1899; London (England); mystery and detective stories; adventure and adventurers
Time Period: Nineteenth Century   ❏ Library owns

Garfield, Leon. *The December Rose.* **New York: Viking, 1987. 207pp. ISBN 0-670-81054-1. LC 86-40576.**
England, nineteenth century. With characters that Dickens would be proud of, this is the story of Barnacle, a young chimney sweep, who falls from a chimney and into a mystery. Three of the characters are honorable barge-dwellers who aid Barnacle, save his life, and give him self-esteem. This paints a colorful picture of Victorian London.
Reviews: *BCCB* 9/87; *HB* 11-12/87; *SLJ* 9/87★
Reading Level: Middle–High School

Subject Areas: Great Britain--1800-1899; London (England); mystery and detective stories

Time Period: Nineteenth Century ❏ Library owns

Harrison, Ray. *Why Kill Arthur Potter?* **New York: Scribner, 1984. 155pp. ISBN 0-684-18131-2. LC 84-1317.**

England, nineteenth century. The investigation into the beating death of a shipping clerk in a back alley leads two London policemen to Monte Carlo where they discover crime in Victorian London's institutions of high finance.

Reviews: *BL* 8/84; *LJ* 7/84

Reading Level: High School [Mature Reader]

Subject Areas: Great Britain--1800-1899; Monte Carlo; London (England); mystery and detective stories

Time Period: Nineteenth Century ❏ Library owns

Harrod-Eagles, Cynthia. *Anna.* **New York: St. Martin's Press, 1991. 640pp. ISBN 0-312-06290-7. LC 91-4336.**

France, Russia, 1800-1815. Anne Peters, who has just lost her job as a governess with an English family living in Paris, finds herself with nowhere to go as war breaks out between England and France. Just as she is about to be arrested, she is rescued by a Russian who takes her home to St. Petersburg where they fall in love. First of a projected trilogy.

Reviews: *BL* 9/15/91; *LJ* 9/15/91

Reading Level: High School

Subject Areas: France--1800-1899; Russia; love

Time Period: 1800-1815 ❏ Library owns

Hodge, Jane Aiken. *Escapade.* **New York: St. Martin's, 1993. 240pp. ISBN 0-312-09799-9.**

England, Sicily, nineteenth century. Heiress Charlotte, escaping a marriage proposal, and Beth, actress and British spy, set off for Palermo, Sicily, where they find adventure, romance, and political intrigue.

Reviews: *BL* 10/1/93; *PW* 9/6/93

Reading Level: High School [Mature Reader]

Subject Areas: Great Britain--1800-1899; spies; actors

Time Period: Nineteenth Century ❏ Library owns

Hodge, Jane Aiken. *Greek Wedding.* **New York: Doubleday, 1970. 303pp. LC 79-116214.**

Greece, early nineteenth century. During the War of Greek Independence, American Phyllida Vannick is captured by the Turks while searching for her brother who joined the Greek revolutionaries. She escapes and is rescued by Brett, a British yacht owner. While on the yacht, they are involved in many exciting incidents, including Phyllida's kidnapping by a Greek who wants to marry her for her money.

Reviews: *BL* 1/15/71; *LJ* 9/1/70
Reading Level: High School
Subject Areas: Greece; adventure and adventurers; kidnapping
Time Period: Nineteenth Century ❑ **Library owns**

Holt, Victoria. *The Landowner Legacy.* **New York: Doubleday, 1984. 374pp. ISBN 0-385-19628-8. LC 84-8020.**

England, nineteenth century. Banished by her stern father for a relatively minor misdeed, 14-year-old Caroline Tressidor is sent to live with a cousin in Cornwall. There she meets the Landowner brothers, one of whom will figure prominently in her life. She discovers after her father's death that she is the daughter of her mother's lover and goes to live with her mother in France. When Paul Landowner visits her, they fall in love, bringing tragic circumstances.

Reviews: *BL* 9/15/84; *SLJ* 3/85
Reading Level: High School [Mature Reader]
Subject Areas: Great Britain--1800-1899; France
Time Period: Nineteenth Century ❑ **Library owns**

Holt, Victoria. *The Silk Vendetta.* **New York: Doubleday, 1987. 425pp. ISBN 0-385-24299-9. LC 87-5266.**

England, France, nineteenth century. The French and English branches of a family compete with their silk cloth manufacturing businesses. The English family has an advantage due to the invention of a new weaving technique. Lenore, from the English branch but brought up by her French grandmother, begins a dressmaking business in Paris, unaware of the family feud nor the misfortunes she will bring.

Reviews: *BL* 8/87; *LJ* 8/87
Reading Level: High School
Subject Areas: Great Britain--1800-1899; France 1800-1899; silk industry
Time Period: Nineteenth Century ❑ **Library owns**

Hoover, H. M. *The Lion's Cub.* **New York: Four Winds, 1974. 211pp. ISBN 0-590-07375-3. LC 74-8594.**

Russia, Caucasus, nineteenth century. During the war between the Russian czar and the Daghestan mountain people, Jemal-Edin, eldest son of Shamil, leader of the Daghestan, is taken as a hostage by the czar's troops in an effort to make Shamil surrender. Jemal-Edin becomes the permanent guest of the czar when his father refuses to surrender.

Reviews: *BCCB* 1/75; *BL* 11/1/74; *SLJ* 12/74

Reading Level: Middle–High School
Subject Areas: Russia; Daghestan; hostages
Time Period: Nineteenth Century ❏ Library owns

Hughes, Glyn. *The Rape of the Rose*. New York: Simon & Schuster, 1993. 319pp. ISBN 0-671-72516-5. LC 92-39326.
England, 1811-1813. Mor Greave, a self-educated weaver, sees the hardships that industrialization is bringing to the workers and joins the Luddites. When he is caught spying, he abandons his family, teams up with a prostitute, and joins other revolutionaries who want to stop industrialization.
Reviews: *BL* 3/15/93; *LJ* 2/1/93; *SLJ* 1/94
Reading Level: High School [Mature Reader]
Subject Areas: Great Britain--1800-1899; Luddites; Industrial Revolution
Time Period: 1811-1813 ❏ Library owns

Jones, Adrienne. *Another Place, Another Spring*. Boston: Houghton, 1971. 285pp.
Russia, 1840. When Countess Elena and her maid Marya are arrested and exiled to Siberia, they are escorted by Boris who is really a member of the Underground. Boris plans their escape, but it is a long and arduous journey, during which Elena dies. Boris and Marya fall in love, marry, and begin a new life when they finally make it to California.
Reviews: *BL* 4/15/72; *HB* 2/72; *LJ* 12/15/71
Reading Level: Middle–High School
Subject Areas: Russia; Underground movements; voyages and journeys; escapes
Time Period: 1840 ❏ Library owns

Lampedusa, Giuseppe di; translated by Archibald Colquhoun. *The Leopard*. New York: Pantheon, 1982, c1960. 319pp. ISBN 0-394-74949-9. LC 60-679.
Italy, nineteenth century. This is based on the life of Don Fabrizio, Prince of Salina, who rules Sicily, and his effect on the aristocracy and his domain after Garibaldi's overthrow of the aristocracy.
Reviews: *BBSH*; *WS* 10, 11
Reading Level: High School
Subject Areas: Italy; Sicily; Fabrizio, Prince of Salina
Time Period: 1850-1870 ❏ Library owns

Lasky, Kathryn; illustrated by Trina Schart Hyman. *The Night Journey*. New York: Warne, 1981. 149pp. ISBN 0-7232-6201-2. LC 81-2225.
Russia, nineteenth century. Rachel and her family decide they must flee Russia as the pogroms and persecutions against the Jews increase. Rachel also learns about her grandmother's life.

Reviews: *BCCB* 12/81; *CRC*; *HB* 4/82; *SLJ* 1/82; *WJ* 5
Reading Level: Middle & Junior High School
Subject Areas: Russia; Jews in Russia; antisemitism; refugees; family life
Time Period: Nineteenth Century ❏ Library owns

Lingard, Joan. *Greenyards.* **New York: Putnam, 1981. 293pp. ISBN 0-399-12513-2. LC 80-19022.**

Scotland, 1850s. Catriona Ross must decide which of two men to marry after she and her neighbors and family are evicted by the lord of the manor where they were tenants. Nineteenth century life is well described.

Reviews: *BL* 3/1/81; *LJ* 1/1/81
Reading Level: High School
Subject Areas: Scotland; Great Britain--1800-1899; love
Time Period: 1850s ❏ Library owns

Lovesey, Peter. *Waxwork.* **New York: Pantheon, 1978. 239pp. ISBN 0-394-50066-0. LC 77-90420.**

England, nineteenth century. Using many details of Victorian London, this is the story of a woman who confesses to poisoning a blackmailer. The plot thickens when a minor officer of Scotland Yard is assigned to investigate a discrepancy in her story before she goes to the gallows.

Reviews: *BL* 6/15/78★; *SLJ* 9/78
Reading Level: High School
Subject Areas: Great Britain--1800-1899; London (England); mystery and detective stories; crime and criminals
Time Period: Nineteenth Century ❏ Library owns

Lutzeier, Elizabeth. *The Coldest Winter.* **New York: Holiday House, 1991. 153pp. ISBN 0-8234-0899-X. LC 91-7159.**

Ireland, 1846. Evicted by their landlords because they can't pay the rent, the Eammon family begins a long walk to Dublin in search of food and work, but instead find squalid conditions. Kate makes friends with a girl from a rich family who finally tries to help, but is too late to save Kate's baby sister. The family decides their only hope is to emigrate to America.

Reviews: *BR* 5/92; *SLJ* 9/91; *VOYA* 4/91
Reading Level: Middle–High School
Subject Areas: Ireland; Great Britain--1800-1899; famines; Potato Famine
Time Period: 1846 ❏ Library owns

Europe—Nineteenth Century

MacBeth, George. *Anna's Book.* **New York: Holt, 1984. 278pp. ISBN 0-03-070487-1. LC 83-22534.**

Sweden, North Pole, 1890s. Strindberg, a man intent on reaching the North Pole by balloon, and Anna, his summer pupil, fall in love, but decide to delay their wedding until he returns from the expedition. Anna and Strindberg each tell their tale. Strindberg and the two other men with him never return, their bodies found in 1930 on a remote island. Based on a true event.

Reviews: *LJ* 5/1/84; *SLJ* 8/84

Reading Level: High School

Subject Areas: Sweden; Arctic Regions; love; explorers; survival

Time Period: 1890s ❏ Library owns

Matas, Carol. *Sworn Enemies.* **New York: Bantam, 1993. 134pp. ISBN 0-553-08326-0. LC 92-6188.**

Russia, 1851. Told alternatively by two young men, this is the story of Aaron, a young Jewish scholar who is kidnapped and forced into the army; and Zev, the man who kidnapped him. Zev suddenly finds himself conscripted as well and placed in the same unit with Aaron who hates him for ruining his life. Aaron plots an escape from the army and Zev demands to be taken along.

Reviews: *BCCB* 4/93; *BL* 2/1/93; *BR* 3-4/93; *SLJ* 2/93; *VOYA* 6/93

Reading Level: Middle–High School

Subject Areas: Russia; Jews in Russia; escapes

Time Period: 1851 ❏ Library owns

McLean, Allan Campbell. *The Year of the Stranger.* **New York: Walck, 1972. 192pp. ISBN 0-8098-3108-2. LC 72-3210.**

Scotland, 1877. In this allegorical tale, 14-year-old Calum Og tries to aid a tinker who is treated cruelly and run out of town. It then begins to rain—rains that continues for 50 days, stopping only when a stranger arrives bringing pleasant weather. When the stranger asks the townspeople to aid the tinkers, they refuse, the stranger leaves, and the rains begin again, flooding the village. Calum, because of his kindness, gets a glimpse of a heaven-like place.

Reviews: *BL* 2/1/73; *LJ* 4/15/73; *HB* 2/73

Reading Level: Middle–High School

Subject Areas: Great Britain--1800-1899; Isle of Skye; Scotland; allegories

Time Period: 1877 ❏ Library owns

Overton, Jenny. *The Ship from Simnel Street.* **New York: Greenwillow, 1986. 144pp. ISBN 0-688-06182-6. LC 85-21965.**

England, 1800-1815. During the Napoleonic Wars two sisters have very different fates. Although one sister, Polly, adventurously and romantically sails to Portugal

to follow her soldier fiance, the author's focus stays on Susannah who remains in Simnel Street to oversee the family's bakery, providing a revealing look nineteenth century village life.
Reviews: *BCCB* 10/86; *BL* 11/1/86; *BR* 11-12/86; *SLJ* 11/86; *VOYA* 12/86
Reading Level: Middle–High School
Subject Areas: Great Britain--1800-1899; London (England); bakers and bakeries; village life
Time Period: 1800-1815 ❑ Library owns

Paton Walsh, Jill. *Grace.* **New York: Farrar, 1992. 256pp. ISBN 0-374-32758-0. LC 91-31054.**
England, 1838. Grace Darling, who becomes a national hero after she and her father complete a dangerous rescue during a raging storm, finds her life much changed after the incident. Her quiet life in the lighthouse is disrupted by rude visitors and accusations that she acted out of greed for a reward, eventually weakening her health.
Reviews: *BCCB* 6/92; *BL* 6/15/92; *BR* 9-10/92; *HB* 7/92; *SLJ* 7/92★
Reading Level: High School
Subject Areas: Great Britain--1800-1899; Darling, Grace; heroes; shipwrecks
Time Period: 1838 ❑ Library owns

Paton Walsh, Jill. *A Chance Child.* **New York: Farrar, 1978. 186pp. ISBN 0-374-31236-2. LC 78-21521.**
England, nineteenth century. Neglected and abused, modern day Creep escapes his dark confinement and passes back to the time of the Industrial Revolution, finding other children just as mistreated as he is. In a ghostlike form he saves two child laborers from their horrible lives. The author paints a grim picture of industrialization that leaves a path of destruction in its wake.
Reviews: *BCCB* 4/79; *BL* 4/1/79; *HB* 2/79; *SLJ* 1/79★
Reading Level: Middle–High School
Subject Areas: Great Britain--1800-1899; Industrial Revolution; child labor; space and time
Time Period: Nineteenth Century ❑ Library owns

Parker, Richard. *A Sheltering Tree.* **Lido Beach, NY: Meredith, 1969. 223pp. LC 76-93841.**
England, nineteenth Century. Set on the Kentish coast near Canterbury, this is the tale of two boys and their encounters with smuggling that almost earn them imprisonment, but lead them to the Navy instead.
Reviews: *BL* 4/15/70; *LJ* 4/15/70
Reading Level: Middle & Junior High School

Subject Areas: Great Britain--1800-1899; smuggling
Time Period: Nineteenth Century ❏ Library owns

Perry, Anne. *A Sudden, Fearful Death.* **New York: Fawcett, 1993. 383pp. ISBN 0-449-90637-X. LC 93-70006.**

England, nineteenth century. Inspector Monk once again investigates murder, this time of two women—the sister of a lady and a nurse at a local hospital. Monk carefully examines the evidence and with the help of two friends, a nurse and a lawyer, is able to find a connection between the two. Perry paints a vivid picture of Victorian life and the rigid roles women were expected to fill. There are several volumes in this series.

Reviews: *BL* 9/1/93; *LJ* 9/1/93; *SLJ* 3/94
Reading Level: High School
Subject Areas: Great Britain--1800-1899; mystery and detective stories; nurses
Time Period: Nineteenth Century ❏ Library owns

Petrakis, Harry Mark. *The Hour of the Bell: A Novel of the 1821 Greek War of Independence Against the Turks.* **New York: Doubleday, 1976. 363pp. ISBN 0-385-04877-7. LC 75-40738.**

Greece, 1821. With brutal detail, the author details the first year of a ten-year war, showing the small battles and skirmishes that make up the larger battle of the Greek people in defense of their homeland.

Reviews: *BL* 11/1/76; *LJ* 12/1/76
Reading Level: High School [Mature Reader]
Subject Areas: Greece--1821-1829
Time Period: 1821 ❏ Library owns

Plaidy, Jean. *The Captive of Kensington Palace.* **New York: Putnam, 1976. 285pp. ISBN 0-399-11851-9. LC 76-27122.**

England, 1819-1901. In this fictionalized account of Queen Victoria's rocky road to the throne, virtue triumphs over the plots, jealousies, and guile of those around her, including her mother. First of the Queen Victoria Series.

Reviews: *BL* 1/1/77; *WS* 11
Reading Level: High School
Subject Areas: Great Britain--1800-1899; Victoria, Queen of Great Britain
Time Period: 1819-1901 ❏ Library owns

Plaidy, Jean. *The Queen and Lord M.* **New York: Putnam, 1977. 268pp. ISBN 0-399-11994-9. LC 77-3644.**

England, 1819-1901. Plaidy weaves a tale of a young Queen Victoria, liberated from her mother's intrigues in order to assume her role as queen. She finds political enemies who must be dealt with and the dashing Lord Melbourne who provides affection. Sequel to *The Captive of Kensington Palace*, and second in the Queen Victoria Series.

Reviews: *BL* 9/15/77; *WS* 11

Reading Level: High School

Subject Areas: Great Britain--1800-1899; Victoria, Queen of Great Britain

Time Period: 1819-1901 ❏ Library owns

Plaidy, Jean. *The Queen's Husband.* **New York: Putnam, 1978. 382pp. ISBN 0-399-12128-5. LC 77-21161.**

England, 1819-1901. Focusing on Albert, prince of Saxe-Coburg-Gotha, we see the intellectual man who courted Queen Victoria. With the marriage preparations, there are also people in the court who must be dealt with, such as the petty Baroness Lezhen who had great influence over Victoria and Lord Melbourne.

Reviews: *BL* 7/1/78; *WS* 11

Reading Level: High School

Subject Areas: Great Britain--1800-1899; Victoria, Queen of Great Britain; Albert, consort of Queen Victoria; marriage

Time Period: 1819-1901 ❏ Library owns

Pullman, Philip. *Shadow in the North.* **New York: Knopf, 1988. 300pp. ISBN 0-394-89453-7. LC 87-29846.**

England, 1878. In this sequel to *The Ruby in the Smoke*, heroine Sally Lockhart is now a Cambridge educated business woman whose client has lost his life's savings, causing Sally to suspect fraud, and to begin an investigation with the aid of her friend Jim and her lover, Fred Garland, a photographer. The investigation puts Sally's life at risk as she works to get back her client's money and destroy the evil Bellman.

Reviews: *BBYA*; *BCCB* 4/88; *BL* 4/1/88★; *BR* 11-12/88; *HB* 5-6/88; *SLJ* 5/88★

Reading Level: High School

Subject Areas: Great Britain--1800-1899; mystery and detective stories; London (England)

Time Period: 1878 ❏ Library owns

Pullman, Philip. *The Ruby in the Smoke.* **New York: Knopf, 1987. 204pp. ISBN 0-394-98826-4. LC 86-20983.**

England, 1872. Pullman's first Sally Lockhart story is a real page turner as it begins 16-year-old Sally's investigative career. In this first installment, Sally's father dies leaving her an orphan in search of a mysterious ruby that is said to be her inheritance. Her search takes her to opium dens and slums and puts her in contact with hags, the children of poverty, and a ruthless blackmailer.

Reviews: *BBYA*; *BCCB* 5/87; *BL* 3/1/87★; *HB* 5-6/87; *SLJ* 4/87★; *VOYA* 10/87; *WJ* 6; *WS* 14

Europe—Nineteenth Century

Reading Level: Middle–High School
Subject Areas: Great Britain--1800-1899; London (England); mystery and detective stories; orphans
Time Period: 1872 ❏ Library owns

Pullman, Philip. *The Tin Princess.* **New York: Knopf, 1994. 290pp. ISBN 0-679-84757-X. LC 92-38305.**
England, 1882. Exiled from Central Europe, Becky has become a language tutor which is how she meets Jim, a detective, and Adelaide, who are both taking German lessons. Becky learns that Adelaide is secretly married to Prince Rudolf of Razkavia and that both Adelaide and Rudolf have become the targets of revolutionaries. Becky, Jim and Adelaide become involved in espionage, attempted assassinations and exciting chases. Jim and Adelaide appeared as characters in Pullman's earlier books.
Reviews: *BCCB* 2/94; *BL* 2/15/94; *BR* 9-10/94; *PW* 3/21/94; *SLJ* 4/94
Reading Level: High School
Subject Areas: Great Britain; espionage; terrorism
Time Period: 1882 ❏ Library owns

Schlee, Ann. *Ask Me No Questions.* **New York: Holt, 1982. 228pp. ISBN 0-03-061523-2. LC 81-6932.**
England, 1848. Based on a true incident, this is the story of Laura and her brother Barty who are sent to live with relatives when cholera comes to their home. Next door to their new home is an orphanage where the children are supposed to be well cared for and given practical training, however, as with much of the Victorian age, this facade covers some horrifying truths.
Reviews: *BCCB* 5/82; *BL* 7/82★; *HB* 10/82; *SLJ* 4/82
Reading Level: Middle–High School
Subject Areas: Great Britain--1800-1899; orphans; poverty; child abuse
Time Period: 1848

Schur, Maxine Rose. *The Circlemaker.* **New York: Dial, 1994. 192pp. ISBN 0-8037-1354-1. LC 93-17983.**
Russia, 1852. Rather than let the Russian troops force him into the army, Mendel, a 12-year-old Jewish boy, runs away and is helped by an underground network that provides him with false papers and helps him make it to Hungary. Accompanying him is Dovid, a bully who has tormented Mendel, and who is injured, forcing Mendel to choose between abandoning him or going back to help him.
Reviews: *BL* 1/15/94; *SLJ* 2/94; *BR* 9-10/94; *PW* 12/6/93
Reading Level: Middle–High School
Subject Areas: Russia; Jews in Russia; runaways; escapes
Time Period: 1852 ❏ Library owns

Stone, Irving. *The Greek Treasure: A Biographical Novel of Henry and Sophia Schliemann.* **New York: Doubleday, 1975. 479pp. ISBN 0-385-07309-7. LC 74-33740.**
Greece, Germany, 1850-1890. This is the story of Henry Schliemann, a retired German whose dream was to find the fabled city of Troy. While excavating in Greece, he meets and marries his young wife Sophia, and together they find eight ancient cities.
Reviews: *BBSH*; *BL* 9/15/75; *WS* 11, 12
Reading Level: High School
Subject Areas: Germany; Greece; Schliemann, Heinrich; Schlieman, Sophia Kastromenos; archeologists
Time Period: 1850-1890 ❏ Library owns

Stone, Irving. *Lust for Life: The Novel of Vincent Van Gogh.* **New York: Doubleday, 1959, c1937. 399pp. ISBN 0-385-04270-1.**
Netherlands, France, 1853-1890. Following the facts as closely as possible, the author paints a tortured picture of Vincent van Gogh's life which ended in suicide.
Reviews: *BBSH*; *FFY*, *WS* 10, 11, 12, 13, 14
Reading Level: High School [Mature Reader]
Subject Areas: Gogh, Vincent van; painters; artists
Time Period: 1853-1890 ❏ Library owns

Stone, Irving. *The Origin: A Biographical Novel of Charles Darwin.* **New York: Doubleday, 1980. 743pp. ISBN 0-385-12064-8. LC 79-6655.**
England, 1831-1889. Trained for the church, Charles Darwin is instead drawn to nature and is invited to join an expedition to South America and the Galapagos Islands where the idea for his *The Origin of Species*, and his most famous and infamous theory of evolution begins. In spite of his far-reaching idea, and the storm of controversy it precipitates, his life is mostly that of a staid gentleman of his time.
Reviews: *BBSH*; *BL* 6/15/80; *LJ* 8/80; *WS* 11, 12, 13
Reading Level: High School
Subject Areas: Darwin, Charles; scientists; voyages and travels
Time Period: 1831-1889 ❏ Library owns

Trollope, Joanna. *Leaves from the Valley.* **New York: St. Martin's, 1984. 254pp. ISBN 0-312-47729-5. LC 83-21096.**
Crimea, 1854. Two sisters, Blanche and Sarah, accompany their brother Edgar, a British army officer, to the Crimea, expecting a rather entertaining time in Constantinople. Instead they find the horrors of war. Blanche runs away with a

playboy, but Sarah tries to stay and be useful. She becomes involved with Florence Nightingale's hospital and its appalling conditions.
Reviews: *BL* 7/84; *SLJ* 5/84
Reading Level: High School
Subject Areas: Great Britain--1800-1899; Crimean War, 1854-56; nurses
Time Period: 1854 ❏ **Library owns**

Unsworth, Walter. *Grimsdyke.* **Nashville: Nelson, 1976. 160pp. ISBN 0-8407-6491-X. LC 76-2522.**
England, 1819. This is the tragic tale of orphaned Kit Standish whose uncle plots to kill him in order to claim the lead deposits underneath Grimsdyke, the Standish family manor on the moors. Luckily, Kit is befriended by three locals who help him to escape from his uncle.
Reviews: *BCCB* 11/76; *BL* 10/1/76; *SLJ* 4/76
Reading Level: Middle–High School
Subject Areas: Great Britain--1800–1899; orphans; Peterloo Massacre
Time Period: 1819 ❏ **Library owns**

Uris, Leon. *Trinity.* **New York: Doubleday, 1976. 751pp. ISBN 0-385-03458-X.**
Northern Ireland, 1840-1916. Three families form the "trinity" of this epic novel of Catholic and Protestant, Irish and English, peasantry and aristocracy, attempting to show the beginnings of the crisis in Northern Ireland.
Reviews: *BBSH*; *WS* 10, 11, 12, 13, 14
Reading Level: High School [Mature Reader]
Subject Areas: Ireland; Great Britain--1800-1899
Time Period: 1840-1916 ❏ **Library owns**

Williams, Jeanne. *The Island Harp.* **New York: St. Martin's, 1992. 338pp. ISBN 0-312-06570-1. LC 91-21185.**
Scotland, nineteenth century. When most of her family chooses to emigrate from Scotland after being evicted by their landlord, Mairi opts to stay and lead what is left of the family, trying to keep the old traditions alive. Life is difficult, but she persists. She falls in love with a wealthy landowner, but knows she has no future with him because of their different social classes.
Reviews: *BL* 12/1/91; *SLJ* 7/92
Reading Level: High School
Subject Areas: Scotland; Great Britain--1800-1899; social classes
Time Period: Nineteenth Century ❏ **Library owns**

Wiseman, David. *Jeremy Visick.* **Boston: Houghton, 1981. 170pp. ISBN 0-395-30449-0. LC 80-28116.**

England, 1852, contemporary. When Matthew first sees the Visick family gravestone while doing a class assignment, he notes that 12-year-old Jeremy's body is not in the grave, but in the local mine, victim of a mining accident. He is drawn back in time and follows Jeremy into the mine where he narrowly escapes death. He is able, however, to put Jeremy's spirit to rest.

Reviews: *BCCB* 9/81; *BL* 7/1/81★; *CRC*; *HB* 4/81; *SLJ* 4/81

Reading Level: Middle & Junior High School

Subject Areas: Great Britain--1800-1899; Cornwall (England); miners; space and time; ghosts

Time Period: 1852 ❏ Library owns

Zei, Alki; translated by Edward Fenton. *The Sound of the Dragon's Feet.* **New York: Dutton, 1979. 128pp. ISBN 0-525-39712-4. LC 79-14917.**

Russia, 1894. Ten-year-old Sasha, with her child's curiosity, tries to understand everything around her. Her doctor father provides some answers, as does her tutor, an exiled revolutionary.

Reviews: *BL* 12/1/79; *HB* 10/79; *SLJ* 9/79

Reading Level: Middle & Junior High School

Subject Areas: Russia; fathers and daughters

Time Period: 1894 ❏ Library owns

Twentieth Century

(Arranged by country or major area)

England

Archer, Jeffrey. *As the Crow Flies.* **New York: HarperCollins, 1991. 617pp. ISBN 0-06-017914-7. LC 90-56105.**

England, 1900-1930. Charlie Trumper hopes to own a large shop one day, following in the footsteps of his grocer grandfather, but his plans are interrupted by World War I. During the war he makes an enemy of vengeful Guy Trentham who, after the war, lives his life to destroy Charlie's.

Reviews: *PW* 4/26/91; *SLJ* 11/91

Reading Level: High School

Subject Areas: Great Britain--1900-

Time Period: 1900-1930 ❏ Library owns

Europe—Twentieth Century

Bainbridge, Beryl. *The Birthday Boys.* **Carroll & Graf, 1994. 189pp. ISBN 0-7867-0071-8. LC 94-1264.**

South Pole, 1910. Beginning in England, Robert Falcon Scott and the men in his expedition party ready themselves for their exploration of the South Pole. Using the medium of journal entries, their excitement and curiosity are evident at the beginning of their entries during their arduous journey. When they discover that Amundsen has beaten them to the discovery of the South Pole and that they will not survive, the entries show their courage.

Reviews: *BL* 4/1/94; *LJ* 3/1/94; *PW* 1/24/94; *SLJ* 10/94
Reading Level: High School
Subject Areas: South Pole; explorers; adventure and adventurers
Time Period: 1910 ❑ Library owns

Binchey, Maeve. *Light a Penny Candle.* **New York: Viking, 1983. 542pp. ISBN 0-670-42827-2. LC 82-19132.**

England, Ireland, 1940-1960. Elizabeth and Aisling become fast friends when Elizabeth is sent to Ireland during the Blitz of London. They both experience life's turmoil, and as young widows, discover their friendship has been their anchor over many difficult years.

Reviews: *BBSH*; *BL* 2/15/83; *LJ* 2/15/83; *SLJ* 8/83
Reading Level: High School
Subject Areas: Great Britain--1900-; Ireland; friendship
Time Period: 1940-1960 ❑ Library owns

Burton, Hester. *In Spite of All Terror.* **Cleveland: World Pub., 1969. 203pp. LC 69-13060.**

England, 1939-1940. Burton's title comes from one of Winston Churchill's wartime speeches. Her story unfolds in World War II England as thousands of schoolchildren like 15-year-old orphaned Liz Hawtin are evacuated from London in preparation for the coming war. Evacuated to Oxford, Liz learns to accommodate herself to a middle class family with high intellectual standards, but difficult relationships, as all in England and Europe learn to face the vicissitudes of war.

Reviews: *BCCB* 10/70; *HB* 8/69; *LJ* 7/69; *NCB*
Reading Level: Middle–High School
Subject Areas: Great Britain--1900-; orphans; family life
Time Period: 1939-1940; World War, 1939-1945 ❑ Library owns

Hiçyilmaz, Gaye. *The Frozen Waterfall.* **New York: Farrar, 1994. 288pp. ISBN 0-374-32482-4. LC 94-9839.**

Switzerland, contemporary. Leaving Turkey, 12-year-old Selda, her sisters and mother, are finally reunited with her father and brothers who have been working in Switzerland. Her excitement subsides quickly as she confronts prejudice and difficulties with acculturation. She finds two friends, Giselle and Ferhat (an illegal Turkish immigrant whom she tries to help). Selda also confronts the conflict between becoming a good Islamic wife or determining her own destiny.

Reviews: *BL* 10/1/94; *SLJ* 10/94; *BR* 3-4/95

Reading Level: Middle–High School

Subject Areas: Switzerland; Turks; emigration and immigration; prejudice

Time Period: Twentieth Century ❏ Library owns

Horgan, Dorothy. *Then the Zeppelins Came.* **New York: Oxford University Press, 1990. 106pp. ISBN 0-19-271598-4. LC 89-17511.**

England, 1901-1918. This novel, which is actually a sequence of short stories, follows upper-middle-class Emily and her friend from the wrong end of the lane, Lizzie, from their childhood through their young adulthood at the end of World War I. Not only does it give a glimpse of Edwardian London, it also shows how people's prejudices grow.

Reviews: *BCCB* 5/90; *SLJ* 7/90

Reading Level: Middle & Junior High School

Subject Areas: Great Britain--1900-; London (England); friendship; World War, 1914-1918

Time Period: 1901-1918 ❏ Library owns

Hylton, Sara. *My Sister Clare.* **New York: St. Martin's, 1989. 512pp. ISBN 0-312-02618-8. LC 88-29870.**

England, India, 1935-1945. Eve Meredith tells the story of her beautiful but manipulative and morally vacant sister Clare and how her actions, including the seduction of her stepfather, affected their family. The settings provide much historical background from England preparing for war to the wartime events in the Far East.

Reviews: *BL* 6/1/89; *PW* 5/12/89; *BBSH*

Reading Level: High School [Mature Reader]

Subject Areas: Great Britain--1900-; India; sisters

Time Period: 1935-1945 ❏ Library owns

Kerr, Judith. *The Other Way Round.* **New York: Coward, McCann, 1975. 256pp. ISBN 0-698-20335-6. LC 75-4254.**

England, 1939-1945. Sequel to *When Hitler Stole Pink Rabbit.* Having finally made their way to London, Anna and Max must adapt to life in London during World War II. They find that people are prejudiced against foreigners, and that money is scarce. Despite the hardships, Anna develops as an artist and finds romance.

Europe—Twentieth Century

Reviews: *BL* 9/1/75★; *HB* 10/75; *SLJ* 9/75
Reading Level: Middle–High School
Subject Areas: Great Britain--1900-; London (England); refugees; Jews in England
Time Period: World War, 1939-1945   ❏ Library owns

Lisle, Janet Taylor. *Sirens and Spies.* **New York: Bradbury, 1985. 169pp. ISBN 0-02-759150-6. LC 84-21518.**
England, contemporary. Sisters Elsie and Mary delve into the mystery of their elderly French teacher, who has been brutally attacked. Elsie believes that she deserved the attack, but Mary does not. After finding some startling information, the girls confront Miss Fitch, who tells of her life in France during World War II and the tragic events that followed her affair with a German soldier.
Reviews: *BBYA*; *BCCB* 6/85; *BL* 5/15/85★; *HB* 9-10/85; *SLJ* 8/85★; *VOYA* 12/85
Reading Level: Middle–High School
Subject Areas: Great Britain--1900-; France; sisters
Time Period: World War, 1939-1945   ❏ Library owns

Pearson, Diane. *The Summer of the Barshinskeys.* **New York: Crown, 1984. 465pp. ISBN 0-517-55520-4. LC 84-4954.**
England, 1902-1924. Pearson sets her story in England at the time of World War I and the Russian Revolution. The story involves two families, the poor Barshinskeys and the proper Willoughbys, neighbors for whom world events have different effects. This is also the love story of each of the three children of each family.
Reviews: *BL* 7/84; *LJ* 8/84; *SLJ* 11/84
Reading Level: High School
Subject Areas: Great Britain--1900-; family life; love; World War, 1914-1918
Time Period: 1902-1924   ❏ Library owns

Rowlands, Avril. *Milk and Honey.* **New York: Oxford, 1990. 144pp. ISBN 0-19-271627-1. LC 89-24719.**
England, 1958. Set against the race riots of 1958 is the story of Nelson and his family who immigrated to England from Jamaica in search of a better life only to find racial discrimination. Twelve-year-old Nelson does find friendship with an eccentric old lady.
Reviews: *BCCB* 6/90; *BL* 6/1/90; *SLJ* 8/90; *VOYA* 8/90
Reading Level: Middle–High School
Subject Areas: Great Britain--1900-; race relations; Blacks; discrimination; emigration and immigration; prejudices
Time Period: 1958   ❏ Library owns

Smith, Rukshana. *Sumitra's Story.* New York: Coward-McCann, 1983. 168pp. ISBN 0-698-20579-0. LC 82-19794.
England, 1972-1979. Having fled Uganda under Idi Amin's regime, Sumitra Patel's East Indian family emigrates to England where young Sumitra must finally choose between the tradition-bound ways of her family or the greater freedoms of English life. This novel won an award for racial harmony in England.
Reviews: *BBYA*; *BCCB* 4/83; *BL* 4/15/83; *HB* 6/83; *SLJ* 8/83; *VOYA* 6/83
Reading Level: Middle–High School
Subject Areas: Great Britain--1900-; East Indians in Great Britain; family life; prejudices; women
Time Period: 1972-1979 ❏ Library owns

Ireland

Alyn, Marjory. *The Sound of Anthems.* New York: St. Martin's, 1983. 209pp. ISBN 0-312-74600-8. LC 83-10901.
Northern Ireland, 1945. Eleven-year-old orphan Jennifer Marshall, being raised by her Catholic grandmother, tries to make sense of her world in which hostilities between the Catholics and Protestants begin again at the close of World War II.
Reviews: *BL* 12/1/83; *SLJ* 2/84; *VOYA* 4/84; *YARC*
Reading Level: High School
Subject Areas: Great Britain--1900-; Northern Ireland; prejudices
Time Period: 1945 ❏ Library owns

Behan, Brian. *Kathleen: A Dublin Saga.* New York: St. Martin's, 1989. 320pp. ISBN 0-312-02593-9. LC 88-30605.
Ireland, early twentieth century. Kathleen Corr is determined to achieve her dreams and overcome the early adversity in her life. All is not as she planned, however, and a series of mismatched relationships resigns her to the fact that she will not achieve her goals. Kathleen sees in her children a way for her dreams to live on despite the political disputes of the times.
Reviews: *BL* 2/15/89; *LJ* 2/15/89
Reading Level: High School [Mature Reader]
Subject Areas: Great Britain--1900-; Ireland
Time Period: 1900-1920 ❏ Library owns

Forman, James. *A Fine, Soft Day.* New York: Farrar, 1978. 245pp. ISBN 0-374-32301-1. LC 78-11127.
Northern Ireland, 1970s. Catholic Brian O'Brien is caught between his pacifist father and his violent uncle who have different solutions to the Catholic-Protestant conflict in Belfast. When his father leaves home, Brian tries to keep the

family together, each member having their own problems and philosophies. Brian becomes a journalist and witnesses years of conflict, eventually ending up in a belfry with a machine gun.
Reviews: *FFY*; *SLJ* 1/79; *WJ* 4, *WS* 11
Reading Level: Middle–High School
Subject Areas: Great Britain--1900-; Northern Ireland; prejudices; family life
Time Period: 1970s ❏ **Library owns**

Lingard, Joan. *Across the Barricades*. Nashville: Nelson, 1973. 159pp. ISBN 0-8407-6280-1. LC 72-8915.
Northern Ireland, 1960s. Sequel to *The Twelfth Day of July*. Two teens, Protestant Sadie and Catholic Kevin, resume a friendship that was curtailed three years earlier. They are warned about the relationship, and Kevin is even beaten, but they continue to meet until a friend of theirs is killed. Unable to live in Ireland, the two leave for London.
Reviews: *BCCB* 11/73; *BL* 6/15/73; *LJ* 7/73; *SLJ* 9/73
Reading Level: Middle–High School
Subject Areas: Great Britain--1900-; Northern Ireland; prejudices; love
Time Period: 1960s ❏ **Library owns**

Lingard, Joan. *The File on Fraulein Berg*. New York: Elsevier/Nelson, 1980. 160pp. ISBN 0-525-66684-2. LC 80-10447.
Northern Ireland, 1944. Three 13-year-old girls suspect that their German teacher, Fraulein Berg, is a Nazi spy. They become a nuisance as they trail her around Belfast, even causing the break up of a romance. Fraulein Berg leaves Belfast. Twenty years later they discover just how wrong they were.
Reviews: *HB* 8/80; *SLJ* 5/80
Reading Level: Middle & Junior High School
Subject Areas: Great Britain--1900-; Northern Ireland; Jews in Great Britain
Time Period: 1944 ❏ **Library owns**

Lingard, Joan. *The Twelfth Day of July: A Novel of Modern Ireland*. Nashville: Nelson, 1972. 158pp. LC 72-1454.
Northern Ireland, 1960s. Siblings Sadie and Tommy Jackson and their Protestant friends are in high spirits while waiting for the "Glorious Twelfth" celebration, which celebrates a 1690 victory over the Catholics. Catholic youths and Protestant youths each invade the other's territory until a near tragic confrontation leaves them all shaken.
Reviews: *BCCB* 4/73; *BL* 4/1/73
Reading Level: Middle & Junior High School

Subject Areas: Great Britain--1900-; Northern Ireland; prejudices
Time Period: 1960s ❏ Library owns

Sullivan, Mary Ann. *Child of War.* **New York: Holiday House, 1984. 144pp. ISBN 0-8234-0537-0. LC 84-47832.**
Northern Ireland, 1969. One by one members of 13-year-old Maeve Doherty's family are killed by the violence of the Catholic-Protestant conflict. Maeve, though repelled by the violence, is drawn into it, seeking revenge. Finally, unable to accept any more, Maeve withdraws into a fantasy world, and is sent away to a school in Scotland.
Reviews: *BCCB* 12/84; *BL* 9/1/84; *SLJ* 2/85
Reading Level: Middle & Junior High School
Subject Areas: Great Britain--1900-; Northern Ireland; war; prejudices
Time Period: 1969 ❏ Library owns

Wibberley, Anna. *Time and Chance: A Novel.* **New York: Simon & Schuster, 1974, c1973. 315pp. ISBN 0-671-21611-2.**
Ireland, 1916-1921. Having moved to Ireland from London, the members of the Carroll family find it impossible to remain neutral during the Irish War of Independence, choosing to side with the Irish. One son joins the Irish Republican Army, one daughter falls in love with an Irish brigade commander, and the rest of the family are equally affected by the events of the time.
Reviews: *WS* 10
Reading Level: High School
Subject Areas: Great Britain--1900-; Ireland
Time Period: 1916-1921 ❏ Library owns

Scotland

Temperley, Alan. *Murdo's War.* **North Pomfret, VT: Canongate; David & Charles, 1989. 264pp. ISBN 0-86241-181-5.**
Scotland, 1943. Twelve-year-old Murdo and an old fisherman, Hector, are sucked into a Nazi spy intrigue when they fall for the story of a man claiming to be a Norwegian who needs a boat to transfer supplies for exiles. The man, however, is a Nazi whose real goal is an invasion of Britain. Despite his age, Murdo becomes a real hero as he braves the harsh elements to stop the Nazi.
Reviews: *BL* 10/15/89; *SLJ* 12/89
Reading Level: Middle–High School
Subject Areas: Great Britain--1900-; Scotland; spies; heroes; World War, 1939-1945
Time Period: 1943 ❏ Library owns

Austria

Stone, Irving. *The Passions of the Mind: A Novel of Sigmund Freud.* New York: Doubleday, 1971. 808pp. ISBN 0-385-02396-0. LC 75-139064.

Austria, 1856-1939. This detailed novel tells of the life and times of Sigmund Freud, giving a history of the psychoanalytical movement and of Freud's techniques.
Reviews: *WS* 10
Reading Level: High School
Subject Areas: Austria; Freud, Sigmund; psychologists
Time Period: 1856-1939 ❏ Library owns

Germany

Baer, Edith. *A Frost in the Night.* New York: Pantheon, 1980. 208pp. ISBN 0-394-84364-9. LC 79-27774.

Germany, 1932. Seen through the eyes of Eva Bentheim, a Jewish child living in relative security, this is the story of the last days of the Wiemar Republic. The first hints at the growing threat are the taunts of a bully and worried letters from American relatives. Eva tries to make sense of confusing and troublesome events. The story ends the day that Hitler is appointed Chancellor.
Reviews: *BCCB* 1/81; *BL* 9/1/80; *SLJ* 10/80; *VOYA* 4/81
Reading Level: Middle–High School
Subject Areas: Germany; Jews in Germany; persecution
Time Period: 1932 ❏ Library owns

Degens, T. *Transport 7-41-R.* New York: Viking, 1974. 171pp. ISBN 0-670-72429-7. LC 74-10930.

Germany, post-WWII. Because her family is unable to feed her, a 13-year-old German girl living in the Russian sector is sent away, traveling by cattlecar to Cologne in the British sector, where she befriends Mr. Lauritzen who is attempting to take his dead wife back to Cologne for burial.
Reviews: *FFY*; *HB* 10/74; *LJ* 10/15/74; *NCB*
Reading Level: Middle–High School
Subject Areas: Germany; refugees
Time Period: 1945-1950 ❏ Library owns

Ecke, Wolfgang; translated by Anthony Knight. *Flight Toward Home.* New York: Macmillan, 1970. 116pp.

Germany, 1945-1947. At the very end of World War II, as the Russians are advancing, Peter and his mother flee their home in Breslau. Peter, whose father

was killed during the war, watches his mother die while they are trying to get to his grandmother in Goslar, many miles away. Peter continues the journey which takes him two hardship-filled years, as he is now in East Germany and must escape to West Germany.
Reviews: *BL* 7/1/70; *LJ* 6/15/70
Reading Level: Middle & Junior High School
Subject Areas: Germany; refugees; orphans
Time Period: 1945-1947 ❏ Library owns

Härtling, Peter; translated by Elizabeth Crawford. *Crutches*. New York: Lothrop, 1988. 163pp. ISBN 0-688-07991-1. LC 88-80400.
Austria, Germany, post-WWII. While traveling with his mother to Austria to search for his Aunt Wanda, young Thomas becomes separated from her. Thomas rides the train all the way to Vienna, but does not find his mother or his aunt. A war veteran, Crutches, takes Thomas under his wing, protects him, becomes his family and takes him back to Germany. Crutches continues to look for Thomas's mother, who is found after a year of searching.
Reviews: *BCCB* 11/88; *BL* 2/1/89; *HB* 11-12/88; *SLJ* 11/88
Reading Level: Middle & Junior High School
Subject Areas: Germany; Austria; physically handicapped; missing persons
Time Period: 1945-1950 ❏ Library owns

Koehn, Ilse. *Tilla*. New York: Greenwillow, 1981. 254pp. ISBN 0-688-00650-7. LC 81-2217.
Germany, post-WWII. At the close of the war, Tilla becomes a refugee when she finds her family dead in the ruins of their bombed home. While traveling through a devastated land to her aunt's house in Berlin, she meets Rolf, escaping the Hitler Youth Army who is looking for his mother. Together they skirt danger, fall in love, become intimate, and eventually find their relatives. Tilla enrolls in art school while Rolf gets a job playing the piano in a nightclub. Their romance hits a snag when Tilla finds that Rolf has been sleeping with a singer.
Reviews: *BBYA*; *BCCB* 11/81; *BL* 10/1/81; *SLJ* 10/81; *WJ* 5, 6; *VOYA* 2/82
Reading Level: High School
Subject Areas: Germany; refugees
Time Period: 1945-1950 ❏ Library owns

Körner, Wolfgang; translated by Patricia Crampton. *The Green Frontier*. New York: Morrow, 1977. 190pp. ISBN 0-688-32124-0. LC 77-24517.
East Germany, 1952. A 14-year-old boy who doesn't understand his parents criticism of their East German government reluctantly agrees to flee with them to West Germany when he is not allowed to go to high school because his father is

not a Communist. Living as a refugee at a Red Cross center, he is pulled into a criminal act by other youths. He escapes capture by the police. He and his parents then leave the camp to begin a new life.
Reviews: *BL* 12/1/77; *SLJ* 12/77; *WJ* 4
Reading Level: Middle–High School
Subject Areas: Germany (East); refugees
Time Period: 1952

Lutzeier, Elizabeth. *The Wall.* **New York: Holiday House, 1992. 153pp. ISBN 0-8234-0987-2. LC 92-52712.**
East Germany, 1989. Hannah's mother, unable to cope with living in a repressive society, attempts to escape from East Germany and is killed. She is not allowed to talk about her mother or grieve in order not to draw attention to her father or herself. She and a friend become involved in a secret freedom movement, but she is afraid to tell her father, who unbeknownst to her is also working toward liberation. After a visit with her grandparents, also in the underground, Hannah decides to take a risk and tell her father. Six months after her mother dies, the Berlin Wall comes down.
Reviews: *BCCB* 1/92; *BL* 10/15/92; *BR* 3/93; *SLJ* 1/93; *VOYA* 4/93
Reading Level: Middle–High School
Subject Areas: Germany (East); anticommunist movements; underground movements
Time Period: 1989   ❏ **Library owns**

Skármeta, Antonio; translated by Hortense Carpentier. *Chileno!* **New York: Morrow, 1979. 92pp. ISBN 0-688-22213-7. LC 79-17540.**
Chile, Germany, 1973. Lucho and his family flee to Berlin after the 1973 military coup in Chile. There Lucho becomes involved in a fight with a gang led by Hans. Because Hans is injured in the fight, Lucho is forced to fight Hans' brother with whom he becomes friends. Mention of Chilean politics and the adjustment of political exiles to a new society round out the story.
Reviews: *BCCB* 12/79; *BL* 12/1/79; *SLJ* 11/79
Reading Level: Middle–High School
Subject Areas: Germany; Chile; political refugees; refugees
Time Period: 1973   ❏ **Library owns**

Trachtenberg, Inge. *So Slow the Dawning.* **New York: Norton, 1973. 249pp. ISBN 0-393-08538-4. LC 72-8970.**
Germany, 1920-1939. Ellen, the daughter of a modern Jewish couple who are not particularly devout, tells of the events leading to her family's escape from Germany. Her parents are blind to all the warning signs of the impending war and Holocaust. Ellen learns about devout Judaism and the impending threats from an

Orthodox Polish immigrant family. When it's almost too late, her family decides to emigrate.

Reviews: *WS* 10

Reading Level: High School

Subject Areas: Germany; Jews in Germany

Time Period: 1920-1939 ❏ Library owns

Uhlman, Fred. *Reunion.* **New York: Farrar, Straus, 1977. 112pp. ISBN 0-374-24951-2. LC 76-50514.**

Germany, 1932. Two boys, one a true Aryan aristocrat and the other a shy Jewish boy, attend school together where they develop a strong friendship. After a year, Hans, the Jewish boy, is sent to live with relatives in America, while Konradin becomes one of the elite of Hitler's circle.

Reviews: *BBYA*; *FFY*; *LJ* 3/1/77; *SLJ* 10/77

Reading Level: High School

Subject Areas: Germany; Jews in Germany; friendship

Time Period: 1932 ❏ Library owns

Greece

Duran, Cheli. *Kindling.* **New York: Greenwillow, 1979. 160pp. ISBN 0-688-84199-6. LC 78-23629.**

Greece, 1967-1974. Suspected of arson, Stelios and four other boys are arrested and cruelly beaten. Stelios makes note that the adults of the community do little to come to his aid, with the exception of his schoolmaster. After he and two others escape to the hills, he takes time to cool his anger and rethink his position. He chooses to return to school to become a lawyer, having gained a new respect for education through the actions of the schoolmaster.

Reviews: *BCCB* 7/79; *HB* 6/79; *SLJ* 2/79

Reading Level: Middle–High School

Subject Areas: Greece--1900-

Time Period: 1967-1974 ❏ Library owns

Fenton, Edward. *The Refugee Summer.* **New York: Delacorte, 1982. 261pp. ISBN 0-440-07404-5. LC 81-12593.**

Greece, 1922. Nikolas, finally understanding the impact of war after being asked to read the diary of a dead Greek soldier to his family, forms a secret society with a group of English children who are living in a villa for the summer. The purpose of the society, the Pallikars, is to do noble deeds, one of which is to aid refugees.

Reviews: *BCCB* 4/82; *BL* 4/15/82; *FFY*; *HB* 6/82; *SLJ* 4/82; *VOYA* 8/82

Reading Level: Middle & Junior High School

Subject Areas: Greece--1900-; Greco-Turkish War, 1921-1922; refugees
Time Period: 1922 ❑ Library owns

Forman, James. *Ring the Judas Bell.* **New York: Farrar, Straus, 1965. 218pp. ISBN 0-374-36304-8. LC 65-11619.**
Greece, post-WWII. Fifteen-year-old Nicholas, son of a pacifist priest, is kidnapped with a group of children by a band of communist guerillas. They are transported to Albania and put in a prison camp. Nicholas organizes their escape and manages to bring 11 of them home, overcoming the elements and hunger.
Reviews: *WJ* 4
Reading Level: Middle–High School
Subject Areas: Greece--1900-; kidnapping; escapes
Time Period: 1950s ❑ Library owns

Rosen, Billi. *Andi's War.* **New York: Dutton, 1989. 136pp. ISBN 0-525-44473-4. LC 88-25786.**
Greece, 1945-1949. Just after World War II during the Greek Civil War, Andi and her brother live with their grandmother while their parents become communist guerillas to fight the Monarchists. Andi and Paul find a hidden cave full of weapons and keep it secret. They discover their grandmother is also helping the communists. Paul becomes the victim when the Monarchists use him to lure his mother into a trap.
Reviews: *BCCB* 4/89; *HB* 7-8/89; *SLJ* 7/89; *VOYA* 8/89
Reading Level: Middle–High School
Subject Areas: Greece--1900-; war
Time Period: 1945-1949 ❑ Library owns

Poland and Eastern Europe

Geras, Adèle. *Voyage.* **New York: Atheneum, 1983. 193pp. ISBN 0-689-30955-4. LC 82-13760.**
Eastern Europe, 1904. Told in shifting points of view, this is the story of a group of people from Eastern Europe who are emigrating to America. Each has a story to tell, a reason for leaving home, and fears of the future to deal with. The story ends as they reach Ellis Island.
Reviews: *BBYA*; *BL* 31/1/83; *SLJ* 5/83
Reading Level: Middle–High School
Subject Areas: Eastern Europe; emigration and immigration; voyages and travels
Time Period: 1904 ❑ Library owns

Hesse, Karen. *Letters from Rifka.* **New York: Holt, 1992. 146pp. ISBN 0-8050-1964-2. LC 91-48007.**

Europe, Belgium, 1919. Twelve-year-old Rifka tells a cousin of her trip across Europe in a series of letters. Rifka and her family leave Russia due to persecution and hope to get to America to start a new life. Rifka has to stay behind in Belgium because she has ringworm. A year later, she is able to travel, hoping to join her family already in America. When she arrives at Ellis Island, she is at first denied entry because the ringworm has left her bald.

Reviews: BBYA; *BL* 7/92; *HB* 9/92; *SLJ* 8/92★

Reading Level: Middle & Junior High School

Subject Areas: Europe; emigration and immigration; Jews in Russia; letters; voyages and travels

Time Period: 1919 ❏ **Library owns**

Mark, Michael. *Toba: At the Hands of a Thief.* **New York: Bradbury, 1985. 136pp. ISBN 0-02-762310-6. LC 84-20456.**

Poland, 1900s. Sequel to *Toba*. Fourteen-year-old Toba must decide whether to leave Poland to emigrate to America. Through 11 lyrical episodes, Toba's last days in Lenchintz are described.

Reviews: *BCCB* 9/85; *BL* 5/15/85; *VOYA* 2/86

Reading Level: Middle–High School

Subject Areas: Poland; Jews in Poland; emigration and immigration

Time Period: 1900s ❏ **Library owns**

Michener, James. *Poland.* **New York: Random House, 1983. 556pp. ISBN 0-394-53189-2. LC 83-4477.**

Poland. In his typical style, Michener follows three Polish families from the 1200s to the 1980s. The events of the Holocaust at the concentration camp of Majdanek are described in horrifying detail.

Reviews: *WS* 13; *BBSH*

Reading Level: High School

Subject Areas: Poland

Time Period: 1200-1980s ❏ **Library owns**

Soviet Union

Appel, Allen. *Time After Time.* **New York: Carrol & Graf, 1985. 372pp. ISBN 0-88184-182-X.**

Russia, 1917. A history teacher travels back in time and becomes involved in the Russian Revolution of 1917. He must decide if he should try to change history or just try to get back to his own time.

Europe—Twentieth Century

Reviews: *BFY*; *BL* 10/1/85
Reading Level: High School
Subject Areas: Soviet Union; Russian Revolution, 1917; time and space
Time Period: 1917 ❏ **Library owns**

Borovsky, Natasha. *A Daughter of the Nobility.* **New York: Holt, 1985. 512pp. ISBN 0-03-003294-6. LC 84-22453.**
Russia, 1913-1920. Princess Tatyana Silomirskaya, daughter of the Tsar's advisor, is betrothed to Stefan, heir to the Polish kingdom. Her study of medicine with Prof. Holveg is set aside for Stefan, but when World War I begins and Stefan goes to the Western Front, Tatyana serves as a nurse. After the 1917 Revolution, she marries Holveg, only to have Stefan reappear demanding that she return to him and royal life.
Reviews: *BL* 9/15/85; *LJ* 9/1/85; *SLJ* 10/85
Reading Level: High School
Subject Areas: Soviet Union; Russian Revolution, 1917; World War, 1914-1918
Time Period: 1913-1920 ❏ **Library owns**

Fisher, Leonard Everett. *A Russian Farewell.* **New York: Scholastic/Four Winds, 1980. 133pp. ISBN 0-590-07525-X. LC 80-342.**
Russia, 1905. As the antisemitic attitudes in Russia escalate, the Shapiro family makes the painful decision to leave their village and emigrate to America. The Shapiro's delicatessen is vandalized and the community's synagogue is burned. Seeing no hope for improvement, the three older daughters are sent off. The rest of the family will follow later.
Reviews: *BCCB* 5/81; *BL* 2/15/81; *SLJ* 1/81
Reading Level: Middle & Junior High School
Subject Areas: Russia; Jews in Russia; antisemitism
Time Period: 1905 ❏ **Library owns**

Gorki, Maxim; translated by Moura Budberg. *The Life of a Useless Man.* **Caroll & Graf, 1990, c1971. 240pp. ISBN 0-88184-647-3.**
Russia, 1905. Yevsey Klimkov, a man with no principles, becomes a spy and an informer for the Czar's forces, and is used as a pawn in a cruel game in which Yevsey is both victim and victimizer.
Reviews: *WS* 10
Reading Level: High School
Subject Areas: Russia; Russian Revolution of 1905; spies
Time Period: 1905 ❏ **Library owns**

Gottschalk, Elin Toona. *In Search of Coffee Mountains.* **Nashville: Nelson, 1977. 203pp. ISBN 0-8407-6558-4. LC 77-15071.**
Estonia, post-WWII. Along with the remaining members of her family, Lotukata is placed in a Displaced Persons camp at the end of World War II. Each member of her family moves away to start a new life, including her mother, leaving her with her grandmother. Finally they must go, moving from transit camp to transit camp.
Reviews: *BL* 1/1/78; *HB* 4/78; *SLJ* 3/78
Reading Level: Middle–High School
Subject Areas: Soviet Union; refugees
Time Period: 1945-1950 ❏ Library owns

Heyman, Anita. *Exit from Home.* **New York: Crown, 1977. 288pp. ISBN 0-517-52903-3. LC 77-23323.**
Russia, 1900-1905. Despite his dedication to religious studies (out of guilt for his baby brother's death), Samuel, a 12-year-old Jewish boy, find himself drawn to the secular world where he learns about the persecution of his people. He joins a secret revolutionary group, but becomes disillusioned, and at 15, leaves home to emigrate to America.
Reviews: *BL* 7/15/77★; *FFY*; *SLJ* 4/77★; *WJ* 4
Reading Level: Middle–High School
Subject Areas: Russia; Russian Revolution of 1905; Jews in Russia
Time Period: 1900-1905 ❏ Library owns

Holman, Felice. *The Wild Children.* **New York: Scribner, 1983. 151pp. ISBN 0-684-17970-9. LC 83-8974.**
Soviet Union, 1920s. After the Bolshevik Revolution of 1917, Alex becomes a "bezprizorni," a homeless wild child, after his family is taken away by the secret police. The gang of youths he joins lives in alleys under terrible conditions, stealing food, and always fearful of the police. He helps Peter, the gang's leader, plan the gang's escape from Russia, but decides to stay behind.
Reviews: *BBYA*; *BCCB* 12/83; *BL* 9/15/83★; *HB* 12/83; *SLJ* 11/83; *VOYA* 4/84; *WJ* 5, 6
Reading Level: Middle & Junior High School
Subject Areas: Soviet Union; Russian Revolution, 1917-1921; abandoned children; survival
Time Period: 1920s ❏ Library owns

Pasternak, Boris; translated by Max Hayward and Manya Harari. *Doctor Zhivago.* **New York: Pantheon, 1958. ISBN 0-394-42223-6. LC 60-11762.**
Soviet Union, 1900-1929. Focusing on one man, Dr. Zhivago, this shows the impact of the Russian Revolution on life in Russia.

Europe—Twentieth Century

Reviews: *WS* 10, 11, 12, 13, 14; *BBSH*
Reading Level: High School [Mature Reader]
Subject Areas: Soviet Union; communism; physicians; Russian Revolution, 1917-1921
Time Period: 1900-1929 ❏ **Library owns**

Plowman, Stephanie. *My Kingdom for a Grave.* **Boston: Houghton, 1971. 239pp. ISBN 0-395-12429-8. LC 71-147903.**

Russia, 1917. Sequel to *Three Lives for the Czar*. Andrei Hamilton, a lieutenant in the Russian Imperial Guard, follows the last Czar and his family as they are taken to Siberia, hoping to rescue them. He knows he is too late when he finds a blood-spattered room. He then aids investigators in reconstructing the murders and finding the bodies.

Reviews: *BL* 7/1/71; *LJ* 10/15/71
Reading Level: High School
Subject Areas: Soviet Union; Russian Revolution, 1917
Time Period: 1917 ❏ **Library owns**

Plowman, Stephanie. *Three Lives for the Czar.* **Boston: Houghton, 1970. 269pp. LC 76-105249.**

Russia, 1900-1917. Andrei Hamilton, a young officer in the Russian Imperial Guard whose parents both serve the Imperial family, experiences the terrible events that lead to the Russian Revolution, including assassinations, Rasputin, peasant revolts, and the beginning of World War I.

Reviews: *BL* 7/15/70; *HB* 6/70; *LJ* 5/15/70
Reading Level: High School
Subject Areas: Russia; Nicholas II, Emperor of Russia
Time Period: 1900-1914 ❏ **Library owns**

Posell, Elsa. *Homecoming.* **San Diego: Harcourt, Brace, 1987. 224pp. ISBN 0-15-235160-4. LC 87-7615.**

Russia, 1917. After the communists take over the government, the six Jewish Koshansky children and their mother are evicted from their home and must live in wretched conditions. They hope to join their father who has already fled to America. Poverty and illness take their toll and Mrs. Koshansky dies, leaving Lev, the oldest, to keep the family together and find a way to leave Russia.

Reviews: *BCCB* 1/88; *BL* 12/1/87; *BFY*; *HB* 3-4/88; *SLJ* 12/87; *VOYA* 4/88
Reading Level: Middle–High School
Subject Areas: Russia; antisemitism; Jews in Russia; Russian Revolution, 1917; survival
Time Period: 1917 ❏ **Library owns**

Sevela, Ephraim; translated by Richard Lourie. *Why There Is No Heaven on Earth.* **New York: Harper, 1982. 205pp. ISBN 0-06-025503-X. LC 81-47736.**

Soviet Union, pre-WWII. This serio-comic work is told as a series of misadventures involving Berele Mats, a picaresque, talented Jewish youth, and his friend, the narrator, who live in a small town outside of Moscow. Despite an abusive home life, Berele is a thoughtful, inventive, strong-willed young man. When the Germans invade the city at the beginning of World War II. Tragedy befalls Berele.

Reviews: *BCCB* 11/82; *BL* 7/82; *HB* 8/82; *SLJ* 4/82

Reading Level: Middle–High School

Subject Areas: Soviet Union; Jews in Russia; friendship; World War, 1939-1945

Time Period: 1937-1940 ❏ Library owns

Sholokhov, Mikhail; translated by Stephen Garry. *And Quiet Flows the Don.* **New York: Knopf, 1934. 755pp. ISBN 0-394-41520-5.**

Russia, 1910-1921. This is the story of Gregor Melekhov, a young Cossack living along the Don River. Gregor's home life, his loves, and his military exploits in the Russian Revolution are told from a Bolshevik point of view. The author won the Nobel Prize for literature in 1965.

Reviews: *WS* 11, 12, 13; *BBSH*

Reading Level: High School [Mature Reader]

Subject Areas: Soviet Union; Cossacks; Russian Revolution, 1917-1921; World War, 1914-1918

Time Period: 1910-1921 ❏ Library owns

Sholokhov, Mikhail; translated by Stephen Garry. *The Don Flows Home to the Sea.* **New York: Knopf, 1941. 777pp. ISBN 0-394-42232-5.**

Soviet Union, 1917-1921. Sequel to *And Quiet Flows the Don*. Continuing to follow Gregor Melekhov and the group of Cossacks through the Russian Revolution, the author shows the culture and personality of the Cossack people, at a time of cruelty and brutality. Followed by *Seeds of Tomorrow*.

Reviews: *WS* 11

Reading Level: High School [Mature Reader]

Subject Areas: Soviet Union; Cossacks; Russian Revolution, 1917-1921

Time Period: 1917-1921 ❏ Library owns

Sholokhov, Mikhail; translated by Stephen Garry. *The Silent Don.* **New York: Knopf, 2 v. in 1.**

Soviet Union, 1910-1921. Contains both of the previous volumes.

❏ Library owns

Solzhenitsyn, Alexander; translated by Gillon Aitken. *One Day in the Life of Ivan Denisovich.* **New York: Farrar, Straus, 1971. 173pp. ISBN 0-374-22643-1.**
Soviet Union, 1950s. This slim volume describes one day in the life of an innocent man imprisoned in a labor camp in Siberia, and is based on the author's experiences. It was first published in Russia in 1962. The author won the Nobel Prize for literature in 1970.
Reviews: *WS* 10, 12, 13, 14
Reading Level: High School
Subject Areas: Soviet Union; political prisoners; prisons and prisoners; survival
Time Period: 1950s ❑ Library owns

Spain

Griffiths, Helen; illustrated by Victor Ambrus. *The Last Summer: Spain 1936.* **New York: Holiday House, 1979. 151pp. ISBN 0-8234-0361-0. LC 79-10469.**
Spain, 1936. During the Spanish Civil War, Eduardo, son of a wealthy attorney, has his life changed forever when he witnesses the brutality of war on his father's estate. With his father gone, he runs away to find his mother and sees first hand the poverty and conditions that brought about the war. He eventually find his mother with help from army troops, but life can't be the same for him again.
Reviews: *BL* 1/1/80; *SLJ* 12/79
Reading Level: Middle & Junior High School
Subject Areas: Spain; horses; war; Spanish Civil War 1936-1939
Time Period: 1936 ❑ Library owns

Polland, Madeleine. *The Heart Speaks Many Ways.* **New York: Delacorte, 1982. 375pp. ISBN 0-440-03598-8. LC 82-2319.**
Spain, Ireland, 1936-1945. Returning to Ireland from a lengthy visit with a wealthy Spanish family following the outbreak of the Civil War, Emily McRoss waits patiently for two years to be reunited with Alejandro, who left for the army the day before they were to marry. When Emily finds he has married another, she meets Dermot Kilpatrick and they plan to marry, but war once again stalls their plans. Dermot is reported missing, and Emily begins a new romance, while Dermot's fate remains uncertain.
Reviews: *BL* 5/1/82; *LJ* 8/82; *SLJ* 11/82
Reading Level: High School [Mature Reader]
Subject Areas: Spain; Ireland; Spanish Civil War, 1936-1939; World War, 1939-1945; love
Time Period: 1936-1945 ❑ Library owns

Watson, James. *The Freedom Tree.* **New York: Gollancz; David & Charles, 1986. 160pp. ISBN 0-575-03779-2.**

Spain, 1936-1939. Will, an English orphan whose father died fighting in Spain, makes his way there to join an international brigade fighting the fascists. He is sickened by what he sees of war as a stretcher-bearer. He is taken prisoner, escapes, and witnesses the bombing of Guernica.

Reviews: *BL* 11/1/86; *SLJ* 2/87

Reading Level: Middle–High School

Subject Areas: Spain; Spanish Civil War, 1936-1939; war

Time Period: 1936-1939 ❑ Library owns

World War I

Dank, Milton. *Khaki Wings.* **New York: Delacorte, 1980. 180pp. ISBN 0-440-04486-3. LC 80-65832.**

England, France, 1914-1918. Seventeen-year-old Edward Burton joins the Royal Flying Corps, as a mechanic. With his natural leadership skills, he becomes a pilot, hoping to become an ace fighting the Germans. He achieves some fame, but also sees the carnage of war and the death of his friend. He finally "cracks" under the pressure and is sent home.

Reviews: *BBSH*; *BL* 10/15/80; *HB* 12/80; *SLJ* 1/81; *VOYA* 4/81

Reading Level: Middle–High School

Subject Areas: Great Britain--1900-; France; air pilots; aerial operations

Time Period: World War, 1914-1918 ❑ Library owns

Dank, Milton. *Red Flight Two.* **New York: Delacorte, 1981. 184pp. ISBN 0-440-07336-7. LC 81-176.**

England, France, 1916-1918. Sequel to *Khaki Wings*. Recovered from his nervous breakdown, Edward Burton is now a flight instructor who feels guilty about sending young men to die in battle. He volunteers to go to France again and spends two more years leading his men, eventually reaching the rank of Major at the age of 20. The dogfights with German planes are well portrayed.

Reviews: *BL* 10/1/81; *SLJ* 9/81

Reading Level: Middle–High School

Subject Areas: Great Britain--1900-; France; air pilots; aerial operations

Time Period: World War, 1914-1918 ❑ Library owns

Frank, Rudolf; translated by Patricia Crampton; illustrated by Klaus Steffens. *No Hero for the Kaiser.* **New York: Lothrop, 1986. 222pp. ISBN 0-688-06093-5. LC 85-23989.**

Poland, Germany, 1914-1918. Fourteen-year-old Jan Kubitsky, the sole survivor of his Polish village, is adopted by a group of German troops. Jan helps the men in many ways, and comes to consider them his friends. They are so impressed with Jan that they want to make him a German citizen and a highly publicized symbol. Jan, however, having seen the horrors of war, walks away, wanting no part of the glorification of war. Originally written in 1931, this was banned by Hitler.

Reviews: *BCCB* 10/86; *BL* 9/1/86; *BR* 11-12/86; *NCB*; *SLJ* 10/86; *WJ* 6

Reading Level: Middle–High School

Subject Areas: Poland; Germany

Time Period: World War, 1914-1918 ❏ Library owns

Gann, Ernest. *In the Company of Eagles.* **New York: Simon & Schuster, 1966. 342pp.**

France, 1917. A young French pilot, seeking vengeance, is pitted against a flawless German pilot who has killed many French pilots.

Reviews: *WS* 10

Reading Level: High School

Subject Areas: France; air pilots; aerial operations

Time Period: World War, 1914-1918 ❏ Library owns

Remarque, Erich Maria; translated by A. W. Wheen. *All Quiet on the Western Front.* **Boston: Little, Brown, 1929. 291pp. ISBN 0-316-73992-8.**

Germany, 1914-1918. Paul and three friends are pulled from school and placed on the front with the German Army. At the end of the war, only Paul is alive, but he is forever damaged by the slaughter he witnessed. This autobiographical novel is an indictment of war.

Reviews: *BBSH*; *WS* 10, 11, 12, 13, 14

Reading Level: High School

Subject Areas: Germany; soldiers; war

Time Period: World War, 1914-1918 ❏ Library owns

Solzhenitsyn, Alexander; translated by Michael Glenny. *August 1914.* **New York: Farrar, Straus, 1972. 622pp. ISBN 0-374-10684-3.**

Russia, 1914. Meticulous in research and detail, the author explores the Battle of Tannenberg where the Russians were defeated, offering theories on where the blame for the defeat should be placed.

Reviews: *WS* 10, 11

Reading Level: High School

Subject Areas: Russia; Tannenberg, Battle of 1914

Time Period: World War, 1914-1918 ❏ Library owns

World War II

Anatoli, A.; translated by David Floyd. *Babi Yar.* **Cambridge, MA: Bentley, 1979, c1970. p. ISBN 0-8376-0432-X. LC 78-74649.**

Soviet Union, 1941-1943. Based on documents such as diaries, interviews, and newspaper clippings, the author (who was twelve at the time), documents the period in which Germans used a ravine on the outskirts of Kiev, known as Babi Yar, to murder 200,000 people, 50,000 of them Jews.

Reviews: *WS* 10

Reading Level: High School [Mature Reader]

Subject Areas: Soviet Union; Holocaust, Jewish (1933-1945); massacres; Kiev (Soviet Union)

Time Period: World War, 1939-1945 ❏ Library owns

Baer, Frank; translated by Ivanka Roberts. *Max's Gang.* **Boston: Little, Brown, 1983. 324pp. ISBN 0-316-07517-5. LC 82-24918.**

Germany, 1945. Just before the end of WWII, three boys are separated from a group being sent home to Berlin when their evacuation camp closes. They are forced to fend for themselves and escape dangerous situations, including mine fields and enemy troops, in order to reach their families.

Reviews: *BCCB* 10/83; *BL* 5/15/83; *HB* 6/83; *SLJ* 9/83; *VOYA* 10/83

Reading Level: Middle–High School

Subject Areas: Germany

Time Period: World War, 1939-1945 ❏ Library owns

Baklanov, Grigory; translated by Antonina W. Bouis. *Forever Nineteen.* **Philadelphia: Lippincott, 1989. 166pp. ISBN 0-397-32297-6. LC 88-26622.**

Soviet Union, 1943. In his tribute to the other 19 boys in his high school class who did not return from the Russian Front, Baklanov tells the story of Jr. Lieutenant Volodya Tretyakov, at 19, already a veteran of the front, who is assigned to the Ukrainian front in command of a Red Army artillery unit. He is wounded, experiences love while hospitalized, and returns to the front.

Reviews: *BBSH*; *BL* 5/1/89; *HB* 9-10/89; *SLJ* 5/89

Reading Level: Middle–High School

Subject Areas: Soviet Union; war

Time Period: World War, 1939-1945 ❏ Library owns

Benchley, Nathaniel. *Bright Candles: A Novel of the Danish Resistance.* **New York: Harper, 1974. 256pp. ISBN 0-06-020461-3. LC 73-5477.**

Denmark, 1940-1945. When the Nazis invade Denmark in 1940, many Danes feel cooperation is their best defense. Two teens decide to give the Germans a hard time, finally joining the Resistance when troops begin to round up Danish Jews. Jens is finally captured by the Nazis and imprisoned, but escapes and awaits the end of the war in hiding.

Reviews: *BBYA*; *BL* 3/1/74; *FFY*; *WJ* 4, 5; *WS* 10, 11, 12, 13

Reading Level: Middle–High School

Subject Areas: Denmark; underground movements

Time Period: World War, 1939-1945 ❏ Library owns

Bergman, Tamar; translated by Michael Swirsky. *Along the Tracks.* **Boston, Houghton, 1991. 245pp. ISBN 0-395-55328-8. LC 90-27521.**

Poland, Soviet Union, 1939-1945. Eight-year-old Yankele and his family flee Poland with many other Jews hoping to escape the German occupation. On their way to Russia, Yankele is separated from his parents, beginning a four-year search not only for his mother, but for survival as he must beg, steal, and rely on his own resources and the occasional kindness of strangers. When he does find his mother, he is a strong, resilient teen. Based on a true story.

Reviews: *BCCB* 10/91★; *BL* 9/15/91; *BR* 5/92; *HB* 11/91; *NCB*; *SLJ* 12/91; *VOYA* 12/91

Reading Level: Middle–High School

Subject Areas: Soviet Union; Jews in Russia; refugees; survival

Time Period: World War, 1939-1945 ❏ Library owns

Bienek, Horst; translated by Ralph R. Reed. *Time Without Bells.* **New York: Atheneum, 1988. 292pp. ISBN 0-689-11930-5. LC 87-17124.**

Poland, 1943. The hopes and faith of the people of a small Polish town deteriorate as the events of WWII escalate. Young and old characters who have finally achieved success, or are on the brink of success, find it short-lived as they realize their roles in the fate of the Jews and the war effort.

Reviews: *BL* 12/15/87★; *LJ* 1/88

Reading Level: High School [Mature Reader]

Subject Areas: Poland

Time Period: World War, 1939-1945 ❏ Library owns

Bloch, Marie Halun; illustrated by Allen Davis. *Displaced Person.* **New York: Lothrop, 1978. 174pp. ISBN 0-688-51860-5. LC 78-13083.**

Germany, 1944-1945. After his mother's death and after traveling from one refugee camp to another with his father, Stefan cannot trust anyone and has a difficult time thinking for himself. Stefan's botanist father, who is dragging a large briefcase with them filled with years of his research, is killed in a raid. Stefan hides the briefcase and moves on, hoping to make his way to the American sector where he has a chance of freedom. Finally using his head, Stefan saves three friends and risks his life to retrieve his father's work.

Reviews: *BL* 12/1/78; *SLJ* 12/78; *WJ* 4

Reading Level: Middle & Junior High School

Subject Areas: Germany; refugees

Time Period: World War, 1939-1945 ❑ Library owns

Briskin, Mae. *The Tree Still Stands.* **New York: Norton, 1991. 256pp. ISBN 0-393-02894-1. LC 90-31463.**

Europe, 1939-1945. A wealthy Polish family must stay one step ahead of the Nazis, hiding in Italian monasteries, and traveling through France.

Reviews: *BL* 1/15/91; *LJ* 12/90

Reading Level: High School

Subject Areas: Europe; Italy; France; family life

Time Period: World War, 1939-1945 ❑ Library owns

Burnford, Sheila. *Bel Ria.* **New York: Bantam, 1977. 215pp. ISBN 0-316-77139-2. LC 77-21082.**

France, England, 1939-1945. Bel Ria, a small dog who was the pet of French woman who was killed in a bombing, finds his way to a group of British soldiers who adopt him and take him to England. There he becomes the pet of an English spinster. Bel Ria has an impact on each of his owners.

Reviews: *LJ* 1/15/78; *SLJ* 5/78; *WJ* 4; *WS* 12

Reading Level: Middle–High School

Subject Areas: dogs; France; Great Britain--1900–

Time Period: 1939-1945; World War, 1939-1945 ❑ Library owns

Bykov, Vasil; translated by Lynn Solotaroff. *Pack of Wolves.* **New York: Crowell, 1981. 181pp. ISBN 0-690-04115-2. LC 80-2456.**

Soviet Union, 1943. Levchuk goes to visit an unnamed acquaintance. While he waits for the man to return home he recalls his experience in World War II as part of a group which included Klava, a pregnant radio operator, who was trying to reach a Russian medical. Trapped in a shed by a "pack of wolves," the Germans and the Polizei, only Levchuk and Klava's newborn baby survive.

Reviews: *BBYA*; *BCCB* 1/82; *BL* 1/1/82; *SLJ* 12/81★; *WJ* 6

Reading Level: Middle–High School

Subject Areas: Soviet Union; escapes

Time Period: 1943; World War, 1939-1945 ❑ Library owns

Europe—Twentieth Century

Carter, Peter. *The Hunted.* **New York: Farrar, 1994. 309pp. ISBN 0-374-33520-6. LC 93-34211.**

France, 1943. While making his way home after the surrender of Italy, Corporal Vito Salvani finds himself traveling with a small Jewish boy, Judah. They are pursued by a French policeman, Palet, who is a Nazi collaborator and who believes Judah is smuggling diamonds. At this time, Hitler's army is stepping up its efforts to murder all the Jews in Europe. Vito, who would rather be home, finds he cannot leave Judah behind.

Reviews: *BCCB* 3/94; *BL* 4/1/94; *BR* 11-12/94; *PW* 5/23/94; *SLJ* 6/94

Reading Level: Middle–High School

Subject Areas: France--1900-

Time Period: World War, 1939-1945   ❏ Library owns

Coulonges, Henri; translated by Lowell Bair. *Farewell, Dresden.* **New York: Summit, 1989. 266pp. ISBN 0-671-61779-6. LC 88-29452.**

Germany, 1945. A special night out with her friend Hella becomes a nightmare for Johanna as the firebombing of Dresden begins. As they desperately try to reach home, Hella is killed. Johanna finds her mother in shock and her sister dead. After finding a safe place for herself and her mother, Johanna makes friends with a wounded boy who helps her as she tries to help him.

Reviews: *BL* 12/15/88; *PW* 12/16/88

Reading Level: High School

Subject Areas: Germany; Dresden (Germany)

Time Period: World War, 1939-1945   ❏ Library owns

Dank, Milton. *The Dangerous Game.* **Philadelphia: Lippincott, 1977. 160pp. ISBN 0-397-31753-0. LC 77-23453.**

France, 1939-1945. Charles joins the French Underground in Paris and begins a series of dangerous missions including delivering secret documents, assassinating a British double agent, and escaping from the Gestapo. When things get too hot for him, he flees to England and joins the Free French Intelligence Service.

Reviews: *HB* 2/78; *SLJ* 9/77

Reading Level: Middle–High School

Subject Areas: France; underground movements; spies

Time Period: World War, 1939-1945   ❏ Library owns

Degens, T. *The Visit.* **New York: Viking, 1982. 168pp. ISBN 0-670-74712-2. LC 82-2600.**

Germany, 1939-1945. Kate Hoffman finds the diary of her dead aunt, also named Kate. As she reads, she discovers that her Aunt Kate and Aunt Sylvia, Kate's sister who is still very much alive, were in the Hitler Youth Corp. Kate is able to

reconstruct the events that lead to Aunt Kate's untimely death. Kate must know why her family never mentions Aunt Kate.
Reviews: *BCCB* 11/82; *BR* 11-12/82; *HB* 2/83; *SLJ* 10/82; *VOYA* 4/83; *WJ* 5, 6
Reading Level: Middle–High School
Subject Areas: Germany; Hitler Youth Corps
Time Period: World War, 1939-1945 ❏ Library owns

Fife, Dale; illustrated by Haakon Soether. *North of Danger.* New York: Dutton, 1978. 72pp. ISBN 0-525-36035-2. LC 77-26199.
Norway, 1939-1945. Twelve-year-old Arne Kristiansen avoids evacuation from Norway to England so that he can travel to warn his father of the impending Nazi invasion. Arne makes a dangerous journey through the frozen north to reach his father and is helped along the way by a German trapper.
Reviews: *WJ* 4
Reading Level: Middle & Junior High School
Subject Areas: Norway; survival
Time Period: World War, 1939-1945 ❏ Library owns

Forester, C. S. *The Last Nine Days of the Bismarck.* Boston: Little, Brown, 1959. 138pp. ISBN 0-685-03074-1.
Atlantic Ocean, 1941. In May, 1941, the German battleship Bismarck began to attack British ships in the Atlantic. The English ships, inferior to the Bismarck, were given the task of destroying the Bismarck. This novel is based on the naval strategies employed and the British Navy's luck.
Reviews: *WS* 10
Reading Level: High School
Subject Areas: Bismarck (Battleship); battleships; Naval Operations; Great Britain. Navy
Time Period: 1941; World War, 1939-1945 ❏ Library owns

Forman, James. *Ceremony of Innocence.* Hawthorn Books, 1970. 249pp. ISBN 0-8015-1140-2. LC 73-106177.
Germany, 1939-1945. Hans Scholl and his sister Sophie, university students, become involved in an underground movement by operating a printing press that produces materials urging resistance to the Third Reich. They are arrested, and urged to cooperate with the government. They refuse, preferring to die than give up their principles. This is based on a true account.
Reviews: *WJ* 4
Reading Level: Middle–High School

Europe—Twentieth Century

Subject Areas: Germany; Scholl family; underground movements
Time Period: World War, 1939-1945   ❏ Library owns

Forman, James. *Horses of Anger.* **New York: Farrar, Straus, 1967. 249pp. LC 67-15004.**
Germany, 1939-1945. Through a series of flashbacks, we see the evolution of 15-year-old Hans, who is trying to defend a jet factory from bombers with ineffective weapons. Hans, as a small child is enthusiastic about Hitler, but as he matures and sees how those around him are affected by Nazism, he recognizes the insanity of it.
Reviews: *BL* 9/1/67; *HB* 6/67; *LJ* 5/15/67
Reading Level: Middle–High School
Subject Areas: Germany
Time Period: World War, 1939-1945   ❏ Library owns

Forman, James. *The Traitors.* **New York: Straus, 1968. 238pp. ISBN 0-374-37722-7. LC 68-23747.**
Germany, 1938-1945. The two sons of a pastor in a small Bavarian town take different sides during the war. Kurt becomes a confirmed Nazi, but Paul, who is not fit for military service, at first is unsure of his beliefs. As the war grinds on, he sees that Germany will lose. He hides a Jewish friends and helps save his town from destruction by the Nazis.
Reviews: *WJ* 4
Reading Level: Middle–High School
Subject Areas: Germany; brothers; underground movements
Time Period: World War, 1939-1945   ❏ Library owns

Garfield, Brian and Christopher Creighton. *The Paladin: A Novel Based on Fact.* **New York: Simon & Schuster, 1980. 512pp. ISBN 0-671-24704-2. LC 79-20290.**
Great Britain, 1939-1945. Allegedly based on fact, this is the story of a 15-year-old boy who is asked by Winston Churchill to go to Belgium before the Nazis takes over and do a little spying. He does an excellent job and is recruited into the Secret Service, where he is trained to do all the jobs a top agent would do, including assassination. Churchill sends him on many dangerous and deadly missions during the war.
Reviews: *BBYA*; *BL* 2/15/80; *WS* 11, 12; *YARC*
Reading Level: High School
Subject Areas: Great Britain--1990-; Secret Service; Churchill, Sir Winston; spies
Time Period: World War, 1939-1945   ❏ Library owns

Gehrts, Barbara; translated by Elizabeth D. Crawford. *Don't Say a Word.* **New York: Macmillan, 1986. 192pp. ISBN 0-689-50412-8. LC 86-7248.**
Germany, 1939-1945. In this autobiographical novel, Anna and her mother are the only remaining members of their family. Her brother and boy friend have been killed, and her Jewish friend commits suicide. Her father, an officer in the Luftwaffe, is executed for anti-Nazi activities. Her home is bombed. With nothing left of their life, Anna and her mother escape into the countryside and away from the war.
Reviews: *BL* 10/1/86; *NCB*; *PW* 5/26/86; *SLJ* 12/86; *WJ* 6
Reading Level: Middle–High School
Subject Areas: Germany
Time Period: World War, 1939-1945 ❏ Library owns

Gessner, Lynne. *Edge of Darkness.* **New York: Walker, 1979. 181pp. ISBN 0-8027-6367-7. LC 79-4859.**
Latvia, 1939-1945. The Ozols family is beset with great difficulties during the war when, at different times, Latvia is invaded by the Nazis and the Russians. When Davids' father is imprisoned, he must run the farm and take care of his family. He also becomes involved in a resistance movement. This has many characters (some stereotyped), but little character development. The action keeps the story moving.
Reviews: *BCCB* 1/80; *HB* 2/80; *SLJ* 11/79; *VOYA* 2/80
Reading Level: Middle–High School
Subject Areas: Latvia; underground movements
Time Period: World War, 1939-1945 ❏ Library owns

Haar, Jaap ter; translated by Martha Mearns; illustrated by Rien Poortvliet. *Boris.* **New York: Delacorte, 1970. 152pp. LC 77-122770.**
Soviet Union, 1941-1944. During the Siege of Leningrad when food was very scarce, Boris and a friend, Nadia, sneak into a forbidden area where they are digging for frozen potatoes. They are captured by German troops, and to their surprise, they are fed and returned to the Russian lines at great risk to the Germans. Despite the horrors of war he will later encounter, Boris remembers the German soldier's kindness that showed him the human face of the enemy.
Reviews: *BL* 2/15/71; *LJ* 1/15/71
Reading Level: Middle & Junior High School
Subject Areas: Soviet Union; Leningrad, Siege of, 1941-1944
Time Period: World War, 1939-1945 ❏ Library owns

Harris, John. *Ride Out the Storm: A Novel of Dunkirk.* Mason/Charter, 1976. 272pp. ISBN 0-88405-144-7.
France, 1940. The nine days of the Battle of Dunkirk are recreated through the experiences of several characters who experience horror and injury while fleeing from Hitler's troops, but who also are courageous.
Reviews: *BL* 8/76; *LJ* 5/15/76
Reading Level: High School [Mature Reader]
Subject Areas: France--1900-; Dunkirk, Battle of, 1940
Time Period: 1940; World War, 1939-1945 ❏ Library owns

Hartman, Evert; translated by Patricia Crampton. *War Without Friends.* New York: Crown, 1982. 192pp. ISBN 0-517-54754-6. LC 82-10093.
Netherlands, 1942-1944. Hated and taunted by his schoolmates because of his Nazi beliefs, Arnold begins as an unlikable character. In his loneliness, he makes friends with the only other boy whose father is a Nazi. Through this other boy and by helping a resistance fighter who has become his friend, he gradually realizes how destructive the Party is. He chooses to stay behind when his parents flee to Germany as the Allies invade.
Reviews: *BCCB* 12/82; *BL* 9/1/82; *HB* 12/82; *SLJ* 10/82; *VOYA* 6/83
Reading Level: Middle–High School
Subject Areas: Netherlands
Time Period: 1942-1944; World War, 1939-1945 ❏ Library owns

Haugaard, Erik Christian. *Chase Me, Catch Nobody.* Boston: Houghton, 1980. 209pp. ISBN 0-395-29208-5. LC 80-371.
Denmark, Germany, 1937. On a class trip from Denmark to Germany, 14-year-old Erik is asked to deliver a package of forged passports to an address in Hamburg by a man who was later arrested by the Gestapo. Erik decides to follow through and becomes involved in a desperate escape while the Gestapo pursue him and a Jewish girl who is also desperate to escape.
Reviews: *BBYA*; *BCCB* 6/80; *BL* 5/1/80; *HB* 6/80; *SLJ* 4/80; *VOYA* 4/80; *WJ* 5
Reading Level: Middle–High School
Subject Areas: Germany
Time Period: 1937; World War, 1939-1945 ❏ Library owns

Haugaard, Erik Christian; illustrated by Milton Johnson. *The Little Fishes.* Boston: Houghton, 1967. 214pp. ISBN 0-395-06802-9. LC 67-14701.
Italy, 1939-1945. Guido, an orphan who remembers his mother telling him to be strong and kind, survives in Italy during the war despite starvation and filth and is able to help other orphans as well.

Reviews: *BBYA*; *WJ* 4
Reading Level: Middle & Junior High School
Subject Areas: Italy; orphans; survival
Time Period: World War, 1939-1945 ❏ Library owns

Horgan, Dorothy. *The Edge of War.* **New York: Oxford Univ. Press, 1988. 112pp. ISBN 0-19-271574-7.**
Germany, 1939-1945. Anna, a dark-haired child, and her non-Nazi Catholic family suffer hardships during the war. As punishment for not joining the Nazi party, her parents are given jobs in separate remote areas, and when her father is wounded, he is given very minimal care. Anna witnesses the death of her mother in a raid, a friend is put in a labor camp, and her uncle is captured by the Russians. When the allies invade, Anna becomes an interpreter and is able to help save her father and her friend.
Reviews: *BCCB* 7-8/88; *BL* 7/88; *SLJ* 6-7/88
Reading Level: Middle & Junior High School
Subject Areas: Germany
Time Period: World War, 1939-1945 ❏ Library owns

Hough, Richard. *Razor Eyes.* **New York: Lodestar, 1983. 116pp. ISBN 0-525-66916-7. LC 83-11574.**
England, 1939-1945. Mick Boyd, nicknamed Razor Eyes for his acute eyesight, makes it through flight school and is involved in raids against the Nazis in Europe. He has a fear of blood and pain, and he is devastated by the loss of his best friend in combat, but he takes on a risky solo mission that earns him the Distinguished Flying Cross.
Reviews: *BL* 10/1/83
Reading Level: Middle–High School
Subject Areas: Great Britain--1900-; air pilots; aerial operations
Time Period: World War, 1939-1945 ❏ Library owns

Kennedy, Raymond. *The Bitterest Age.* **New York: Ticknor & Fields, 1994. 218pp. ISBN 0-395-68629-6.**
Germany, 1939-1945. Ten-year-old Ingeborg Maas believes that her father, missing in action on the Russian front, is still alive. Despite the nightly bombing, hunger, and other terrors of war, she will not leave Potsdam so that her father will know where she and her family are when he returns. Her faith provides hope for her mother and brother as well.
Reviews: *BL* 4/15/94; *LJ* 2/15/94
Reading Level: High School

Subject Areas: Germany; survival
Time Period: World War, 1939-1945   ❏ Library owns

Korschunow, Irina; translated by Leigh Hafrey. *A Night in Distant Motion.* **Boston: Godine, 1983. 151pp. ISBN 0-87923-399-0. LC 71-47325.**
Germany, 1944. After her Polish lover is captured by the Nazis, 17-year-old Regine is hunted as a traitor and finds refuge with a family. While in hiding, she reflects on how her lover helped to change her belief in the Nazi philosophy.
Reviews: *BBYA*; *FFY*; *BL* 10/15/83
Reading Level: High School
Subject Areas: Germany
Time Period: 1944; World War, 1939-1945   ❏ Library owns

Kotowska, Monika; translated by Maia Wojciechowska. *The Bridge to the Other Side.* **New York: Doubleday, 1970. 164pp. LC 75-116264.**
Poland, 1939-1945. In 19 vignettes, the author writes of children surviving during World War II in Poland. The first half of the book details the appalling living conditions and survival techniques of children who are also trying to understand why this has happened to them. The second shows how the children retaliated against adults, blaming them for the war.
Reviews: *BL* 1/15/71; *HB* 10/70; *LJ* 11/15/70
Reading Level: High School
Subject Areas: Poland; survival; children
Time Period: World War, 1939-1945   ❏ Library owns

Lingard, Joan. *Tug of War.* **New York: Dutton/Lodestar, 1990. 192pp. ISBN 0-525-67306-7. LC 89-13967.**
Latvia, Germany, 1944. A Latvian family tries to escape the advance of the Russian Army on its way to Germany. Hugo, the 14-year-old son, is separated from his family and his twin sister. Dual narratives tell the story of the family's and Hugo's separate attempts to reach Germany and survive as the Nazis lose the war.
Reviews: *BCCB* 9/90; *BL* 6/15/90; *HB* 9/90★; *SLJ* 9/90; *VOYA* 10/90
Reading Level: Middle–High School
Subject Areas: Latvia; Germany; refugees
Time Period: 1944; World War, 1939-1944   ❏ Library owns

Lowry, Lois. *Number the Stars.* **Boston: Houghton, 1989. 125pp. ISBN 0-395-50930-0. LC 88-37134.**
Denmark, 1943. Annamarie, whose life hasn't been affected much by the German occupation, finds things changing when her family becomes involved in the Resistance effort as the Nazis begins rounding up Jews. Annamarie's Jewish

friend takes on the identity of her dead sister until her parents can smuggle her out of Denmark. After Annamarie's mother moves the girls to a small town, Annamarie becomes involved in smuggling Jews out of Denmark, along with her parents. This book won the Newbery Award in 1989.
Reviews: *BCCB* 3/89; *BL* 3/1/89★; *HB* 5-6/89; *SLJ* 3/89★; *WJ* 6
Reading Level: Middle & Junior High School
Subject Areas: Denmark; underground movements; friendship; Jews in Denmark
Time Period: 1943; World War, 1939-1945 ❑ Library owns

MacLean Alistair. *The Guns of Navarone.* **New York: Fawcett, 1979, c1957. 288pp. ISBN 0-449-21472-9.**
Eastern Mediterranean, 1939-1945. A five-man British team is chosen to destroy the Nazi-controlled big guns on the island of Navarone. The team must land secretly, elude Nazis, climb a gargantuan cliff, and destroy the gun in this grand adventure story. Followed by *Force 10 from Navarone*.
Reviews: *WS* 12, 13, 14
Reading Level: High School
Subject Areas: adventure and adventurers
Time Period: World War, 1939-1945 ❑ Library owns

MacLean, Alistair. *H.M.S. Ulysses.* **New York: Fawcett, 1979, c1955. 320pp. ISBN 0-449-14083-0.**
Arctic Ocean, 1939-1945. Set in the stormy Arctic waters between Iceland and Sweden, this is the story of the crew of the HMS *Ulysses*, a British light cruiser, and their disintegration as they guard a convoy from German ships.
Reviews: *BBSH*; *WS* 12, 13
Reading Level: High School
Subject Areas: sea stories; Great Britain. Navy
Time Period: World War, 1939-1945 ❑ Library owns

Matas, Carol. *Code Name Kris.* **New York: Scribners, 1989. 152pp. ISBN 0-684-19208-X. LC 90-32656.**
Denmark, 1943. Sequel to *Lisa's War*. Seventeen-year-old Jesper, reflecting on his activities in the Resistance from a jail cell, tells of some of his successful missions and is able to explain how the war affected people in Denmark emotionally.
Reviews: *BCCB* 1/91; *BR* 5-6/91; *HB* 1/91; *SLJ* 12/90
Reading Level: Middle–High School
Subject Areas: Denmark; underground movements
Time Period: 1943; World War, 1939-1945 ❑ Library owns

Europe—Twentieth Century

Matas, Carol. *Lisa's War.* **New York: Scribners, 1989. 111pp. ISBN 0-684-19010-9. LC 88-29525.**

Denmark, 1939-1945. Twelve-year-old Lisa and her family join the resistance in Denmark during the Nazi occupation. Lisa begins with small duties but her assignments grow in responsibility. In contrast is Lisa's cousin's family who deny that there is truly any danger until it is too late. When the news reaches Lisa and her family that the Jews are to be deported to camps, they help in organizing a mass evacuation.

Reviews: *BCCB* 5/89; *BL* 4/1/89; *HB* 5-6/89; *SLJ* 5/89
Reading Level: Middle–High School
Subject Areas: Denmark; underground movements
Time Period: World War, 1939-1945 ❑ Library owns

Nöstlinger, Christine; translated by Anthea Bell. *Fly Away Home.* **New York: Watts, 1975. 134pp. ISBN 0-531-01096-1. LC 75-16255.**

Austria, 1945. During the closing days of World War II, Christel and her family are left homeless when their apartment building is bombed. They, along with other refugees, are offered a villa near the city. Everyone is apprehensive when the Russians arrive, expecting brutality, but instead the Russians move into the villa, too, where they show kindness.

Reviews: *BCCB* 2/76; *BL* 9/1/75★; *HB* 2/76; *SLJ* 12/75★
Reading Level: Middle–High School
Subject Areas: Austria; refugees
Time Period: 1945; World War, 1939-1945 ❑ Library owns

Rees, David. *The Exeter Blitz.* **New York: Elsevier/Nelson, 1980. 128pp. ISBN 0-525-66683-4. LC 80-13670.**

England, 1942. The bombardment of Exeter is described by the members of the Lockwood family, each being in a different place when the blitz begins. The father and younger sister are at home, the older sister is at the movies, the mother is in an elevator at a dress shop, and Colin is in the tower of the cathedral, watching the attack which destroys almost the entire town, sparing only the cathedral. Winner of the 1978 Carnegie Medal.

Reviews: *BCCB* 9/80; *BL* 9/1/80; *HB* 10/80; *SLJ* 9/80
Reading Level: Middle–High School
Subject Areas: Great Britain--1900-; Exeter (England), bombardment, 1942
Time Period: 1942; World War, 1939-1945 ❑ Library owns

Reuter, Bjarne; translated by Anthea Bell. *The Boys from St. Petri.* **New York: Dutton, 1994. 192pp. ISBN 0-525-45121-8. LC 93-24161.**
Denmark, 1939-1945. Brothers Lars and Gunnar meet secretly in St. Petri's church with a group of high school boys who decide to harass the Nazis. The level of harassment increases, turning into sabotage, and then to the destruction of a German train. After the train is blown up, the boys are arrested.
Reviews: *BCCB* 3/94; *BL* 2/1/94; *BR* 9-10/94; *HB* 3/94; *SLJ* 2/94
Reading Level: Middle–High School
Subject Areas: Denmark; underground movements
Time Period: World War, 1939-1945 ❏ Library owns

Richter, Hans Peter; translated by Edite Kroll. *I Was There.* **New York: Holt, 1972. 204pp. ISBN 0-14-032206-X. LC 72-76581.**
Germany, 1939-1945. For different reasons, three young boys join the Hitler Youth movement. This follows them as they mature, doing what is expected of them—collecting scraps for the war movement, participating in war games, harassing Jews, and finally, going away to war.
Reviews: *BL* 3/1/73; *HB* 12/72; *LJ* 1/15/73
Reading Level: Middle–High School
Subject Areas: Germany; Hitler Youth Corps
Time Period: World War, 1939-1945 ❏ Library owns

Rydberg, Ernie and Lou Rydberg. *The Shadow Army.* **New York: Nelson, 1976. 160pp. ISBN 0-8407-6493-6. LC 76-6115.**
Greece, 1941. When the Germans invade Crete, 14-year-old Demetrios escapes with his brother and grandfather to the hills, but his mother forced to become their cook. Over a period of three years, Demetrios' activities in the Shadow Army, an underground militia, include rescuing his mother and kidnapping a Nazi officer.
Reviews: *BL* 7/15/76; *SLJ* 9/76
Reading Level: Middle–High School
Subject Areas: Greece; underground movements
Time Period: World War, 1939-1945 ❏ Library owns

Samuels, Gertrude. *Mottele: A Partisan Odyssey.* **New York: Harper, 1976. 160pp. ISBN 0-06-013759-2. LC 75-25101.**
Poland, 1942. Twelve-year-old violin virtuoso Mottele joins the Jewish underground, hiding in the forests. Through acts of courage and vengeance he participates in a series of raids. His courage cannot keep him from death in a raid.
Reviews: *BL* 4/1/76★; *FFY*; *SLJ* 10/76; *WS* 11
Reading Level: High School

Subject Areas: Poland; Jews in Poland; underground movements; Holocaust, 1933-1945
Time Period: 1942; World War, 1939-1945 ❏ Library owns

Sevela, Ephraim; translated by Antonina W. Bouis. *We Were Not Like Other People.* **New York: Harper, 1989. 216pp. ISBN 0-06-025508-0. LC 89-11015.**
Soviet Union, 1939-1945. Told as a series of episodes, this is the story of a boy, separated from his family, who over a period of six years survives with help from peasants, soldiers, and others. He steals food, works in a factory manned by children, helps with a grain harvest, anything to help him survive. At the end, he is reunited with his family.
Reviews: *BCCB* 10/89; *BL* 9/1/89★; *SLJ* 12/89; *VOYA* 12/89; *WS* 13
Reading Level: Middle–High School
Subject Areas: Soviet Union; survival
Time Period: World War, 1939-1945 ❏ Library owns

Shemin, Margaretha. *The Empty Moat.* **New York: Coward-McCann, 1969. 159pp. LC 77-86301.**
Netherlands, 1939-1945. This autobiographical novel tells of 16-year-old Elizabeth Van Swaenenburgh and her involvement with the resistance movement. Elizabeth begins as a fearful girl, with a quiet hatred for the Nazis. Through her participation with the resistance, she becomes courageous despite the risks.
Reviews: *BL* 2/1/70; *HB* 12/69; *LJ* 12/15/69
Reading Level: Middle–High School
Subject Areas: Netherlands; underground movements
Time Period: World War, 1939-1945 ❏ Library owns

Stachow, Hasso G.; translated by J. Maxwell Brownjohn. *If This Be Glory.* **New York: Doubleday, 1982. 257pp. ISBN 0-385-15974-9. LC 80-2437.**
Germany, 1942. Years after the war, Herbert Quast tells an interviewer of his experiences as an 18-year-old German soldier on the Russian front. He relates the grimness of existence and the horrors of war as well as his realization of the futility of his position.
Reviews: *BL* 4/15/82; *SLJ* 9/82
Reading Level: High School
Subject Areas: Germany; soldiers; war
Time Period: World War, 1939-1945 ❏ Library owns

Europe—Twentieth Century

Terlouw, Jan. *Winter in Wartime.* **New York: McGraw-Hill, 1976. 197pp. ISBN 0-07-063504-8. LC 75-41345.**

Netherlands, 1939-1945. Fifteen-year-old Michiel, son of the town's mayor, finds himself aiding a downed British pilot by himself. Despite short supplies and Nazi occupation, he must find food and hiding places for the pilot. In retaliation against the active resistance movement, Michiel's father is executed. Michiel, who once thought it romantic to join the resistance, now understands that war is not romantic just as his father had told him. Winner of Best Dutch Juvenile Book for 1973.

Reviews: *BL* 6/1/76; *SLJ* 9/76
Reading Level: Middle–High School
Subject Areas: Netherlands; underground movements
Time Period: World War, 1939-1945 ❏ Library owns

Vos, Ida; translated by Terese Edelstein and Inez Smidt. *Hide and Seek.* **Boston: Houghton, 1991. 144pp. ISBN 0-395-56470-0. LC 90-4980.**

Netherlands, 1939-1945. Rachel, eight years old when the story begins, observes life as a Jewish child during the Nazi occupation of Holland. So much changes that she does not understand, like why she must wear a yellow star. As she gets older, she must deal with the need to change her name, the removal of her grandparents, and the need to go into hiding.

Reviews: *BCCB* 3/91; *BL* 3/15/91★; *CED*; *HB* 5/91; *SLJ* 5/91
Reading Level: Middle & Junior High School
Subject Areas: Netherlands; Jews in Netherlands; Holocaust, Jewish, 1933-1945
Time Period: World War, 1939-1945 ❏ Library owns

Van Stockum, Hilda. *The Borrowed House.* **New York: Farrar, Straus, 1975. 215pp. ISBN 0-374-30888-8. LC 75-8853.**

Netherlands, 1939-1945. Janna goes to live with her parents in Amsterdam in a house that was taken from a Jewish family. Janna, who is a fervent believer in the Third Reich and a Hitler Youth, becomes confused by her new experiences, the mystery of the previous residents of the house, a friendship with a Jew, and her parents' attitudes. She becomes aware of the horrible implications of the Hitler's plan for the Jews.

Reviews: *BCCB* 11/75; *BL* 9/15/75; *HB* 10/75; *SLJ* 5/75
Reading Level: Middle & Junior High School
Subject Areas: Netherlands
Time Period: World War, 1939-1945 ❏ Library owns

Watkins, Paul. *Night Over Day Over Night.* **New York: Knopf, 1988. 293pp. ISBN 0-394-57047-2. LC 87-46102.**

Germany, 1944. When his father is killed at Normandy, 17-year-old Sebastian enlists in the SS. He knows that Germany will lose the war, but feels an obliga-

tion to enlist. He experiences the camaraderie of the troops and the horror of the battlefield, but moves toward a crisis in conscience.
Reviews: *BBSH*; *BL* 3/15/88; *LJ* 4/1/88
Reading Level: High School [Mature Reader]
Subject Areas: Germany; soldiers
Time Period: 1944; World War, 1939-1945 ❏ Library owns

Westall, Robert. *Blitzcat*. New York: Scholastic, 1989. 230pp. ISBN 0-590-42770-9. LC 89-4219.
England, 1939-1945. Lord Gort, a cat, searches all over England for her owner, an RAF pilot. Her search takes her through many harrowing circumstances, including a parachute jump into France. She does eventually find her owner, who has been emotionally scarred by his experiences in the war.
Reviews: *BCCB* 11/89; *BL* 12/15/89; *HB* 1/90; *SLJ* 11/89; *VOYA* 2/90
Reading Level: Middle–High School
Subject Areas: Great Britain--1900-; cats
Time Period: World War, 1939-1945 ❏ Library owns

Westall, Robert. *Echoes of War*. New York: Farrar, Straus, 1991. 96pp. ISBN 0-374-31964-2.
England, 1939-1945. Of the five short stories in this book, only one is not about World War II. That one exception is about a boy and his grandfather, a shell-shocked World War I veteran. The remaining four deal with life on the home front and the effects of war on the people.
Reviews: *BCCB* 10/91; *BL* 8/91; *HB* 1/92; *SLJ* 8/91; *VOYA* 10/91
Reading Level: Middle–High School
Subject Areas: Great Britain--1900-; short stories
Time Period: World War, 1939-1945 ❏ Library owns

Westall, Robert. *Fathom Five*. New York: Greenwillow, 1980. 242pp. ISBN 0-688-84286-0. LC 80-11223.
England, 1943. Sequel to *The Machine Gunners*. Chas and his three friends uncover a spy operating under everyone's nose. The spy has been floating messages about the location of ships out to German U-boats. The investigation leads the teens into the seamy part of town and danger. When Chas discovers the spy's identity, he must then decide whether to turn the person in.
Reviews: *BBYA*; *BR* 5/81; *SLJ* 10/80; *WJ* 5; *WS* 12
Reading Level: Middle–High School
Subject Areas: Great Britain--1900-; spies
Time Period: 1943; World War, 1939-1945 ❏ Library owns

Westall, Robert. *The Kingdom by the Sea.* **New York: Farrar, Straus, 1991. 176pp. ISBN 0-374-34205-9. LC 91-12500.**

England, 1939-1945. Twelve-year-old Harry is on his own after the loss of his family in an air raid bombing. Hoping to avoid placement with his awful Cousin Elsie, Harry hits the road, adopts a stray dog, and must survive on his own. He is helped by many individuals along the way, but is also threatened by gangs, a potential child molester, and life in the wild. Harry matures amidst war's destructiveness.

Reviews: *BBYA*; *BL* 11/1/91; *BR* 5/92; *HB* 1/92★; *SLJ* 11/91; *VOYA* 2/92
Reading Level: Middle–High School
Subject Areas: Great Britain--1900-; orphans; survival; dogs
Time Period: World War, 1939-1945 ❏ **Library owns**

Westall, Robert. *The Machine Gunners.* **New York: Greenwillow, 1976. 186pp. ISBN 0-688-84055-8. LC 76-13630.**

England, 1939-1945. Chas McGill and his friends find a crashed German plane and salvage the machine gun from it. Expecting a German invasion, they build a fortress in an abandoned building, arming it with the machine gun. Instead of an invasion, they find only one downed German pilot and keep him in the fortress. The adults in their lives become the enemy and the pilot becomes their friend.

Reviews: *BBYA*; *BL* 11/1/76★; *SLJ* 12/76; *WJ* 4, 5
Reading Level: Middle–High School
Subject Areas: Great Britain--1900-
Time Period: World War, 1939-1945 ❏ **Library owns**

Woodford, Peggy. *Backwater War.* **New York: Farrar, Straus, 1975. 213pp. ISBN 0-374-304-77-7. LC 75-8817.**

England, 1940. Set in the German-occupied Channel Islands, 17-year-old Anna Hardy and her family must move out of their home to make way for Germans, and end up near a German labor camp. They hide an escaped prisoner, and when Anna's friend plans his escape to England, the two men work together toward that goal.

Reviews: *BL* 7/1/75; *HB* 8/75; *SLJ* 9/75
Reading Level: Middle–High School
Subject Areas: Great Britain--1900-
Time Period: World War, 1939-1945 ❏ **Library owns**

Wuorio, Eva-Lis. *To Fight in Silence.* **New York: Holt, 1973. 216pp. ISBN 0-03-080241-5. LC 78-150031.**

Denmark, Norway, 1939-1945. Thor, who is twelve at the start of the story, and his many family members all work in the underground movement helping Jews to escape to safety. Thor's immaturity and rashness brings about tragic consequences.

Reviews: *BL* 10/1/73; *LJ* 11/15/73

Reading Level: Middle & Junior High School
Subject Areas: Denmark; underground movements
Time Period: World War, 1939-1945   ❏ Library owns

Zei, Al'ki; translated by Edward Fenton. *Petros' War.* **New York: Dutton, 1972. 236pp. ISBN 0-525-36962-7. LC 73-179059.**
Greece, 1939-1945. During the desperate days of first Italian and then German occupation of Greece, ten-year-old Petros see the changes in his family as food becomes scarce and people are executed. He joins the Resistance, performing small acts of defiance and joins in demonstrations. His maturity is complete when he sees his best friend shot.
Reviews: *BL* 9/15/72; *HB* 10/72; *LJ* 1/15/73
Reading Level: Middle & Junior High School
Subject Areas: Greece; underground movements; government, resistance to
Time Period: World War, 1939-1945   ❏ Library owns

Holocaust

Aaron, Chester. *Gideon.* **Philadelphia: Lippincott, 1981. 192pp. ISBN 0-397-31993-2. LC 81-48066.**
Poland, 1939-1945. Gideon, a street-wise Jewish youth, manages to stay alive in the Warsaw Ghetto by smuggling and stealing, escaping through the sewers to the non-Jewish sectors. After the Warsaw ghetto uprising in which he participates, Gideon is captured and sent to camp at Treblinka. There, once again, he manages to survive and escapes during the Treblinka revolt of 1943.
Reviews: *BCCB* 6/82; *BL* 4/1/82; *BR* 9-10/82; *PW* 6/4/82; *SLJ* 4/82
Reading Level: Middle–High School
Subject Areas: Poland; Holocaust, Jewish, 1933-1945; concentration camps; survival
Time Period: World War, 1939-1945   ❏ Library owns

Broner, Peter. *Night of the Broken Glass.* **Barrytown, NY: Station Hill Press/ Institute for Publishing Arts, 1991. 316pp. ISBN 0-88268-132-X. LC 90-23312.**
Germany, 1939-1945. Three men each respond differently to the question posed by a man dying of injuries sustained during Kristallnacht. The question was how does one deal with evil. Martin chooses to fight from within the system; Samuel, the adopted son of the dying man, denounces his newly revealed noble heritage; and Johann joins the inmates at a concentration camp to share their despair.
Reviews: *LJ* 7/91; *SLJ* 12/91
Reading Level: High School

Subject Areas: Germany; Holocaust, Jewish, 1933-1945
Time Period: World War, 1939-1945   ❏ Library owns

Del Castillo, Michel; translated by Peter Green. *Child of Our Time.* **New York: Knopf, 1958. 281pp.**
France, 1936-1945. In exile in France due to his mother's activities during the Spanish Civil War, Tanguy's French father betrays his mother causing her arrest. Tanguy ends up in a concentration camp during World War II where he shows great strength and courage.
Reviews: *WS* 10, 11
Reading Level: High School
Subject Areas: Spain; France; concentration camps
Time Period: 1936-1945; World War, 1939-1945   ❏ Library owns

Demetz, Hana. *The House on Prague Street.* **New York: St. Martin's, 1980. 160pp. ISBN 0-312-39322-9. LC 79-27312.**
Czechoslovakia, 1939-1945. Helenka, a half-Jewish teen, finds herself between two worlds. She can walk with her Aryan father in public, but not with her Jewish mother. Her world begins to crumble as friends and relatives are lost to her by removal to death camps or from hunger and disease. She is forced to work in an armament factory. Her loyalties are conflicted, feeling she doesn't belong to either side. Finally her beloved home is used as a shelter for Auschwitz survivors.
Reviews: *BBYA*; *BL* 7/1/80; *LJ* 8/80; *SLJ* 10/80; *WS* 13; *YARC*
Reading Level: High School
Subject Areas: Czechoslovakia; Holocaust, Jewish, 1933-1945
Time Period: World War, 1939-1945   ❏ Library owns

Dillon, Ellis. *Children of Bach.* **New York: Scribners, 1992. 164pp. ISBN 0-684-19440-6. LC 91-45432.**
Hungary, 1939-1945. Three days after the arrival of the Germans in Hungary, three teenaged Jewish children arrive home from school to find that their musician parents have been arrested and sent to a concentration camp. Their aunt escapes the roundup and returns to help them. She locates a person who is willing to help them escape to a remote Italian village. The journey is dangerous and they do not know whom to trust, but there are no other options. Music provides them with comfort and solace.
Reviews: *BCCB* 1/93; *BL* 12/1/92; BR 5-6/93; *SLJ* 12/92; *VOYA* 2/93
Reading Level: Middle–High School
Subject Areas: Hungary; Holocaust, Jewish, 1933-1945; escapes; musicians; Jews in Hungary
Time Period: World War, 1939-1945   ❏ Library owns

Europe—Twentieth Century

Drucker, Malka and Michael Halperin. *Jacob's Rescue: A Holocaust Story.* **New York: Bantam/Skylark, 1993. 128pp. ISBN 0-553-08976-5. LC 92-30523.**

Poland, 1942-1945. Responding to a question asked by his daughter, Jacob tells the story of his and his brother's rescue by Righteous Gentiles, the Roslans, in Poland during World War II. The Roslans hid Jacob and David in a variety of claustrophobia-causing places during the war at great risk to themselves as well as to the boys. Based on a true story.

Reviews: *BL* 2/15/93; *HB* 9/93; *SLJ* 5/93; *VOYA* 6/93

Reading Level: Middle–High School

Subject Areas: Poland; Holocaust, Jewish, 1933-1945; Jews in Poland

Time Period: World War, 1939-1945 ❏ Library owns

Fink, Ida; translated by Johanna Weschler and Francine Prose. *The Journey.* **New York: Farrar, Straus, 1992. 234pp. ISBN 0-374-28541-1. LC 91-40828.**

Poland, Germany, 1939-1945. Based on the author's experiences, two Jewish sisters assume new identities as non-Jews to escape the Warsaw ghetto. They are sent to Germany to work in a factory, but must flee when their true identity is leaked. They pose as peasants, adopting new identities, and manage to survive.

Reviews: *BL* 7/92; *LJ* 7/92; *PW* 6/1/92

Reading Level: High School

Subject Areas: Poland; Germany; Holocaust, Jewish, 1933-1945

Time Period: World War, 1939-1945 ❏ Library owns

Fink, Ida; translated by Madeline Levin and Francine Prose. *A Scrap of Time: And Other Stories.* **New York: Pantheon, 1987. 155pp. ISBN 0-394-55806-5. LC 86-42982.**

Poland, 1939-1945. This contains 23 short stories set in concentration camps during World War II. Some of the characters have survived and are recalling their experiences, while some characters are living the horror.

Reviews: *BBSH*; *BBYA*; *BL* 6/1/87★; *LJ* 8/87; *PW* 5/29/87

Reading Level: High School

Subject Areas: Poland; Holocaust, Jewish, 1933-1945; concentration camps; Jews in Poland; short stories

Time Period: World War, 1939-1945 ❏ Library owns

Forman, James. *The Survivor.* **New York: Farrar, Straus, 1976. 272pp. ISBN 0-374-37312-4. LC 76-2478.**

Netherlands, 1939-1945. The large and prosperous family of a Jewish doctor in Amsterdam is decimated by the events of the Holocaust, dying of shock, exposure, suicide, and death camps. Finally, only David, near death, is still alive when the Allies liberate the camps. He wills himself to live and becomes stronger, hoping to find his younger sister still alive.

Reviews: *FFY*; *WJ* 4, 5; *WS* 10, 11

Reading Level: Middle–High School

Subject Areas: Netherlands; Holocaust, Jewish, 1933-1945; Jews in the Netherlands

Time Period: World War, 1939-1945 ❏ Library owns

Hackl, Erich; translated by Edna McCown. *Farewell Sidonia.* **Fromm International, 1991. 135pp. ISBN 0-88064-124-X. LC 90-45461.**

Austria, 1939-1945. Sidonia, whose coloring identifies her as a gypsy child, is abandoned as an infant and adopted by a loving Austrian couple. She has a normal childhood until 1943, when her parents are forced to give her up because she is not Aryan. Sidonia is shipped to a concentration camp.

Reviews: *BL* 12/15/90; *LJ* 12/90; *SLJ* 7/91

Reading Level: High School

Subject Areas: Austria; Holocaust, Gypsy; Gypsies

Time Period: World War, 1939-1945 ❏ Library owns

Hersey, John. *The Wall.* **New York: Random House, 1988, c1950. 644pp. ISBN 0-317-75696-7. LC 87-45944.**

Poland, 1939-1945. Written in the form of diary, this story focuses on a group of friends living in the Warsaw Ghetto. The resistance efforts of the people against the Nazis is detailed, as well as the horrid living conditions. Finally, the group of friends is able to face their inevitable death with courage.

Reviews: *BBSH*; *FFY*; *WS* 10, 11, 12, 13, 14

Reading Level: High School

Subject Areas: Poland; Holocaust, Jewish, 1933-1945; Jews in Poland

Time Period: World War, 1939-1945 ❏ Library owns

Jacot, Michael. *The Last Butterfly.* **Columbus, OH: Bobbs-Merrill, 1974. ISBN 0-672-51926-7. LC 73-16803.**

Germany, Poland, 1939-1945. Antonin Karis, a second-rate half-Jewish clown, is ordered to entertain children at the concentration camp Terezin during a Red Cross visit. His anti-Hitler joke places him with a doctor and a woman, also being punished, who are accompanying a large group of children being shipped to Auschwitz from Terezin. It is evident that they will not return after the children are delivered, but are also being sent to their death.

Reviews: *BBYA*; *BL* 5/1/74; *LJ* 6/1/74
Reading Level: High School [Mature Reader]
Subject Areas: Poland; Holocaust, Jewish, 1933-1945; concentration camps
Time Period: World War, 1939-1945 ❏ **Library owns**

Kerr, Judith. *When Hitler Stole Pink Rabbit.* **New York: Coward-McCann, 1972. 191pp. ISBN 0-698-20182-5. LC 71-185765.**
Germany, Switzerland, 1933. When Hitler comes to power in 1933, Anna and her family, German Jews, must flee Germany. Anna is only nine and does not understand what is happening. As the family travels around Europe looking for safety, Anna comes to realize that they will not be returning to Germany, and she will not be able to have her pink rabbit, left behind when they escaped. Followed by *The Other Way Round.*
Reviews: *BL* 4/15/72; *HB* 8/72; *LJ* 5/15/72; *NCB*
Reading Level: Middle & Junior High School
Subject Areas: Germany; Holocaust, Jewish, 1933-1945; Jews in Germany; escapes
Time Period: 1933 ❏ **Library owns**

Kertész, Imre; translated by Christophr C. Wilson and Katharina M. Wilson. *Fateless.* **Chicago: Northwestern Univ., 1992. 189pp. ISBN 0-8101-1024-5. LC 92-16930.**
Hungary, Poland, 1942-1945. Fourteen-year-old Gyorgy Koves, a Hungarian Jew, is sent to a work camp and then to Buchenwald. He endures starvation, disease, cruelty, and the smell of burning bodies in "the lowest circle of hell." He is freed after one year when the Allies liberate the camps.
Reviews: *BL* 9/15/92; *PW* 8/24/92
Reading Level: High School [Mature Reader]
Subject Areas: Hungary; Poland; Holocaust, Jewish, 1933-1945; Jews in Hungary; concentration camps
Time Period: 1942-1945; World War, 1939-1945 ❏ **Library owns**

Laird, Christa. *Shadow of the Wall.* **New York: Greenwillow, 1990. 144pp. ISBN 0-688-09336-1. LC 89-34469.**
Poland, 1939-1945. Thirteen-year-old Misha takes responsibility for his dying mother and two younger sisters after the death of his father. He and his sister live in an Orphans' Home run by a doctor, but Misha becomes involved in the resistance movement, partly to provide food for his sisters and mother. He manages to smuggle one sister out of the ghetto through the sewers. However, he must watch helplessly as the remaining children in the home, including his sister, are taken to trains to be transported to a concentration camp.
Reviews: *BCCB* 5/90; *BL* 5/15/90; *BR* 10/90; *SLJ* 7/90

Reading Level: Middle–High School

Subject Areas: Poland; Holocaust, Jewish, 1933-1945; underground movements; Jews in Poland

Time Period: World War, 1939-1945 ❏ Library owns

Levitin, Sonia; illustrated by Charles Robinson. *Journey to America.* **New York: Atheneum, 1970. 150pp. ISBN 0-689-71130-1. LC 86-22234.**

Germany, Switzerland, 1938. A Jewish family escapes Nazi Germany in a desperate attempt to reach freedom. The mother and three daughters flee to Switzerland where they await passports and tickets from the father who has traveled ahead to America. While waiting they suffer poverty and sadness at the news of friends and family who have been killed. Winner of the Jewish Book Award.

Reviews: *BFY*; *BL* 6/1/70; *HB* 4/70; *LJ* 5/15/70

Reading Level: Middle & Junior High School

Subject Areas: Germany; Holocaust, Jewish, 1933-1945; Jews in Germany

Time Period: 1938 ❏ Library owns

Lewitt, Maria. *Come Spring.* **New York: St. Martin's, 1982. 169pp. ISBN 0-312-15099-7. LC 82-5575.**

Poland, 1939-1945. Half-Jewish teen Irena is somewhat protected with false papers and the isolation of her uncle's rural home. The addition of one more family member to hide adds to the chance of discovery, making all fearful. Irena tells of her joys and sorrows and the events that she witnesses. Based on the author's experiences.

Reviews: *LJ* 9/1/82; *SLJ* 3/83

Reading Level: High School

Subject Areas: Poland; Holocaust, Jewish, 1933-1945; Jews in Poland

Time Period: World War, 1939-1945 ❏ Library owns

Linn, Merritt. *A Book of Songs.* **New York: St. Martin's, 1982. 309pp. ISBN 0-312-09013-7.**

Poland, 1939-1945. The narrator tells of his life in a concentration camp, detailing the living conditions. He and others in the camp hold onto their belief in the goodness of the human spirit through the music of a child who kept alive because of his talent for playing the violin.

Reviews: *BL* 9/1/82; *LJ* 9/1/82

Reading Level: High School [Mature Reader]

Subject Areas: Holocaust, Jewish, 1933-1945; concentration camps

Time Period: World War, 1939-1945 ❏ Library owns

Lustig, Arnost; translated by Jeanne Nemcová. *Darkness Casts No Shadow.* **Inscape, 1977. 144pp. ISBN 0-87953-406-0. LC 76-41232.**
Germany, Czechoslovakia, 1944-1945. Having escaped from a death train headed for a concentration camp, two youths must hide and find a means to survive in an unfamiliar territory. The film *Diamonds of the Night* was based on this novel.
Reviews: *BL* 7/1/77; *LJ* 5/15/77
Reading Level: High School [Mature Reader]
Subject Areas: Germany; Czechoslovakia; Holocaust, Jewish, 1933-1945; survival
Time Period: 1944-1945; World War, 1939-1945   ❏ Library owns

Lustig, Arnost; translated by Jeanne Nemcová. *A Prayer for Katerina Horovitzova.* **New York: Overlook Press, 1987, c1973. 176pp. ISBN 0-87951-223-7. LC 84-25593.**
Czechoslovakia, 1939-1945. An evil, greedy concentration camp commandant plans to make himself rich by offering 21 Jews their freedom in return for their fortunes. As trains travel back and forth in a mock escape, the tables turn as the Jews blackmail the commandant. This won a Czechoslovak literary award.
Reviews: *WS* 10
Reading Level: High School
Subject Areas: Holocaust, Jewish, 1933-1945; concentration camps; Jews in Europe
Time Period: World War, 1939-1945   ❏ Library owns

Manea, Norman; translated by Cornelia Golna and others. *October, Eight O'Clock.* **New York: Grove Weidenfeld, 1992. 224pp. ISBN 0-8021-1280-3. LC 91-36377.**
Ukraine. This collection of 15 short stories is loosely bound together by the narrator who appears in each. They each relate the horrors and tragedy of the Holocaust. Based on the author's experiences in a concentration camp in the Ukraine.
Reviews: *BL* 4/15/92; *LJ* 6/1/92; *PW* 3/23/92
Reading Level: High School [Mature Reader]
Subject Areas: Holocaust, Jewish, 1933-1945; Jews in Europe; concentration camps
Time Period: World War, 1939-1945   ❏ Library owns

Morpurgo, Michael. *Waiting for Anya.* **New York: Viking, 1991. 160pp. ISBN 0-670-83735-0. LC 90-50560.**
France, 1939-1945. Twelve-year-old Jo discovers that Benjamin and a group of Jewish children are in hiding in his town, awaiting a time when they can be smug-

gled across the border to Spain. However, when a garrison of German soldiers arrives, things become more dangerous. With the cooperation of the entire village, the children are taken over the mountains, however Benjamin and one child are captured and sent to Auschwitz. Jo also discovers that the Germans were not entirely evil, that they too wished for peace.

Reviews: *BBYA*; *BCCB* 3/91; *BL* 5/15/91; *HB* 7/91; *SLJ* 4/91★; *VOYA* 6/91
Reading Level: Middle & Junior High School
Subject Areas: France--1900-; Holocaust, Jewish, 1933-1945; escapes
Time Period: World War, 1939-1945 ❑ Library owns

Moskin, Marietta D. *I Am Rosemarie.* **New York: Day, 1972. 190pp. ISBN 0-381-98158-4. LC 72-2413.**
Germany, 1939-1945. Rosemarie Brenner, a young Dutch Jew, amazingly survives for five years in three concentration camps. This is the story of her survival and her maturation under very adverse conditions.

Reviews: *WJ* 4; *WS* 10
Reading Level: Middle–High School
Subject Areas: Holocaust, Jewish, 1933-1945; concentration camps; Jews in the Netherlands; survival
Time Period: World War, 1939-1945 ❑ Library owns

Nolan, Han. *If I Should Die Before I Wake.* **San Diego: Harcourt, 1994. 201pp. ISBN 0-15-238040-X. LC 93-30720.**
Germany, contemporary, 1939-1945. Hilary Burke, a rebellious neo-Nazi, is hospitalized after a motorcycle accident. While unconscious, she slips into the memory of the old woman, an Auschwitz survivor, who is sharing the room. Hilary experiences the physical and emotional horrors of the concentration camp, and returns to consciousness a changed person. Though the modern scenes are contrived, those set in Auschwitz are memorable.

Reviews: *BL* 4/1/94; *BR* 9-10/94; *SLJ* 4/94; *PW* 1/31/94
Reading Level: Middle–High School
Subject Areas: Germany; Holocaust, Jewish, 1933-1945; Jews in Poland; white supremacy movements; space and time
Time Period: World War, 1939-1945 ❑ Library owns

Orgel, Doris. *The Devil in Vienna.* **New York: Dial, 1978. 256pp. ISBN 0-8037-1920-5. LC 78-51319.**
Austria, 1939-1945. Jewish Inge and her friend Lieslotte, whose father is a Nazi officer, continue their friendship against her parents wishes even after Lieslotte's father moves his family to Germany. When Inge's family must leave the country, Inge turns to Lieslotte's uncle, a Catholic priest, for help.

Reviews: *BCCB* 12/78; *BL* 10/15/78★; *HB* 2/79; *NCB*; *PW* 8/28/78; *SLJ* 11/78; *WJ* 5

Europe—Twentieth Century

Reading Level: Middle & Junior High School
Subject Areas: Austria; Holocaust, Jewish, 1933-1945; friendship; Jews in Austria
Time Period: World War, 1939-1945 ❑ Library owns

Orlev, Uri; translated by Hillel Halkin. *The Island on Bird Street.* **Boston: Houghton, 1984. 162pp. ISBN 0-395-33887-5. LC 83-26524.**
Poland, 1939-1945. Having hidden while the Jewish ghetto was evacuated, 11-year-old Alex follows his father's orders to wait for him. Alex wanders the empty ghetto looking for food and warmth, hoping his father will come soon, but knowing that his chances of survival are slim.
Reviews: *BCCB* 6/84; *HB* 4/84; *NCB*; *SLJ* 8/84; *WJ* 5, 6
Reading Level: Middle & Junior High School
Subject Areas: Poland; Holocaust, Jewish, 1933-1945; Jews in Poland; survival
Time Period: World War, 1939-1945 ❑ Library owns

Orlev, Uri; translated by Hillel Halkin. *The Man from the Other Side.* **Boston: Houghton, 1991. 186pp. ISBN 0-395-53808-4. LC 90-47898.**
Poland, 1943. Anthony helps his despised step-father smuggle food to the Jews in the Warsaw ghetto mostly for the money. When he finds out that his real father was Jewish and was tortured to death, his attitudes change. He hides a Jewish medical student, Jorek, and comes to love him as a father. The two go back into the ghetto through the sewers to participate in the 1943 ghetto uprising where Jorek is killed. Anthony's step-father risks his life to save him.
Reviews: *BBYA*; *BCCB* 6/91; *BL* 6/15/91★; *BR* 9/91; *CED*; *SLJ* 9/91★
Reading Level: Middle–High School
Subject Areas: Poland; Holocaust, Jewish, 1933-1945; Jews in Poland; underground movements
Time Period: 1943; World War, 1939-1945 ❑ Library owns

Ossowski, Leonie; translated by Ruth Crowley. *Star Without a Sky.* **Minneapolis: Lerner, 1985. 214pp. ISBN 0-8225-0771-4. LC 84-21834.**
Germany, 1945. At the end of World War II in a small town near Berlin, five teens find a young Jew hiding in a bombed out building. They try to decide his fate — whether to turn him in to authorities as they have been taught, or to help him.
Reviews: *BFY*; *BL* 7/85; *SLJ* 10/85
Reading Level: Middle–High School
Subject Areas: Germany; Holocaust, Jewish, 1933-1945
Time Period: 1945; World War, 1939-1945 ❑ Library owns

Europe—Twentieth Century

Ramati, Alexander. *And the Violins Stopped Playing.* **New York: Watts, 1986. 237pp. ISBN 0-531-15028-3. LC 86-50188.**

Poland, 1939-1945. Learning that the Nazis have begun to imprison Gypsies, Roman's family, musicians in Warsaw, return to the Gypsy winter camp to try to convince 85 others to escape to Hungary. They arrive in Hungary on the day of the Nazi invasion, are captured and sent to Birkenau, the Gypsy camp at Auschwitz. Roman alone survives because he acts as a translator for Dr. Mengele. (This book is sometimes cataloged as non-fiction.)

Reviews: *BBSH*; *BBYA*; *BFY*; *BL* 9/1/86; *BR* 11-12/86; *SLJ* 1/87; *VOYA* 2/87

Reading Level: High School

Subject Areas: Poland; Holocaust, Gypsy; Gypsies

Time Period: World War, 1939-1945 ❏ Library owns

Ray, Karen. *To Cross a Line.* **New York: Orchard, 1994. 160pp. ISBN 0-531-08681-X. LC 93-11813.**

Germany, 1938. While delivering goods for a bakery, Egon has a minor traffic accident with the car of a Nazi officer. He discovers after going to court that the Gestapo are looking for him. After packing a few belongings, he travels to his extended family members, hoping to get out of Germany. One plan at the Dutch border fails, which leads him to the Danish border in an even more desperate attempt.

Reviews: *BL* 2/15/94; *BR* 9-10/94; *PW* 2/14/94

Reading Level: Middle–High School

Subject Areas: Germany; Holocaust, Jewish, 1933-1945; escapes; Jews in Germany

Time Period: 1938 ❏ Library owns

Reiss, Johanna. *The Upstairs Room.* **New York: Crowell, 1972. 196pp. ISBN 0-690-85127-8. LC 77-187940.**

Netherlands, 1939-1945. Unable to escape the Netherlands after the Nazi occupation, the Jewish Reiss family splits up and hides with Dutch families. This is the story of two sisters, Annie and her older sister Sini, who are hidden for more than two year with the Oosterveld family. The isolation is trying on the girls. Annie's legs atrophy from disuse and she talks to imaginary friends. Sini worries about missing out on dating and nags Annie to exercise. Despite the stress and worries the girls love each other and the Oostervelds. (This is sometimes cataloged as biography.)

Reviews: *BCCB* 11/72; *BL* 10/15/72; *HB* 2/73; *LJ* 12/15/72; *PW* 9/25/72; *SLJ* 12/72★

Reading Level: Middle–High School

Subject Areas: Netherlands; Holocaust, Jewish, 1933-1945; sisters; Jews in the Netherlands

Time Period: World War, 1939-1945 ❏ Library owns

Richter, Hans Peter; translated by Edite Kroll. *Friedrich.* **New York: Holt, 1970. 149pp. ISBN 0-03-085116-5.**

Germany, 1925-1942. The story of Friedrich and his middle class Jewish family is told by his friend, whose father is a poor civil servant. As Hitler comes to power, Friedrich and his family experience increasing antisemitism. His mother is attacked at home and dies, his father is deported, and Friedrich is denied entry into an air raid shelter and is killed during a raid. An appendix chronicles the laws and decrees affecting the Jews in Germany.

Reviews: *BL* 4/1/71; *FFY*; *HB* 4/71; *LJ* 5/15/71

Reading Level: Middle–High School

Subject Areas: Germany; Holocaust, Jewish, 1933-1945; friendship; Jews in Germany; World War, 1939-1945

Time Period: 1925-1942 ❏ **Library owns**

Roth-Hano, Renée. *Touch Wood: A Girlhood in Occupied France.* **New York: Macmillan/Four Winds, 1988. 274pp. ISBN 0-02-777340-X. LC 87-34326.**

France, 1939-1945. The Roth family, having fled Alsace when the Nazis invaded, go to Paris where they feel they will be safe. However, as the Nazis advance, the three daughters are placed in a Normandy convent. In the form of a diary, Renee tells of their experiences, both good and bad, as they await the end of the war, beginning with her confusion as they begin to feel the effects of the restrictions on Jews, their fear of deportation, the time living with the nuns, to their reunion with their parents after the Allied invasion.

Reviews: *BCCB* 5/88; *BL* 8/88; *HB* 1-2/89; *SLJ* 6-7/88

Reading Level: Middle–High School

Subject Areas: France--1900-; Holocaust, Jewish, 1933-1945; Jews in France

Time Period: World War, 1939-1945 ❏ **Library owns**

Rudner, Lawrence. *The Magic We Do Here.* **Boston: Houghton, 1988. 212pp. ISBN 0-395-45034-9. LC 88-558.**

Poland, 1939-1945. Chaim Turkow, a strikingly handsome young Jew with Nordic features and artistic ability, manages to survive the war by pretending to be a mute, mentally deficient servant of a Nazi sympathizer. Chaim's neighbors have given him the task of keeping photographs of Nazi atrocities to be used as proof after the war. Chaim's roles, both as archivist and mute, take their toll and Chaim appears to be permanently mute. A dwarf traveling with the Russians recognizes Chaim asa victim and helps him recover.

Reviews: *BBSH*; *BL* 5/15/88; *LJ* 5/15/88

Reading Level: High School [Mature Reader]

Subject Areas: Poland; Holocaust, Jewish, 1933-1945; Jews in Poland
Time Period: World War, 1939-1945 ❏ Library owns

Schaeffer, Susan Fromberg. *Anya: A Novel.* **New York: Macmillan, 1974. 489pp. ISBN 0-02-607020-0.**
Poland, 1939-1945. Anya, a beautiful blond Jew, is imprisoned in the Warsaw ghetto. Fearing the worst, she gives her daughter to a gentile family. Anya survives the concentration camps, and begins a quest, to find her daughter, which continues after she emigrates to America.
Reviews: *WS* 11, 12
Reading Level: High School
Subject Areas: Poland; Holocaust, Jewish, 1933-1945; Jews in Poland
Time Period: World War, 1939-1945 ❏ Library owns

Treseder, Terry Walton; illustrated by Bloom Lloyd. *Hear O Israel: A Story of the Warsaw Ghetto.* **New York: Atheneum, 1990. 48pp. ISBN 0-689-31456-6. LC 89-7029.**
Poland, 1939-1945. This slim volume tells the story of Isaac, a young Jewish boy who is held in the Warsaw Ghetto. Isaac begins to lose his faith as he watches his family members die of starvation. Finally, Isaac is transported to Treblinka where he dies. The reading is easy, but the content is troubling.
Reviews: *BCCB* 10/90; *BL* 11/15/90; *BR* 1-2/91; *HB* 1/91; *PW* 8/10/90; *SLJ* 11/90
Reading Level: Middle–High School
Subject Areas: Poland; Holocaust, Jewish, 1933-1945; concentration camps; Jews in Poland
Time Period: World War, 1939-1945 ❏ Library owns

Vos, Ida. *Anna Is Still Here.* **Bsoton: Houghton, 1993. 139pp. ISBN 0-395-65368-1. LC 92-1618.**
Netherlands, 1945. Anna is having a hard time adjusting to life at the end of the war. She was hidden in an attic for three years by herself. Her parents have survived, but will not speak of their experiences. Anna meets another survivor, Mrs. Neumann, who is waiting for her daughter to return, unable even to leave the house in case her daughter arrives to find her gone. Together they begin to heal each other.
Reviews: *BL* 4/15/93★; *BR* 9-10/93; *HB* 7/93; *SLJ* 5/93
Reading Level: Middle & Junior High School
Subject Areas: Netherlands; Holocaust survivors; Jews in the Netherlands
Time Period: 1945 ❏ Library owns

Wood, Barbara and Gareth Wootton. *Night Trains.* **New York: Morrow, 1979. 382pp. ISBN 0-688-03470-5. LC 79-14286.**
Poland, 1939-1945. Two Polish doctors plan a fake typhus epidemic in the town of Sofia, hoping to keep the Nazis out and slow down the shipment of arms from the town train depot. The plan is jeopardized by a group of Jewish partisans whose plan is more violent, and involves hijacking the trains.
Reviews: *WS* 11
Reading Level: High School
Subject Areas: Poland, underground movements
Time Period: World War, 1939-1945 ❏ Library owns

Uris, Leon. *Mila 18.* **New York: Bantam, 1983, c1961. 539pp. ISBN 0-553-24160-5. LC 61-9562.**
Poland, 1943. For 42 days and nights the freedom fighters in the Warsaw Ghetto fight the Nazis, trying to keep them from completing their plan of exterminating the Warsaw Jews. This is the story of those men and women and their hopeless fight.
Reviews: *BBSH*; *WS* 10, 11, 12, 13, 14
Reading Level: High School
Subject Areas: Poland; Holocaust, Jewish, 1939-1945; Jews in Poland; underground movements
Time Period: 1943; World War, 1939-1945 ❏ Library owns

Yolen, Jane. *The Devil's Arithmetic.* **New York: Viking, 1988. 160pp. ISBN 0-670-81027-4. LC 88-14235.**
Poland, 1942. Twelve-year-old Hannah, cranky and bored by talk of remembrance, is asked to open the door to the prophet Elijah at Passover Seder. When she does, she is drawn into a time warp that sends her back to 1942 just as she is captured by the Nazis and sent to a concentration camp. She experiences the full range of inhumanities and sacrifices herself to save another. As she enters the gas chamber, she is transported back to modern times and the safety of her home. Winner of the Newbery Medal 1988.
Reviews: *BCCB* 10/88; *BL* 9/1/88; *BR* 1-2/89; *SLJ* 11/88★; *WJ* 6
Reading Level: Middle–High School
Subject Areas: Poland; Holocaust, Jewish, 1939-1945; Jews in Poland; concentration camps
Time Period: 1942; World War, 1939-1945 ❏ Library owns

The Americas

The Caribbean

Anderson, John L. *Night of the Silent Drums.* **New York: Scribner, 1975. 406pp. ISBN 0-684-14324-0. LC 75-4137.**
St. John (Virgin Islands), 1733. Based on a slave uprising on St. John, a Danish-held island, this includes not only the events, but the thoughts of the characters as they either participated in the revolt or fought to suppress it.
Reviews: *WS*
Reading Level: High School
Subject Areas: Virgin Islands; St. John, Virgin Islands; slavery
Time Period: 1733
❏ Library owns

Beatty, John and Patricia Beatty. *Pirate Royal.* **New York: Macmillan, 1969. 209pp. LC 69-16209.**
Jamaica, seventeenth century. Fourteen-year-old Anthony Grey is kidnapped on his way to Boston to be a bond servant, and instead becomes buccaneer Henry Morgan's clerk.
Reviews: *BL* 9/15/69; *LJ* 9/15/69
Reading Level: Middle–High School
Subject Areas: Jamaica; pirates; Morgan, Henry
Time Period: Seventeenth Century
❏ Library owns

Berry, James. *Ajeemah and His Son.* **New York: HarperCollins, 1992. 96pp. ISBN 0-06-021044-3. LC 92-6615.**
Ghana, Jamaica, 1807-1840. As they traveled to present a bride-gift to his betrothed family, Ajeemah and his 18-year-old son Atu are captured by slavers. They are taken to Jamaica where they are sold to different plantations, never to see each other again. Ajeemah's plans for escape are foiled. Atu eventually commits suicide. After becoming very ill, Ajeemah is nursed back to health by Bella whom he marries.
"Writing from an African perspective, the author conveys the differences between those slaves born in the New World and those brought from Africa..." *School Library Journal*
Reviews: *BCCB* 11/92★; *BL* 10/1/92★; *BR* 5-6/93; *HB* 3/93; *SLJ* 9/92★; *VOYA* 2/93
Reading Level: Middle–High School
Subject Areas: Jamaica; slaves; fathers and sons; Blacks
Time Period: 1807-1840
❏ Library owns

Haugaard, Erik Christian. *Under the Black Flag.* **Roberts Niwot, CO: Rinehart, 1994. 163pp. ISBN 1-879373-63-7. LC 93-85476.**
Jamaica, ca 1700. Kidnapped while sailing back to England to attend boarding school, fourteen-year-old William Bernard becomes the cabin boy for Blackbeard, the pirate. When Blackbeard joins forces with another pirate, William meets and befriends Sam, a 15-year-old slave. Together they plot an escape.
Reviews: *BL* 4/1/94; *PW* 11/22/93; *SLJ* 5/94
Reading Level: Middle & Junior High School
Subject Areas: Jamaica; pirates; Teach, Edward; slavery; sea stories; adventure and adventurers
Time Period: 1700s ❑ Library owns

Howard, Ellen. *When Daylight Comes.* **New York: Atheneum, 1985. 210pp. ISBN 0-689-31133-8. LC 85-7963.**
St. John (Virgin Islands), 1733. Howard uses the slave uprising in Danish-held St. John as her background for this tale of the Danish magistrate's daughter, held captive by the liberated slaves, and of the girl's sympathy with and for her captors.
"Howard strives to be historically accurate, adding only three fictional characters to the known participants...The book also remains true to the cultural characteristics of both the Danes and the blacks." *School Library Journal*
Reviews: *BCCB* 10/85; *SLJ* 11/85
Reading Level: Middle–High School
Subject Areas: Virgin Islands; St. John, Virgin Islands; slavery
Time Period: 1733 ❑ Library owns

Michener, James A. *Caribbean.* **New York: Random House, 1989. 672pp. ISBN 0-394-56561-4. LC 89-42785.**
Caribbean. In another epic tome, Michener fictionalizes the history of the Caribbean area, including the Arawak and Carib indians, explorers, conquistadors, buccaneers and pirates, Haitian and Cuban revolutions, and Rastafarianism in Jamaica.
Reviews: *BBSH*; *BL* 9/1/89; *PW* 9/29/89
Reading Level: High School
Subject Areas: Caribbean Islands
Time Period: Fourteenth–Twentieth Centuries ❑ Library owns

O'Dell, Scott. *My Name Is Not Angelica.* **Boston: Houghton, 1989. 144pp. ISBN 0-395-51061-9. LC 89-1864.**
St. John (Virgin Islands), 1733-1734. Once again the slave uprising in the Danish Virgin Islands is the historical backdrop for a story that reveals the ugly inhumanity of slavery. In this story, Konje, a Senagalese girl, is betrayed into slavery, along

with her royal fiance and her servant, and eventually becomes the sole survivor of a mass suicide by rebelling slaves who choose death over continued bondage.
Reviews: *BCCB* 10/89; *BL* 11/15/89★; *BR* 3/90; *HB* 3/90; *SLJ* 10/89
Reading Level: Middle & Junior High School
Subject Areas: Virgin Islands; St. John, Virgin Islands; slavery; Blacks
Time Period: 1733 ❏ Library owns

Temple, Frances. *Taste of Salt.* **New York: Orchard, 1992. 179pp. ISBN 0-531-05459-4. LC 92-6716.**
Haiti, contemporary. Djo, beaten almost to death by the Tonton Macoute, tells his story to Jeremie, a young woman who has fought her way out of the slums to achieve an education. Djo and Jeremie both have a connection to Aristide, Djo being one of the street urchins that Aristide sheltered and Jeremie, through her efforts to fight Duvalier's dictatorship. Djo's (and Jeremie's) experiences reveal a lifetime of poverty, fear, and injustice.
Reviews: *BCCB* 11/92; *BL* 8/92; *BR* 1/93; *HB* 11/92; *SLJ* 9/92★; *VOYA* 12/92
Reading Level: Middle–High School
Subject Areas: Haiti; Blacks; Aristide, Jean-Bertrand; poverty
Time Period: 1980s ❏ Library owns

Central America

Castañeda, Omar S. *Among the Volcanoes.* **New York: Dutton/Lodestar, 1991. 192pp. ISBN 0-525-67332-6. LC 90-43874.**
Guatemala, contemporary. Isabel Pacay, a young Mayan living in a small village, wishes to become a teacher and to marry a young man she loves, but she is expected to care for her ailing mother. When local folk medicine fails to cure her mother, she is swayed by a visiting American to take her to a doctor, causing problems in the village.
Reviews: *BCCB* 6/91; *BL* 5/15/91; *HB* 5/91; *SLJ* 3/91; *VOYA* 4/91
Reading Level: Middle–High School
Subject Areas: Guatemala; Mayas; Indians of Central America
Time Period: 1980s ❏ Library owns

Castañeda, Omar S. *Imagining Isabel.* **New York: Dutton/Lodestar, 1994. 200pp. ISBN 0-525-67431-4. LC 93-50593.**
Guatemala, contemporary. Sequel to *Among the Volcanoes*. Isabel, now 16-years-old and married to Lucas, has the responsibility for her whole family when her mother dies. A surprise invitation to attend a teacher training program in the city brings logistical problems which Isabel manages to sort out. While attending classes, Isabel becomes involved in resistance movements and is tested to see if she is committed and able to keep silent.

Reviews: *BL* 10/1/94; *BR* 11-12/94; *SLJ* 9/94
Reading Level: High School
Subject Areas: Guatemala; Mayas; Indians of Central America; underground movements
Time Period: 1980s ❏ Library owns

Highwater, Jamake. *Journey to the Sky: A Novel About the True Adventures of Two Men in Search of the Lost Maya Kingdom.* **New York: T.Y. Crowell, 1978. 242pp. ISBN 0-690-01758-8. LC 78-3324.**
Central America, 1839-1840. Highwater bases his novel on the true adventure of American attorney John Lloyd Stephens and British architectural draftsman and artist, Frederick Catherwood, who travel by mule through hostile Central American jungles to search for the rumored lost great cities of the Maya civilization. A treat for archaeological buffs and adventure buffs alike.
Reviews: *BL* 2/15/79; *LJ* 12/1/78
Reading Level: High School [Mature Reader]
Subject Areas: Central America; Mayas; Catherwood, Frederick; Stephens, John Lloyd; Mexico; archeologists
Time Period: 1839-1840 ❏ Library owns

Moeri, Louise. *The Forty-Third War.* **Bsoton: Houghton, 1989. 208pp. ISBN 0-395-50215-2. LC 89-31178.**
Contemporary Central America. Set in a fictionalized Central American country, twelve-year-old Uno is conscripted into the revolutionary army and bound to his comrades-in-arms through the course of his harrowing experiences. Moeri's theme is not just political, but also ethical as she explores "the way attitudes are shaped and the way one searches for a moral balance in circumstances where morality seems absent." *Booklist*
Reviews: *BBYA*; *BCCB* 11/89; *BL* 10/15/89; *HB* 1-2/90; *SLJ* 10/89
Reading Level: Middle–High School
Subject Areas: Central America; war
Time Period: 1980s ❏ Library owns

Peters, Daniel. *Tikal: A Novel About the Maya.* **New York: Random House, 1983. 422pp. ISBN 0-394-53278-3. LC 83-3273.**
Central America, 900 A.D. Set during a five-year period, this novel describes the political problems and struggles between clans which hastened the fall of the Mayan civilization. The book is rich with descriptions of the social life and customs of the Mayas.
Reviews: *BL* 9/1/83; *LJ* 9/1/83
Reading Level: High School [Mature Reader]

Subject Areas: Central America; Mayas; Indians of Central America
Time Period: 900 ❑ Library owns

Temple, Frances. *Grab Hands and Run.* **New York: Orchard, 1993. 160pp. ISBN 0-531-08630-5. LC 92-34063.**
El Salvador, contemporary. When his political activist father disappears, 12-year-old Felipe, his mother, and younger sister must flee the country. In their attempt to get to Canada, they are confronted by many obstacles and dangerous situations as they travel across a continent, hoping that their father was able to escape, too.
Reviews: *BBYA*; *BCCB* 4/93; *BL* 5/1/93; *CED;* *PW* 4/12/93; *SLJ* 4/93; *VOYA* 6/93
Reading Level: Middle–High School
Subject Areas: El Salvador; refugees
Time Period: 1980s ❑ Library owns

Mexico

Hennessy, Max. *The Crimson Wind.* **New York: Atheneum, 198. 247pp. ISBN 0-689-11530-X. LC 84-45623.**
Mexico, 1910-1917. The first in a trilogy on the Revolution-torn Mexico of the early twentieth century, this story introduces hero Henry Marquis, a half-British, half-Mexican reporter sent to Mexico to cover the revolution. Spending time with revolutionary leader Pancho Villa, Henry becomes involved with the politics and battles of the time.
Reviews: *BL* 5/15/85; *LJ* 5/1/85
Reading Level: High School
Subject Areas: Mexico; Villa, Pancho; revolutions; reporters and reporting
Time Period: 1910-1917 ❑ Library owns

McGee, Charmayne. *So Sings the Blue Deer.* **New York: Atheneum, 1994. 186pp. ISBN 0-689-31888-X. LC 93-26580.**
Mexico, contemporary. Thirteen-year-old Moon Feather, a Huichol Indian, goes with the village elders to Mexico City to receive some deer that are being given to the tribe by the government. The deer represent an ancient god. Moon Feather is fascinated by the bustling modern city and is tempted to stay with relatives and go to school. He decides, instead, to return to his tribe and his heritage.
Reviews: *BR* 11-12/94; *SLJ* 5/94; *VOYA* 6/94
Reading Level: Middle & Junior High School
Subject Areas: Mexico; Huichol Indians; Indians of Mexico
Time Period: Twentieth Century ❑ Library owns

The Americas—Mexico

Merino, José María; translated by Helen Lane. *The Gold of Dreams.* **New York: Farrar, 1992. 224pp. ISBN 0-374-32692-4. LC 91-12073.**
Mexico, 1500s. Fifteen-year-old Miguel, whose father was a Conquistador and whose mother was a Mayan Indian, accompanies his godfather and two hundred Spanish soldiers on a search for a temple laden with riches located south of Mexico City. The group argues and splits up. Miguel finds a treasure, but not in a temple. He also finds out that his father is not dead, but living in an Indian village.
Reviews: *BCCB* 3/92; *BL* 1/15/92; *PW* 12/6/91; *SLJ* 2/92; *VOYA* 4/92
Reading Level: Middle–High School
Subject Areas: Mexico; America--discovery and exploration; Mayas; adventure and adventurers
Time Period: 1500s ❏ Library owns

Merino, José María; translated by Helen Lane. *Beyond the Ancient Cities.* **New York: Farrar, 1994. 182pp. ISBN 0-374-34307-1. LC 93-35482.**
Peru, 1500s. Sequel to *The Gold of Dreams*. Miguel and his godfather now journey toward Peru where Don Santiago will assume a government post. Along the way they encounter danger in the form of natural disasters and treacherous humans. Miguel observes the changes in culture after the Spaniards' arrival.
Reviews: *BL* 4/1/94; *SLJ* 5/94
Reading Level: Middle–High School
Subject Areas: Mexico; America--discovery and exploration
Time Period: 1500s ❏ Library owns

Michener, James A. *Mexico.* **New York: Random House, 1992. 625pp. ISBN 0-679-41649-8. LC 92-50151.**
Mexico, contemporary. Born in Mexico City, journalist Norman Clay returns there to cover bullfights at a festival, focusing on the rivalry between two matadors. His reports highlight the contrasts in contemporary Mexico, bullfighting, and the two matadors.
Reviews: *WS* 14
Reading Level: High School
Subject Areas: Mexico; bullfighting; reporters and reporting
Time Period: 1980s ❏ Library owns

O'Dell, Scott. *The Captive.* **Boston: Houghton, 1979. 210pp. ISBN 0-395-27811-2. LC 79-15809.**
Mexico, 1517. O'Dell's first in his City of the Seven Serpents trilogy introduces Julián Escobar, a 16-year-old seminarian whose unexpected journey to the New World leaves him a witness to Spanish greed and brutality toward natives. Sole survivor of a shipwreck, he leads a "Robinson Crusoe" existence until found by

Guillermo Cantú, a Spanish dwarf, who convinces him to masquerade as Kukulcán, the Mayan god who promised to return as a young blond man.
Reviews: *BL* 11/1/79; *HB* 12/79; *PW* 12/10/79; *SLJ* 11/79; *WS* 11
Reading Level: Middle–High School
Subject Areas: Mexico; Mayas; America--discovery and exploration; adventure and adventurers
Time Period: 1517   ❏ Library owns

O'Dell, Scott. *The Feathered Serpent.* **Bsoton: Houghton, 1979. 224pp. ISBN 0-395-30851-8. LC 81-7888.**
Mexico, 1519. Sequel to *The Captive*. Julián Escobar gets caught up in his role as Mayan god Kukulcán, and revels in his power, even watching human sacrifices to him. Traveling to visit Aztec Moctezuma, from whom he hopes to learn how to rule, Julián is caught in Cortés' invasion of Moctezuma's empire and the brutality of the Conquistadors. Followed by *The Amethyst Ring*.
Reviews: *BCCB* 12/81; *HB* 2/82; *SLJ* 10/81
Reading Level: Middle–High School
Subject Areas: Mexico; Mayas; Aztecs; America--discovery and exploration; Cortes, Hernan
Time Period: 1519   ❏ Library owns

O'Dell, Scott. *The King's Fifth.* **Boston: Houghton, 1966. 264pp. ISBN 0-395-06963-7. LC 66-7763.**
Mexico, sixteenth century. As imprisoned Estéban de Sandoval, a young cartographer who traveled with Coronado, waits for the end of his 20-day trial for withholding the royal share of treasure, the King's Fifth, he writes of his journey to the Seven Cities of Cibola and the gold found there. He also comes to realize what his greed will cost him.
Reviews: *BBYA*; *WJ* 4; *SLJ* Best of the Best 1966-1978
Reading Level: Middle & Junior High School
Subject Areas: Mexico; America--discovery and exploration; Estévan; slaves
Time Period: 1500s   ❏ Library owns

Parish, Helen Rand. *Estebanico.* **New York: Viking, 1974. 128pp. ISBN 0-670-29814-X. LC 74-1454.**
Mexico, 1539. Based on much research but still speculative in accuracy, this is the story of a black slave named Estebanico whom the author considers "the first great black man in America." Estebanico leads his Spanish master over much territory in search of the Seven Cities of Cibola, which proves their downfall.
Reviews: *BL* 10/1/74; *LJ* 11/15/74; *SLJ* 11/74
Reading Level: Middle & Junior High School

Subject Areas: Mexico; America--discovery and exploration; Estévan; slaves; adventure and adventurers
Time Period: 1539 ❏ Library owns

Shellabarger, Samuel. *Captain from Castile.* **Boston: Little, 1945. 632pp. LC 48-17424.**
Mexico, Spain, 1519. The historical romance set against the Renaissance and Inquisition in Europe and the promise of the New World, finds Pedro de Vargas evading an enemy by joining Cortes' Conquistadors to seek his fortune.
Reviews: *WS* 10, 11
Reading Level: High School
Subject Areas: Mexico; Cortes, Hernan; America--discovery and exploration; adventure and adventurers
Time Period: 1519 ❏ Library owns

Zollinger, Norman. *Not of War Only.* **New York: Tor/Forge/St. Martin's, 1994. 416pp. ISBN 0-312-85229-X.**
Mexico, 1914-17. Jorge Martinez, a young Mexican soldier, is pursued across the border by an American lawman, Corey Lane. Jorge joins Pancho Villa's forces, and maturing quickly, rises in rank. Corey becomes a secret agent for the U.S. government who infiltrates Villa's revolutionaries. Both men become entangled with beautiful women and in vivid battles.
Reviews: *BL* 6/1/94; *LJ* 5/15/94; *PW* 4/25/94
Reading Level: High School [Mature Reader]
Subject Areas: Mexico; Villa, Pancho; revolutions
Time Period: 1914-1917 ❏ Library owns

Canada

Bond, Nancy. *Another Shore.* **New York: McElderry/Macmillan, 1988. 316pp. ISBN 0-689-50463-2. LC 87-3907.**
Louisbourg, Nova Scotia, 1744/ twentieth century. Lyn Paget takes a summer job at the port town of Louisbourg reconstructed to look as it did in the eighteenth century, and suddenly finds herself back in 1744 assuming the identity of the girl whose life she has researched for her work at the park. Lyn finds some other twentieth century contemporaries who have not been able to return to the present and must adapt to her new world and the possibility that she may not be able to return to the present and must adapt to French colonial life.
Reviews: *BCCB* 10/88; *BL* 9/1/88; *BR* 5-6/89; *HB* 3-4/89; *SLJ* 10/88★; *WJ* 6
Reading Level: High School
Subject Areas: Canada; Nova Scotia; space and time
Time Period: 1744 ❏ Library owns

Houston, James. *Running West.* **New York: Crown, 1990. 320pp. ISBN 0-517-57732-1. LC 89-25156.**
Canada, early eighteenth century. This romance story is based on fact, telling the story of William Stewart, an exiled Scot, and of Thanadelthur, a woman of the Dene nation. The author's knowledge of the Canadian wilderness adds authenticity to this tragic story.
Reviews: *BBSH*; *BL* 6/1/90; *PW* 2/9/90
Reading Level: High School [Mature Reader]
Subject Areas: Canada; Stewart, William; Indians of North America
Time Period: Eighteenth Century ❏ Library owns

Houston, James A. *The White Dawn: An Eskimo Saga.* **San Diego: Harcourt, 1971. 275pp. ISBN 0-15-196115-8. LC 72-134575.**
1897. Three white whalers become stranded in a Canadian Eskimo village. Their presence brings about changes in the social structure of the village and tragedy.
Reviews: *BBYA*; *BL* 7/1/71; *HB* 10/71; *LJ* 6/15/71
Reading Level: High School [Mature Reader]
Subject Areas: Canada; Eskimos
Time Period: 1897 ❏ Library owns

Lingard, Joan. *Between Two Worlds.* **New York: Dutton/Lodestar, 1991. 192pp. ISBN 0-525-67360-1. LC 90-18475.**
Canada, late 1940s. Sequel to *Tug of War*. The Peterson family, post-World War II Latvian refugees, arrive in Toronto and find adjusting to a new country and culture a bewildering experience. The father collapses just after they arrive and the children must take over providing for the family.
Reviews: *BL* 11/15/91; *PW* 9/6/91; *SLJ* 11/91
Reading Level: Middle–High School
Subject Areas: Canada; refugees; emigration and immigration
Time Period: 1940s ❏ Library owns

Marko, Katherine McGlade. *Away to Fundy Bay.* **New York: Walker, 1987. 590pp. ISBN 0-8027-6594-7. LC 84-25680.**
Nova Scotia, 1775-1783. As the Revolutionary War rages and England needs every able bodied boy and man for its fight to keep its American colonies, 13-year-old Doone Ramsey flees from Halifax to Fundy Bay to evade impressment into the Royal Navy. Taken in by the Dickerson family, he must be careful not to reveal his political sympathies as the area is ripe with spies and counterspies, whom Doone helps to uncover.
Reviews: *BL* 11/15/85; *SLJ* 10/85
Reading Level: Middle–High School

The Americas—Canada

Subject Areas: Canada; Nova Scotia; United States--Revolutionary War, 1775-1783; spies
Time Period: 1775-1783 ❏ Library owns

Nicol, Clive W. *White Shaman.* **Boston: Little, 1979. 234pp. ISBN 0-316-60650-2. LC 79-1305.**
Canada, twentieth century. Arriving in the Canadian arctic to be a student and assistant to a field biologist, Richard Tavett is soon adopted by the Inuit Eskimos and renamed Tik because of his affinity for their culture and his mystical nature. When the field biologist returns, the two are at odds and the biologist is accidentally killed, sending Tik into the wilderness to evade the authorities.
Reviews: *BBYA*; *BL* 9/1/79★; *LJ* 9/1/79; *SLJ* 12/79; *WS* 11
Reading Level: High School [Mature Reader]
Subject Areas: Canada; Eskimos; wilderness survival; Inuit
Time Period: Twentieth Century ❏ Library owns

Pearson, Kit. *The Sky Is Falling.* **New York: Viking, 1990. 248pp. ISBN 0-670-82849-1.**
Toronto, World War II 1939-1945. Strong characterizations make this a compelling story of children traumatized by separation, in this case brought on by a major war. Sent by her British parents to safety in Canada, Norah has a much harder time adjusting to their new home than her younger brother Gavin.
Reviews: *BCCB* 6/90; *BL* 5/15/90★; *SLJ* 6/90
Reading Level: Middle & Junior High School
Subject Areas: Canada; refugees
Time Period: World War, 1939-1945 ❏ Library owns

Pearson, Kit. *The Lights Go On Again.* **New York: Viking, 1994. 201pp. ISBN 0-670-84919-7. LC 93-093819.**
Canada, 1945. Sequel to *The Sky Is Falling* and *Looking at the Moon*. As World War II ends, plans are made to send Norah and Gavin back home to their British parents. Gavin, however, feels like a Canadian boy and does not wish to return, preferring to be adopted by the elderly woman who cared for him during the war.
Reviews: *BCCB* 6/94; *SLJ* 7/94
Reading Level: Middle & Junior High School
Subject Areas: Canada; refugees
Time Period: 1945; World War, 1939-1945 ❏ Library owns

Webster, Jan. *Muckle Annie.* **New York: St. Martin's, 1986. 299pp. ISBN 0-312-55205-X. LC 85-25058.**
Scotland/Canada, late 1850s. "Muckle Annie" lives up to the determination of her name as she searches for her true love Hector Mennock in the Cariboo gold fields

of British Columbia where women are scarce and conditions are harsh. Breaking hearts along the way, Annie does find Hector, but when he dies, she selects her second choice to be her husband.

Reviews: *BL* 12/1/85; *SLJ* 5/86
Reading Level: High School
Subject Areas: Canada; Scotland; women; frontier and pioneer life
Time Period: 1850s ❑ Library owns

South America

Blair, David Nelson. *Fear the Condor.* **New York: Dutton/Lodestar, 1992. 137pp. ISBN 0-525-67381-4. LC 91-46921.**
Bolivia, 1932. Raised in a society ruled by plantation patrons who have no regard for the sharecroppers they employ, ten-year-old Bartolina is intrigued by what lay beyond the plantation. When her family is killed in a war, Bartolina leaves the plantation and finds a world where the downtrodden are beginning to stand up for themselves, forming labor unions and seeking equality.

Reviews: *BCCB* 7/92; *BL* 5/12/92; *PW* 5/18/92; *SLJ* 7/92; *VOYA* 10/92
Reading Level: Middle & Junior High School
Subject Areas: Bolivia; poverty; orphans
Time Period: 1932 ❑ Library owns

Callison, Brian. *The Judas Ship.* **New York: Dutton, 1978. 192pp. ISBN 0-525-13780-7. LC 78-52330.**
Atlantic Ocean/Coast of South America, World War II 1939-1945. The *Maya Star*, a British merchant ship, has been attacked in the Atlantic Ocean by a Nazi raider, leaving the captain dead and its cargo of ammunition on fire. The crew must keep the ship afloat until it reaches the coast of South America, but the Nazis are waiting for them, forcing a difficult decision.

Reviews: *WS* 11
Reading Level: High School
Subject Areas: sea stories
Time Period: World War, 1939-1945 ❑ Library owns

Greene, Jacqueline Dembar. *Out of Many Waters.* **New York: Walker, 1988. 200pp. ISBN 0-8027-6811-3. LC 88-1291.**
Brazil, 1654. Two Jewish sisters, 12-year-old Isobel and her older sister Maria, who were kidnapped in Portugal during the Inquisition are held as virtual slaves in a Brazilian monastery. Maria plots an escape, but the girls must stowaway on separate ships. Isobel very reluctantly agrees. On the ship she becomes very ill and is nursed to health by a Jewish family on board. They shelter her until the

ship reaches New Amsterdam where together they found the first synagogue in America. Followed by *One Foot Ashore*.
Reviews: *BL* 1/15/89; *SLJ* 10/88
Reading Level: Middle & Junior High School
Subject Areas: Brazil; Inquisition; Jews in Brazil; sisters
Time Period: 1654 ❏ Library owns

Jenkins, Lyll Becerra de. *The Honorable Prison*. New York: Dutton/Lodestar, 1988. 203pp. ISBN 0-525-67238-9. LC 87-25197.
South America, 1955. Set in an unnamed Latin American country controlled by a military junta, Jenkins tells the story of 17-year-old Marta Maldonado whose family is imprisoned because of her journalist father's anti-government writings. Subjected to harsh conditions and treatment, Marta dreams of her father's death that might mean an end to the confinement, but in the end internalizes her father's beliefs.
Reviews: *BCCB* 1/88; *BL* 3/15/88★; *HB* 7-8/88; *SLJ* 2/88; *VOYA* 10/88
Reading Level: High School
Subject Areas: Latin America; political prisoners; government, resistance to; freedom of speech
Time Period: 1955 ❏ Library owns

McCunn, Ruthanne Lum. *Sole Survivor*. San Francisco: Design Enterprises of San Francisco, 1985. 235pp. ISBN 0-932538-61-4; pap. 0-92538-62-2. LC 85-71877.
Brazil, 1942. Poon Lim, a 24-year-old second steward aboard the British merchant ship *Benlomond*, is the sole survivor of a German U-Boat attack off the coast of Brazil. McCunn writes Lim's story of survival at sea for 133 days (still a *Guinness Book* record) based on a 1982 interview with him, 40 years after his adventure.
Reviews: *LJ* 10/1/85; *SLJ* 8/86
Reading Level: High School
Subject Areas: sea stories; survival
Time Period: 1942; World War, 1939-1945 ❏ Library owns

O'Dell, Scott. *The Amethyst Ring*. Boston: Houghton, 1983. 212pp. ISBN 0-395-33886-7. LC 82-23388.
Mexico, Peru, 1520-1525. Sequel to *The Captive* and *The Feathered Serpent*. Seminarian Julián Escobar flees after the death of Moctezuma and the sacrifice of the Bishop Don Luis, managing to survive the attack of Cortes' army. He joins Pizarro's army and witnesses even more brutality in Peru. He returns to Spain where he retreats from the world, tortured by his experiences.
Reviews: *BCCB* 3/83; *BL* 3/15/83; *HB* 6/83; *PW* 5/13/83; *SLJ* 9/83
Reading Level: Middle–High School

Subject Areas: Mexico; Peru; Mayas; Incas; Indians of South America
Time Period: 1520-1525   ❑ Library owns

Peters, Daniel. *The Incas.* **New York: Random House, 1991. 1,073pp. ISBN 0-394-58492-9. LC 90-44467.**
Peru, pre-Columbian. Focusing on two characters, a young warrior and the daughter of a chief, this shows the Inca civilization at its zenith, just before the arrival of the Conquistadors.
Reviews: *BL* 1/1/91; *LJ* 6/1/91; *PW* 5/31/91
Reading Level: High School [Mature Reader]
Subject Areas: Peru; Incas
Time Period: 1450-1500   ❑ Library owns

Raspail, J.; translated by Jeremy Leggatt. *Who Will Remember the People....* **San Francisco: Mercury H.S., 1988. 213pp. ISBN 0-916515-42-7. LC 88-10016.**
Prehistory–twentieth century, Tierra del Fuego. Raspail follows the People, a Stone Age tribe as they migrate from Siberia to Tierra del Fuego and maintain their Stone Age culture over the centuries, through their early twentieth century extinction caused by contact with missionaries and modern society. This is a grim, non-romanticized, look at a primitive people.
Reviews: *BBSH*; *Choice* 2/89; *PW* 8/5/88; *SLJ* 12/89
Reading Level: High School [Mature Reader]
Subject Areas: Latin America; prehistoric man
Time Period: Stone Age   ❑ Library owns

Watson, James. *Talking in Whispers.* **New York: Knopf, 1984. 144pp. ISBN 0-394-96538-8. LC 83-17595.**
Chile, contemporary. The author who is active in Amnesty International, tells the story of Andres Larreta whose father is taken away by the military because of his opposition to the government. Andres is now a fugitive and becomes involved in the Resistance, and along with a brother-sister team of puppeteers, works to expose the junta. He is captured, tortured, and released half-dead, which provides material for photographs exposing the brutality.
Reviews: *BL* 6/15/84; *SLJ* 4/84
Reading Level: Middle–High School
Subject Areas: Chile; government, resistance to; underground movements
Time Period: 1980s   ❑ Library owns

Bibliography and Suggested Reading

Brandhorst, Allan R. "Historical Fiction in the Classroom: Useful Tool or Entertainment?" *Southern Social Studies Quarterly* 14.1 (Fall 1988): 19-30

Blos, Joan W. "The Overstuffed Sentence and Other Means for Assessing Historical Fiction for Children." *School Library Journal* (Nov. 1985): 38-39.

Caldwell, John J. "Historical Fiction as a Modern Tool." *Canadian Journal of English Language Arts* 11.1(1988): 24-32.

Chauvette, Cathy. "Journey in the Past: the Power of Historical Fiction." *School Library Journal* (June 1992): 51-52.

Cianciolo, Patricia. "Yesterday Comes Alive for Readers of Historical Fiction." *Language Arts* (April 1981): 452-462.

Collier, Christopher. "Criteria for Historical Fiction." *School Library Journal* (Aug. 1982): 32-33.

Donelson, Kenneth L. and Alleen Pace Nilsen. *Literature for Today's Young Adults*. Glenview, Illinois: HarperCollins College Publishers, c1993.

Heinly, R. E. and Kenneth Hilton. "Using Historical Fiction to Enrich Social Studies Courses." *The Social Studies* (Jan./Feb 1982): 21-24.

Lehman, Barbara A. and David Hayes. "Advancing Critical Reading Through Historical Fiction and Biography." *The Social Studies* (July/Aug. 1985): 165-169.

MacRae, Cathi. "The Young Adult Perplex." *Wilson Library Bulletin* (Sept. 1991): 102-103.

Rochman, Hazel, Masha Kabakow Rudman and Diane Stanley. "Is That Book Politically Correct?" *Journal of Youth Services in Libraries* 7 (Winter 1994): 159-175.

Stanek, Lou Willett. "Whole Language for Whole Kids." *School Library Journal* (Sept. 1991): 187-189.

Van Kirk, Eileen. "Imagining the Past Through Historical Novels." *School Library Journal* (Aug. 1993): 50-51.

Title Index

A

Abduction, The 131
Across the Barricades 178
Across the Sea from Galway 160
Adam of the Road 89
Admiral and the Deck Boy, The 132
Advent of Brother Cadfael, The 95
African Mask, The 10
Against the Storm 28
Age of Miracles, The 106
Agony and the Ecstacy, The 112
Ah, But Your Land Is Beautiful 13
Ajeemah and His Son 223
AK 7
Albany 157
Alethea 115
Alexandrian, The 4
All Men Tall 113
All Quiet on the Western Front 192
Along the Tracks 194
Amethyst Ring, The 234
Among the Volcanoes 225
And Quiet Flows the Don 189
And the Violins Stopped Playing 219
Andi's War 184
Anna 162
Anna Is Still Here 221
Anna's Book 166
Another Place, Another Spring 164
Another Shore 230
Anthony Adverse 139
Anya 221
Apprentice, The 105
Apprentices, The 145

Armada 120
Arrow of God 9
As the Crow Flies 173
Ask Me No Questions 170
August 1914 192
Avalon 73
Away to Fundy Bay 231
Ayo Gurkha! 37

B

Babi Yar 193
Backwater War 209
Barnaby Rudge 143
Baron's Hostage, The 99
Bartholomew Fair 135
Beacon at Alexandria, The 2
Bearkeeper's Daughter, The 23
Becoming Gershona 26
Beggar King of China, The 29
Bel Ria 195
Belt of Gold, The 24
Ben Hur 65
Bern, Son of Mikula 69
Between Two Worlds, The 231
Beware of Moonlight 146
Beyond Safe Boundaries 14
Beyond the Ancient Cities 228
Beyond the Mists 69
Beyond the Weir Bridge 115
Big Fisherman, The 21
Birthday Boys, The 174
Bisha of Burundi 7
Bitterest Age, The 201
Bittersweet 34
Black Arrow, The 111

World Historical Fiction Guide

Black Lamp, The 158
Black Rose, The 86
Black Tulip, The 118
Blitzcat 208
Blood Red, Sister Rose 104
Blood Royal 121, 137
Bloody Field, The 107
Bomber's Moon, The 35
Bond of Honour 75
Bonnie Dundee 135
Book of Merlyn, The 81
Book of Songs, A 215
Boris 199
Born of the Sun 75
Borrowed House, The 207
Bounty Trilogy, The 48
Boy and the Samurai, The 38
Boy of the Painted Cave 50
Boys from St. Petri, The 205
Bride Price, The 10
Bridge of Sighs 128
Bridge Over the River Kwai, The 18
Bridge to the Other Side, The 202
Bridle the Wind 156
Bright and Morning Star, The 3
Bronze Bow, The 23
Bull from the Sea, The 57

C

Capricorn Bracelet, The 64
Captain from Castile 230
Captain Horatio Hornblower 144
Captive of Kensington Palace, The 168
Captive Queen of Scots, The 132
Captive, The 228
Captives of Time 84
Cargo for a King 83
Cargo of the Madalena, The 102
Caribbean 224
Catherine, Called Birdy 86
Ceremony of Innocence 197
Chain of Fire 13
Chance Child, A 167
Charterhouse of Parma, The 153
Chase Me, Catch Nobody 200
Child from the Sea, The 121
Child of Our Time 211
Child of the Morning 3

Child of the Northern Spring 82
Child of War 179
Children of Bach 211
Children of the Book 116
Children of the Fox 56
Children of the Wolf 36
Chileno! 182
Chinwe 9
Circle of Pearls 127
Circlemaker, The 170
Clan of the Cave Bear, The 49
Clay Marble, The 17
Cleopatra 4
Cloister and the Hearth, The 134
Code Name Kris 203
Cold Wind Blowing, A 138
Coldest Winter, The 165
Colors Aloft! 148
Come Spring 215
Coming of the Bear, The 38
Confession of Brother Haluin, The 94
Connecticut Yankee in King Arthur's Court, A 80
Conspiracy, The 62
Consul's Daughter, The 6
Covenant, The 12
Cranes at Dusk 42
Crimson Wind, The 227
Crocodile Burning 16
Cromwell's Boy 123
Crowning Mercy, A 126
Crows of War, The 68
Crusade in Jeans 83
Crutches 181
Cry of the Peacock 25
Cry, The Beloved Country 14
Crystal Cave, The 79

D

Dancing Bear, The 24
Dangerous Game, The 196
Dark Quartet 157
Darkness and the Dawn, The 59
Darkness Casts No Shadow 216
Daughter of the Nobility, A 186
Daughter of the Red Deer 52
Daughter of the Sea 56
Daughter of Time, The 112

240

Title Index

Dawn 27
Dawn Palace, The 55
Days of the Dragon's Seed, The 55
Dear and Glorious Physician 21
Death Comes As Epiphany 92
December Rose, The 161
Deep Dream of the Rain Forest 47
Désirée 152
Devil in Vienna, The 217
Devil on Horseback, The 147
Devil to Pay 151
Devil Water 153
Devil's Arithmetic, The 222
Devil's Workshop, The 106
Displaced Person 194
Doctor Zhivago 187
Dog of Bondi Castle 89
Dom and Va 1
Don Flows Home to the Sea, The 189
Don Quixote de La Mancha 84
Don't Say a Word 199
Door in the Wall, The 62
Dragon Seed 32
Dragon Village, The 33
Druid's Gift, The 52
Druid's Tune, The 53
Druids 68
Drummer Boy, The 145

E

Eagle in the Snow 59
Eagle of the Ninth, The 64
Earth Will Shake, The 155
Echoes of the White Giraffe 45
Echoes of War 208
Edge of Darkness 199
Edge of Light, The 76
Edge of War, The 201
Egyptian, The 5
Elizabeth, Captive Princess 126
Empire of the Sun 32
Empty Moat, The 206
Empty Sleeve, The 145
Enchantress, The 155
Enemy in Sight! 148
Escapade 162
Escape from Egypt 22
Escape from the Evil Prophecy 72

Estebanico 229
Everlasting Covenant, The 100
Exeter Blitz, The 204
Exit from Home 187
Exodus 26
Eye for Color, An 15
Eyes of the Blind, The 22

F

Falls the Shadow 93
Farewell Sidonia 213
Farewell, Dresden 196
Fatal Crown, The 91
Fateless 214
Fathom Five 208
Fear the Condor 233
Feathered Serpent, The 229
Fernande 160
File on Fraulein Berg, The 178
Fine, Soft Day, A 177
Fire from Heaven 57
Firebrand, The 54
Flame-Colored Taffeta 154
Flight Toward Home 180
Florentine, The 111
Flowers in the Blood 35
Flowers of Adonis, The 58
Flowers of Hiroshima, The 42
Fly Away Home 204
Footsteps 161
Forbidden City 32
Forest House 67
Forest of the Clouded Leopar 48
Forever Nineteen 193
Form Line of Battle! 148
Fortune Made His Sword 109
Forty-third War, The 226
Four Horses for Tishtry 66
1492 119
Freedom Tree, The 191
Frenchwoman, The 151
Friedrich 220
Frontier Wolf 64
Frost in the Night, A 180
Frozen Waterfall, The 174

G

Gideon 210

World Historical Fiction Guide

Gilgamesh the King 20
Glass-Blowers, The 144
Go Saddle the Sea 156
God Against the Gods, A 3
God Is an Englishman 160
Gold of Dreams, The 228
Golden Bees, The 56
Golden Tulip, The 127
Golden Warrior, The 73
Good Earth, The 30
Goodbye, Vietnam 20
Grab Hands and Run 227
Grace 167
Grania 129
Great House, The 122
Great Lion of God 21
Great Thirst, The 11, 14
Great Train Robbery, The 159
Greek Treasure, The 171
Greek Wedding 162
Green Frontier, The 181
Greenyards 165
Grendel 53
Grimsdyke 172
Gudrun 91
Guinevere 78, 82
Guns of Darkness, The 5
Guns of Navarone, The 203
Guns of Valmy, The 140

H

Hadder Maccoll 141
Hakon of Rogen's Saga 71
Half Child, The 124
Handful of Stars, A 28
Hanging at Tyburn, A 143
Harold Was My King 72
Haunting of Kildoran Abbey, The 158
Haveli 37
Hawk of May 77
Hawk That Dare Not Hunt by Day, The 132
Hawk, The 138
Healing Blade, The 141
Hear O Israel 221
Heart of the Continent, The 45
Heart Speaks Many Ways, The 190
Heaven Tree Trilogy, The 93

Heaven's Only Daughter 63
Heirs of the Kingdom, The 93
Here Be Dragons 94
Hide and Seek 207
High Voyage, The 128
Hiroshima No Pika 41
His Majesty, Queen Hatshepsut 2
His Majesty's Elephant 75
Holdfast 114
Hollow Hills, The 79
Holy Thief, The 95
Homecoming 188
Honorable Prison, The 234
Horation Hornblower Series, The 144
Horse Goddess, The 53
Horses of Anger 198
Horses of Heaven 54
Hour of the Bell, The 168
House on Prague Street, The 211
How Far to Bethlehem? 22
Hunchback of Notre Dame, The 103
Hunted, The 196

I

I Am England 76
I Am Mary Tudor 128
I Am Rosemarie 217
I Remember Love 122
I Sailed With Columbus 130
I Was There 205
I, Claudius 62
I, Elizabeth 131
I, Juan de Pareja 136
Ides of April, The 63
Ides of March, The 66
If I Should Die Before I Wake 217
If This Be Glory 206
Imagining Isabel 225
Imperial Purple 24
Imperial Woman 29
In Pursuit of the Green Lion 109
In Search of Coffee Mountains 187
In Spite of All Terror 174
In the Autumn Wind 43
In the Company of Clown 114
In the Company of Eagles 192
In the Forest at Midnight 36
In the Shadow of the Brontës 157

Title Index

In the Time of Trouble 7
In Winter's Shadow 77
Incas, The 235
Inheritance, The 137
Ink-keeper's Apprentice, The 43
Innocent Wayfaring, The 100
Into the Valley 16
Iron Hand of Mars, The 60
Iron Lily, The 138
Iron Way, The 159
Island Harp, The 172
Island of Ogres 39
Island on Bird Street, The 218
Ivanhoe 96
Ivy Crown, The 129

J

Jacob's Ladder 45
Jacob's Rescue 212
Jeremy Visick 173
Joseph and His Brothers 22
Journal of the Plague Year, A 118
Journey to America 215
Journey to Jo'burg 13
Journey to the Sky 226
Journey, The 212
Judas Ship, The 233

K

Kate Ryder 116
Katherine 110
Kathleen 177
Kenilworth 134
Keys of the Kingdom, The 33
Khaki Wings 191
Kim 35
Kindling 183
King Must Die, The 57
King's Cavalier, The 111
King's Daughters, The 90
King's Fifth, The 229
King's General, The 119
King's Grey Mare, The 104
King's Knight's Pawn 114
King's Pleasure, The 129
King's Road, The 91
Kingdom by the Sea, The 209
Kingdom of Summer 77

Kingdom of the Grail 83
Kiss the Dust 25
Knight's Acre 106
Kristin Lavransdatter 99

L

Lady Jane 135
Lady of Rhuddesmere, The 97
Lady's Maid 161
Landowner Legacy, The 163
Lantern Bearers, The 68
Last Butterfly, The 213
Last Days of Pompeii, The 59
Last Enchantment, The 79
Last Love, The 142
Last Nine Days of the Bismarck, The 197
Last of the Wine, The 57
Last Pendragon 78
Last Summer, The 190
Last Voyage, The 48
Leaves from the Valley 171
Left-Handed Spirit, The 62
Legend of Tarik, The 6
Leif the Unlucky 103
Leopard, The 164
Letters from Rifka 185
Letters to Horseface 150
Life of a Useless Man, The 186
Light a Penny Candle 174
Light in the Mountain 47
Lights Go On Again, The 232
Lily and the Bull, The 54
Linnet 137
Lion and the Lily, The 96
Lion and the Rose, The 137
Lion in the Evening 8
Lion of Ireland 72
Lion of the Kalahari, The 9
Lion's Cub, The 163
Lisa's War 204
Little Brother 17
Little Fishes, The 200
Little Lower Than the Angels, A 107
Little Sister 33
Locadio's Apprentice 66
Longsword 98
Lords of Vaumartin, The 103
Lost Magic 83

243

Lost Queen, The 149
Lothian Run, The 147
Love Child, The 159
Love Knot, The 101
Lust for Life 171

M

Machine Gunners, The 209
Madonna of the Seven Hills 108
Magic We Do Here, The 220
Magician's Apprentice, The 96
Maiden Crown 86
Man from the Other Side, The 218
Man from the Sea, The 52
Man in the Iron Mask, The 118
Man Who Buried Jesus, The 23
Man's Fate 34
Manwolf 97
Many Waters Cannot Quench Love 115
Mary Stewart's Merlin Trilogy 79
Mask of Apollo, The 58
Master of Ballantrae, The 154
Master of Hestviken, The 99
Master Puppeteer, The 40
Master Rosalind 115
Max's Gang 193
Mckenzie's Boots 46
Memory String, The 17
Men of Iron 108
Merchant's Mark, The 102
Mermaid's Daughter, The 67
Merrymaid, The 122
Messenger for Parliament, A 123
Mexico 228
Mila 18 222
Milk and Honey 176
Miracle Tree, The 42
Mists of Avalon, The 76
Moon in the Cloud, The 4
Moonclock, The 136
Mottele 205
Mountain Light 31
Muckle Annie 232
Murder for Her Majesty, A 124
Murder in the Tower, The 133
Murder Wears a Cowl 87
Murdo's War 179
My Enemy the Queen 125

My Enemy, My Brother 25
My Kingdom for a Grave 188
My Name Is Not Angelica 224
My Sister Clare 175
Myself As Witness 88
Myself My Enemy 133

N

Nicholas Cooke 117
Night in Distant Motion, A 202
Night Journey, The 164
Night of the Broken Glass 210
Night of the Silent Drums 223
Night Over Day Over Night 207
Night Trains 222
Nightingale Gallery, The 89
No Hero for the Kaiser 191
No Need for Heroes 55
No Surrender 15
No Tigers in Africa 15
North of Danger 197
Not of War Only 230
Novel About the Maya, A 226
Novel Based on the Lives of Edmund and William Shakespeare, A 116
Novel of the Danish Resistance, A 193
Nugget of Gold, A 47
Number the Stars 202

O

October, Eight O'Clock 216
Odyssey of the Irish, The 53
Of Nightingales That Weep 40
Old Tale Carved Out of Stone, An 16
Once and Future King, The 81
One Day in the Life of Ivan Denisovich 190
One Foot Ashore 121
Origin, The 171
Other Way Round, The 175
Out of Many Waters 233

P

Pack of Wolves 195
Paladin, The 198
Pangur Ban 74
Paper Bird 12
Paradise 71
Paradise of the Blind 20

Title Index

Parcel of Patterns, A 132
Passage to Pontefract 108
Passions of the Mind, The 180
Peace Child, The 107
Personal Recollections of Joan of Arc 113
Petros' War 210
Pillar of the Sky 50
Pillars of the Earth, The 87
Piper to the Clan 117
Pirate Royal 223
Pit, The 117
Playhouse Tales 124
Playing Beatie Bow 46
Plymouth Cloak, The 110
Poland 185
Porcelain Pagoda, The 30
Potato Eaters, The 157
Potter's Field, The 95
Praise Singer, The 58
Prayer for Katerina Horovitzova 216
Prince and the Pauper, The 136
Prince Charlie's Year 144
Prince of Foxes 111
Prison Window, Jerusalem Blue 70
Prisoner of the Queen 131
Private Life of Mona Lisa, The 105
Proud Taste for Scarlet and Miniver, A 92

Q

Queen and Lord M, The 168
Queen and the Gypsy, The 123
Queen in Waiting 152
Queen of the Summer Stars 82
Queen of This Realm 133
Queen's Confession, The 147
Queen's Head, The 130
Queen's Husband, The 169
Queen's War, The 92
Quentin Durward 110
Quest for a Maid 90
Quo Vadis 64

R

Rain from the West 63
Rape of the Rose, The 164
Razor Eyes 201
Rebel, The 140
Rebels of the Heavenly Kingdom 31

Reckoning, The 94
Red and the Black, The 154
Red Flight Two 191
Red Shift 120
Red Slayer 90
Refugee Summer, The 183
Regards from the Dead Princess 28
Reindeer Moon 17
Rembrandt 134
Requiem for Princess 113
Return to Thebes 3
Return, The 5
Reunion 183
Rice Without Rain 18
Ride Out the Storm 200
Riders of the Storm 140
Right-Hand Man, The 152
Ring the Judas Bel 184
River With No Bridge, The 43
Road to Camlann, The 80
Road to Damietta, The 92
Robe, The 61
Robin and the King 88
Roller Birds of Rampur, The 36
Roman, The 65
Rose for Virtue, A 150
Ruby in the Smoke, The 169
Running Vixen 84
Running West 231
Russian Farewell, A 186

S

Salah of Sierra Leona 11
Samurai 41
Samurai and the Long-nosed Devils, The 39
Samurai's Tale, The 38
Saving Grace 87
Scaramouche 152
Scarlet Pimpernel, The 150
Scent of the Gods, The 18
Scrap of Time, A 212
Sea Beggars, The 125
Second Mrs. Giaconda, The 105
Second Son of Heaven, The 30
Secret of the Mountain, The 12
Seeds of Hiroshima, The 42
Serpent's Children, The 31

World Historical Fiction Guide

Seth of the Lion People 51
Severed Crown, The 128
Shabanu 37
Shadow Army, The 205
Shadow in the North 169
Shadow of the Wall 214
Shadow of Vesuvius, The 61
Shadow on the Sun, The 4
Shadows in Bronze, The 60
Sharpe's Enemy 141
Sharpe's Regiment 142
Sharpe's Siege 142
Sheltering Tree, A 167
Sherwood 88
Shining Company, The 74
Ship from Simnel Street, The 166
Shiva 49
Shiva Accused 50
Shiva's Challenge 49
Shogun 38
Shrine of Murders 101
Sign of the Green Falcon, The 102
Sign of the Owl, The 85
Silent Don, The 189
Silk Vendetta, The 163
Silver Chalice, The 60
Silver Crest, The 158
Silver Pigs 61
Silver Touch, The 149
Singletusk 51
Sirens and Spies 176
Sister of the Moon. 4
Sisters' Tale, The 70
Six Wives of Henry VIII, The 130
Sixth Century: Hollow Hills 79
Skindeep 12
Sky Is Falling, The 232
Slave Girl, The 10
Slave of the Huns 67
Slave's Tale, A 71
Smile of the Stranger, The 139
Smith 146
So Far from the Bamboo Grove 44
So Sings the Blue Deer 227
So Slow the Dawning 182
Soldier of Arete 58
Sole Survivor 234

Somehow Tenderness Survives 14
Song for a Dark Queen 68
Song for Young King Wenceslas, A 72
Song of Be 8
Song of the Buffalo Boy 19
Sound of Anthems, The 177
Sound of Coaches, The 146
Sound of the Dragon's Feet, The 173
Source, The 26
Spirit on the Wall 50
Sprig of Broom, The 139
Spring Moon 34
Stand Into Danger 149
Star in the Forest, The 73
Star of Lancaster, The 108
Star Without a Sky 218
Stars of Fortune 122
Story for a Black Night 8
Story Like the Wind, A 15
Story of the Grail and the Passing of Arthur, The 78
Strange Devices of the Sun and Moon 120
Street Child 160
String in the Harp, A 70
Striped Ships, The 73
Stronghold, The 67
Success to the Brave 149
Sudden, Fearful Death, A 168
Sumitra's Story 177
Summer of the Barshinskeys, The 176
Sun Horse, Moon Horse 69
Survivor, The 213
Sword in the Stone, The 81
Sworn Enemies 166

T

Take Heed of Loving Me 136
Tale of Two Cities, A 143
Tales of the Crusades 85
Talisman, The 27
Talking in Whispers 235
Tall Stones, The 52
Tartar's Sword, The 127
Taste of Salt 225
Teeth of the Gale, The 156
Testing of Tertius, The 78
Then the Zeppelins Came 175
Things Fall Apart 9

Title Index

13th Member, The 125
Three Crowns, The 134
Three from Galilee 21
Three Lives for the Czar 188
Three Musketeers, The 118
Threshing Floor, The 110
Throne of Isis 65
Tilla 181
Time After Time 185
Time and Chance 179
Time of Anger, The 26
Time of the Dragon, The 30
Time of the Forest, The 51
Time Without Bells 194
Tin Princess, The 170
To Cross a Line 219
To Fight in Silence 209
To Kill a King 95
To Ravensrigg 140
To Touch a Dream 25
Toba 185
Tokaido Road, The 41
Tomorrow's Sphinx 2
Too Few for Drums 143
Touch and Go 151
Touch Wood 220
Traitor Within, The 33
Traitors, The 198
Transport 7-41-R 180
Tree Still Stands, The 195
Trinity 172
Tristan and Iseult 75
Trumpeter of Krakow, The 104
Tudor Rose, The 99
Tug of War 202
Tulku 19
Twelfth Day of July, The 178

U

Ulysses 203
Under the Black Flag 224
Untold Tale, The 123
Unwilling Vestal, The 66
Upon This Rock 23
Upstairs Room, The 219

V

Valda 46

Valley of Deer, The 119
Valley of the Broken Cherry Trees 39
Venus in Copper 61
Victor of Salamis, A 55
Village of the Vampire Cat 40
Vindication 153
Vision of Light, A 109
Vision of Stephen, The 70
Visit, The 196
Voyage 184
Voyage of the Lucky Dragon, The 19

W

Waiting for Anya 216
Waiting for the Rain 11
Wall, The 182, 213
War and Peace 155
War Without Friends 200
Warlord of the Genji 37
Waxwork 165
Way Home, The 112
We Speak No Treason 104
We Were Not Like Other People 206
Westward Ho! 127
What Happened in Hamelin 97
When Daylight Comes 224
When Hitler Stole Pink Rabbit 214
Where the Towers Pierce the Sky 101
White Company, The 101
White Dawn, The 231
White Rose Murders 117
White Serpent Castle 40
White Shaman 232
Who Will Remember the People... 235
Why Kill Arthur Potter? 162
Why There Is No Heaven on Earth 189
Whyte Hart, The 87
Wicked Day, The 80
Wild Children, The 187
Wild Hunt, The 85
Wind at Morning, The 130
Wind from the Sea, The 147
Windows of Elissa, The 6
Winter in Wartime 207
Winter Prince, The 80
Wise Child 71
Witch's Brat, The 98
Witches' Sabbath 141

World Historical Fiction Guide

With the Eagles 59
Wolves of Paris, The 106
Woman in the Cloak, The 90
Woman of Nazareth, A 27
Women of Ashdon 113
Women of the Silk 35
World of the Pharoahs, The 1
Writing on the Hearth, The 102

Y

Year of Impossible Goodbyes 44
Year of the Stranger, The 166
You Never Knew Her As I Did 125
Young Bess 126
Young Joan 100

Author Index

A

Aaron, Chester 210
Achebe, Chinua 9
Aiken, Joan 139, 156
Allen, Hervey 139
Alyn, Marjory 177
Amoss, Berthe 83
Anand, Valerie 113
Anatoli, A. 193
Anderson, John L. 223
Anderson, Margaret J. 47, 52
Andrews, J. S. 52, 83
Appel, Allen 185
Archer, Jeffrey 173
Arthur, Ruth M. 113
Attanasio, A. A 83
Auel, Jean 49

B

Bacon, Martha Sherman 114
Baer, Edith 180
Baer, Frank 193
Baillie, Allan 17
Bainbridge, Beryl 174
Baklanov, Grigory 193
Ballard, J. G. 32
Banks, Lynne Reid 157
Barkhordar-Nahai, Gina 25
Barnes, Margaret Campbell 99
Baumann, Hans 1
Beake, Lesley 8
Beatty, John 223
Beatty, John Louis 114, 115
Beatty, Patricia 114, 115, 223
Beckman, Thea. 83

Behan, Brian 177
Bell, Clare 2
Bell, William 32
Belle, Pamela 115
Benchley, Nathaniel 69, 193
Bennett, Jack 19
Bergman, Tamar 194
Berry, James 223
Bess, Clayton 8
Bibby, Violet 115
Bienek, Horst 194
Binchey, Maeve 174
Black, Laura 157
Blair, David Nelson 233
Bloch, Marie Halun 69, 194
Bond, Nancy 70, 230
Born, Lynne 48
Borovsky, Natasha 186
Bosse, Malcolm 47, 84
Boulle, Pierre 18
Bourliaguet, Léonce 140
Bradley, Marion Zimmer 54, 67, 76
Bradshaw, Gillian 2, 23, 24, 54, 77
Branson, Karen 157
Brennan, J. H. 49
Brindley, Louise 157
Briskin, Mae 195
Broner, Peter 210
Brown, Diana 44
Buck, Pearl 29, 30, 32
Bunting, Eve 158
Burchard, Peter 9
Burford, Lolah 70
Burnford, Sheila 195
Burton, Hester 115, 116, 140, 174

Burton, Philip 116
Bykov, Vasil 195

C

Caldecott, Moyra 52, 54
Caldwell, Taylor 21
Callison, Brian 233
Calvert, Patricia 141
Carlson, Dale Bick 29, 37
Carr, Robyn 100
Carter, Dorothy Sharp 2
Carter, Peter 116, 158
Castañeda, Omar S. 225
Castle, Frances 70
Cato, Nancy 45
Cervantes, Miguel de 84
Chadwick, Elizabeth 84, 85
Cheetham, Ann 117
Chen, Yuan-Tsung 33
Cheong, Fiona 18
Chester, Deborah 85
Choi, Sook Nyul 44, 45
Christopher, John 1
Chukovsky, Kornei 158
Chute, Marchette 100
Clarke, Mary Stetson 117
Clavell, James 38
Clements, Bruce 70
Clifford, Mary Louise 7, 11
Clynes, Michael 117
Collins, Alan 45
Collins, Meghan 86
Cookson, Catherine 159
Coolidge, Olivia 85
Cordell, Alexander 33, 141
Cornwell, Bernard 141, 142
Costain, Thomas B. 59-60, 86, 142
Cotich, Felicia 46
Coulonges, Henri 196
Courter, Gay 35
Cowell, Stephanie 117
Creighton, Christopher 198
Crichton, Michael 159
Cronin, A.J. 33
Cross, Gilbert B. 143
Cross, Gillian 159
Cushman, Karen 86

D

Dana, Barbara 100
Dank, Milton 191, 196
Darby, Catherine 101
David, Kurt 29
Davis, Lindsey 60, 61
Davis, William Stearns 55
Defoe, Daniel 118
Degens, T. 180, 196
Del Castillo, Michel 211
Delderfield, Ronald Frederick 143, 160
Demetz, Hana 211
Denzel, Justin 50
Dickens, Charles 143
Dickinson, Peter 7, 19, 24
Dillon, Ellis 61, 211
Doherty, Berlie 160
Doherty, P.C. 87
Douglas, Lloyd C. 21, 61
Doyle, Sir Arthur Conan 101
Drucker, Malka 212
Drury, Allen 3
Du Maurier, Daphne 119, 144
Duggan, William 11
Dumas, Alexandre 118, 160
Dunlop, Eileen 119
Duran, Cheli 183

E

Eberhart, Dikkon 71
Ecke, Wolfgang 180
Eden, Dorothy 30
Emecheta, Buchi 10

F

Fenton, Edward 183
Fife, Dale 197
Fink, Ida 212
Fisher, Leonard Everett 160, 186
Follett, Ken 87
Forester, C. S. 144, 197
Forman, James 25, 144, 177, 184, 197-198, 213
Forster, Margaret 161
Frank, Rudolf 191
Frohlich, Newton 119

G

Gaan, Margaret 33

Author Index

Gann, Ernest 192
García, Ann O'Neal 50
Gard, Joyce 67
Gardner, John 53
Gárdonyi, Géza 67
Garfield, Brian 198
Garfield, Leon 145, 146, 161
Garland, Sherry 19
Garner, Alan 120
Garwood, Julie 87
Gedge, Pauline 3
Gehrts, Barbara 199
Geras, Adèle 184
Gessner, Lynne 199
Gidley, Charles 120
Godwin, Parke 88
Goldman, James 88
Golstein, Lisa 120
Goodwin, Marie D. 101
Gordon, Sheila 11
Gorki, Maxim 186
Gottschalk, Elin Toona 187
Goudge, Elizabeth 121
Grace, C. L. 101
Graves, Robert 62
Gray, Elizabeth Janet 89
Greene, Jacqueline Dembar 121, 233
Griffiths, Helen 190

H

Haar, Jaap ter 199
Hackl, Erich 213
Hall, Aylmer 146
Hall, James Norman 48
Hall, Lynn 89
Halperin, Michael 212
Harding, Paul 89, 90
Hardwick, Mollie 121, 122
Harnett, Cynthia 102, 122
Harris, John 200
Harris, Rosemary 3, 4
Harrison, Ray 162
Harrod-Eagles, Cynthia 162
Härtling, Peter 181
Hartman, Evert 200
Haugaard, Erik Christian 38, 71, 103, 123, 200, 224
Haycraft, Molly (Costain) 90
Heaven, Constance 123, 147

Hellman, Aviva 25
Hendrey, Frances Mary 90
Hennessy, Max 227
Hersey, John 62, 213
Hersom, Kathleen 124
Hesse, Karen 185
Heyman, Anita 187
Hiçyilmaz, Gaye 28, 174
Highwater, Jamake 226
Hilgartner, Beth 124
Hill, Pamela 90
Ho, Minfong 17, 18
Hodge, Jane Aiken 162
Hodges, Cyril Walter 124
Holland, Cecelia 24, 50, 91, 103, 125
Holman, Felice 187
Holmes, Marjorie 21
Holt, Victoria 125, 147, 163
Hoover, H. M. 55, 163
Horgan, Dorothy 175, 201
Hough, Richard 201
Houston, James A. 231
Howard, Ellen 224
Hughes, Glyn 164
Hugo, Victor 103
Hunter, Mollie 67, 125, 147
Huong, Duong Thu 20
Hylton, Sara 175

I

Innes, Hammond 48
Irwin, Margaret 126

J

Jabbour, Hala Deeb 27
Jacot, Michael 213
Jarman, Rosemary Hawley 104
Jaro, Benita Kane 62
Jenkins, Lyll Becerra de 234
Johnston, Norma 55
Jones, Adrienne 164
Jones, Ellen 91
Jones, Toeckey 12

K

Keaney, Brian 55
Kells, Susannah 126
Kelly, Eric P. 104
Keneally, Thomas 104
Kennedy, Raymond 201

Kent, Alexander 148, 149
Kerr, Judith 175, 214
Kertész, Imre 214
Kimmel, Eric A. 127
Kingman, Lee 72
Kingsley, Charles 127
Kipling, Rudyard 35
Koehn, Ilse 181
Koenig, Alma Johanna 91
Konigsburg, E. L. 92, 105
Körner, Wolfgang 181
Korschunow, Irina 202
Kotowska, Monika 202
Kurtén, Björn 51

L

La Mure, Pierre 105
Laird, Christa 214
Laird, Elizabeth 25
Laker, Rosalind 127, 149
Lampedusa, Giuseppe di 164
Lane, Jane 128
Lasky, Kathryn 164
Lee, C. Y. 30
Leighton, Margaret (Carver) 4
Levitin, Sonia 5, 22, 215
Lewis, Hilda Winifred 72, 128
Lewitt, Maria 215
Li, Leslie 34
Linevski, A. 16
Linfield, Esther 9, 12
Lingard, Joan 165, 178, 202, 231
Linn, Merritt 215
Lisle, Janet Taylor 176
Litowinsky, Olga 128
Llorente, Pilar Molina 105
Llywelyn, Morgan 53, 68, 72, 129
Lofts, Norah 22, 106, 129, 149, 150
Lord, Bette Bao 34
Lovesey, Peter 165
Lowry, Lois 202
Luke, Mary 129
Lustig, Arnost 216
Lutzeier, Elizabeth 165, 182

M

Maartens, Maretha 12
MacBeth, George 166
MacCoun, Catherine 106
Mackin, Jeanne 92

MacLean, Alistair 203
Maiden, Cecil 72
Malraux, André 34
Malvern, Gladys 130
Manea, Norman 216
Mann, Thomas 22
Mannix, Daniel Pratt 106
Marcuse, Katherine 106
Mark, Michael 185
Marko, Katherine McGlade 231
Marks, James M. 37
Marshall, James Vance 130
Marston, Edward 130
Martin, Susan 130
Maruki, Toshi 41
Matas, Carol 166, 203
Matsubara, Hisako 41, 42
Mattingley, Christobel 42
McCaughrean, Geraldine 107
McCunn, Ruthanne Lum 234
McGee, Charmayne 227
McGowen, Tom 51
McGraw, Eloise 73
McLean, Allan Campbell 166
McLeod, Alison 131
Melling, Orla 53
Merino, José María 228
Michener, James 12, 26, 185, 224, 228
Moeri, Louise 226
Monjo, F. N. 30, 150
Morgan, Alison 22
Morpurgo, Michael 216
Morris, Edita 42
Moskin, Marietta D. 217
Mourad, Kenize 28
Muntz, Hope 73
Murphy, Walter F. 23
Myers, Christopher A. 48
Myers, Walter Dean 6

N

Naidoo, Beverley 13
Namioka, Lensey 38, 39, 40
Newman, Robert 78
Newman, Sharan 78, 92
Newth, Mette 131
Nichols, Ruth 62
Nicol, Clive W. 232
Nolan, Han 217
Noonan, Michael 46

Author Index

Nordhoff, Charles 48
Nöstlinger, Christine 204
Nurenberg, Thelma 26

O

O'Dell, Scott 92
O'Connor, Genevieve A. 132
O'Dell, Scott 132, 224, 228, 229, 234
Oldenbourg, Zoé 93
Orczy, Baroness 150
Orgel, Doris 217
Orlev, Uri 218
Osborne, Chester G. 17
Ossowski, Leonie 218
Overton, Jenny 166

P

Pargeter, Edith 93, 107
Parish, Helen Rand 229
Park, Rut 46
Parker, Richard 167
Parkinson, Cyril Northcote 151
Pasternak, Boris 187
Paterson, Katherine 31, 40
Paton Walsh, Jill 56, 132, 167
Paton, Alan 13, 14
Paul, Barbara 151
Pearson, Diane 176
Pearson, Kit 232
Penman, Sharon Kay 93, 94
Perry, Anne 168
Peters, Daniel 226, 235
Peters, Ellis 94, 95
Petrakis, Harry Mark 168
Peyton, K.M. 152
Phillips, Ann 107
Plaidy, Jean 108, 132, 133, 152, 168, 169
Plowman, Stephanie 188
Polland, Madeleine 190
Polland, Madeleine A. 56, 95
Pople, Maureen 47
Posell, Elsa 188
Pryor, Bonnie 51
Pullman, Philip 169, 170
Pyle, Howard 78, 108

R

Ramati, Alexander 219
Rana, Indi 36
Raspail, J. 235
Ray, Karen 219

Ray, Mary 6, 56, 63
Rayson, Steven 68
Reade, Charles 134
Rees, David 204
Reiss, Johanna 219
Remarque, Erich Maria 192
Renault, Mary 57
Reuter, Bjarne 205
Rice, Robert 78
Richter, Hans Peter 205, 220
Riley, Judith Merkle 109
Robinson, Kathleen 63
Robson, Lucia St. Clair 41
Rochman, Hazel (ed.) 14
Rofheart, Martha 4, 109
Rosefield, James. 96
Rosen, Billi 184
Rosen, Dorothy 96
Rosen, Sidney 96
Roth-Hano, Renée 220
Rowlands, Avril 176
Rudner, Lawrence 220
Rupert, Janet E. 10
Russell, Jennifer 110
Rydberg, Ernie 205
Rydberg, Lou 205

S

Sabatini, Rafael 152
Sacks, Margaret 14
Samuels, Gertrude 205
Say, Allen 43
Schaeffer, Susan Fromberg 221
Schami, Rafik 28
Schlee, Ann 5, 6, 170
Schmitt, Gladys 134
Scholefield, Alan 8
Schur, Maxine Rose 170
Scott, Sir Walter 27, 96, 110, 134
Sedley, Kate 110
Seed, Jenny 14
Selinko, Annemarie 152
Semel, Nava 26
Seton, Anya 73, 110, 153
Sevela, Ephraim 189, 206
Shellabarger, Samuel 111, 230
Shemin, Margaretha 206
Sherwood, Frances 153
Sholokhov, Mikhail 189
Shulman, Sandra 111

Sienkiewicz, Henryk 64
Silver, Norman 15
Silverberg, Robert 20
Skármeta, Antonio 182
Skurzynski, Gloria 97
Smith, A. C. H. 135
Smith, Rita Pratt 36
Smith, Rukshana 177
Solzhenitsyn, Alexander 190, 192
Speare, Elizabeth George 23
Stachow, Hasso G. 206
Staples, Suzanne Fisher 37
Stendhal 153, 154
Stevenson, Robert Louis 111, 154
Stewart, Mary 79, 80
Stiles, Martha Bennett 73
Stolz, Mary 74, 135
Stone, Irving 112, 171, 180
Strauss, Victoria 97
Stroup, Dorothy 43
Sullivan, Mary Ann 179
Sumii, Sué 43
Sutcliff, Rosemary 58, 64, 68, 74, 75, 80, 98, 135, 154
Suyin, Han 155

T

Tarr, Judith 65, 75
Temperley, Alan 179
Temple, Frances 98, 225, 227
Terlouw, Jan 207
Tey, Josephine 112
Thomas, Elizabeth Marshall 17
Thorne, Victoria 98
Todd, Catherine 75
Tolstoy, Leo 155
Trachtenberg, Inge 182
Trease, Geoffrey 99
Treseder, Terry Walton 221
Treviño, Elizabeth Borton de 136
Trollope, Joanna 171
Tsukiyama, Gail 35
Turner, Ann 112
Twain, Mark 80, 113, 136

U

Uhlman, Fred 183
Undset, Sigrid 99
Unsworth, Walter 172
Uris, Leon 26, 172, 222

V

Van der Post, Laurens 15
Van Stockum, Hilda 207
Vander Els, Betty 35
Vining, Elizabeth Gray 136
Von Canon, Claudia 136, 137
Vos, Ida 207, 221

W

Wallace, Lew 65
Walsh, John Evangelist 23
Waltari, Mika 5, 65
Watkins, Paul 207
Watkins, Yoko Kawashima 44
Watson, James 15, 191, 235
Watson, Sally 137
Weaver-Gelzer, Charlotte 7
Webster, Jan 232
Wein, Elizabeth 80
Weir, Rosemary 137
Welch, Ronald 138
Westall, Robert 208, 209
Wheeler, Thomas Gerald 113
Whelan, Gloria 20
White, Edward Lucas 66
White, T. H. 81
Wibberley, Anna 179
Wiesel, Elie 27
Wilder, Thornton 66
Willard, Barbara 138, 139
Williams, Jeanne 172
Williams, Michael 16
Wilson, Robert Anton 155
Wiseman, David 173
Wolf, Joan 52, 75, 76
Wolfe, Gene 58
Wood, Barbara 222
Woodford, Peggy 209
Woolley, Persia 82
Wootton, Gareth 222
Wright, Patricia 76
Wuorio, Eva-Lis 209

Y

Yarbro, Chelsea Quinn 66
Yep, Laurence 31
Yolen, Jane 36, 222

Z

Zei, Al'ki 73, 210
Zollinger, Norman 230

Subject Index

A
abandoned children
    Wild Children 187
Abelard, Peter
    Death Comes As Epiphany 92
abolitionists
    Ravensrigg 141
Aborigines
    Dreamtime 46
actors
    Dragon Village 33
    Escapade 162
    In the Company of Clown 114
    Little Lower Than the Angels 107
    Mask of Apollo 58
    Merrymaid 122
    Playhouse Tales 124
    Queen's Head 130
    Sound of Coaches 146
    You, My Brother 116
adolescence
    Becoming Gershona 26
    Earth Will Shake 155
    Jacob's Ladder 45
adoption
    Requiem for Princess 114
adventure and adventurers
    Anthony Adverse 140
    Beyond the Mists 69
    Birthday Boys 174
    Black Rose 86
    Blood Feud 74
    Bridle the Wind 156
    Captain from Castile 230

    Captain Horatio Hornblower 144
    Captive 229
    Colors Aloft! 148
    Crowning Mercy 127
    Devil to Pay 151
    Don Quixote de La Mancha 84
    Enemy in Sight! 148
    Enchantress 155
    Estebanico 230
    Flame-Colored Taffeta 154
    Footsteps 161
    Form Line of Battle! 148
    Go Saddle the Sea 156
    Gold of Dreams 228
    Golden Bees 56
    Grania 129
    Greek Wedding 163
    Guns of Navarone 203
    Hawk 138
    High Voyage 129
    Horation Hornblower Series 144
    In Pursuit of the Green Lion 109
    Kim 36
    Legend of Tarik, The 6
    Man in the Iron Mask 118
    Moon in the Cloud 4
    Paradise 71
    Peace Child 107
    Prince and the Pauper 136
    Quest for a Maid 90
    Running Vixen 85
    Scarlet Pimpernel 151
    Smile of the Stranger 139

World Historical Fiction Guide

Stand Into Danger 149
Success to the Brave 149
Tartar's Sword 127
Teeth of the Gale 157
Three Musketeers 119
Touch and Go 151
Under the Black Flag 224
White Company 101
aerial operations
In the Company of Eagles 192
Khaki Wings 191
Razor Eyes 201
Red Flight Two 191
Africa
African Mask 11
Ah, But Your Land Is Beautiful 13
AK 7
Arrow of God 9
Beyond Safe Boundaries 14
Bride Price 10
Chain of Fire 13
Chinwe 10
Covenant 13
Crocodile Burning 16
Cry, The Beloved Country 14
Dom and Va 1
Eye for Color 15
Great Thirst 11, 14
Into the Valley 16
Journey to Jo'burg 13
Legend of Tarik, The 6
Lion of the Kalahari 9
No Surrender 16
No Tigers in Africa 15
Paper Bird 12
Salah of Sierra Leona 11
Secret of the Mountain 12
Skindeep 12
Slave Girl 10
Somehow Tenderness Survives 14
Song of Be 9
Story Like the Wind 15
Things Fall Apart 9
Waiting for the Rain 11
Windows of Elissa, The 6
Africa, East
Lion in the Evening 8

Ainu
Coming of the Bear 39
air pilots
In the Company of Eagles 192
Khaki Wings 191
Razor Eyes 201
Red Flight Two 191
Albert, consort of Queen Victoria
Queen's Husband 169
Alcibiades
Flowers of Adonis 58
Alexander the Great
Fire from Heaven 57
Alfred the Great, King of England
Edge of Light 76
Algeria
Consul's Daughter, The 6
allegories
Year of the Stranger 166
Amenhetep IV, King of Egypt
God Against the Gods 3
Return to Thebes 3
Amerasians
Song of the Buffalo Boy 19
Amergin
Bard 53
America
Admiral and the Deck Boy 132
Anthony Adverse 140
High Voyage 129
I Sailed With Columbus 131
America--discovery and exploration
Beyond the Ancient Cities 228
Captain from Castile 230
Captive 229
Estebanico 230
Feathered Serpent 229
Gold of Dreams 228
King's Fifth 229
Americans in Japan
Flowers of Hiroshima 42
Anglo-Saxons
Born of the Sun 76
Edge of Light 76
Lantern Bearers 68
Sherwood 88
Shining Company 75

Subject Index

Striped Ships 73
Vision of Stephen 70
Angola
No Surrender 16
anthropology
Clan of the Cave Bear 49
anticommunist movements
Wall 182
Antigone (Greek mythology)
Days of the Dragon's Seed 55
Antioch
Silver Chalice 60
antisemitism
Homecoming 188
Jacob's Ladder 45
Night Journey 165
Return, The 5
Russian Farewell 186
apartheid
Ah, But Your Land Is Beautiful 13
Beyond Safe Boundaries 14
Chain of Fire 13
Eye for Color 15
Journey to Jo'burg 13
No Tigers in Africa 15
Skindeep 12
Somehow Tenderness Survives 14
Waiting for the Rain 11
apprentices
Apprentice 105
Apprentices 145
Devil's Workshop 107
Empty Sleeve 146
Lion and the Rose 138
Arabs
Source 26
archeologists
Greek Treasure 171
Journey to the Sky 226
archeology
Source 26
Valley of Deer 119
World of the Pharoahs 2
architects
Great House 123
architecture
Lion and the Rose 138

Arctic Regions
Anna's Book 166
Ariadne (Greek mythology)
No Need for Heroes 56
Aristide, Jean-Bertrand
Taste of Salt 225
Armada, 1588
Westward Ho! 127
Arthur, King
Book of Merlyn 81
Child of the Northern Spring 82
Connecticut Yankee in King Arthur's Court 80
Guinevere 78, 82
Hawk of May 77
Hollow Hills 79
In Winter's Shadow 77
Kingdom of Summer 77
Last Enchantment 80
Mary Stewart's Merlin Trilogy 79
Mists of Avalon 77
Once and Future King 81
Queen of the Summer Stars 82
Road to Camlann 80
Story of the Grail and the Passing of Arthur 78
Sword in the Stone 81
Testing of Tertius 78
Wicked Day 80
Winter Prince 81
Arthurian romances
Crystal Cave 79
Last Pendragon 78
Testing of Tertius 78
Winter Prince 81
artillery
All Men Tall 113
artists
Agony and the Ecstasy 112
Alethea 115
Apprentice 105
Florentine 111
Golden Tulip 128
I, Juan de Pareja 136
Ink-keeper's Apprentice 43
Lust for Life 171
One Foot Ashore 121

World Historical Fiction Guide

Pangur Ban 74
Rembrandt 134
Asia
Black Rose 86
Left-Handed Spirit 63
Assyrians
Eyes of the Blind 23
athletics
Victor of Salamis 55
atomic bomb
Flowers of Hiroshima 42
Hiroshima No Pika 41
In the Autumn Wind 43
Miracle Tree 42
Seeds of Hiroshima 43
Attila
Darkness and the Dawn 60
Slave of the Huns 67
Augustus, 63 B.C.-14 A.D., Emperor of Rome
I, Claudius 62
Aurelius Antonius Marus, Emperor of Rome
Unwilling Vestal 66
Australia
Dreamtime 46
Heart of the Continent 45
Jacob's Ladder 45
Mckenzie's Boots 46
Nugget of Gold 47
Playing Beatie Bow 47
Valda 46
Voyage of the Lucky Dragon 19
Australian Aborigines
Dreamtime 46
Heart of the Continent 45
Austria
Children of the Book 116
Crutches 181
Devil in Vienna 218
Farewell Sidonia 213
Fly Away Home 204
Horse Goddess 53
Moonclock 137
Passions of the Mind 180
authors
Dark Quartet 157

Lady's Maid 161
Aztecs
Feathered Serpent 229
B
Bacon, Roger
Magician's Apprentice 96
bakers and bakeries
Ship from Simnel Street 167
Balcombe, Betsy
Last Love 142
Baron's War, 1263-1267
Baron's Hostage 99
battleships
Last Nine Days of the Bismarck 197
Bayeaux Tapestry
Striped Ships 73
Beatrice d'Este, consort of Lodovico Sforza, il Moro, Duke of Milan
Second Mrs. Giaconda 105
Beowulf
Grendel 53
Bible stories
Big Fisherman 21
Dear and Glorious Physician 21
Escape from Egypt 22
Great Lion of God 21
How Far to Bethlehem? 22
Joseph and His Brothers 22
Man Who Buried Jesus 23
Moon in the Cloud 4
Silver Chalice 60
Three from Galilee 22
Upon This Rock 23
Bismarck (Battleship)
Last Nine Days of the Bismarck 197
Black Death
Way Home 112
Blacks
Ajeemah and His Son 223
Milk and Honey 176
My Name Is Not Angelica 225
Taste of Salt 225
Blacks--Nigeria
Bride Price 10
Slave Girl 10
Blacks--Sierra Leone
Salah of Sierra Leona 11

Subject Index

Blacks--South Africa
Crocodile Burning 16
Journey to Jo'burg 13
Paper Bird 12
Waiting for the Rain 11
Bligh, William
Bounty Trilogy 48
blind
Eyes of the Blind 23
Woman in the Cloak 91
Bohemia
Song for Young King Wenceslas 73
Boleyn family
Blood Royal 121
Boleyn, Anne
Blood Royal 121
Bolivia
Fear the Condor 233
Borgia family
Madonna of the Seven Hills 108
Borgia, Cesare
Prince of Foxes 111
Borgia, Lucrezia
Madonna of the Seven Hills 108
Borneo
Deep Dream of the Rain Forest 48
Forest of the Clouded Leopard 48
Boudicca, Queen
Song for a Dark Queen 69
Bounty (ship)
Bounty Trilogy 48
Brazil
Out of Many Waters 234
Brian Boru
Lion of Ireland 72
Britain
Grendel 53
Tall Stones 53
British in Borneo
Deep Dream of the Rain Forest 48
British in India
In the Forest at Midnight 36
British in Nigeria
Arrow of God 9
Brontë family
Dark Quartet 157
In the Shadow of the Brontës 158

brothers
Empty Sleeve 146
Master of Ballantrae 154
Secret of the Mountain 12
Traitors 198
Warlord of the Genji 38
Winter Prince 81
brothers and sisters
Escape from the Evil Prophecy 72
In the Time of Trouble 8
bullfighting
Mexico 228
Burundi
Bisha of Burundi 7
Bushmen
Lion of the Kalahari 9
Song of Be 9
Story Like the Wind 15
Byzantine Empire
Bearkeeper's Daughter 24
Belt of Gold 24
Dancing Bear 24
Imperial Purple 24
Byzantium
Blood Feud 74

C
Caesar, Julius
Ides of March 66
Caligula
Robe 61
Cambodia
Clay Marble 18
Little Brother 17
Cameroun
In the Time of Trouble 8
Canada
Another Shore 230
Away to Fundy Bay 232
Between Two Worlds 231
Lights Go On Again 232
Muckle Annie 233
Running West 231
Sky Is Falling 232
White Dawn 231
White Shaman 232
canals
Hanging at Tyburn 143

Canterbury (England)
  Shrine of Murders 102
  Threshing Floor 110
Caribbean Islands
  Caribbean 224
Caroline Mathilde, consort of Christian VII
  Lost Queen 150
Carthage
  Windows of Elissa, The 6
cartoonists
  Ink-keeper's Apprentice 43
Cassandra (Greek mythology)
  Firebrand 54
cathedrals
  Heaven Tree Trilogy 93
  Murder for Her Majesty 124
  Pillars of the Earth 87
Catherine of Aragon, consort of Henry VIII
  King's Pleasure 129
Catherwood, Frederick
  Journey to the Sky 226
cats
  Blitzcat 208
cave drawings
  Boy of the Painted Cave 50
  Spirit on the Wall 50
cave dwellers
  Boy of the Painted Cave 50
  Seth of the Lion People 51
  Spirit on the Wall 50
Caxton, William
  Cargo of the Madalena 102
Celts
  Bard 53
  Crows of War 68
  Druids 68
  Forest House 67
  Horse Goddess 53
  Song for a Dark Queen 69
  Stronghold 68
  Sun Horse, Moon Horse 69
censorship
  Handful of Stars 28
Central America
  Forty-Third War 226

  Journey to the Sky 226
  Tikal 227
Charlemagne, Emperor
  His Majesty's Elephant 75
Charles I, King of England
  Myself My Enemy 133
  Severed Crown 128
Charles II, King of Great Britain
  Child from the Sea 121
Charles XIV John, King of Sweden and Norway
  Désirée 153
Chaucer, Geoffrey
  Love Knot 101
cheetahs
  Tomorrow's Sphinx 2
child abuse
  Ask Me No Questions 170
child labor
  Chance Child 167
children
  Bridge to the Other Side 202
Children's Crusade, 1212
  Crusade in Jeans 84
Chile
  Chileno! 182
  Talking in Whispers 235
China
  Beggar King of China 29
  Bittersweet 34
  Black Wolf of the Steppes 29
  Bomber's Moon 35
  Dragon Seed 33
  Dragon Village 33
  Enchantress 155
  Forbidden City 32
  Good Earth 30
  Imperial Woman 29
  Keys of the Kingdom 33
  Left-Handed Spirit 63
  Little Sister 34
  Man's Fate 34
  Mountain Light 31
  Porcelain Pagoda 31
  Rebels of the Heavenly Kingdom 31
  Second Son of Heaven 30
  Serpent's Children 32

Subject Index

Spring Moon 34
Time of the Dragon 30
Traitor Within 33
Tulku 19
Women of the Silk 35
chivalry
   Connecticut Yankee in King Arthur's Court 80
   Guinevere 78
   Longsword 98
   Queen of the Summer Stars 82
   White Company 101
choirs
   Murder for Her Majesty 124
Christian saints
   Big Fisherman 21
   Blood Red, Sister Rose 104
   Dear and Glorious Physician 21
   Great Lion of God 21
   Personal Recollections of Joan of Arc 113
   Road to Damietta 93
   Upon This Rock 23
   Woman in the Cloak 91
   Young Joan 100
Christian VII, King of Denmark
   Lost Queen 150
Christianity
   Escape from the Evil Prophecy 72
Christmas stories
   Miracle Tree 42
church history
   Ben Hur 65
   Quo Vadis 64
   Robe 61
   Roman 65
   Silver Chalice 60
Churchill, Sir Winston
   Paladin 198
Claudius, 10 B.C.-54 A.D., Emperor of Rome
   I, Claudius 62
Cleopatra, Queen of Egypt
   Alexandrian, The 5
   Cleopatra 4
   Throne of Isis 65

clocks and watches
   Captives of Time 84
Columbus, Christopher
   1492 119
   Admiral and the Deck Boy 132
   High Voyage 129
   I Sailed With Columbus 131
Columbus, Ferdinand
   High Voyage 129
Commedia dell' Arte
   In the Company of Clown 114
communism
   Doctor Zhivago 188
concentration camps 217
   Book of Songs 215
   Child of Our Time 211
   Dawn 27
   Devil's Arithmetic 222
   Empire of the Sun 32
   Fateless 214
   Gideon 210
   Hear O Israel 221
   I Am Rosemarie 217
   Last Butterfly 214
   October, Eight O'Clock 216
   Prayer for Katerina Horovitzova 216
   Scrap of Time 212
Constantinople
   Bearkeeper's Daughter 24
   Imperial Purple 24
Cook, James
   Last Voyage 48
Cornwall (England)
   Jeremy Visick 173
   King's General 119
Cortes, Hernan
   Captain from Castile 230
   Feathered Serpent 229
Cossacks
   And Quiet Flows the Don 189
   Don Flows Home to the Sea 189
   Tartar's Sword 127
country life
   Great House 123
Crete
   Daughter of the Sea 56
   King Must Die 57

World Historical Fiction Guide

Lily and the Bull 54
No Need for Heroes 56
crime and criminals
   Great Train Robbery 159
   Waxwork 165
Crimean War, 1854-56
   Leaves from the Valley 172
Cro-Magnons
   Adventure of the Ice Age 49
   Clan of the Cave Bear 49
   Daughter of the Red Deer 52
   Shiva Accused 50
   Shiva's Challenge 49
   Spirit on the Wall 50
Crusades
   Crusade in Jeans 84
   Heirs of the Kingdom 93
   Kingdom of the Grail 83
   Road to Damietta 93
   Tales of the Crusades 86
   Talisman 27
cults
   Mermaid's Daughter 67
   Rebels of the Heavenly Kingdom 31
Czechoslovakia
   Darkness Casts No Shadow 216
   House on Prague Street 211

D

Daghestan
   Lion's Cub 164
Darling, Grace
   Grace 167
Darwin, Charles
   Origin 171
Denmark
   Boys from St. Petri 205
   Bright Candles 194
   Code Name Kris 203
   Lisa's War 204
   Lost Queen 150
   Maiden Crown 86
   Number the Stars 203
   Time of the Forest 51
   To Fight in Silence 210
   Untold Tale 123
depressions, economic
   Valda 46

Desideria, consort of Charles XIV John, King of Sweden and Norway
   Désirée 153
diaries
   Catherine, Called Birdy 86
   Handful of Stars 28
discrimination
   Milk and Honey 176
dogs
   Bel Ria 195
   Blood Royal 137
   Dog of Bondi Castle 89
   Holdfast 114
   Kingdom by the Sea 209
Donne, John
   Take Heed of Loving Me 136
dreams
   Requiem for Princess 114
Dresden (Germany)
   Farewell, Dresden 196
Druids
   Bard 53
   Druid's Gift 52
   Druid's Tune 54
   Druids 68
   Forest House 67
   Mists of Avalon 77
   Stronghold 68
Dudley, Amy Robsart, Lady
   Kenilworth 135
   Queen and the Gypsy 124
Dundee, John Graham of Claverhouse, Viscount
   Bonnie Dundee 135
Dunkirk, Battle of, 1940
   Ride Out the Storm 200

E

East Indians in Great Britain
   Sumitra's Story 177
Eastern Europe
   Voyage 184
Edward I, King of England
   King's Daughters 90
   Reckoning 94
Edward IV, King of England
   King's Grey Mare 104

Subject Index

Edward VI, King of England
  Prince and the Pauper 136
Egypt
  Alexandrian, The 5
  Beacon at Alexandria 2
  Bright and Morning Star, The 4
  Child of the Morning 3
  Cleopatra 4
  Egyptian, The 5
  Escape from Egypt 22
  God Against the Gods 3
  His Majesty, Queen Hatshepsut 2
  Moon in the Cloud 4
  Return to Thebes 3
  Shadow on the Sun 4
  Throne of Isis 65
  Tomorrow's Sphinx 2
  World of the Pharoahs 2
El Salvador
  Grab Hands and Run 227
Eleanor, Queen of England
  Proud Taste for Scarlet and Miniver 92
  Queen's War 92
Elizabeth I, Queen of England
  Elizabeth, Captive Princess 126
  I, Elizabeth 131
  Kenilworth 135
  Linnet 137
  My Enemy the Queen 125
  Queen and the Gypsy 124
  Queen of This Realm 133
  Stars of Fortune 122
  Young Bess 126
Elizabeth, consort of Edward IV
  King's Grey Mare 104
Elizabeth, consort of Henry VII
  Tudor Rose 100
Elizabeth, Princess of England
  King's Daughters 90
emigration and immigration
  Between Two Worlds 231
  Frozen Waterfall 175
  Letters from Rifka 185
  Milk and Honey 176
  Mountain Light 31
  Toba 185
  Voyage 184
England--1154-1399
  Reckoning 94
Erikson, Leif
  Beyond the Mists 69
escapes
  Another Place, Another Spring 164
  Bomber's Moon 35
  Children of Bach 211
  Circlemaker 170
  Pack of Wolves 195
  Ring the Judas Bell 184
  Sworn Enemies 166
  To Cross a Line 219
  Waiting for Anya 217
  When Hitler Stole Pink Rabbit 214
  You Never Knew Her As I Did 126
Eskimos 232
  White Dawn 231
espionage
  Tin Princess 170
Estévan
  Estebanico 230
  King's Fifth 229
Ethiopia
  Guns of Darkness, The 6
  Return, The 5
Europe
  Druids 68
  Letters from Rifka 185
  Slave of the Huns 67
  Tree Still Stands 195
Europe--1517-1648
  Hawk That Dare Not Hunt by Day 132
Europe--1798-1900
  Sharpe's Enemy 142
Europe--476-1492
  Captives of Time 84
  Crusade in Jeans 84
  Tales of the Crusades 86
Exeter (England), bombardment, 1942
  Exeter Blitz 204
Exodus, The
  Escape from Egypt 22
explorers
  1492 119

263

World Historical Fiction Guide

    Admiral and the Deck Boy 132
    Anna's Book 166
    Beyond the Mists 69
    Birthday Boys 174
    High Voyage 129
    I Sailed With Columbus 131
    Last Voyage 48
    Paradise 71
    Wind at Morning 130
extrasensory perception
    Horse Goddess 53
    In the Shadow of the Brontës 158
    Tall Stones 53

F

Fabrizio, Prince of Salina
    Leopard 164
fairies
    *Strange Devices of the Sun
        and Moon* 120
fairs
    Bartholomew Fair 135
family life
    Ayo Gurkha! 37
    Cranes at Dusk 42
    Dark Quartet 157
    Fine, Soft Day 178
    Glass-Blowers 144
    In Spite of All Terror 174
    In the Autumn Wind 43
    Iron Way 159
    Little Sister 34
    Night Journey 165
    Playing Beatie Bow 47
    Potato Eaters 157
    Samurai 41
    Scent of the Gods 18
    Serpent's Children 32
    Shabanu 37
    Silver Touch 149
    Spring Moon 34
    Sumitra's Story 177
    Summer of the Barshinskeys 176
    Tree Still Stands 195
family problems
    No Tigers in Africa 15
famines
    Across the Sea from Galway 161

    Coldest Winter 165
    Haunting of Kildoran Abbey 158
    Potato Eaters 157
fantastic fiction
    Druid's Tune 54
    Hawk of May 77
    His Majesty's Elephant 75
    Kingdom of Summer 77
    Legend of Tarik, The 6
    *Strange Devices of the Sun
        and Moon* 120
    String in the Harp 70
    Tomorrow's Sphinx 2
    Vision of Stephen 70
fathers and daughters
    Sound of the Dragon's Feet 173
fathers and sons
    Ajeemah and His Son 223
feminists
    Vindication 153
feral children
    Children of the Wolf 36
Florence (Italy)
    Apprentice 105
folklore
    Dreamtime 46
France
    Anthony Adverse 140
    Bel Ria 195
    Blood Red, Sister Rose 104
    Child of Our Time 211
    Dangerous Game 196
    Death Comes As Epiphany 92
    Dog of Bondi Castle 89
    Guns of Valmy 140
    Heirs of the Kingdom 93
    Hunchback of Notre Dame 103
    In Pursuit of the Green Lion 109
    In the Company of Eagles 192
    Khaki Wings 191
    King's Cavalier 111
    Landowner Legacy 163
    Lion and the Lily 96
    Lords of Vaumartin 103
    Magician's Apprentice 96
    Man in the Iron Mask 118
    *Personal Recollections of
        Joan of Arc* 113

Subject Index

Queen's Confession 147
Quentin Durward 110
Red Flight Two 191
Rose for Virtue 150
Sharpe's Siege 142
Sign of the Green Falcon 102
Sign of the Owl 85
Sirens and Spies 176
Three Musketeers 119
Tree Still Stands 195
Where the Towers Pierce the Sky 101
White Company 101
Wolves of Paris 106
Young Joan 100
France 1800-1899
Silk Vendetta 163
France--1789
Devil on Horseback 147
Glass-Blowers 144
Rebel 140
Tale of Two Cities 144
France--1789-1799
Scaramouche 152
Scarlet Pimpernel 151
Wind from the Sea 147
France--1798
Healing Blade 141
France--1799-1815
Désirée 153
Red and the Black 154
France--1800-1899
Anna 162
Bridle the Wind 156
Fernande 160
France--1900-
Hunted 196
Ride Out the Storm 200
Touch Wood 220
Waiting for Anya 217
France--to 986
Testing of Tertius 78
France--to 987
Star in the Forest 74
Francis of Assisi, Saint
Road to Damietta 93
Francis, I, King of France
King's Cavalier 111

freedom of speech
Honorable Prison 234
Freemasonry
Earth Will Shake 155
Freud, Sigmund
Passions of the Mind 180
Friedrich II, Emperor of Germany
King's Road 91
friendship 26
Beyond the Weir Bridge 116
Bridle the Wind 156
Devil in Vienna 218
Friedrich 220
Go Saddle the Sea 156
Light a Penny Candle 174
Mckenzie's Boots 46
Number the Stars 203
Reunion 183
Then the Zeppelins Came 175
Three Musketeers 119
Why There Is No Heaven on Earth 189
frontier and pioneer life
Muckle Annie 233
G
Gaul
Druids 68
Star in the Forest 74
With the Eagles 59
Genghis Khan
Black Wolf of the Steppes 29
George I, King of England
Queen in Waiting 152
Germany
All Quiet on the Western Front 192
Bitterest Age 202
Ceremony of Innocence 198
Chase Me, Catch Nobody 200
Chileno! 182
Crusade in Jeans 84
Crutches 181
Darkness Casts No Shadow 216
Devil's Workshop 107
Displaced Person 195
Don't Say a Word 199
Eagle in the Snow 59
Edge of War 201

Farewell, Dresden 196
Flight Toward Home 181
Friedrich 220
Frost in the Night 180
Greek Treasure 171
Guns of Valmy 140
Horses of Anger 198
I Was There 205
If I Should Die Before I Wake 217
If This Be Glory 206
Iron Hand of Mars 60
Journey 212
Journey to America 215
Max's Gang 193
Night in Distant Motion 202
Night of the Broken Glass 211
Night Over Day Over Night 208
No Hero for the Kaiser 192
Reunion 183
So Slow the Dawning 183
Star Without a Sky 218
Tilla 181
To Cross a Line 219
Traitors 198
Transport 7-41-R 180
Tug of War 202
Visit 197
What Happened in Hamelin 97
When Hitler Stole Pink Rabbit 214

Germany (East)
Green Frontier 182
Wall 182

ghosts
Empty Sleeve 146
Jeremy Visick 173

Gilgamesh
Gilgamesh the King 20

Godwin, William
Vindication 153

Gogh, Vincent van
Lust for Life 171

Gordon Riots, 1780
Barnaby Rudge 143

Gordon, Charles George
Second Son of Heaven 30

Goths
Heaven's Only Daughter 63

government, resistance to
Handful of Stars 28
Honorable Prison 234
Petros' War 210
Talking in Whispers 235

Grail
Silver Chalice 60

grandmothers
Spirit on the Wall 50

grandparent and child
Becoming Gershona 26

Great Britain
I, Elizabeth 131
Murder Wears a Cowl 87
No Tigers in Africa 15
Red Slayer 90
Street Child 160
Tin Princess 170
Vision of Stephen 70

Great Britain--to 1066
Avalon 73
Book of Merlyn 81
Born of the Sun 76
Child of the Northern Spring 82
Connecticut Yankee in King Arthur's Court 80
Crystal Cave 79
Edge of Light 76
Guinevere 78, 82
Hawk of May 77
Hollow Hills 79
In Winter's Shadow 77
Kingdom of Summer 77
Lantern Bearers 68
Last Enchantment 80
Last Pendragon 78
Mary Stewart's Merlin Trilogy 79
Mists of Avalon 77
Once and Future King 81
Queen of the Summer Stars 82
Road to Camlann 80
Shining Company 75
Story of the Grail and the Passing of Arthur 78
Sword in the Stone 81
Testing of Tertius 78
Wicked Day 80

Subject Index

Winter Prince 81
Great Britain--1154-1399
Adam of the Road 89
Age of Miracles 106
All Men Tall 113
Baron's Hostage 99
Black Rose 86
Cargo for a King 83
Catherine, Called Birdy 86
Falls the Shadow 93
Heaven Tree Trilogy 93
Here Be Dragons 94
In Pursuit of the Green Lion 109
Innocent Wayfaring 100
Ivanhoe 97
Katherine 110
King's Daughters 90
Lady of Rhuddesmere 98
Lion and the Lily 96
Little Lower Than the Angels 107
Longsword 98
Lost Magic 83
Love Knot 101
Magician's Apprentice 96
Myself As Witness 89
Nightingale Gallery 89
Peace Child 107
Proud Taste for Scarlet and Miniver 92
Queen's War 92
Ramsay Scallop 98
Threshing Floor 110
Vision of Light 109
Way Home 112
White Company 101
Whyte Hart 87
Great Britain--1389-1455
Black Arrow 112
Great Britain--1399-1485
Bloody Field 107
Cargo of the Madalena 102
Daughter of Time 112
Everlasting Covenant 100
Fortune Made His Sword 110
I Remember Love 122
King's Grey Mare 104
Knight's Acre 106

Men of Iron 109
Merchant's Mark 102
Passage to Pontefract 108
Plymouth Cloak 111
Sign of the Green Falcon 102
Star of Lancaster 108
Tudor Rose 100
We Speak No Treason 104
Writing on the Hearth 103
Great Britain--1485-1603
13th Member 125
Armada 120
Bartholomew Fair 135
Blood Royal 121
Captive Queen of Scots 133
Cold Wind Blowing 138
Elizabeth, Captive Princess 126
Hawk 138
Hawk That Dare Not Hunt by Day 132
Holdfast 114
I Am Mary Tudor 128
I Remember Love 122
Iron Lily 139
Ivy Crown 130
Kenilworth 135
King's Pleasure 129
Lady Jane 135
Linnet 137
Master Rosalind 115
Merrymaid 122
Murder for Her Majesty 124
My Enemy the Queen 125
Nicholas Cooke 118
Playhouse Tales 124
Prince and the Pauper 136
Prisoner of the Queen 131
Queen and the Gypsy 124
Queen of This Realm 133
Queen's Head 130
Requiem for Princess 114
Shrine of Murders 102
Six Wives of Henry VIII 130
Sprig of Broom 139
Stars of Fortune 122
Strange Devices of the Sun and Moon 120

World Historical Fiction Guide

Westward Ho! 127
White Rose Murders 117
Women of Ashdon 113
You Never Knew Her As I Did 126
Young Bess 126

Great Britain--1603-1714
Alethea 115
Bridge of Sighs 128
Child from the Sea 121
Great House 123
Half Child 124
Journal of the Plague Year 118
Lion and the Rose 138
Many Waters Cannot Quench Love 115
Murder in the Tower 133
Myself My Enemy 133
Parcel of Patterns 132
Pit 117
Take Heed of Loving Me 136
Three Crowns 134
You, My Brother 116

Great Britain--1642-1660
Beyond the Weir Bridge 116
Blood Royal 137
Circle of Pearls 127
Cromwell's Boy 123
Crowning Mercy 127
Kate Ryder 116
King's General 119
King's Knight's Pawn 115
Messenger for Parliament 123
Piper to the Clan 117
Red Shift 120
Severed Crown 128

Great Britain--1714-1837
Apprentices 145
Barnaby Rudge 143
Beware of Moonlight 146
Captain Horatio Hornblower 144
Colors Aloft! 148
Devil on Horseback 147
Devil to Pay 151
Devil Water 153
Drummer Boy 145
Empty Sleeve 146
Enemy in Sight! 148

Flame-Colored Taffeta 154
Form Line of Battle! 148
Frenchwoman 151
Hadder Maccoll 141
Hanging at Tyburn 143
Horation Hornblower Series 144
Lothian Run 148
Master of Ballantrae 154
Prince Charlie's Year 145
Queen in Waiting 152
Ravensrigg 141
Rebel 140
Riders of the Storm 140
Right-Hand Man 152
Sharpe's Regiment 142
Silver Touch 149
Smile of the Stranger 139
Smith 146
Sound of Coaches 146
Stand Into Danger 149
Success to the Brave 149
Touch and Go 151
Vindication 153
Wind from the Sea 147

Great Britain--1800-1899
Albany 157
Ask Me No Questions 170
Black Lamp 158
Captive of Kensington Palace 168
Chance Child 167
Coldest Winter 165
Dark Quartet 157
December Rose 162
Escapade 162
Footsteps 161
Go Saddle the Sea 156
God Is an Englishman 160
Grace 167
Great Train Robbery 159
Greenyards 165
Grimsdyke 172
Haunting of Kildoran Abbey 158
In the Shadow of the Brontës 158
Iron Way 159
Island Harp 172
Jeremy Visick 173
Lady's Maid 161

Subject Index

Landowner Legacy 163
Leaves from the Valley 172
Love Child 159
Potato Eaters 157
Queen and Lord M 169
Queen's Husband 169
Rape of the Rose 164
Ruby in the Smoke 170
Shadow in the North 169
Sheltering Tree 168
Ship from Simnel Street 167
Silk Vendetta 163
Sudden, Fearful Death 168
Trinity 172
Waxwork 165
Why Kill Arthur Potter? 162
Year of the Stranger 166

Great Britain--1900-
Across the Barricades 178
As the Crow Flies 173
Backwater War 209
Bel Ria 195
Blitzcat 208
Child of War 179
Echoes of War 208
Exeter Blitz 204
Fathom Five 208
File on Fraulein Berg 178
Fine, Soft Day 178
In Spite of All Terror 174
Kathleen 177
Khaki Wings 191
Kingdom by the Sea 209
Light a Penny Candle 174
Machine Gunners 209
Milk and Honey 176
Murdo's War 179
My Sister Clare 175
Other Way Round 176
Paladin 198
Razor Eyes 201
Red Flight Two 191
Sirens and Spies 176
Sound of Anthems 177
Sumitra's Story 177
Summer of the Barshinskeys 176
Then the Zeppelins Came 175

Time and Chance 179
Twelfth Day of July 179

Great Britain. Army
Bridge Over the River Kwai 18

Great Britain. Navy
Captain Horatio Hornblower 144
Devil to Pay 151
Enemy in Sight! 148
Form Line of Battle! 148
Horation Hornblower Series 144
Last Nine Days of the Bismarck 197
NavyColors Aloft! 148
Stand Into Danger 149
Success to the Brave 149
Touch and Go 151
Ulysses 203

Great Britain--Colonies
Deep Dream of the Rain Forest 48

Great Britain--Norman Period
Confession of Brother Haluin 94
Fatal Crown 91
Golden Warrior 73
Harold Was My King 72
Holy Thief 95
I Am England 76
Pillars of the Earth 87
Potter's Field 95
Rare Benedictine 95
Robin and the King 88
Sherwood 88
Striped Ships 73
To Kill a King 96
Witch's Brat 98

Great Britain--Norman period
Bond of Honour 75

Great Britain--Roman Period
Crows of War 68
Forest House 67
Red Shift 120
Sun Horse, Moon Horse 69

Great Britain--Roman period
Capricorn Bracelet 65
Eagle of the Ninth 64
Frontier Wolf 64
Mermaid's Daughter 67
Rain from the West 63
Song for a Dark Queen 69

269

World Historical Fiction Guide

Greco-Turkish War, 1921-1922
   Refugee Summer 184
Greece
   Bull from the Sea 57
   Children of the Fox 56
   Dawn Palace 55
   Days of the Dragon's Seed 55
   Fire from Heaven 57
   Firebrand 54
   Flowers of Adonis 58
   Golden Bees 56
   Greek Treasure 171
   Greek Wedding 163
   Horses of Heaven 54
   Last of the Wine 58
   Mask of Apollo 58
   Petros' War 210
   Praise Singer 58
   Shadow Army 205
   Soldier of Arete 59
   Victor of Salamis 55
Greece--1821-1829
   Hour of the Bell 168
Greece--1900-
   Andi's War 184
   Kindling 183
   Refugee Summer 184
   Ring the Judas Bell 184
Greenland
   Abduction 131
   Leif the Unlucky 103
Grenville, Sir Richard
   King's General 119
Grey, Lady Jane
   Lady Jane 135
Guatemala
   Among the Volcanoes 225
   Imagining Isabel 226
Gudrun
   Gudrun 91
Guinevere
   Child of the Northern Spring 82
   Guinevere 78, 82
   In Winter's Shadow 77
   Mists of Avalon 77
   Queen of the Summer Stars 82

gun powder
   All Men Tall 113
Gutenberg, Johann
   Devil's Workshop 107
gypsies
   And the Violins Stopped Playing 219
   Farewell Sidonia 213

H

Haiti
   Taste of Salt 225
Harold II, King of England
   Golden Warrior 73
   Harold Was My King 72
Hastings, The Battle of
   Golden Warrior 73
Hatshepsut, Queen of Egypt
   Child of the Morning 3
   His Majesty, Queen Hatshepsut 2
healers
   Lost Magic 83
Henriette Marie, consort of Charles I
   Myself My Enemy 133
Henry I, King of England
   Running Vixen 85
Henry II, King of England
   Lion and the Lily 96
   Proud Taste for Scarlet and Miniver 92
   Queen's War 92
Henry III, King of England
   Falls the Shadow 93
Henry IV, King of England
   Bloody Field 107
   Men of Iron 109
   Passage to Pontefract 108
   Star of Lancaster 108
Henry V, King of England
   Bloody Field 107
   Fortune Made His Sword 110
   Sign of the Green Falcon 102
   Star of Lancaster 108
Henry VII, King of England
   Tudor Rose 100
Henry VIII, King of England
   Blood Royal 121
   I Am Mary Tudor 128
   Ivy Crown 130

Subject Index

King's Pleasure 129
Six Wives of Henry VIII 130
heresies and heretics
   Lady of Rhuddesmere 98
heroes
   Grace 167
   Murdo's War 179
Hiroshima
   Flowers of Hiroshima 42
   Hiroshima No Pika 41
   In the Autumn Wind 43
   Seeds of Hiroshima 43
Hitler Youth Corps
   I Was There 205
   Visit 197
Holocaust survivors
   Is Still Here 221
Holocaust, 1933-1945
   Mottele 206
Holocaust, Gypsy
   And the Violins Stopped Playing 219
   Farewell Sidonia 213
Holocaust, Jewish, 1933-1945 217
   Anya 221
   Babi Yar 193
   Book of Songs 215
   Children of Bach 211
   Come Spring 215
   Darkness Casts No Shadow 216
   Devil in Vienna 218
   Devil's Arithmetic 222
   Fateless 214
   Friedrich 220
   Gideon 210
   Hear O Israel 221
   Hide and Seek 207
   House on Prague Street 211
   I Am Rosemarie 217
   If I Should Die Before I Wake 217
   Island on Bird Street 218
   Jacob's Rescue 212
   Journey 212
   Journey to America 215
   Last Butterfly 214
   Magic We Do Here 221
   Man from the Other Side 218
   Mila 18 222

   Night of the Broken Glass 211
   October, Eight O'Clock 216
   Prayer for Katerina Horovitzova 216
   Scrap of Time 212
   Shadow of the Wall 215
   Star Without a Sky 218
   Survivor 213
   To Cross a Line 219
   Touch Wood 220
   Upstairs Room 219
   Waiting for Anya 217
   Wall 213
   When Hitler Stole Pink Rabbit 214
homeless persons
   Street Child 160
horse racing
   Right-Hand Man 152
horses
   Four Horses for Tishtry 66
   Last Summer 190
Hortense, consort of Louis, King of Holland
   Rose for Virtue 150
hostages
   Lion's Cub 164
Hottentots
   Great Thirst 14
household employees
   Lady's Maid 161
Huichol Indians
   So Sings the Blue Deer 227
humorous stories
   Dancing Bear 24
Hundred Years' War, 1339-1453
   White Company 101
Hung Shiu-chu'an
   Second Son of Heaven 30
Hungary
   Children of Bach 211
   Fateless 214
Huns
   Dancing Bear 24
   Darkness and the Dawn 60
   Slave of the Huns 67

I
Iban
   Deep Dream of the Rain Forest 48

World Historical Fiction Guide

Iban Tribe
   Forest of the Clouded Leopard 48
Ibo Tribe
   Arrow of God 9
   Chinwe 10
   Things Fall Apart 9
Ice Age
   Daughter of the Red Deer 52
Iceland
   Escape from the Evil Prophecy 72
Incas
   Amethyst Ring 235
   Incas 235
India
   Bomber's Moon 35
   Children of the Wolf 36
   Flowers in the Blood 35
   In the Forest at Midnight 36
   Kim 36
   My Sister Clare 175
   Roller Birds of Rampur 36
Indians of Central America
   Among the Volcanoes 225
   Imagining Isabel 226
   Tikal 227
Indians of North America
   Running West 231
Indians of South America
   Amethyst Ring 235
individuality
   Roller Birds of Rampur 36
Industrial Revolution
   Black Lamp 158
   Chance Child 167
   Rape of the Rose 164
Inquisition
   Inheritance 137
   Magician's Apprentice 96
   Out of Many Waters 234
   Sea Beggars 125
Inuit
   Abduction 131
   White Shaman 232
Iran
   Cry of the Peacock 25
   Kiss the Dust 25

Iraq
   Kiss the Dust 25
Ireland
   Across the Sea from Galway 161
   Bard 53
   Beware of Moonlight 146
   Coldest Winter 165
   Druid's Tune 54
   Grania 129
   Haunting of Kildoran Abbey 158
   Healing Blade 141
   Heart Speaks Many Ways 190
   Kathleen 177
   King's Knight's Pawn 115
   Light a Penny Candle 174
   Lion of Ireland 72
   Man from the Sea 52
   Pangur Ban 74
   Paradise 71
   Potato Eaters 157
   Sisters' Tale 70
   Time and Chance 179
   Trinity 172
   Tristan and Iseult 75
   Witches' Sabbath 141
Irene, Empress of Byzantium
   Belt of Gold 24
islands
   Druid's Gift
      Druid's Gift 52
   Light in the Mountain 47
Islands of the Pacific
   Bounty Trilogy 48
   Last Voyage 48
Isle of Skye
   Year of the Stranger 166
Israel
   Becoming Gershona 26
   Escape from Egypt 22
   Exodus 27
   My Enemy, My Brother 25
   Source 26
   Talisman 27
   Time of Anger 26
   To Touch a Dream 26
   Woman of Nazareth 27

Subject Index

Israel-Arab War, 1948-49
   My Enemy, My Brother 25
Israel-Arab War, 1967
   Time of Anger 26
Istanbul (Turkey)
   Blood Feud 74
   Children of the Book 116
Italy
   Agony and the Ecstasy 112
   Anthony Adverse 140
   Apprentice 105
   Charterhouse of Parma 154
   Earth Will Shake 155
   Florentine 111
   I, Juan de Pareja 136
   In the Company of Clown 114
   King's Road 91
   Lady's Maid 161
   Leopard 164
   Letters to Horseface 150
   Little Fishes 201
   Madonna of the Seven Hills 108
   Prince of Foxes 111
   Private Life of Mona Lisa 105
   Road to Damietta 93
   Second Mrs. Giaconda 105
   Tree Still Stands 195

J

Jacobite Rebellion, 1745
   Flame-Colored Taffeta 154
   Hadder Maccoll 141
   Lothian Run 148
   Master of Ballantrae 154
   Prince Charlie's Year 145
Jacobite Rebellions
   Devil Water 153
Jacobites
   Bonnie Dundee 135
Jamaica
   Ajeemah and His Son 223
   Pirate Royal 223
   Under the Black Flag 224
James II, King of England
   Bridge of Sighs 128
James VI, King of Scotland
   13th Member 125

Japan
   Boy and the Samurai 38
   Coming of the Bear 39
   Cranes at Dusk 42
   Flowers of Hiroshima 42
   Hiroshima No Pika 41
   In the Autumn Wind 43
   Ink-keeper's Apprentice 43
   Island of Ogres 39
   Master Puppeteer 41
   Miracle Tree 42
   Of Nightingales That Weep 40
   River With No Bridge 43
   Samurai 41
   Samurai and the Long-nosed Devils 39
   Samurai's Tale 38
   Seeds of Hiroshima 43
   Shogun 38
   So Far from the Bamboo Grove 44
   Tokaido Road 41
   Valley of the Broken Cherry Trees 39
   Village of the Vampire Cat 40
   Warlord of the Genji 38
   White Serpent Castle 40
Japanese in the United States
   Samurai 41
Jason (Greek mythology)
   Dawn Palace 55
Jerusalem
   Heirs of the Kingdom 93
   Man Who Buried Jesus 23
   Silver Chalice 60
Jesus Christ
   Big Fisherman 21
   Bronze Bow 23
   Great Lion of God 21
   How Far to Bethlehem? 22
   Man Who Buried Jesus 23
   Robe 61
   Three from Galilee 22
Jewish-Arab relations
   Exodus 27
   My Enemy, My Brother 25
   Time of Anger 26
   To Touch a Dream 26

World Historical Fiction Guide

Jews 25
   Becoming Gershona 26
   Ben Hur 65
   Cry of the Peacock 25
   Escape from Egypt 22
   Eyes of the Blind 23
   Flowers in the Blood 35
   Jacob's Ladder 45
   Kingdom of the Grail 83
   Source 26
   To Touch a Dream 26
Jews and gentiles
   Jacob's Ladder 45
Jews in Austria
   Devil in Vienna 218
Jews in Brazil
   Out of Many Waters 234
Jews in Denmark
   Number the Stars 203
Jews in England
   Other Way Round 176
Jews in Europe
   October, Eight O'Clock 216
   Prayer for Katerina Horovitzova 216
Jews in France
   Touch Wood 220
Jews in Germany
   Friedrich 220
   Frost in the Night 180
   Journey to America 215
   Reunion 183
   So Slow the Dawning 183
   To Cross a Line 219
   When Hitler Stole Pink Rabbit 214
Jews in Great Britain
   File on Fraulein Berg 178
Jews in Hungary
   Children of Bach 211
   Fateless 214
Jews in Poland
   Anya 221
   Come Spring 215
   Devil's Arithmetic 222
   Hear O Israel 221
   If I Should Die Before I Wake 217
   Island on Bird Street 218
   Jacob's Rescue 212

   Magic We Do Here 221
   Man from the Other Side 218
   Mila 18 222
   Mottele 206
   Scrap of Time 212
   Shadow of the Wall 215
   Toba 185
   Wall 213
Jews in Russia
   Along the Tracks 194
   Circlemaker 170
   Exit from Home 187
   Homecoming 188
   Letters from Rifka 185
   Night Journey 165
   Russian Farewell 186
   Sworn Enemies 166
   Why There Is No Heaven on Earth 189
Jews in the Netherlands 217
   Hide and Seek 207
   I Am Rosemarie 217
   Is Still Here 221
   One Foot Ashore 121
   Survivor 213
   Upstairs Room 219
Jews--Ethiopia
   Return, The 5
Joan of Arc, Saint
   Blood Red, Sister Rose 104
   Personal Recollections of Joan of Arc 113
   Where the Towers Pierce the Sky 101
   Young Joan 100
John of Gaunt, Duke of Lancaster
   Katherine 110
John, King of England
   Myself As Witness 89
Joseph the Patriarch
   Joseph and His Brothers 22
Judea
   Dear and Glorious Physician 21
   How Far to Bethlehem? 22
Julius Caesar
   Door in the Wall 62

Subject Index

K
Kalahari Desert
Lion of the Kalahari 9
Katherine, Duchess of Lancaster
Katherine 110
kidnapping
Abduction 131
Dancing Bear 24
Greek Wedding 163
Imperial Purple 24
Left-Handed Spirit 63
Ring the Judas Bell 184
Teeth of the Gale 157
Kiev (Soviet Union)
Babi Yar 193
Bern, Son of Mikula 69
Kilda, Saint
Druid's Gift 52
knights and knighthood
Don Quixote de La Mancha 84
Gudrun 91
Hawk of May 77
In Winter's Shadow 77
Ivanhoe 97
Kingdom of Summer 77
Knight's Acre 106
Last Enchantment 80
Last Pendragon 78
Men of Iron 109
Mists of Avalon 77
Road to Camlann 80
Story of the Grail and the Passing of Arthur 78
Tales of the Crusades 86
Knollys, Lettice
My Enemy the Queen 125
Korea
Blue Dragon 44
So Far from the Bamboo Grove 44
Year of Impossible Goodbyes 44
Korean War, 1950-1953
Echoes of the White Giraffe 45
Kurds
Kiss the Dust 25
L
Lancelot
Story of the Grail and the Passing of Arthur 78
Latin America
Honorable Prison 234
Who Will Remember the People.... 235
Latvia
Edge of Darkness 199
Tug of War 202
Lebanon
Regards from the Dead Princess 29
Woman of Nazareth 27
Leicester, Robert Dudley, Earl of
Kenilworth 135
Queen and the Gypsy 124
Leningrad, Siege of, 1941-1944
Boris 199
Leonardo da Vinci
Second Mrs. Giaconda 105
Leonidas
Victor of Salamis 55
letters
Letters from Rifka 185
Liberia
Story for a Black Night 8
lions
Lion in the Evening 8
London (England)
Apprentices 145
Bartholomew Fair 135
December Rose 162
Footsteps 161
Great Train Robbery 159
Journal of the Plague Year 118
Linnet 137
Lion and the Rose 138
Other Way Round 176
Pit 117
Ruby in the Smoke 170
Shadow in the North 169
Ship from Simnel Street 167
Silver Touch 149
Smith 146
Street Child 160
Then the Zeppelins Came 175
Waxwork 165
Why Kill Arthur Potter? 162

London, England
   Time of the Dragon 30
Louis XI, King of France
   Quentin Durward 110
love
   Across the Barricades 178
   Age of Miracles 106
   Anna 162
   Anna's Book 166
   Child from the Sea 121
   Cloister and the Hearth 134
   Daughter of the Sea 56
   Dog of Bondi Castle 89
   Everlasting Covenant 100
   Fatal Crown 91
   Forest House 67
   Golden Tulip 128
   Greenyards 165
   Heart Speaks Many Ways 190
   Heaven's Only Daughter 63
   Here Be Dragons 94
   Horses of Heaven 54
   I Remember Love 122
   In the Forest at Midnight 36
   Innocent Wayfaring 100
   Katherine 110
   Last Days of Pompeii 59
   Left-Handed Spirit 63
   Many Waters Cannot Quench Love 115
   Queen and the Gypsy 124
   Saving Grace 88
   Sisters' Tale 70
   Skindeep 12
   Summer of the Barshinskeys 176
   Tale of Two Cities 144
   Tristan and Iseult 75
   Wild Hunt 85
Lucan
   Conspiracy 62
Luddites
   Rape of the Rose 164
Luke, Saint
   Dear and Glorious Physician 21
M
Magellan, Ferdinand
   Wind at Morning 130

magic
   His Majesty's Elephant 75
Magna Carta
   Falls the Shadow 93
Malaysia
   Ayo Gurkha! 37
Malcolm III, King of Scotland
   To Kill a King 96
Manichaeism
   Lady of Rhuddesmere 98
Maoris
   Light in the Mountain 47
Marc Antony
   Throne of Isis 65
Margaret of Metola, Saint
   Woman in the Cloak 91
Margaret, Saint, Queen of Scotland
   To Kill a King 96
Marie Antoinette, consort of Louis XVI
   Queen's Confession 147
marriage
   Bride Price 10
   Here Be Dragons 94
   In Pursuit of the Green Lion 109
   King's Daughters 90
   Love Knot 101
   Moonclock 137
   Queen's Husband 169
   Ramsay Scallop 98
   Saving Grace 88
   Shabanu 37
   Tudor Rose 100
   Wild Hunt 85
Mary I, Queen of England
   I Am Mary Tudor 128
Mary II, Queen of Great Britain
   Three Crowns 134
Mary Queen of Scots
   Prisoner of the Queen 131
Mary Stuart, Queen of Scots
   Captive Queen of Scots 133
   You Never Knew Her As I Did 126
Mary, of Modena, consort of James II
   Bridge of Sighs 128
massacres
   Babi Yar 193
   Untold Tale 123

Subject Index

Matilda, Empress of Germany
   Fatal Crown 91
May Thirtieth Movement, 1925
   Little Sister 34
Mayas
   Amethyst Ring 235
   Among the Volcanoes 225
   Captive 229
   Feathered Serpent 229
   Gold of Dreams 228
   Imagining Isabel 226
   Journey to the Sky 226
   Tikal 227
Medea (Greek mythology)
   Dawn Palace 55
medical care
   Heart of the Continent 45
Medici, Lorenzo de, il Magnifico
   Florentine 111
mentally handicapped
   Half Child 124
Merlin 80
   Book of Merlyn 81
   Crystal Cave 79
   Hollow Hills 79
   Mary Stewart's Merlin Trilogy 79
   Sword in the Stone 81
   Testing of Tertius 78
Mexico
   Amethyst Ring 235
   Beyond the Ancient Cities 228
   Captain from Castile 230
   Captive 229
   Crimson Wind 227
   Estebanico 230
   Feathered Serpent 229
   Gold of Dreams 228
   Journey to the Sky 226
   King's Fifth 229
   Mexico 228
   Not of War Only 230
   So Sings the Blue Deer 227
Michelangelo Buonarroti
   Agony and the Ecstasy 112
Middle East
   Tales of the Crusades 86

Milan
   Second Mrs. Giaconda 105
Minamoto, Yoshitsune
   Warlord of the Genji 38
miners
   Jeremy Visick 173
Ming, T'ai-tsu, Emperor of China
   Beggar King of China 29
Minotaur (Greek mythology)
   No Need for Heroes 56
minstrels
   Adam of the Road 89
   Merrymaid 122
missing persons
   Crutches 181
missionaries 39
   Blue Dragon 44
   Bomber's Moon 35
   In the Time of Trouble 8
   Keys of the Kingdom 33
Mona Lisa
   Private Life of Mona Lisa 105
   Second Mrs. Giaconda 105
monks
   Confession of Brother Haluin 94
   Holy Thief 95
   Pangur Ban 74
   Potter's Field 95
   Rare Benedictine 95
Monsters
   Grendel 53
Monte Carlo
   Why Kill Arthur Potter? 162
Montfort, Simon de, Earl of Leicester
   Baron's Hostage 99
   Falls the Shadow 93
Moors
   Knight's Acre 106
Mordred (legendary character)
   Wicked Day 80
   Winter Prince 81
More, Anne
   Take Heed of Loving Me 136
Morgan, Henry
   Pirate Royal 223
Moses
   Escape from Egypt 22

moving, household
   No Tigers in Africa 15
Mozart, Wolfgang Amadeus
   Letters to Horseface 150
music
   Letters to Horseface 150
musicians
   Children of Bach 211
mystery and detective stories
   Albany 157
   Cargo of the Madalena 102
   Coming of the Bear 39
   Confession of Brother Haluin 94
   Crowning Mercy 127
   Daughter of Time 112
   Death Comes As Epiphany 92
   December Rose 162
   Eagle of the Ninth 64
   Footsteps 161
   Frenchwoman 151
   Holy Thief 95
   Ides of April 63
   Iron Hand of Mars 60
   Island of Ogres 39
   Master Rosalind 115
   Merchant's Mark 102
   Murder for Her Majesty 124
   Murder Wears a Cowl 87
   Nightingale Gallery 89
   Plymouth Cloak 111
   Potter's Field 95
   Queen's Head 130
   Rare Benedictine 95
   Red Slayer 90
   Ruby in the Smoke 170
   Samurai and the Long-nosed Devils 39
   Shadow in the North 169
   Shadows in Bronze 60
   Shrine of Murders 102
   Silver Pigs 61
   Star in the Forest 74
   Stars of Fortune 122
   Sudden, Fearful Death 168
   Valley of the Broken Cherry Trees 39
   Venus in Copper 61
   Village of the Vampire Cat 40

   Waxwork 165
   White Rose Murders 117
   White Serpent Castle 40
   Why Kill Arthur Potter? 162
   Whyte Hart 87
mythology, Greek
   Bull from the Sea 57
   Dawn Palace 55
   Days of the Dragon's Seed 55
   Firebrand 54
   King Must Die 57
   No Need for Heroes 56

N
Namibia
   Song of Be 9
Napoléon I, Emperor of the French
   Last Love 142
Napoleon I, Emperor of the French War and Peace 155
naval operations
   Last Nine Days of the Bismarck 197
Neanderthals
   Adventure of the Ice Age 49
   Clan of the Cave Bear 49
   Shiva Accused 50
   Singletusk 51
Nefertiti, Queen of Egypt
   God Against the Gods 3
   Return to Thebes 3
Nepal
   Ayo Gurkha! 37
Nero, Emperor of Rome
   Conspiracy 62
Netherlands
   Black Tulip 118
   Borrowed House 207
   Empty Moat 206
   Golden Tulip 128
   Hide and Seek 207
   Is Still Here 221
   One Foot Ashore 121
   Rembrandt 134
   Sea Beggars 125
   Survivor 213
   Upstairs Room 219
   War Without Friends 200
   Winter in Wartime 207

Subject Index

New Guinea
   Mckenzie's Boots 46
New Zealand
   Light in the Mountain 47
Nicholas II, Emperor of Russia
   Three Lives for the Czar 188
Nigeria
   African Mask 11
   Arrow of God 9
   Bride Price 10
   Slave Girl 10
   Things Fall Apart 9
Noah's Ark
   Moon in the Cloud 4
Normandy
   Gudrun 91
North America
   Paradise 71
Northern Ireland
   Across the Barricades 178
   Child of War 179
   File on Fraulein Berg 178
   Fine, Soft Day 178
   Sound of Anthems 177
   Twelfth Day of July 179
Norway
   Abduction 131
   Kristin Lavransdatter 99
   Master of Hestviken 99
   North of Danger 197
Notre Dame Cathedral
   Hunchback of Notre Dame 103
Nova Scotia
   Another Shore 230
   Away to Fundy Bay 232
nurses
   Leaves from the Valley 172
   Sudden, Fearful Death 168

O

Oedipus (Greek mythology)
   Days of the Dragon's Seed 55
orphans 52
   Adventure of the Ice Age 49
   Anthony Adverse 140
   Ask Me No Questions 170
   Boy and the Samurai 38
   Children of the Wolf 36

   Deep Dream of the Rain Forest 48
   Fear the Condor 233
   Flight Toward Home 181
   Grimsdyke 172
   Hanging at Tyburn 143
   Haunting of Kildoran Abbey 158
   Holdfast 114
   In Spite of All Terror 174
   In the Company of Clown 114
   Ink-keeper's Apprentice 43
   Iron Lily 139
   Jacob's Ladder 45
   Kim 36
   Kingdom by the Sea 209
   Little Brother 17
   Little Fishes 201
   Lost Magic 83
   Magician's Apprentice 96
   Merrymaid 122
   Ruby in the Smoke 170
   Scent of the Gods 18
   Slave Girl 10
   Smile of the Stranger 139
   Sprig of Broom 139
   Street Child 160
   To Kill a King 96
   Tulku 19
   Untold Tale 123

P

Painters
   Rembrandt 134
painters
   Florentine 111
   Golden Tulip 128
   I, Juan de Pareja 136
   Lust for Life 171
Pakistan
   Haveli 37
   Shabanu 37
Palestine
   Bronze Bow 23
   Dawn 27
   Exodus 27
   Great Lion of God 21
   Source 26
   Three from Galilee 22
   Woman of Nazareth 27

World Historical Fiction Guide

parapsychology
    Left-Handed Spirit 63
Pareja, Juan de
    I, Juan de Pareja 136
Paris (France)
    White Rose Murders 117
    Wolves of Paris 106
Parr, Katherine, consort of Henry VIII
    Ivy Crown 130
Paul, Saint
    Great Lion of God 21
peace
    Miracle Tree 42
Peking, siege of, 1900
    Time of the Dragon 30
Peloponnesian Wars
    Flowers of Adonis 58
Percy, Sir Henry
    Bloody Field 107
persecution
    Frost in the Night 180
    Robe 61
Peru
    Amethyst Ring 235
    Incas 235
Peter, Saint
    Big Fisherman 21
    Upon This Rock 23
Peterloo Massacre
    Grimsdyke 172
pharoahs
    Child of the Morning 3
    God Against the Gods 3
    His Majesty, Queen Hatshepsut 2
    Return to Thebes 3
Philip II, King of France
    Lion and the Lily 96
physically handicapped
    Boy of the Painted Cave 50
    Crutches 181
    Hunchback of Notre Dame 103
    King's General 119
    Seth of the Lion People 51
    Spirit on the Wall 50
    Stronghold 68
    Witch's Brat 98

physicians
    Beacon at Alexandria 2
    Dear and Glorious Physician 21
    Doctor Zhivago 188
    Egyptian, The 5
    Locadio's Apprentice 66
    Shrine of Murders 102
    Witch's Brat 98
pickpockets
    Smith 146
Pied Piper of Hamelin
    What Happened in Hamelin 97
pilgrims and pilgrimages
    Ramsay Scallop 98
    Threshing Floor 110
pirates
    Cargo for a King 83
    Consul's Daughter, The 6
    Pirate Royal 223
    Under the Black Flag 224
plague
    Journal of the Plague Year 118
    Parcel of Patterns 132
    Pit 117
poets
    Lady's Maid 161
    Praise Singer 58
    Take Heed of Loving Me 136
Poland
    And the Violins Stopped Playing 219
    Anya 221
    Bridge to the Other Side 202
    Children of the Book 116
    Come Spring 215
    Devil's Arithmetic 222
    Fateless 214
    Gideon 210
    Hear O Israel 221
    Island on Bird Street 218
    Jacob's Rescue 212
    Journey 212
    Last Butterfly 214
    Magic We Do Here 221
    Man from the Other Side 218
    Manwolf 97
    Mila 18 222
    Mottele 206

Subject Index

No Hero for the Kaiser 192
Poland 185
Scrap of Time 212
Shadow of the Wall 215
Time Without Bells 194
Toba 185
Trumpeter of Krakow 105
Wall 213
Poland, underground movements
Night Trains 222
political prisoners
Honorable Prison 234
One Day in the Life of Ivan Denisovich 190
political refugees
Chileno! 182
Pompeii
Last Days of Pompeii 59
Locadio's Apprentice 66
Shadow of Vesuvius 61
Portugal
Armada 120
Potato Famine
Coldest Winter 165
poverty
Against the Storm 28
Ask Me No Questions 170
Beware of Moonlight 146
Fear the Condor 233
Paper Bird 12
Street Child 160
Taste of Salt 225
Valda 46
prehistoric man
Adventure of the Ice Age 49
Boy of the Painted Cave 50
Clan of the Cave Bear 49
Daughter of the Red Deer 52
Dom and VA 1
Memory String 17
Old Tale Carved Out of Stone 16
Pillar of the Sky 51
Reindeer Moon 17
Seth of the Lion People 51
Shiva Accused 50
Shiva's Challenge 49
Singletusk 51

Time of the Forest 51
Who Will Remember the People.... 235
prejudice
Frozen Waterfall 175
Time of Anger 26
prejudices
Across the Barricades 178
Adventure of the Ice Age 49
Child of War 179
Fine, Soft Day 178
Milk and Honey 176
River With No Bridge 43
Shiva Accused 50
Song of the Buffalo Boy 19
Sound of Anthems 177
Sumitra's Story 177
Time of the Forest 51
Twelfth Day of July 179
priests
Prisoner of the Queen 131
printing
Cargo of the Madalena 102
Devil's Workshop 107
Hawk That Dare Not Hunt by Day 132
Inheritance 137
prisoners
No Surrender 16
prisoners of war
Bridge Over the River Kwai 18
Empire of the Sun 32
prisons and prisoners
One Day in the Life of Ivan Denisovich 190
Piper to the Clan 117
psychologists
Passions of the Mind 180
puppets and puppet plays
Master Puppeteer 41
Q
queens
Six Wives of Henry VIII 130
R
race relations
Ah, But Your Land Is Beautiful 13
Beyond Safe Boundaries 14

Chain of Fire 13
Cry, The Beloved Country 14
Eye for Color 15
Journey to Jo'burg 13
Milk and Honey 176
Paper Bird 12
Skindeep 12
Somehow Tenderness Survives 14
Song of Be 9
Waiting for the Rain 11
Radcliffe, Charles
   Devil Water 153
railroads
   Great Train Robbery 159
   Iron Way 159
   Lion in the Evening 8
rainforest
   Forest of the Clouded Leopard 48
Reformation 132
   Cloister and the Hearth 134
reformers
   Riders of the Storm 140
refugees
   Along the Tracks 194
   Between Two Worlds 231
   Chileno! 182
   Clay Marble 18
   Displaced Person 195
   Echoes of the White Giraffe 45
   Flight Toward Home 181
   Fly Away Home 204
   Goodbye, Vietnam 20
   Grab Hands and Run 227
   Green Frontier 182
   In Search of Coffee Mountains 187
   Kiss the Dust 25
   Lights Go On Again 232
   Little Brother 17
   Night Journey 165
   Other Way Round 176
   Refugee Summer 184
   Return, The 5
   Sky Is Falling 232
   So Far from the Bamboo Grove 44
   Tilla 181
   Transport 7-41-R 180
   Tug of War 202

Voyage of the Lucky Dragon 19
Woman of Nazareth 27
Year of Impossible Goodbyes 44
religious life
   Pangur Ban 74
Rembrandt, Harmenszoon van Rijn
   One Foot Ashore 121
   Rembrandt 134
reporters and reporting
   Crimson Wind 227
   Mexico 228
revolutions
   Chain of Fire 13
   Crimson Wind 227
   Dragon Village 33
   Glass-Blowers 144
   Healing Blade 141
   Little Sister 34
   Man's Fate 34
   Mountain Light 31
   Not of War Only 230
   Rebel 140
   Rebels of the Heavenly Kingdom 31
   Rice Without Rain 18
   Second Son of Heaven 30
   Serpent's Children 32
   Tale of Two Cities 144
   Witches' Sabbath 141
Richard I, King of England
   Ivanhoe 97
   Talisman 27
Richard II, King of England
   Passage to Pontefract 108
   Whyte Hart 87
Richard III, King of England
   Black Arrow 112
   Daughter of Time 112
   We Speak No Treason 104
Robin Hood
   Ivanhoe 97
   Robin and the King 88
   Sherwood 88
Roman Legion
   Eagle in the Snow 59
   With the Eagles 59
Rome
   Beacon at Alexandria 2

Subject Index

Ben Hur 65
Capricorn Bracelet 65
Conspiracy 62
Darkness and the Dawn 60
Door in the Wall 62
Eagle in the Snow 59
Eagle of the Ninth 64
Four Horses for Tishtry 66
Frontier Wolf 64
Heaven's Only Daughter 63
I, Claudius 62
Ides of April 63
Ides of March 66
Iron Hand of Mars 60
Last Days of Pompeii 59
Left-Handed Spirit 63
Locadio's Apprentice 66
Quo Vadis 64
Rain from the West 63
Robe 61
Roman 65
Shadow of Vesuvius 61
Shadows in Bronze 60
Silver Chalice 60
Silver Pigs 61
Throne of Isis 65
Unwilling Vestal 66
Upon This Rock 23
Venus in Copper 61

runaways
Circlemaker 170
Innocent Wayfaring 100
King's Knight's Pawn 115
Linnet 137

Russia
Anna 162
Another Place, Another Spring 164
August 1914 192
Bern, Son of Mikula 69
Circlemaker 170
Exit from Home 187
Homecoming 188
Life of a Useless Man 186
Lion's Cub 164
Night Journey 165
Russian Farewell 186
Silver Crest 159

Sound of the Dragon's Feet 173
Sworn Enemies 166
Tartar's Sword 127
Three Lives for the Czar 188

Russia--1799-1820
War and Peace 155

Russian Revolution of 1905
Exit from Home 187
Life of a Useless Man 186

Russian Revolution, 1917
Daughter of the Nobility 186
Homecoming 188
My Kingdom for a Grave 188
Time After Time 186

Russian Revolution, 1917-1921
And Quiet Flows the Don 189
Doctor Zhivago 188
Don Flows Home to the Sea 189
Wild Children 187

S
saints
Big Fisherman 21
Blood Red, Sister Rose 104
Dear and Glorious Physician 21
Great Lion of God 21
Personal Recollections of Joan of Arc 113
Road to Damietta 93
Upon This Rock 23
Woman in the Cloak 91
Young Joan 100

Saladin
Talisman 27

Salai, Andrea
Second Mrs. Giaconda 105

Samurai
Boy and the Samurai 38
Coming of the Bear 39
Island of Ogres 39
Of Nightingales That Weep 40
Samurai and the Long-nosed Devils 39
Samurai's Tale 38
Shogun 38
Valley of the Broken Cherry Trees 39
Village of the Vampire Cat 40
White Serpent Castle 40

World Historical Fiction Guide

San (African People)
   Song of Be 9
Scandinavia
   Beyond the Mists 69
   Hakon of Rogen's Saga 71
   Prison Window 71
   Slave's Tale 72
Schlieman, Sophia Kastromenos
   Greek Treasure 171
Schliemann, Heinrich
   Greek Treasure 171
Scholl family
   Ceremony of Innocence 198
scientists
   Magician's Apprentice 96
   Origin 171
Scilly Islands
   Mermaid's Daughter 67
Scotland
   13th Member 125
   Bonnie Dundee 135
   Druid's Gift 52
   Greenyards 165
   Hadder Maccoll 141
   Island Harp 172
   Lothian Run 148
   Master of Ballantrae 154
   Muckle Annie 233
   Murdo's War 179
   Piper to the Clan 117
   Prince Charlie's Year 145
   Quest for a Maid 90
   Saving Grace 88
   Stronghold 68
   Valley of Deer 119
   Wise Child 71
   Year of the Stranger 166
   You Never Knew Her As I Did 126
Scythians
   Horse Goddess 53
sea stories
   Admiral and the Deck Boy 132
   Armada 120
   Beyond the Mists 69
   Bounty Trilogy 48
   Captain Horatio Hornblower 144
   Cargo for a King 83

   Colors Aloft! 148
   Devil to Pay 151
   Enemy in Sight! 148
   Form Line of Battle! 148
   Goodbye, Vietnam 20
   Grania 129
   Hawk 138
   High Voyage 129
   Horation Hornblower Series 144
   I Sailed With Columbus 131
   Judas Ship 233
   Last Voyage 48
   Paradise 71
   Porcelain Pagoda 31
   Sole Survivor 234
   Stand Into Danger 149
   Success to the Brave 149
   Touch and Go 151
   Ulysses 203
   Under the Black Flag 224
   Westward Ho! 127
   Wind at Morning 130
secret service
   Kim 36
   Paladin 198
Shakespeare, Edmund
   You, My Brother 116
Shakespeare, William
   You, My Brother 116
Shanghai (China)
   Empire of the Sun 32
Shanghai Insurrection, 1927
   Man's Fate 34
shipwrecks
   Across the Sea from Galway 161
   Grace 167
short stories
   Apprentices 145
   Children of the Fox 56
   Dreamtime 46
   Echoes of War 208
   Scrap of Time 212
   Somehow Tenderness Survives 14
   Tales of the Crusades 86
Siberia
   Memory String 17
   Old Tale Carved Out of Stone 16

Subject Index

 Reindeer Moon 17
Sicily
 King's Road 91
 Leopard 164
Sierra Leone
 Salah of Sierra Leona 11
silk industry
 Silk Vendetta 163
 Women of the Silk 35
silversmiths
 Silver Touch 149
Simonides, 556-667 B.C.
 Praise Singer 58
Singapore
 Scent of the Gods 18
Sino-Japanese Conflict, 1937-1945
 Empire of the Sun 32
Sino-Japanese relations
 Dragon Seed 33
sisters
 Beyond Safe Boundaries 14
 Half Child 124
 My Sister Clare 175
 Out of Many Waters 234
 Sirens and Spies 176
 So Far from the Bamboo Grove 44
 Upstairs Room 219
slave trade
 Chinwe 10
 Ravensrigg 141
slavery
 My Name Is Not Angelica 225
 Night of the Silent Drums 223
 Under the Black Flag 224
 When Daylight Comes 224
slaves
 Abduction 131
 Ajeemah and His Son 223
 Estebanico 230
 Four Horses for Tishtry 66
 I, Juan de Pareja 136
 Ides of April 63
 Imperial Purple 24
 King's Fifth 229
 Prison Window 71
 Shadow of Vesuvius 61
 Slave's Tale 72

smallpox
 Story for a Black Night 8
smugglers
 Lothian Run 148
smuggling
 Flame-Colored Taffeta 154
 Hawk That Dare Not Hunt by Day 132
 Sheltering Tree 168
social classes
 Island Harp 172
 Lady's Maid 161
 River With No Bridge 43
Society of Friends
 Ravensrigg 141
Socrates
 Last of the Wine 58
soldiers
 All Quiet on the Western Front 192
 Ayo Gurkha! 37
 Capricorn Bracelet 65
 Frontier Wolf 64
 If This Be Glory 206
 Mckenzie's Boots 46
 Night Over Day Over Night 208
 Sharpe's Enemy 142
 Sharpe's Regiment 142
 Sharpe's Siege 142
 Too Few for Drums 143
 With the Eagles 59
Somerset, Frances (Howard) Carr, Countess of
 Murder in the Tower 133
Somerset, Robert Carr, Earl of
 Murder in the Tower 133
South Africa
 Ah, But Your Land Is Beautiful 13
 Beyond Safe Boundaries 14
 Chain of Fire 13
 Covenant 13
 Crocodile Burning 16
 Cry, The Beloved Country 14
 Eye for Color 15
 Great Thirst 11
 Into the Valley 16
 Journey to Jo'burg 13
 No Surrender 16

World Historical Fiction Guide

    No Tigers in Africa 15
    Paper Bird 12
    Secret of the Mountain 12
    Skindeep 12
    Somehow Tenderness Survives 14
    Story Like the Wind 15
    Waiting for the Rain 11
South Pole
    Birthday Boys 174
Soviet Union
    Along the Tracks 194
    And Quiet Flows the Don 189
    Babi Yar 193
    Boris 199
    Daughter of the Nobility 186
    Doctor Zhivago 188
    Don Flows Home to the Sea 189
    Forever Nineteen 193
    In Search of Coffee Mountains 187
    My Kingdom for a Grave 188
    One Day in the Life of Ivan Denisovich 190
    Pack of Wolves 195
    Time After Time 186
    We Were Not Like Other People 206
    Why There Is No Heaven on Earth 189
    Wild Children 187
space and time
    Another Shore 230
    Chance Child 167
    Connecticut Yankee in King Arthur's Court 80
    Crusade in Jeans 84
    Druid's Gift 52
    Druid's Tune 54
    If I Should Die Before I Wake 217
    Jeremy Visick 173
    Pit 117
    Playing Beatie Bow 47
    Red Shift 120
    String in the Harp 70
    Vision of Stephen 70
    Where the Towers Pierce the Sky 101
Spain
    1492 119
    Admiral and the Deck Boy 132

    Anthony Adverse 140
    Armada 120
    Bridle the Wind 156
    Child of Our Time 211
    Don Quixote de La Mancha 84
    Freedom Tree 191
    Go Saddle the Sea 156
    Heart Speaks Many Ways 190
    I Sailed With Columbus 131
    I, Juan de Pareja 136
    Inheritance 137
    Knight's Acre 106
    Last Summer 190
    Ramsay Scallop 98
    Sharpe's Enemy 142
    Teeth of the Gale 157
    Too Few for Drums 143
    Woman in the Cloak 91
Spanish Armada, 1588
    Armada 120
Spanish Civil War 1936-1939
    Last Summer 190
Spanish Civil War, 1936-1939
    Freedom Tree 191
    Heart Speaks Many Ways 190
spies
    Armada 120
    Away to Fundy Bay 232
    Cromwell's Boy 123
    Dangerous Game 196
    Escapade 162
    Fathom Five 208
    Hawk 138
    Kim 36
    Life of a Useless Man 186
    Murdo's War 179
    Paladin 198
St. John, Virgin Islands
    My Name Is Not Angelica 225
    Night of the Silent Drums 223
    When Daylight Comes 224
Stephen, King of England
    Fatal Crown 91
Stephens, John Lloyd
    Journey to the Sky 226
Stewart, William
    Running West 231

Subject Index

stone
   Lion and the Rose 138
Stonehenge
   Pillar of the Sky 51
storytelling
   Seth of the Lion People 51
Sumer
   Gilgamesh the King 20
superstition
   Half Child 124
   Manwolf 97
survival 217
   Along the Tracks 194
   Anna's Book 166
   Bitterest Age 202
   Bridge to the Other Side 202
   Captives of Time 84
   Darkness Casts No Shadow 216
   Gideon 210
   Homecoming 188
   I Am Rosemarie 217
   Island on Bird Street 218
   Kingdom by the Sea 209
   Little Fishes 201
   North of Danger 197
   One Day in the Life of Ivan Denisovich 190
   Sole Survivor 234
   Way Home 112
   We Were Not Like Other People 206
   Wild Children 187
Sweden
   Anna's Book 166
   Désirée 153
Switzerland
   Enchantress 155
   Frozen Waterfall 175
   Inheritance 137
Syria
   Handful of Stars 28

T

Taiping Rebellion, 1850-1864
   Mountain Light 31
   Rebels of the Heavenly Kingdom 31
   Second Son of Heaven 30
   Serpent's Children 32

Taliesin
   String in the Harp 70
Tannenberg, Battle of 1914
   August 1914 192
Teach, Edward
   Under the Black Flag 224
teachers
   Devil on Horseback 147
   Riders of the Storm 140
terrorism
   Tin Princess 170
Tewodros, Emperor of Ethiopia
   Guns of Darkness, The 6
Thailand
   Bridge Over the River Kwai 18
   Enchantress 155
   Rice Without Rain 18
theater
   Crocodile Burning 16
   In the Company of Clown 114
   Little Lower Than the Angels 107
   Master Rosalind 115
   Playhouse Tales 124
   Queen's Head 130
   You, My Brother 116
Themistokles
   Children of the Fox 56
   Victor of Salamis 55
Theodora, Empress of Byzantium
   Bearkeeper's Daughter 24
Theseus (Greek mythology)
   Bull from the Sea 57
   King Must Die 57
   No Need for Heroes 56
Tiananmen Square Incident, 1989
   Forbidden City 32
Tiberius
   Robe 61
Tibet
   Tulku 19
time and space
   Time After Time 186
   Valley of Deer 119
trick riding
   Four Horses for Tishtry 66
Troy
   Firebrand 54

Turkey
  Against the Storm 28
  Regards from the Dead Princess 29
Turks
  Frozen Waterfall 175
Tutankhamen, King of Egypt
  Tomorrow's Sphinx 2
Tutenkhamon, King of Egypt
  Return to Thebes 3
twins
  Empty Sleeve 146
  Enchantress 155
  In the Time of Trouble 8
Tyndale, William
  Hawk That Dare Not Hunt by Day 132
Tz'u-hsi, Empress Dowager of China
  Imperial Woman 29

U

Ukraine
  Tartar's Sword 127
underground movements
  Another Place, Another Spring 164
  Boys from St. Petri 205
  Bright Candles 194
  Ceremony of Innocence 198
  Code Name Kris 203
  Dangerous Game 196
  Edge of Darkness 199
  Empty Moat 206
  Imagining Isabel 226
  Lisa's War 204
  Man from the Other Side 218
  Mila 18 222
  Mottele 206
  Number the Stars 203
  Petros' War 210
  Shadow Army 205
  Shadow of the Wall 215
  Talking in Whispers 235
  To Fight in Silence 210
  Traitors 198
  Wall 182
  Winter in Wartime 207
United States--Revolutionary War, 1775-1783
  Away to Fundy Bay 232

V

Valdemar I, King of Denmark
  Maiden Crown 86
Valmy, Battle of, 1792
  Guns of Valmy 140
Velázquez, Diego Rodriguez de Silva y
  I, Juan de Pareja 136
vestal virgins
  Unwilling Vestal 66
Vesuvius, Mt.
  Locadio's Apprentice 66
Victoria, Queen of Great Britain
  Captive of Kensington Palace 168
  Queen and Lord M 169
  Queen's Husband 169
Vienna (Austria), Siege of, 1683
  Children of the Book 116
  Moonclock 137
Vietnam
  Goodbye, Vietnam 20
  Paradise of the Blind 20
  Song of the Buffalo Boy 19
  Voyage of the Lucky Dragon 19
Vietnam War, 1961-1975
  Voyage of the Lucky Dragon 19
Vikings
  Avalon 73
  Beyond the Mists 69
  Blood Feud 74
  Hakon of Rogen's Saga 71
  Leif the Unlucky 103
  Prison Window 71
  Slave's Tale 72
Villa, Pancho
  Crimson Wind 227
  Not of War Only 230
village life
  Parcel of Patterns 132
  Ship from Simnel Street 167
villages
  Story for a Black Night 8
Virgin Islands
  My Name Is Not Angelica 225
  Night of the Silent Drums 223
  When Daylight Comes 224
Virginia
  Devil Water 153

Subject Index

voyages and travels
   Another Place, Another Spring 164
   Admiral and the Deck Boy 132
   High Voyage 129
   I Sailed With Columbus 131
   Last Voyage 48
   Letters from Rifka 185
   Origin 171
   Stand Into Danger 149
   Voyage 184
   Wind at Morning 130

W
Wales
   Heaven Tree Trilogy 93
   Here Be Dragons 94
   Kingdom of the Grail 83
   Reckoning 94
   Running Vixen 85
   String in the Harp 70
   Wild Hunt 85

Walter, Lucy
   Child from the Sea 121

war
   AK 7
   All Quiet on the Western Front 192
   Andi's War 184
   Book of Merlyn 81
   Child of War 179
   Forever Nineteen 193
   Forty-Third War 226
   Freedom Tree 191
   Frontier Wolf 64
   If This Be Glory 206
   Into the Valley 16
   Last Summer 190
   Shining Company 75
   Time of the Forest 51
   Victor of Salamis 55

War of the Roses, 1455-1485
   Black Arrow 112
   Everlasting Covenant 100
   King's Grey Mare 104
   Tudor Rose 100

Watkins, Yoko Kawashima
   So Far from the Bamboo Grove 44

Wenceslaus, Saint, Duke of Bohemia
   Song for Young King Wenceslas 73

white supremacy movements
   If I Should Die Before I Wake 217

wilderness survival
   White Shaman 232

William I, the Conqueror, King of England
   Bond of Honour 75
   Golden Warrior 73
   Harold Was My King 72

William II, of Orange, King of the Netherlands
   Black Tulip 118

William III, King of Great Britain
   Three Crowns 134

witchcraft
   13th Member 125
   Lost Magic 83
   Quest for a Maid 90
   Valley of Deer 119
   Wise Child 71

Wollstonecraft, Mary
   Vindication 153

wolves
   Wolves of Paris 106

women
   Bisha of Burundi 7
   Bittersweet 34
   Catherine, Called Birdy 86
   Grania 129
   Haveli 37
   Kristin Lavransdatter 99
   Muckle Annie 233
   Regards from the Dead Princess 29
   Shabanu 37
   Sumitra's Story 177
   Vision of Light 109
   Woman of Nazareth 27
   Women of Ashdon 113
   Women of the Silk 35

World War, 1914-1918
   And Quiet Flows the Don 189
   Daughter of the Nobility 186
   Lion in the Evening 8
   Summer of the Barshinskeys 176
   Then the Zeppelins Came 175

World War, 1939-1945
   Bomber's Moon 35

Friedrich 220
Heart Speaks Many Ways 190
Murdo's War 179
*Why There Is No Heaven on
  Earth* 189

X
Xerxes
Victor of Salamis 55
Xhosa Tribe
Secret of the Mountain 12

Y
Yoruba (Tribe)
African Mask 11

Z
Zionism
Exodus 27
Zulu
Into the Valley 16

Chronological Index

How to use this index: The Chronological Index is designed to let you scan time periods for fiction titles of interest. To make this as useful as possible, time breakdowns will vary with the number of book titles in a given time period. (This results in broader spans of time coverage for many of the early time periods and shorter ones in contemporary times.)

There are also differences in the time span covered in different fiction titles. Some books can only be assigned to broad time periods—and these will appear listed under the category they fall into (such as **Ancient Civilizations**). Others have a story that focuses on a specific historic event or series of years. These will be listed within a broad category, but also have the specific year range indicated just after the title in parenthesis (*Daughter of the Sea* (1300B.C.)).

Prehistoric Times

Boy of the Painted Cave **50**
Clan of the Cave Bear **49**
Daughter of the Red Deer **52**
Dom and Va **1**
Memory String **17**
Old Tale Carved Out of Stone **16**
Pillar of the Sky **50**
Reindeer Moon **17**
Seth of the Lion People **51**
Shiva Accused **50**
Shiva's Challenge **49**
Singletusk **51**
Spirit on the Wall **50**
Time of the Forest **51**
Who Will Remember the People.... **235**

Ancient Civilizations

Bright and Morning Star, The (2500 B.C.) **3**
Bull from the Sea (1600–1200 B.C.) **57**
Child of the Morning (1470 B.C.) **3**
Daughter of the Sea (1300 B.C.) **56**
Druid's Tune (Iron Age) **53**
Egyptian, The (1100 B.C.) **5**
Escape from Egypt (1200 B.C.) **22**
Eyes of the Blind (900 B.C.) **22**
Firebrand (1200 B.C.) **54**
Gilgamesh the King (3000 B.C.) **20**
God Against the Gods, A (1300 B.C.) **3**
Golden Bees (1500 B.C.) **56**
His Majesty, Queen Hatshepsut (1470 B.C.) **2**
Horse Goddess (900 B.C.) **53**
Joseph and His Brothers (1200 B.C.) **22**
King Must Die (1600–1200 B.C.) **57**
Lily and the Bull (2000 B.C.) **54**
Man from the Sea (Bronze Age) **52**
Moon in the Cloud, The (2500 B.C.) **4**
No Need for Heroes (1600–1200 B.C.) **55**
Return to Thebes (1300 B.C.) **3**
Shadow on the Sun, The (2500 B.C.) **4**
Source (2000 B.C.–1960) **26**
Stronghold (Bronze Age) **67**

World Historical Fiction Guide

Sun Horse, Moon Horse (**Iron Age**) **69**
Tall Stones (Bronze Age) **52**
Tomorrow's Sphinx (1350 B.C.) **2**
World of the Pharoahs (3000 B.C.) **1**

Classical Age

Sixth Century B.C.
Druid's Gift (500) **52**
Praise Singer (556-667) **58**
Soldier of Arete (500) **58**

Fifth Century B.C.
Children of the Fox (500–449) **56**
Flowers of Adonis (431–404) **58**
Last of the Wine (431–404) **57**
Victor of Salamis (481–479) **55**

Fourth Century B.C.
Fire from Heaven **57**
Mask of Apollo **58**

Third Century B.C.
Windows of Elissa, The **6**

Second Century B.C.
Horses of Heaven **54**

First Century B.C.
Alexandrian, The (50) **4**
Ben Hur (35–30) **65**
Cleopatra (50) **4**
Door in the Wall **62**
Druids (58–51) **68**
I, Claudius (10 B.C.–30 A.D.) **62**
Ides of March (62–30) **66**
Throne of Isis (30) **65**
With the Eagles (56–49) **59**

First Century A.D.
Big Fisherman **21**
Bronze Bow **23**
Capricorn Bracelet (61–383) **64**
Conspiracy (64) **62**
Crows of War (43) **68**
Dear and Glorious Physician **21**
Eagle of the Ninth **64**
Four Horses for Tishtry **66**
Great Lion of God **21**
How Far to Bethlehem? (1 A.D.) **22**
Ides of April (60) **63**
Iron Hand of Mars (71) **60**
Last Days of Pompeii (79) **59**
Locadio's Apprentice (79) **66**
Man Who Buried Jesus **23**
Mermaid's Daughter **67**
Quo Vadis (50–60) **64**
Rain from the West (71) **63**
Robe (30-40) **61**
Roman (30-64) **65**
Shadows in Bronze (70) **60**
Silver Chalice (40) **60**
Silver Pigs (70) **61**
Song for a Dark Queen (60) **68**
Three from Galilee **21**
Upon This Rock **23**
Venus in Copper (70) **61**

Second Century
Eagle in the Snow **59**
Left-Handed Spirit **62**
Red Shift (200) **120**
Unwilling Vestal (161–191) **66**

Fourth Century
Beacon at Alexandria **2**
Frontier Wolf **64**
Shadow of Vesuvius **62**

Fifth Century
Darkness and the Dawn (470) **59**
Heaven's Only Daughter (410) **63**
Imperial Purple **24**
Lantern Bearers **68**
Slave of the Huns (450) **67**

Middle Ages (500–1500)
Captives of Time **84**
Dog of Bondi Castle **89**
Don Quixote de La Mancha **84**
I Am England **76**
Lady of Rhuddesmere **97**
Legend of Tarik **6**
Longsword **98**
Lost Magic **83**
Master of Hestviken **99**
Nightingale Gallery **89**
Sign of the Owl **85**

Sixth Century (500–599)
Bearkeeper's Daughter **23**
Book of Merlyn **81**

Subject Index

Born of the Sun **75**
Child of the Northern Spring **82**
Connecticut Yankee in King Arthur's Court **81**
Crystal Cave **79**
Dancing Bear **24**
Guinevere **78, 82**
Hawk of May **77**
In Winter's Shadow **77**
Kingdom of Summer **77**
Last Enchantment **79**
Last Pendragon **78**
Mary Stewart's Merlin Trilogy **79**
Mists of Avalon **76**
Once and Future King **81**
Paradise **71**
Queen of the Summer Stars **82**
Road to Camlann **80**
Sisters' Tale **70**
Star in the Forest **73**
Story of the Grail and the Passing of Arthur **78**
String in the Harp **70**
Sword in the Stone **81**
Testing of Tertius **78**
Tristan and Iseult **75**
Vision of Stephen **70**
Wicked Day **80**
Winter Prince **80**
Wise Child **71**

Seventh Century (600–699)
Shining Company **74**

Eighth Century
His Majesty's Elephant (780) **75**

Ninth Century
Belt of Gold **24**
Edge of Light **76**
Light in the Mountain **47**
Pangur Ban **74**
Prison Window **70**

Tenth Century
Bern, Son of Mikula **69**
Blood Feud **74**
Lion of Ireland **72**
Song for Young King Wenceslas **72**

Eleventh Century
Avalon **72**
Beyond the Mists **69**
Bond of Honour (1050–1066) **75**
Escape from the Evil Prophecy **72**
Golden Warrior (1022–1066) **73**
Hakon of Rogen's Saga **71**
Harold Was My King (1066) **73**
Heirs of the Kingdom (1096-1099) **93**
Robin and the King **88**
Sherwood **88**
Slave's Tale **71**
Striped Ships (1066) **73**
Tales of the Crusades (1094-1464) **85**
To Kill a King **95**

Twelfth Century
African Mask **10**
Black Wolf of the Steppes (1167–1227) **29**
Confession of Brother Haluin **94**
Death Comes As Epiphany **92**
Fatal Crown (1130-1142) **91**
Holy Thief **95**
Ivanhoe (1190) **96**
Kingdom of the Grail **83**
Lion and the Lily (1180–1189) **96**
Maiden Crown **86**
Myself As Witness (1167–1216) **88**
Of Nightingales That Weep **40**
Pillars of the Earth **87**
Potter's Field **95**
Proud Taste for Scarlet and Miniver (1180–1189) **92**
Queen's War (1173) **92**
Rare Benedictine (1120) **95**
Running Vixen **87**
Talisman (1189–1192) **27**
Warlord of the Genji **37**
Wild Hunt **85**
Witch's Brat **98**

Thirteenth Century
Adam of the Road **89**
Baron's Hostage (1263 –1267) **99**
Black Rose **86**
Cargo for a King **83**
Catherine, Called Birdy (1290) **86**
Crusade in Jeans (1212) **83**

World Historical Fiction Guide

Falls the Shadow (1216–1272) **93**
Gudrun **91**
Heaven Tree Trilogy **93**
Here Be Dragons **94**
King's Daughters (1272–1307) **90**
King's Road (1210) **91**
Kristin Lavransdatter **99**
Magician's Apprentice **96**
Poland (1200–1980s) **185**
Quest for a Maid **90**
Reckoning (1283) **94**
Road to Damietta (1205–1220) **92**
Saving Grace (1206) **87**
What Happened in Hamelin (1284) **97**
Woman in the Cloak **90**

Fourteenth Century
Age of Miracles **106**
All Men Tall (1323) **113**
Beggar King of China (1350–1400) **29**
Fortune Made His Sword (1387–1422) **109**
Hunchback of Notre Dame **103**
In Pursuit of the Green Lion **109**
Innocent Wayfaring **100**
Katherine **110**
Little Lower Than the Angels (1347–1351) **107**
Lords of Vaumartin **103**
Love Knot (1360–1400) **101**
Manwolf **97**
Men of Iron (1370–1400) **108**
Murder Wears a Cowl (1300) **87**
Passage to Pontefract (1370–1400) **108**
Peace Child **107**
Ramsay Scallop (1300) **99**
Red Slayer **90**
Star of Lancaster (1380–1422) **108**
Threshing Floor **110**
Vision of Light **109**
Way Home (1349) **112**
Whyte Hart **87**
White Company (1340–1377) **101**

Fifteenth Century
Apprentice **105**
Cargo of the Madalena **102**
Florentine **111**
Leif the Unlucky **103**
Shrine of Murders **101**
Trumpeter of Krakow **104**

1400–1449
Blood Red, Sister Rose (1420–1431) **104**
Bloody Field (1403) **107**
Devil's Workshop (1430) **106**
Everlasting Covenant (1444–1485) **100**
Merchant's Mark (1439) **102**
Personal Recollections of Joan of Arc (1412–1431) **113**
Sign of the Green Falcon (1415) **102**
Where the Towers Pierce the Sky (1429) **101**
Writing on the Hearth (1430–1455) **102**
Young Joan (1422–1461) **100**
Wolves of Paris (1439) **106**

1450-1499
Admiral and the Deck Boy (1492) **132**
Agony and the Ecstasy (1475–1565) **112**
Black Arrow (1455–1485) **111**
Blood Royal (1490–1540) **121**
Cloister and the Hearth (1460) **134**
Daughter of Time (1480–1485) **112**
1492 (1492) **119**
I Remember Love (1455–1485) **122**
I Sailed With Columbus (1492) **130**
Incas (1450–1500) **235**
King's Grey Mare (1470–1483) **104**
King's Pleasure (1485–1536) **129**
Knight's Acre (1451) **106**
Madonna of the Seven Hills (1480–1519) **108**
Plymouth Cloak (1470) **110**
Quentin Durward (1461–1480) **110**
Prince of Foxes (1476–1507) **111**
Private Life of Mona Lisa (1480–1510) **105**
Second Mrs. Giaconda (1480–1500) **105**
Six Wives of Henry VIII (1491–1547) **130**
Tudor Rose (1455–1485) **101**

Subject Index

We Speak No Treason (1452–1485) **104**

Sixteenth Century

Beyond the Ancient Cities **228**
Boy and the Samurai **38**
Coming of the Bear **38**
Gold of Dreams **228**
Grania **129**
Holdfast **114**
In the Company of Clown **114**
Island of Ogres **39**
King's Fifth **229**
Nicholas Cooke **117**
Requiem for Princess **113**
Samurai and the Long-nosed Devils **39**
Samurai's Tale **38**
Sea Beggars **125**
Tokaido Road **41**
Valley of the Broken Cherry Trees **39**
Village of the Vampire Cat **40**
White Serpent Castle **40**
Women of Ashdon **113**
You, My Brother **116**

1500-1549

Amethyst Ring (1520–1525) **234**
Captain from Castile (1519) **230**
Captive (1517) **228**
Cold Wind Blowing (1509–1547) **138**
Estebanico (1539) **229**
Feathered Serpent (1519) **229**
Hawk That Dare Not Hunt by Day (1524–1534) **132**
High Voyage (1502–1504) **128**
Iron Lily (1509–1547) **138**
I, Elizabeth (1533–1603) **131**
I Am Mary Tudor (1516–1553) **128**
I Remember Love (1530s) **122**
Ivy Crown (1509–1547) **129**
King's Cavalier (1520s) **111**
Lady Jane (1537–1554) **135**
Prince and the Pauper (1537–1547) **136**
Queen of This Realm (1533–1603) **133**
Sprig of Broom (1500–1509) **139**
Stars of Fortune (1545–1550) **122**
White Rose Murders (1513) **117**
Wind at Morning (1519–1521) **130**
Young Bess (1533–1547) **126**

1550-1599

Armada (1588) **120**
Bartholomew Fair (1597) **135**
Captive Queen of Scots (1571–1587) **132**
Elizabeth, Captive Princess (1553–1555) **126**
Hawk (1558–1603) **138**
Inheritance (1580– 1620) **137**
Kenilworth (1558–1603) **134**
Linnet (1558–1603) **137**
Merrymaid (1553–1558) **122**
Murder for Her Majesty (1558–1603) **124**
My Enemy the Queen (1558–1603) **125**
Playhouse Tales (1558–1603) **124**
Prisoner of the Queen (1567–1586) **131**
Queen and the Gypsy (1558–1603) **123**
Queen's Head (1588–1603) **130**
Strange Devices of the Sun and Moon (1590) **120**
Take Heed of Loving Me (1573–1613) **136**
13th Member (1567– 1603) **125**
Westward Ho! (1558–1603) **127**
You Never Knew Her As I Did (1567) **125**

Seventeenth Century

Abduction **131**
Alethea **115**
Golden Tulip **127**
Master Rosalind **115**
Pirate Royal **223**
Shogun **38**
Tartar's Sword **127**
Untold Tale **123**
Valley of Deer **119**
You, My Brother **116**

1600–1649

Beyond the Weir Bridge (1642–1660) **115**

World Historical Fiction Guide

Blood Royal (1642–1660) **137**
Circle of Pearls (1642–1660) **127**
Cromwell's Boy (1642–1660) **123**
Crowning Mercy (1642–1660) **126**
I, Juan de Pareja (1620–1660) **136**
Kate Ryder (1642–1660) **116**
King's General (1642– 1660) **120**
King's Knight's Pawn (1649)**115**
Man in the Iron Mask (1630–1650) **118**
Many Waters Cannot Quench Love (1603–1649) **115**
Messenger for Parliament (1642–1660) **123**
Murder in the Tower (1603–1625) **133**
Myself My Enemy (1625–1639) **133**
Red Shift (1642– 1660) **120**
Rembrandt (1606–1669) **134**
Severed Crown (1642–1660) **128**
Three Musketeers (1625) **118**

1650–1699
Black Tulip (1672–1675) **118**
Bonnie Dundee (1689–1714) **135**
Bridge of Sighs (1650–1701) **128**
Child from the Sea (1650–1700) **121**
Children of the Book (1683) **116**
Great House (1669) **122**
Half Child (1650) **124**
High Voyage (1650–1701) **128**
Journal of the Plague Year (1695) **118**
Lion and the Rose (1670–1700) **137**
Moonclock (1683) **136**
One Foot Ashore (1654) **121**
Out of Many Waters (1654) **233**
Parcel of Patterns (1695) **132**
Piper to the Clan (1650) **117**
Pit (1695) **117**
Three Crowns (1662–1694) **134**

Eighteenth Century

Apprentices **145**
Drummer Boy **145**
Earth Will Shake **155**
Empty Sleeve **145**
Enchantress **155**
Master Puppeteer **40**
Riders of the Storm **140**
Running West **231**

Secret of the Mountain **12**
Silver Touch **149**
Smile of the Stranger **139**
Smith **147**
Sound of Coaches **146**
Under the Black Flag **224**

1700-1729
Devil Water (1714–1750) **153**
Queen in Waiting (1714–1727) **152**
Right-Hand Man (1714–1837) **152**

1730–1739
My Name Is Not Angelica (1733) **224**
Night of the Silent Drums (1733) **223**
When Daylight Comes (1733) **224**

1740–1749
Another Shore (1744) **230**
Flame-Colored Taffeta (1745) **154**
Glass-Blowers (1745–1845) **144**
Hadder Maccoll (1745) **141**
Master of Ballantrae (1745) **154**
Prince Charlie's Year (1745) **144**

1750–1759
Hanging at Tyburn (1750s) **143**
Last Voyage (1750–1779) **48**
Queen's Confession (1755–1793) **147**
Vindication (1759–1797) **153**

1760–1769
Beware of Moonlight (1765) **146**
Désirée (1760–1840) **152**
Lost Queen (1762–1780) **149**

1770–1779
Anthony Adverse (1775–1850) **139**
Away to Fundy Bay (1775–1783) **231**
Stand Into Danger (1774) **149**

1780–1789
Barnaby Rudge (1780) **143**
Bounty Trilogy (1787) **48**
Charterhouse of Parma (1789–1820) **153**
Devil on Horseback (1788–1789) **147**
Ravensrigg (1780) **141**
Rebel (1789) **140**
Rose for Virtue (1783–1840) **150**

1790–1799
Devil to Pay (1794) **151**

Subject Index

Enemy in Sight! (1794–1799) **148**
Form Line of Battle! (1793) **148**
Frenchwoman (1799–1815) **151**
Guns of Valmy (1792) **140**
Horation Hornblower Series (1790–1830) **144**
Red and the Black (1799–1815) **154**
Scarlet Pimpernel (1792) **150**
Touch and Go (1794–1799) **151**
War and Peace (1799–1820) **155**
Witches' Sabbath (1798) **141**

Nineteenth Century

Black Lamp **158**
Blue Dragon **44**
Chance Child **167**
Chinwe **9**
December Rose **161**
Escapade **162**
Flowers in the Blood **35**
Footsteps **161**
Greek Wedding **162**
Guns of Darkness, The **5**
Iron Way **159**
Island Harp **172**
Kim **35**
Landowner Legacy **163**
Lion's Cub **163**
Love Child **159**
Night Journey **164**
Sheltering Tree **167**
Silk Vendetta **163**
Sudden, Fearful Death **168**
Things Fall Apart **9**
Vision of Stephen **70**
Waxwork **165**
Why Kill Arthur Potter? **162**

1800–1809

Ajeemah and His Son (1807–1840) **223**
Anna (1800–1815) **162**
Cry of the Peacock (1800–1982) **25**
Ship from Simnel Street (1800–1815) **166**
Success to the Brave (1802) **149**

1810–1819

Captive of Kensington Palace (1819–1901) **168**
Consul's Daughter, The (1816) **6**
Dark Quartet (1816–1850) **157**
Grimsdyke (1819) **172**
Last Love (1815–1821) **142**
Queen and Lord M (1819–1901) **168**
Queen's Husband (1819–1901) **169**
Rape of the Rose (1811–1813) **164**
Sharpe's Enemy (1812) **141**
Sharpe's Regiment (1813) **142**
Sharpe's Siege (1814) **142**

1820–1829

Bridle the Wind **156**
Go Saddle the Sea (1821) **156**
Hour of the Bell (1821) **168**
Porcelain Pagoda (1822) **30**
Teeth of the Gale (1827) **156**

1830–1839

Fernande (1835) **160**
Grace (1838) **167**
Great Thirst (1830) **14**
In the Shadow of the Brontës **157**
Journey to the Sky (1839–1840) **226**
Origin (1830–1889) **171**

1840–1849

Across the Sea from Galway (1847) **160**
Another Place, Another Spring (1840) **164**
Ask Me No Questions (1848) **170**
Coldest Winter (1846) **165**
Haunting of Kildoran Abbey (1847) **158**
Imperial Woman (1840–1908) **29**
Lady's Maid (1845–1861) **161**
Potato Eaters (1846) **157**
Trinity (1840–1916) **172**

1850–1859

Albany **157**
Circlemaker (1852) **170**
Exodus (1850–1940) **26**
God Is an Englishman (1857–1866) **160**
Great Train Robbery (1855) **159**
Greek Treasure (1850–1890) **171**

297

Greenyards **165**
Jeremy Visick (1852) **173**
Leopard (1850–1870) **164**
Leaves from the Valley (1854) **171**
Lust for Life (1853–1890) **171**
Mountain Light (1855) **31**
Muckle Annie **232**
Passions of the Mind (1856–1939) **180**
Rebels of the Heavenly Kingdom (1850–1864) **31**
Second Son of Heaven (1850–1864) **30**
Serpent's Children (1850–1864) **31**
Sworn Enemies (1851) **166**

1860–1869
Guns of Darkness, The (1860) **5**
I Remember Love (1865) **122**
Street Child (1860–1880) **160**

1870–1879
Nugget of Gold **47**
Playing Beatie Bow **46**
Ruby in the Smoke (1872) **169**
Shadow in the North (1878) **169**
Year of the Stranger (1877) **166**

1880–1889
Good Earth (1880–1911) **30**
Tin Princess (1882) **170**

1890–1899
Anna's Book **166**
Silver Crest (1893) **158**
Sound of the Dragon's Feet (1894) **173**
Spring Moon (1890–1970) **34**
Time of the Dragon (1899) **30**
White Dawn (1897) **231**

Twentieth Century (1900–1945)
Bride Price **10**
Great Thirst **11**
Into the Valley **16**
The Return **5**
Samurai **41**
Story for a Black Night **8**
White Shaman **232**

1900–1910
As the Crow Flies (1900–1930) **173**
Bittersweet (1900–1980) **34**

Doctor Zhivago (1900–1929) **187**
Exit from Home (1900–1905) **187**
Kathleen (1900–1920) **177**
Keys of the Kingdom (1900–1930) **33**
Life of a Useless Man (1905) **186**
River With No Bridge **43**
Russian Farewell (1905) **186**
Summer of the Barshinskeys (1902–1924) **176**
Then the Zeppelins Came (1901–1918) **175**
Three Lives for the Czar (1900–1914) **188**
Toba **185**
Tulku **19**
Voyage (1904) **184**

1910–1919
And Quiet Flows the Don (1910–1921) **189**
Birthday Boys (1910) **174**
Crimson Wind (1910–1917) **227**
Daughter of the Nobility (1913–1927) **186**
Don Flows Home to the Sea (1917–1921) **189**
Heart of the Continent (1910–1950) **45**
Homecoming (1917) **188**
Letters from Rifka (1919) **185**
Lion in the Evening (1914–1918) **8**
My Kingdom for a Grave (1917) **188**
Regards from the Dead Princess (1918–1938) **28**
Time After Time (1917) **185**
Time and Chance (1916–1921) **179**
To Touch a Dream (1912–1975) **25**
Women of the Silk (1919–1938) **35**

World War, 1914-1918
All Quiet on the Western Front **192**
August 1914 **192**
In the Company of Eagles **192**
Khaki Wings **191**
No Hero for the Kaiser **191**
Not of War Only **230**
Red Flight Two **191**

1920–1929
Children of the Wolf **36**
Deep Dream of the Rain Forest **47**

Subject Index

Friedrich (1925–1942) **220**
Little Sister (1925) **33**
Man's Fate (1927) **34**
So Slow the Dawning (1929–1939) **182**
Wild Children **187**

1930–1939
Dragon Seed **32**
Fear the Condor (1932) **233**
Freedom Tree (1936–1939) **191**
Frost in the Night (1932) **180**
Jacob's Ladder (1930-1945) **45**
Journey to America (1938) **215**
Reunion (1932) **183**
To Cross a Line (1938) **219**
Valda **46**
When Hitler Stole Pink Rabbit (1933) **214**

1940–1945
Between Two Worlds **231**
Dawn **27**
Light a Penny Candle (1940–1960) **174**

World War, 1939-1945
Along the Tracks **194**
And the Violins Stopped Playing **219**
Anya **221**
Ayo Gurkha! **37**
Babi Yar **193**
Backwater War **209**
Bel Ria **195**
Bitterest Age **202**
Blitzcat **208**
Bomber's Moon **35**
Book of Songs **215**
Boris **199**
Borrowed House **207**
Boys from St. Petri **205**
Bridge Over the River Kwai **18**
Bridge to the Other Side **202**
Bright Candles **194**
Ceremony of Innocence **198**
Chase Me, Catch Nobody **200**
Child of Our Time **211**
Children of Bach **211**
Code Name Kris **203**
Come Spring **215**
Cranes at Dusk **42**

Dangerous Game **196**
Darkness Casts No Shadow **216**
Devil in Vienna **218**
Devil's Arithmetic **222**
Displaced Person **195**
Don't Say a Word **199**
Dreamtime **46**
Echoes of War **208**
Edge of Darkness **199**
Edge of War **201**
Empire of the Sun **32**
Empty Moat **206**
Exeter Blitz **204**
Farewell Sidonia **213**
Farewell, Dresden **196**
Fateless **214**
Fathom Five **208**
File on Fraulein Berg **179**
Fly Away Home **204**
Forever Nineteen **193**
Gideon **210**
Guns of Navarone **203**
Hear O Israel **221**
Heart Speaks Many Ways **191**
Hide and Seek **207**
Hiroshima No Pika **41**
Horses of Anger **198**
House on Prague Street **211**
Hunted **196**
I Am Rosemarie **217**
I Was There **205**
If I Should Die Before I Wake **217**
If This Be Glory **206**
In Spite of All Terror **174**
Is Still Here **222**
Island on Bird Street **218**
Jacob's Rescue **212**
Journey **212**
Judas Ship **233**
Kingdom by the Sea **209**
Last Butterfly **214**
Last Nine Days of the Bismarck **197**
Last Summer **191**
Lights Go On Again **232**
Lisa's War **204**
Little Fishes **201**
Machine Gunners **210**

World Historical Fiction Guide

Magic We Do Here **221**
Max's Gang **193**
Mckenzie's Boots **46**
Mila 18 **222**
Mottele **206**
Murdo's War **180**
My Sister Clare **176**
Night in Distant Motion **202**
Night of the Broken Glass **211**
Night Over Day Over Night **208**
Night Trains **222**
North of Danger **197**
Number the Stars **203**
October, Eight O'Clock **216**
Other Way Round **176**
Pack of Wolves **195**
Paladin **198**
Petros' War **210**
Prayer for Katerina Horovitzova **216**
Razor Eyes **201**
Ride Out the Storm **200**
Scrap of Time **212**
Shadow Army **205**
Shadow of the Wall **215**
Sirens and Spies **176**
Sky Is Falling **232**
So Far from the Bamboo Grove **44**
Sole Survivor **234**
Sound of Anthems **178**
Star Without a Sky **218**
Survivor **213**
Time Without Bells **194**
To Fight in Silence **210**
Touch Wood **220**
Traitors **198**
Tree Still Stands **195**
Tug of War **203**
Ulysses **203**
Upstairs Room **219**
Visit **197**
Waiting for Anya **217**
Wall **213**
War Without Friends **200**
We Were Not Like Other People **206**
Why There Is No Heaven on Earth **190**
Winter in Wartime **207**

Contemporary (1945–)

Chain of Fire **13**
Cry, The Beloved Country **14**
Eye for Color **15**
Forest of the Clouded Leopard **48**
Frozen Waterfall **174**
Haveli **37**
Journey to Jo'burg **13**
No Surrender **16**
No Tigers in Africa **15**
Shabanu **37**
Skindeep **12**
So Sings the Blue Deer **227**
Somehow Tenderness Survives **14**
Story Like the Wind **15**
Waiting for the Rain **11**

1945–1949

Andi's War (1945–1949) **184**
Crutches **181**
Dragon Village (1949) **33**
Flight Toward Home (1945–1947) **180**
In Search of Coffee Mountains **187**
In the Autumn Wind (1945– 1954) **43**
In the Forest at Midnight (1948–1950) **36**
Ink-keeper's Apprentice (1945–1950) **43**
Miracle Tree (1945–1964) **42**
My Enemy, My Brother (1945–1948) **25**
Tilla **181**
Traitor Within **33**
Transport 7-41-R **180**
Woman of Nazareth (1948–1982) **27**
Year of Impossible Goodbyes (1945–1948) **44**

1950–1959

Ah, But Your Land Is Beautiful (1952–1958) **13**
Becoming Gershona (1958) **27**
Echoes of the White Giraffe (1950–1953) **45**
Flowers of Hiroshima (1959) **43**
Green Frontier (1952) **181**
Honorable Prison (1955) **234**
In the Time of Trouble (1955–1960) **8**
Milk and Honey (1958) **176**

Subject Index

*One Day in the Life of Ivan
   Denisovich* **190**
Ring the Judas Bell **184**

1960–1969

Across the Barricades **178**
Arrow of God **9**
Beyond Safe Boundaries (1960) **14**
Kindling (1967–1974) **183**
Salah of Sierra Leona **11**
Scent of the Gods **18**
Seeds of Hiroshima (1960) **42**
Time of Anger **26**

1970–1979

Bisha of Burundi (1972–1979) **7**
Chileno! (1973) **182**
Fine, Soft Day **177**
Goodbye, Vietnam **20**
Little Brother **17**
Nugget of Gold **47**
Paradise of the Blind **20**
Rice Without Rain **19**
Sumitra's Story (1972–1979) **177**
Voyage of the Lucky Dragon **19**

1980–1989

AK (1980) **7**
Against the Storm **28**
Among the Volcanoes **225**
Clay Marble **17**
Forbidden City (1989) **32**
Forty-Third War **226**
Grab Hands and Run **227**
Handful of Stars **28**
Imagining Isabel **225**
Kiss the Dust (1984) **25**
Mexico **228**
Return (1984–1985) **5**
Roller Birds of Rampur **36**
Song of the Buffalo Boy **20**
Talking in Whispers **235**
Taste of Salt **225**
Wall (1989) **182**

1990

Crocodile Burning (1990) **16**
Song of Be (1990s) **9**